Latin America
in a Changing
Global Environment

Latin America
in a Changing
Global Environment

edited by
Riordan Roett
Guadalupe Paz

LYNNE
RIENNER
PUBLISHERS

BOULDER
LONDON

Published in the United States of America in 2003 by
Lynne Rienner Publishers, Inc.
1800 30th Street, Boulder, Colorado 80301
www.rienner.com

and in the United Kingdom by
Lynne Rienner Publishers, Inc.
3 Henrietta Street, Covent Garden, London WC2E 8LU

Library of Congress Cataloging-in-Publication Data
Latin America in a changing global environment / Riordan Roett and Guadalupe Paz, editors.
    p. cm.
    Includes bibliographical references and index.
    ISBN 1-58826-191-3 (hc : alk. paper)
    1. Latin America—Foreign relations—1980– 2. Latin America—Foreign economic
relations. 3. National security—Latin America. I. Roett, Riordan, 1938– II. Paz,
Guadalupe, 1970–
    F1414.2 .L327145 2003
    327'.098—dc21
                                             2002036824

British Cataloguing in Publication Data
A Cataloguing in Publication record for this book
is available from the British Library.

Contents

Preface, Guadalupe Paz   vii
Acknowledgments   ix

1   Introduction: Latin America in the New Century
    Michael Shifter   1

Part 1   The Transformation in Intrahemispheric Relations

2   Free Trade in the Americas: Collective Action
    or Collective Apathy?
    Carol Wise   15

3   The New Security Agenda for the Americas:
    Focus on "Insecurity"
    Margaret Daly Hayes   41

4   U.S. Policy Toward Latin America: A View from the South
    Roberto Russell   61

5   Canada's New Opening to Latin America
    Charles F. Doran   91

Part 2   Changing Ties with International Actors

6   The Role of International Financial Institutions
    Rosa Alonso i Terme   117

7   Human Rights and the Role of International Actors
    Alison Brysk   141

8   Latin America and the European Union:
    A Strategic Partnership?
    Wolf Grabendorff   153

Part 3   Two Pivotal States

9   Mexico's Changing Domestic and International Dynamics
    Russell Crandall   171

10 Brazil's Role as a Regional Power
    Riordan Roett   189

Part 4   Conclusion

11 Latin America and the Western Hemisphere
    in the Age of Globalization
    Russell Crandall   209

Bibliography   215
The Contributors   229
Index   231
About the Book   243

Preface

Today, Latin America faces numerous new challenges that stem from a rapidly evolving global environment. The end of the Cold War, coupled with what is widely known as globalization—the rapid and largely unrestricted flow of information, capital, goods and services, people, ideas, and cultural values—has redefined policy priorities throughout the world. Because globalization has made the world far more integrated and interdependent economically, socially, and technologically than just two decades ago, what happens in Latin America can have a crucial impact on global financial markets and on international dynamics. Likewise, Latin America is increasingly affected by international events. The September 11, 2001, terrorist attacks on the United States, for example, drastically shifted the focus of U.S. foreign policy toward the war against terrorism, while hemispheric issues previously on the agenda—trade, migration, counter-narcotics efforts, to name a few—lost momentum. International financial conditions are also increasingly relevant to Latin America's economic health; the 1997 Asian financial crisis, for instance, triggered widespread contagion in the region.

These global trends have also brought significant change to intrahemispheric relations, as the region moves increasingly toward a Western Hemisphere concept, rather than the more traditional separation between Latin America and North America. As Russell Crandall states in this volume's concluding chapter, globalization will set the parameters for the Western Hemisphere as it confronts a great many issues—strategic, social, political, and economic—that "will shape its evolution in this new century." It is against this backdrop that this volume addresses Latin America's emerging challenges and opportunities at the start of the twenty-first century. The authors examine key political, economic, and security concerns in the region, focusing on the changing dynamics within the Western Hemisphere, as well as Latin America's evolving relationship with international actors and institutions. A final section assesses the pivotal role of Latin America's two largest countries, Mexico and Brazil.

This volume is part of a series published by the SAIS Western Hemisphere Program with the support of the William and Flora Hewlett Foundation. Other volumes published with the support of the Hewlett Foundation include *Mercosur: Regional Integration, World Markets* (1999); *Mexico's Private Sector: Recent History, Future Challenges* (1998); *The Mexican Peso Crisis: International Perspectives* (1996); *The Challenge of Institutional Reform in Mexico* (1995); *Political and Economic Liberalization in Mexico: At a Critical Juncture?* (1993); *Mexico's External Relations in the 1990s* (1991); and *Mexico and the United States: Managing the Relationship* (1988). Two others are in progress: *Mexico in the Age of Globalization: Changing Domestic and External Dynamics* and *Security, Democracy, and Economic Reform in the Andes*.

The SAIS Western Hemisphere Program, created in 1999, brings together the Latin American Studies Program and the Center of Canadian Studies to offer an integrated view and understanding of the dynamics of change in North America and Latin America in the twenty-first century. This volume seeks to further that goal by making available the views of specialists in the field of international relations on the changing nature of intrahemispheric relations and the challenges the region faces in today's globalized world.

—*Guadalupe Paz*

Acknowledgments

We are grateful to all the individuals who participated in the completion of this volume. We owe a special thank you to the contributing authors for their insightful essays, for their patience during the lengthy publication process, and for the considerable time and effort they invested in this project. We would also like to acknowledge Donna Verdier's invaluable editing assistance, as well as the helpful input of Russell Crandall, Guy Poitras, Michael Shifter, and Carol Wise. A special acknowledgment goes to Lynne Rienner, Sally Glover, and the entire publishing team at Lynne Rienner Publishers for making it both a pleasure and a privilege to work with them. Finally, we owe our deepest gratitude to the William and Flora Hewlett Foundation, not only for making the publication of this volume possible, but also for its generous program support over the years.

—*Riordan Roett & Guadalupe Paz*

Introduction: Latin America in the New Century

Michael Shifter

At the start of the twenty-first century, Latin America faces an increasingly formidable and complex agenda, with unprecedented political polarization, economic meltdown, and unremitting lawlessness afflicting many of the region's countries. In the context of globalization, such acute problems acquire even greater significance than they did in previous periods. Although the 1990s were hardly free of these problems, that period at least generated high hopes about continued progress toward more democratic politics, market economics, and freer trade. Such hopes have gradually dissipated, however, in the face of disappointing policy outcomes in a wide array of areas. The outlook for coming years is far from upbeat.[1] Latin America—still generally regarded as a relatively stable region in the wider scheme of global politics—appears more and more fractured and lacking in overall coherence and clear direction.

To be sure, viewed in a longer-term frame and historical perspective, Latin America has advanced in a number of fundamental respects. Elected governments, not dictatorships, dominate the region, which was not the case a generation ago. Despite overwhelming disenchantment with the performance of democratic governments as measured by reliable, cross-country public opinion surveys,[2] there is scant public demand to return to military rule. That option remains unappealing and has few adherents. There is little evidence, moreover, that the armed forces throughout the region have either the capacity or appetite to govern. The coups in Ecuador in January 2000 and Venezuela in April 2002 serve to illustrate both the precariousness and the resilience of democratic rule; in the end, after all, legal mechanisms functioned and legitimacy prevailed.

In a similar sense, the market reforms undertaken in the 1990s have also failed to produce uniformly positive results. Despite high expectations, there have been few reassuring examples of successful second-generation, more thoroughgoing, institutional reforms.[3] Inflation—once the scourge of many Latin American countries—has been held reasonably in check. Yet, privatizations and liberalization of the economies have failed to yield sustained growth; in 2001, Latin America's economies were distressingly stagnant. There was no per capita growth for the region as a whole during the five-year period from 1998 to 2002.

Although poverty has been reduced in some countries—Chile stands out as the most prominent and frequently cited example—the region for the most part remains stubbornly poor, and levels of income-inequality have widened while unemployment rates have increased. Still, despite disappointing economic performance across the region and the attendant public disenchantment with market economics, there is virtually no alternative economic model that enjoys significant public support and approval. Critics—and they are doubtless growing both in numbers and strength—may have pointed out serious shortcomings in political and economic outcomes of prevailing models, but few have made convincing arguments that other available options would produce better outcomes. An examination of the election results in the region to date hardly suggests a groundswell pressing for a particular alternative formulation.

Against this backdrop, this volume, while sobered by more recent developments, seeks to take proper measure of the significance of the noteworthy progress made on key economic, political, and social dimensions, including such questions as security, trade, democracy, and human rights. The collection takes a long-term view, interpreting and appreciating globalization's multiple benefits. These serve to temper the region's relatively gloomy, short-term prognosis. In addition, the authors highlight the fundamental role of regional powers in shaping Western Hemisphere dynamics. This perspective recognizes the preeminent facts of economic and political power, and the key dynamics of globalization. It largely attributes either positive or negative trends to the directions taken by a set of critical countries, so-called "pivotal states."[4] The authors also take into careful account an increasingly variegated hemisphere, with pronounced differences among countries and subregions. While the hemisphere has long been noted for its heterogeneity, some analysts have argued that the major forces of globalization have helped accentuate these differences even more so than in the past.[5]

Changing Intrahemispheric Relations and U.S. Regional Influence

As the world's only superpower, the United States no doubt plays a crucial role and exercises a disproportionate influence on the fundamental nature of Western Hemisphere relations, in particular U.S.–Latin American relations. Several of the authors, especially Roberto Russell, take as a starting point the vast asymmetry that has long characterized relations between the United States and Latin America. That asymmetry was put in sharp relief following the tragic events of September 11, 2001. The terrorist attacks in New York City and Washington, D.C., underscored the vulnerability of the United States and also set in motion a series of foreign policy decisions that reflected new priorities, reallocation of resources, and significant proposals for revamped national institutions concerned with overriding security challenges. Those attacks, in other words, have sharpened and redefined U.S. foreign policy and have resulted in filling the decade-long void that came to be known, for lack of a better term, as the post–Cold War world. The still-evolving strategy that the United States will pursue on a global scale to deal with the terrorist threat will profoundly affect relations with Latin America.

The key question is whether the United States will attempt to define a hemispheric agenda in a unilateral fashion, merely reflecting its own interests, or whether it will seek to respond constructively to many of the valid concerns and problems facing other countries in the hemisphere. The United States may well deem that Latin America is of such low priority that it warrants little attention and resources, except as support for broader U.S. goals on the global stage. Such different options and scenarios, to be sure, have analogues throughout history in the Western Hemisphere, most notably during the Cold War period. In this regard, the September 11 attacks once again laid bare the underlying choices and dynamics of hemispheric relations.[6]

In the current context, the new focus of fighting terrorism was reflected in the agenda and deliberations of the first general assembly meeting of the Organization of American States (OAS) following the September 11 attacks. Indeed, the principal focus and outcome of that meeting, which took place in June 2002 in Barbados, was the approval of an inter-American convention against terrorism. While such a convention was cast widely, and arguably has considerable relevance for many of the hemisphere's countries, its principal sponsor and motor was the U.S. government, acting in accordance with its global antiterrorism campaign. Secretary of State Colin Powell's presence at the meeting underscored the convention's importance for the United States. Moreover, on Colombia policy, in which the United States has been deeply involved even before the Plan Colombia aid package was approved in July 2000, the rationale shifted in the post–September 11 period to be cast more explicitly in terms of fighting terrorism. Before then, the justification was fighting drugs. Such an overlay carries important implications for the strategy to end that country's decades-old conflict.

Nonetheless, while there are occasional signs of such strategic concerns in the hemisphere, it has been difficult to discern a set of carefully developed, proactive policies seeking to fashion and coordinate multilateral arrangements to deal more effectively with common problems. The central question in the post–September 11 period is not unlike that frequently raised in the post–Cold War era: Will the countries of the hemisphere be able to take advantage of a huge opportunity to forge productive partnerships in pursuit of a shared agenda? Despite unparalleled possibilities for joint action to solve common problems in the 1990s, the foundations for a long-term relationship remain tenuous.

In the post–September 11 period, economic and political crises are deepening, yet there are few clear signs of effective responses or overall direction and purpose. Instead, there is considerable confusion and puzzlement throughout the region, as the United States tends to react to events and lacks an overarching framework or strategic concept.[7] Although the world's only superpower is surely tempted to "go it alone" in dealing with terrorist threats, there are well-founded doubts whether such an approach will be fruitful—strictly in terms of advancing U.S. interests in the long term—as incentives for Latin American cooperation weaken.[8]

For Latin America, perhaps the single most disappointing issue has been that of a Free Trade Area of the Americas (FTAA), the principal objective that emerged from the 1994 Summit of the Americas. After an eight-year lapse, the U.S. Congress in July 2002 approved—albeit by the narrowest of margins—the Trade Promotion Authority (TPA), which, as Carol Wise says in Chapter 2, had hung over the free trade question "like a dark cloud." That same legislation also renewed vital trade preferences for the troubled Andean countries of Bolivia, Colombia, Ecuador, and Peru, which had been suspended, at considerable cost, for eight months.

The trade question and the move toward an FTAA are far from settled. The United States continues to display considerable ambivalence on free trade matters. Moreover, many Latin American governments have been dismayed by the rather surprising protectionist tendencies exhibited by the Bush administration, illustrated by decisions on steel and farm subsidies in the United States. Such moves have effectively undercut the arguments being advanced by many advocates for greater reform and trade liberalization in Latin America. Decisions in the United States, coupled with deepening economic and political problems in many of the region's countries, continue to make prospects for an FTAA uncertain at best.

Nonetheless, despite disappointing signs on the political front there has been progress at the technical level made by the nine negotiating groups working on the hemispheric free trade effort. As Wise states in Chapter 2, with "the Southern Cone's own political economic crisis, and the virtual stalling of Mercosur [a customs union including Brazil, Argentina, Paraguay, and Uruguay that was established in 1991], . . . the FTAA is the only truly viable option for pulling out of this slump." She concludes that in order for the FTAA to move forward countries in the region must, at the domestic level, alleviate their distributional strains, and, at the subregional level, generate greater support for hemispheric free trade by demonstrating the political and economic soundness of the FTAA initiative. Finally, Wise argues that Brazil and the United States, the Western Hemisphere's hegemonic leaders, must work toward bridging the gap between trade preferences and policy practices, particularly as they fulfill their assigned responsibility to jointly chair the final stages of the FTAA negotiations from 2003 to 2005.

On the security question, as Margaret Daly Hayes points out in Chapter 3, the hemisphere has also seen significant advances since the end of the Cold War. The regular meetings of the hemisphere's defense ministers, launched in Williamsburg in 1995, continue, reflecting greater collaboration and levels of mutual confidence. Hayes affirms that military cooperation in the hemisphere is at an "all-time high"; progress in the Southern Cone has been particularly dramatic. At the same time, however, there are growing security threats, increasingly

fueled by the spreading drug problem, among the most salient globalization challenges. Common crime has skyrocketed throughout Latin
America, especially in urban areas. Moreover, the Latin American
Barometer surveys consistently reveal that personal security is one of
the leading worries of the region's citizens.

Colombia stands out as the hemisphere's major security challenge,
with already significant "spillover" effects and ominous regional repercussions. A relatively weak state has been unable to deal effectively
with rising levels of lawlessness and violence carried out by two leftist
insurgencies and the rightist paramilitary forces. All three appear on the
U.S. State Department's list of terrorist organizations and are largely
fueled by the drug trade, kidnapping, and extortion. (Roughly 70 percent of the world's kidnappings take place in Colombia.) With a new
government headed by Alvaro Uribe that took power in August 2002,
Colombia will give higher priority to security issues, with a clear commitment to boost defense spending, and seek to professionalize the
country's armed forces and police. The coming years will present a
severe test to Colombia's civilian leadership, and also to U.S. policy,
which has long been misguided by a narrow focus on the drug problem.
Whether Colombia, the United States, and other relevant external actors
will be able to forge a common strategy to turn around the country's
dramatic deterioration remains to be seen.

Canada is another increasingly important player in the region.
Canada's proximity to the United States and status as its principal trading partner have significantly facilitated deeper engagement in hemispheric affairs over the past decade. In Chapter 5, Charles Doran
describes the setting of the early 1990s that prompted Canada to take
advantage of the end of the Cold War and a more propitious environment for meaningful multilateralism, as exemplified by its joining the
OAS in 1990. The adoption of NAFTA in 1993 also gave a substantial
boost to Canada's participation in Latin American affairs. The country's
strategy was to exercise "soft power" and diplomatic influence, positioning itself as a broker between the United States and the Latin
American countries on an array of key political issues. Canada projected a leadership role in 2000 and 2001, when it hosted a variety of
important hemispheric gatherings, including the third Summit of the
Americas, held in Quebec in April 2001. Canada also sought to facilitate Cuba's incorporation into the inter-American system, though this
goal has proved exceedingly difficult, in light of major differences
between Canada, the United States, and Cuba.

Canada has accorded considerable importance to attempting to promote and advance democracy in Latin America through the OAS. It has been the prime mover, and funder, for the Unit for the Promotion of Democracy, created in 1990. Canada has regarded the Democracy Charter as a noteworthy achievement and potentially effective instrument. The charter, which codifies all OAS-related declarations and resolutions related to democratic defense and promotion, was adopted on September 11, 2001, at a special session of the general assembly held in Lima, Peru. As several chapters in this volume note, the OAS, invoking a landmark resolution adopted in June 1991, has responded promptly—albeit with mixed results—to various interruptions of democratic rule in the 1990s, including Haiti (1991), Peru (1992), Guatemala (1993), and Paraguay (1996).

In all four cases the United States government played a leading role in condemning the interruptions of constitutional rule and thus appeared to gain some credibility among Latin Americans on the democracy question. It did so again by taking a firm stand in January 2000, when a coup ousted Ecuadorian president Jamil Mahuad. But on April 11, 2002, following a coup attempt in Venezuela, the initial response by the United States government was ambiguous at best, and even appeared to celebrate the forced removal of President Hugo Chávez. In contrast, the Latin American governments meeting as the Rio Group in Costa Rica—with some no doubt fearing a contagion effect in their own countries—condemned the interruption of the constitutional order in Venezuela. In the first critical test of the Democratic Charter, the United States lost some of the credibility it had managed to establish throughout the preceding decade.[9]

Complicated democratic crises in such countries as Haiti, Peru, and Venezuela have highlighted the important role that the OAS needs to play in advancing democracy—a critical aim on the globalization agenda—throughout Latin America. Yet, while the OAS has responded constructively to a number of serious situations, the regional organization has not undergone the necessary reforms to make it as effective and vigorous as many observers believed it had the potential to become with the end of the Cold War.[10] The organization still lacks the high-level political resources required to deal with an increasingly precarious democratic landscape, as well as an effective system of prevention. In the Venezuelan case, the OAS failed to take any action to anticipate the April 2002 crisis. Despite being assigned a number of key tasks and responsibilities following the three Summits of the Americas in Miami

(1994), Santiago (1998), and Quebec (2001), the OAS has still not assumed the chief coordinating role of such a promising hemispheric initiative.[11] For a variety of reasons—including the mistrust that naturally springs from the asymmetry of power between the United States and other countries—member governments have shown a lack of will to enhance the authority of the OAS in tackling serious hemispheric problems.

Latin America's New Challenges

As Rosa Alonso argues in Chapter 6, there is a compelling case for a new and improved architecture to deal more effectively with financial crises in Latin America and thereby preserve "the existing liberal international economy." This represents one of the most critical challenges for Latin America in light of the forces of globalization. The crisis prevention and crisis management mechanisms of the international financial institutions (IFIs) are woefully inadequate. The response by the International Monetary Fund (IMF) to Argentina's financial meltdown in 2002 underscores the need for institutional reform. Alonso suggests that the World Bank decrease funding of specific projects and instead focus on fostering the adoption of sound development policies through program lending based on conditionality. Such policies should be more attuned to political questions than they have in the past and special attention should particularly be devoted to pushing for serious reforms—and taking on vested interests—in the area of education.

On the issue of human rights, Colombia represents the most critical situation in Latin America, with approximately 3,500 killed each year as a direct result of the unspeakably cruel conflict. Yet, as Alison Brysk contends in Chapter 7, the past decades have seen a number of notable advances in the region's human rights conditions. In the majority of Latin American countries the situation has improved. Although the forces of globalization can help strengthen violent nonstate actors, such as the rebel groups and paramilitaries in Colombia, they can also help foster a growing transnational cosmopolitanism and more robust civil society. This has been one of the more heartening trends within the context of Latin America's still uncertain democratization. Globalization has, however, created what Brysk calls a "citizenship gap," a challenge for citizens to be actively involved and to insist on greater accountability of burgeoning nonstate actors.

What has perhaps been most striking since September 11, 2001, has been indications of growing U.S. indifference toward and disengagement from Latin America and the Caribbean. Mexico has been particularly affected. Just days before the terrorist attacks, Mexican president Vicente Fox was in Washington, where he was received with enormous enthusiasm. At the White House, President George W. Bush, whose friendship with Fox dates from when they were both state governors, proclaimed that Mexico was "our most important relationship." Yet with Bush and senior policy officials consumed by the war on terrorism after September 11, the promising policy initiatives on such key questions as immigration were put on the back burner.

As Russell Crandall makes clear in Chapter 9, Mexico's ties with the United States on a wide array of issues have been accompanied by considerable economic and political benefits, but by some new vulnerabilities as well, including being increasingly subject to the vicissitudes of the U.S. economy. Vicente Fox's election in July 2000 signaled a political sea change in Mexico, to some degree linked to its integration into North America, as exemplified by the North American Free Trade Agreement (NAFTA). Yet Mexico's prospects for playing an increasingly significant role in the hemisphere—functioning as the chief interlocutor between the United States and the rest of Latin America—have been dampened both by the exacerbation of the region's problems and by the perceptible withdrawal of the United States from the bilateral agenda.

Also striking to many observers of the hemisphere is the sharp contrast in the way the United States responded to Mexico's peso crisis in 1994–1995 and its approach to Argentina's financial crisis in 2001–2002. Even acknowledging Mexico's unquestionably special relationship with its northern neighbor, the U.S. government has dealt with Argentina's crisis largely as a fiscal, not political or security problem, and primarily through the IMF, with little direct engagement by senior U.S. policy officials. The largely indifferent approach taken by the United States in addressing the Argentine crisis reinforces the sense of a shift in its policy on one of the major global challenges, and it suggests declining U.S. concern with the region's core problems.

Given its undeniable niche as a "pivotal state" in Latin America, Brazil, too, has not received the attention it deserves from Washington. To be sure, the IMF's $30 billion rescue package to Brazil in August 2002, backed by the U.S. Treasury, was an important sign of support aimed at assuring global financial markets. However, as Carol Wise argues, it would be difficult to imagine the successful completion of a hemisphere-wide free trade agreement without more effective collaboration and a higher degree of convergence between Brazil and the United States. They are, after all, the respective leaders of Mercosur and NAFTA.

In 2002, after eight years of impressive economic order and democratic stability under the two-term presidency of Fernando Henrique Cardoso, there is considerable political uncertainty about what comes next in Brazil, and which policies the administration that took over in January 2003 will pursue. It is unclear whether the next Brazilian government will sustain Cardoso's leadership in regional and foreign policy issues, reflected in his organizing the first summit of South American heads of state in August 2000. Yet, as Riordan Roett argues forcefully in Chapter 10, Brazil's immense social agenda will, in the long term, most likely limit the country's ability to be a decisive actor on the global stage. Without effective national policies aimed at correcting fiscal problems and addressing underlying social and economic inequality, Brazil's role in shaping the hemisphere's agenda—and performing effectively as a pivotal state—will be very difficult to assert.

Careful examination of the different strategies pursued by Mexico and Brazil can be instructive. As Peter Hakim suggests in "Two Ways to Go Global," geography, along with domestic politics and national ideologies, can help account for Mexico's decision to hitch its future to the United States, whereas Brazil has opted for a more independent course with multiple relationships.[12] There is a noticeable difference in the perspectives of Mexican analysts and those in the Southern Cone, who have a much more distant posture regarding the United States, as reflected in an essay written by noted Chilean official Heraldo Muñoz, "Good-bye USA?"[13] For Southern Cone governments, Europe is especially critical to economic and political relations. As Wolf Grabendorff maintains in Chapter 8, while there are considerable grounds for a growing strategic partnership between Europe and Latin America—in May 2002, for example, heads of state from 48 European and Latin American countries convened in Madrid for the second summit between the regions—the relationship can also be quite contentious. Moreover, some European countries have evinced little interest in engaging more deeply with Latin America.

In the new millennium, how Latin America responds to emerging challenges and opportunities will depend on a variety of factors, some that are part of the regional and international context, others that derive directly from particular societies. The United States is surely not the only factor in shaping trends, but it is no doubt a significant one and is likely to remain so for the foreseeable future. There is no question that the power enjoyed by the United States in the economic, military, technological, and cultural spheres is unrivaled. Less clear are the purposes for which that power will be employed—and how it will be employed—in the coming years.

For the United States, the post–September 11 period poses a critical test: Will it be able to buy into the goals and values that key allies in such regions as Latin America deem important? In this regard, it would be worth heeding Stanley Hoffmann's wise words: "If we want to limit terrorism's appeal, we must keep our eyes and ears open to conditions abroad, revise our perceptions of ourselves, and alter our world image through our actions."[14]

Notes

1. Peter Hakim, "The Uneasy Americas," *Foreign Affairs* 80, no. 2 (March–April 2001): 46–61.

2. Marta Lagos, "Public Opinion," in *Constructing Democratic Governance in Latin America,* ed. Jorge I. Domínguez and Michael Shifter (Washington, D.C.: The Inter-American Dialogue, April 2003).

3. Manuel Pastor and Carol Wise, "The Politics of Second-Generation Reform," *Journal of Democracy* 10, no. 3 (1999): 34–48.

4. See Robert Chase, Emily Hill, and Paul Kennedy, eds., *The Pivotal States: A New Framework for U.S. Policy in the Developing World* (New York: Norton, 1999).

5. Abraham F. Lowenthal, "United States–Latin American Relations at the Century's Turn: Managing the 'Intermestic' Agenda," in *The United States and the Americas: A Twenty-First Century View,* ed. Albert Fishlow and James Jones (New York: Norton, 1999), 109–136.

6. Michael Shifter, "A Shaken Agenda: Bush and Latin America," *Current History* 101, no. 652 (February 2002): 51–57.

7. Joseph S. Tulchin and Ralph H. Espach, "Latin America in the New International System: A Call for Strategic Thinking," in *Latin America in the New International System,* ed. Joseph S. Tulchin and Ralph H. Espach (Boulder: Lynne Rienner, 2001), 1–33. "The CEO Presidency," *The Economist,* 21 June 2002, 34.

8. Moisés Naím, "Even a Hegemon Needs Friends and Allies," *Financial Times,* 13 September 2001, 23.

9. Michael Shifter, "Democracy in Venezuela, Unsettling as Ever," *Washington Post,* Outlook Section, 21 April 2002, B2.

10. Viron P. Vaky and Heraldo Muñoz, *The Future of the Organization of American States* (New York: The Twentieth Century Fund Press, 1993).

11. Richard E. Feinberg, *Summitry in the Americas: A Progress Report* (Washington, D.C.: Institute for International Economics, 1997).

12. Peter Hakim, "Two Ways to Go Global," *Foreign Affairs* 81, no. 1 (January–February 2002): 148–162.

13. Heraldo Muñoz, "Good-bye U.S.A.?" in Tulchin and Espach, *Latin America in the New International System,* 73–90.

14. Keith Melville, "Coming to Terms with Terrorism," *Kettering Review* (Winter 2002): 48.

Part 1

The Transformation in
Intrahemispheric Relations

2

Free Trade in the Americas: Collective Action or Collective Apathy?

Carol Wise

Since the launching of formal negotiations for a 34-member Free Trade Area of the Americas (FTAA) agreement in April 1998, the debate over the fate of the FTAA has been increasingly cast in black and white terms. Pessimists have declared the FTAA institutionally incapable of rising above the patchwork of subregional accords that now supports it; the pressures from continued international economic volatility and the apparent weakening of political will for deeper liberalization throughout the hemisphere have further fueled predictions concerning the stalling of the FTAA.[1] Optimists insist that the negotiations are running on track for the 2005 deadline originally set at the 1994 Summit of the Americas in Miami; they argue that the steady stream of external economic shocks, combined with favorable returns from the impressive liberalization advances made over the past decade, has strengthened the resolve of hemispheric leaders and policymakers to see the FTAA negotiations through to a successful finish.[2] Even in the wake of the admittedly inconclusive 2001 Quebec City summit, both sides claimed victory by drawing selectively from the numerous initiatives put forward.[3]

Somewhere in between these polemics lies a middle ground, and it is the purpose of this chapter to explore it. In doing so, I advance three propositions concerning the FTAA. First, it is important to distinguish between the domestic political stalemate and bureaucratic gridlock that has plagued U.S. trade policy since the 1994 expiration of "fast-track" negotiating authority, and the actual progress that has been made within the FTAA's negotiating groups. The repeated failure of the Clinton administration to secure the congressional fast-track authorization necessary to negotiate the FTAA hung like a dark cloud over the FTAA process. In the absence of fast-track, the FTAA cup was decidedly half empty; however, with the August 2002 passage of fast-track (renamed "Trade Promotion Authority" [TPA] by the George W. Bush administration), the cup is beginning to appear half full.[4] Since the appointment of Robert Zoellick as chief trade negotiator on the Bush economic team, the effort to complete the FTAA in a timely fashion has sped up considerably.

The Bush administration's TPA victory is just the beginning, however. To truly move forward (and this is my second proposition), more attention must be paid to the role that traditional collective action problems have played in slowing the progress of the FTAA negotiations. Whereas much of the recent debate has focused on process, timing, and issues intrinsic to the FTAA agreement, the ultimate outcome of the FTAA negotiations lies as much in the resolution of underlying political economic tensions within the key member countries.[5] The most extreme example is the United States, where fast-track authorization was ostensibly thwarted because of a decade-long standoff between, on the one hand, labor and environmental groups that insist that any future trade agreements must include provisions to protect workers' rights and the environment, along the lines of those incorporated into the North American Free Trade Agreement (NAFTA), and, on the other hand, powerful private sector representatives who fear that such stipulations will encroach too heavily on their own interests. This chapter will argue that the fast-track dispute was driven by much deeper distributional cleavages in the United States, related to the stark contrast between rigid patterns of income inequality and a buoyant economic expansion that characterized the 1990s.

In Latin America, the current collective action challenges stem from the sweeping programs of market reform that have been implemented since the mid-1980s. While trade liberalization in particular has correlated with an increase in the real incomes of the lower 60 percent of the population in a large sample of Latin American countries,[6] it has also inflicted considerable adjustment stress on workers and producers alike. The deepening of liberalization via the FTAA presents two main problems. First, preexisting levels of income inequality, which are a main legacy of the 1980s debt crisis, have been exacerbated by subsequent efforts at market restructuring. Thus, although absolute income gains point toward poverty reduction, inequality has still worsened in relative terms. Second, after a decade of public support for market reform, based on fears of the hyperinflationary past, voters in countries

like Argentina and Brazil are now looking forward and fearing the con-
tinuance of unprecedented levels of hyper-unemployment. As voters
who fear further economic liberalization are becoming more vocal,
political leaders must be more strategic in bundling the FTAA with a set
of credible adjustment policies that strengthen the economic position of
a sizable segment of losers who continue to thrash around in the market.

My final proposition concerns the ways in which these collective
action challenges have converged to shape a different path for the
FTAA than the one originally articulated by U.S. leaders at the 1994
Miami summit. On this front, leaders from the five major subregional
schemes in the hemisphere have not rushed forward to complete the
FTAA,[7] but neither are they necessarily working against it. Rather, previous (and mainly U.S.-inspired) notions of a quick outcome have given
way to a more realistic scenario in which the FTAA moves forward
gradually and in tandem with multilateral trade negotiations at the
World Trade Organization (WTO). Given the mounting distributional
tensions on the domestic front across the region, accentuated by the
Argentine debt default and implosion of the Southern Cone economies
in early 2002, this slower pace may be a source of disappointment for
the FTAA's designers; however, even the reform advances that have
occurred thus far within the main subregional schemes have been sufficient for the steady expansion of trade and investment in the Western
Hemisphere.

The FTAA: Political, Economic, and Institutional Evolution

One way of understanding the gap between rhetoric and reality with
regard to the FTAA is to look at the different motivations between north
and south that initially inspired it. For the United States, proposals to
negotiate the bilateral Canada-U.S. Free Trade Agreement (CUSFTA) in
the 1980s, and subsequently NAFTA, stemmed from fears over the
country's declining competitiveness, as well as frustration over the
Uruguay Round's slow progress in reducing trade barriers in Europe
and Asia. Canada, which faced these same troublesome international
trends, pragmatically accepted U.S. overtures toward bilateralism in
recognition that its earlier foothold in European markets could no
longer be taken for granted. While Mexico's request in 1990 to negotiate a bilateral free trade agreement with the United States was badly
received in Ottawa, in the end, Canada joined the NAFTA negotiations

in order to avoid the diversion of trade and investment that it would have otherwise suffered.

Whereas Canada and the United States turned to bilateral initiatives long after each had liberalized its trade and investment regime, the rapid proliferation of subregional trade schemes in Latin America was part and parcel of the region's economic opening. As trade liberalization became an integral part of macroeconomic stabilization efforts in the late 1980s, an initial round of unilateral tariff and nontariff reductions quickly brought most Latin American countries in line with the mandates of the General Agreement on Tariffs and Trade (GATT). Simultaneously, policymakers sought to maximize the potential of trade reform as a powerful tool for microeconomic restructuring. In contrast to the macroeconomic turmoil and inward-looking integration schemes of the 1960s in Latin America, subregional integration in the 1990s became a main venue for "locking in" hard-fought macroeconomic stabilization gains and for institutionalizing new liberal trade and investment initiatives.

For Latin America, it was the 1990 announcement by President George H. W. Bush of a new Enterprise for the Americas Initiative (EAI) that shaped expectations for the creation of a full hemispheric accord that would amount to more than the sum of its subregional parts. The stated strategy of the Bush trade policy team was to proceed simultaneously with the Uruguay Round at the multilateral level and with the NAFTA negotiations at the subregional level. It was assumed that once these more immediate goals were achieved, the negotiation of a larger hemispheric accord would follow. Although the NAFTA and Uruguay Round agreements were later secured by the Clinton administration, it had become apparent that in pursuing a joint subregional/multilateral strategy, U.S. trade policy makers were now operating under new kinds of opportunities and constraints.

Some of NAFTA's achievements clearly went beyond the GATT. For example, NAFTA removed virtually all border barriers to trade between Canada, Mexico, and the United States over a 15-year time period, and it included more comprehensive coverage of foreign direct investment (FDI), trade in services, intellectual property rights, and dispute settlement.[8] These advances revealed the extent to which NAFTA was as much about investment as it was about free trade. And, despite open disagreements in Washington as to whether the United States had any business launching subregional negotiations in the midst of the Uruguay Round,[9] hindsight does show that the very prospect of NAFTA provided the United States with the bargaining chip it needed to finally wrap up the Uruguay Round agreement in early 1994.

Yet the NAFTA negotiations also drove home the constraints inherent in a hemispheric approach to integration. Having entered the NAFTA negotiations at a fairly early stage in its own trade opening, Mexico was primarily interested in market access and bargaining over crucial sectoral concerns (autos, energy, and agriculture). As advanced liberal capitalist economies, Canada and the United States were more intent on securing the kinds of legal trade norms mentioned above, goals that continue to prove extremely challenging to accomplish at the multilateral level. Underpinning these different motives for subregionalism, of course, were the huge disparities between north and south. Because of its close preexisting economic ties with the North American bloc, Mexico had a tremendous amount to gain by conceding on legal norms in exchange for guaranteed access to this market. The Mexican government was even willing to forgo any special breaks in the NAFTA negotiations for its developing country status.

But neither the U.S. public nor political leaders nor their constituencies in the southern part of the hemisphere have been able to overlook these asymmetries. In the United States, while there was substantial consensus among economists that NAFTA would have a modest net gain of 100,000–200,000 jobs over its first ten years, the long-term trend toward corporate downsizing and wage stagnation gave U.S. workers understandable cause for concern. If NAFTA signified a free flow of goods, services, and capital between all three countries, what was to stop the flow northward of environmental pollution and illegal immigrants willing to work for a fraction of the minimum wage? Why risk the lowering of labor and environmental standards that workers and consumers in the United States had fought to achieve since the 1930s?

With the negotiation of special labor and environmental side agreements to address these concerns, the Clinton administration finally won enough congressional votes to pass the controversial NAFTA bill in November 1993. However, by the time of NAFTA's implementation in January 1994, all of the protagonists that took part in the original debate had dug their heels in even deeper than before. Labor and environmental activists were embittered that the side agreements provided for enforcement of national legislation that already existed but stopped short of strengthening and harmonizing North American standards in these areas. Indeed, the side agreements actually impinged very little on national sovereignty, yet the North American private sector saw them as going much too far in this direction. These divisions grew with the rise of a conservative Republican congressional majority out of the 1994 midterm elections in the United States, which uncharacteristically viewed the idea of further market opening with suspicion. Mexico's December 1994 peso crisis, which generated the need for a massive $50 billion[10] multilateral bailout, did little to assuage these fears. Less than a year after NAFTA's launching, the questions of further accession to the agreement or congressional reauthorization of fast-track negotiating authority were basically precluded by these other political and economic forces.

South of the Mexican border, just as NAFTA had elicited contrasting views in North America about what we should expect from government, the role of markets, and strategies for economic development, so too did the prospect of its expansion southward trigger similar debates in these countries. As the possibility of NAFTA accession became increasingly remote, however, policymakers in other Latin American countries were spared this particular debate. Of necessity, they turned their attention to the strengthening of subregional and extraregional ties and to the prospects for negotiating a full hemispheric FTAA accord. The progress that Latin America has made in shifting to an outward development model driven by subregional integration schemes is reflected in figures that show the region's commercial exchange with the rest of the world has doubled since 1990. Similarly, the larger subregional groupings such as NAFTA and the Southern Cone Common Market (Mercosur) have seen average annual export growth rates of 11–25 percent among the respective members of each bloc during this same time period.[11] Nevertheless, wide economic disparities within Latin America, and the varying levels of readiness to commit fully to the FTAA's ultimate liberalization goals, also slowed the march toward full hemispheric integration.

None of this should detract from the vitally important work being conducted within the FTAA's nine negotiating groups (market access; agriculture; antidumping, subsidies, and countervailing duties; competition policy; services; investment; intellectual property rights; government procurement; and dispute settlement), which were consolidated from the 12 preparatory committees created at the 1994 Miami summit. These groups, along with a consultative committee designed to address the concerns of smaller economies and two additional committees dealing with the participation of civil society and with electronic commerce, have been laying the groundwork for a comprehensive negotiating agenda that simply has no precedent in the Western Hemisphere. Apart from the development of crucial institutional capacities, as well as the increased opportunities for political learning and collegial exchange, the current negotiating group format directly lends itself to the achievement of consistency and complementarity between the FTAA and the WTO.

The immediate challenge in the wake of the Bush administration's TPA victory is for state leaders and policymakers across the region to reconfirm the political economic rationale for a hemispheric integration scheme. Just since 1994, U.S. FDI in Latin America has increased by 50 percent, and U.S. exports to the region (excluding Mexico) by 52 percent; in fact, U.S. trade with Latin America is growing twice as fast as with countries outside of the Western Hemisphere.[12] Within the region, even under conditions of severe external volatility, total intraregional trade grew at an average rate of around 20 percent between 1997 and 1999.[13] While the potential for further hemisphere-wide gains in trade and investment are estimated to be considerable, those who initially pushed for the FTAA seem to have lost sight of this earlier rationale. Nowhere is this more true than in the United States, the country that accounts for some 75 percent of hemispheric output, and where a record-setting economic expansion prevailed from 1994 to 2000. In Latin America, despite strong trade performance against the backdrop of the Asian, Russian, and Brazilian financial shocks of 1997–1999, the prospect of further liberalization has been met with caution. The onset of deep recession in the wake of the September 11, 2001, terrorist attacks on the United States has cast another layer of doubt on the prospects for hemispheric integration. The next section explores how continued economic stress has posed distinct challenges to further collective action in pursuing the FTAA, and it argues for a more targeted and credible set of remedial policies to address these tensions.

Challenges to Collective Action: Dynamism Versus Distribution

While the reform strategies embraced by the majority of Latin American countries conform closely to the liberal prescriptions of the Washington Consensus,[14] closer scrutiny of the track record reflects the diversity of those policies that have been pursued under the banner of market reform. In countries like Argentina and Mexico, for example, policymakers have relied on a fairly hands-off approach to liberalization that assigns the task of economic adjustment primarily to market forces. In contrast, Chile has relied on more of a competitive liberalization strategy, which means that public policy (e.g., tax and credit incentives for smaller trading companies, export promotion, and job training programs) has been used actively as part of a development model based on free trade. Brazilian policymakers have also leaned toward a competitive strategy, although the continued propensity of the government to concede readily to private sector demands for protectionism suggests that it would still be premature to classify Brazil's strategy as a "competitive" one.

Table 2.1 reflects the overall progress that has been made at both the macro- and the microeconomic levels in the four countries on which the future of hemispheric integration will most depend. On the macroeconomic side, there is no denying the success of economic liberalization in halting the chaotic inflation that prevailed, for example, in Argentina, Brazil, and Mexico. With Brazil's long overdue adjustment, the average inflation rate for the region as a whole fell from about 900 percent in 1993 to just 10.5 percent in 1997.[15] Despite the added stress from severe financial disruptions in Asia and Russia, which forced a 40 percent devaluation of the real in early 1999, Brazil's continued commitment to adjustment has been such that inflation rates are now running in the single-digit range.

Under the thrust of lower inflation, regional growth rates have similarly improved. In 1997, for the first time in some 25 years, average regional growth surpassed 5 percent of gross domestic product (GDP) and per capita gains approached 4 percent. Yet, only Chile, with an average annual growth rate of 6.6 percent of GDP from 1991 to 2000, surpassed the 6 percent threshold that economic theory holds as necessary for triggering higher sustainable income gains; the remainder of the cases averaged growth rates between 2.7 percent (Brazil) and 4.7 percent (Argentina) over this same time period. Total gross investment as a percent of GDP has followed a similar trend whereby Chile has seen a gradual increase in total investment, from 18.6 percent of GDP in 1981 to 23.2 percent in 1995, while the remaining three cases have registered substantial declines during this same time frame. Net FDI has been more responsive to the stabilization signals that all four countries have succeeded in sending, with the four-country total rising from an average of about $11.3 billion between 1990 and 1994 to a projected $70.9 billion for 1999 alone.[16]

Table 2.1   Growth, Investment, and Distributional Returns in the 1990s: Argentina, Brazil, Chile, and Mexico

		Argentina	Brazil	Chile	Mexico
GDP	1991–2000	4.7	2.7	6.6	3.5
GDI	1990–1998	17.7	20.8	25.3	22.9
EXGDP	1990–2000	9.2	8.8	30.0	22.9
INF	2000	–0.9	7.0	3.8	9.5
RW	1990–2000	0.0	0.4	3.7	0.8
EMP	1990–1999	1.3	1.7	2.1	3.0
LPRO	1990–1995	4.1	–0.1	3.3	–2.2
URUN	1990–2000	12.2	5.8	7.7	3.5
EDGAP	1994	1.9[a]	4.7	1.5	3.1
DIST: poorest 40%	1986	16.2	9.7	12.6	12.7[c]
DIST: poorest 40%	1990	14.9	9.6	13.4	11.7[b]
DIST: poorest 40%	1994	13.9	11.8	13.3	10.8
DIST: poorest 40%	1998	14.9[d]	8.2	—	—
DIST: richest 10%	1986	34.5	44.3	39.6	34.3[c]
DIST: richest 10%	1990	34.8	41.7	39.2	39.0[b]
DIST: richest 10%	1994	34.2	42.5	40.3	41.2
DIST: richest 10%	1998	35.8[e]	44.3[a]	39.1	42.8[d]

Sources: GDP and INF: Economic Commission for Latin America and the Caribbean (ECLAC) Web page [www.eclac.org]. GDI: World Bank, *World Development Indicators* CD-ROM, 2001. EXGDP: Calculated from National Accounts, *IMF International Financial Statistics* CD-ROM, September 2001. RW, EMP, LPRO, URUN: ECLAC Web page. EDGAP: Jere Behrman, Nancy Birdsall, and Miguel Székely, presentation at "Workshop on Social Mobility," Brookings Institution, Washington, D.C., 4–5 June 1998. DIST: Chilean and Brazilian data based on urban areas and Argentine data based on Buenos Aires, from ECLAC (1997); Mexico data from the Instituto Nacional de Estadística, Geografía e Informática (INEGI) [www.inegi.gob.mx]. Most recent distribution figures: ECLAC Web page and World Bank CD-ROM, 2000.

Notes: a. 1996.
  b. 1989.
  c. 1984.
  d. 1995.
  e. 1997.
  GDP = gross domestic product.
  GDI = gross domestic investment as percentage of GDP.
  EXGDP = ratio of exports of goods and services to GDP.
  INF = percent change in consumer prices over previous year.
  RW = real wages, average annual growth rate.
  EMP = employment, average annual growth rate.
  LPRO = labor productivity, average annual growth rate.
  URUN = urban unemployment, average annual rate.
  EDGAP = average years behind in school for ages 15–18.
  DIST = percentage of national income accruing to groups.

Despite considerable advances on the macroeconomic front, Table 2.1 also reflects the risks of relying too heavily on the combination of anchored exchange rates and import competition to fight inflation. In Argentina, Brazil, and Mexico, overvalued currencies, mounting current account deficits, and increasing dependence on short-term portfolio flows have left these countries vulnerable to the whims of mutual fund managers and currency speculators. This strong dependence on external capital flows has also distracted policymakers from designing the kinds of incentives that would garner higher levels of domestic savings and investment. Mexico learned this lesson the hard way in December 1994, as did Brazil in late 1998 and Argentina in late 2001. In all three cases, investors simply lost confidence in each country's ability to maintain the exchange rate amid mounting trade, current account, and fiscal imbalances. The flight of investors provoked a run on the domestic currency and sparked financial crises that quickly spread to other countries in the region. The steep losses of GDP in all three countries in the wake of massive currency devaluations suggested the need to pursue macroeconomic stability through a broader mix of policies (fiscal and monetary reform, more flexible exchange rate management) and to articulate more clearly a role for trade policy as part of a larger development strategy.

Evidence to support this last statement is even more compelling at the microeconomic level. Setting aside the question of distributional trends for the time being, Chile stands out as having achieved higher gains in growth, productivity, and wages than any of its Latin counterparts in the 1990s. One could point to Chile's longer experience with trade liberalization, which preceded these other countries by at least a decade, as ample justification for its relative success. Yet Table 2.1's comparative analysis of the actual trade and development strategies employed by the other countries suggests that the timing variable alone does not suffice as an explanation for differential economic performance in the region. The erratic microeconomic performance of the other three countries can be explained by variations in policy choice.

In Argentina, for example, a hands-off management approach from 1991 to 2001 produced respectable aggregate growth rates; however, at the level of the real economy—everyday economic returns for the average worker—wage gains and employment expansion virtually stood still. The country's comparatively high labor productivity rates have been offset by similarly high levels of urban unemployment, which reflect the extent to which productivity gains in Argentina have stemmed from the downsizing of the labor force. While the volume of trade as a percentage of GDP has nearly doubled since 1990, chronic currency overvaluation during that decade under a fixed exchange rate regime fostered a pattern of trade (led by primary exports) that directly hampered further job creation.

For Mexico, the lower growth rates that appear in Table 2.1, in terms of aggregate GDP, real wages, and labor productivity, testify both to the limits of a market model that relies on a fixed exchange rate as the centerpiece of stabilization and to the high price that the country has paid for the reckless economic management errors that led up to the December 1994 peso crisis. The unexpectedly rapid turnaround of the Mexican economy in the aftermath of the peso's devaluation was spurred by high value-added industrial exports and more privileged access to the U.S. market under NAFTA. Mexico's recent export dynamism reflects the enormous amount of restructuring that has occurred since the onset of trade liberalization, as well as the importance of a competitive exchange rate for unleashing the country's new productive potential.[17] By 1997, as real growth rates had rebounded to 7 percent of GDP, the government had committed itself, at least on paper, to a new Program of Industrial Policy and International Trade. Similar to Chile's shift a decade earlier, Mexican policymakers, under heavy pressure from the domestic private sector, have now opted for a flexible exchange rate and "active government participation, in the form of highly effective public policies that promote industrial growth."[18]

Although Brazil has expressed an affinity for a Chilean-style competitive model,[19] the microeconomic track record there has yet to reflect this policy preference. In Brazil, as stabilization and adjustment continue to work their way through the economy, the country's microeconomic fate now lies in the hands of policymakers who find themselves increasingly torn between private sector demands for government protection and assistance, and a growing mass of poor Brazilians whose social status continues to deteriorate in the wake of the 1999 devaluation. Hence, Brazil's tendency to waver between policies that are clearly market-supporting (monetary and fiscal reform) and those that are market-distorting (unilateral tariff hikes, for example, on consumer durables and some vulnerable nondurable sectors such as apparel). Although recent Brazilian public opinion polls have soured on market reforms and "soft" market candidates dominated the 2002 presidential election campaign, the degree of economic reform in Brazil is now such that the new administration will have little leeway to pursue old-style populism.

Finally, what explains the universally disappointing distributional trends that appear in Table 2.1, a pattern that reflects Latin America's status as the most unequal region in the world? Although econometric evidence from 1985 to 1995 points to a positive relationship between macroeconomic stabilization/trade liberalization and distributional gains,[20] why are these trends not more robust for the 1990s, especially for earlier liberalizers like Chile and Mexico? This distributional deterioration is doubly puzzling when the generally higher levels of spending on health and education in the 1990s, representing some 2 percent of regional GDP, are taken into account. Apart from the unevenness with which trade liberalization and market reforms have been applied in Latin America, two interrelated explanations stand out for the tenacity of income inequality in the region: (1) continued levels of asset concentration since the onset of liberalization, and (2) a widening gap in skill differentials, itself a product of the poor quality and access to training and educational opportunities.

While the failure of wages and income distribution to improve accordingly is still not entirely understood, economic theory points to asset concentration—both productive and human assets—as a main culprit.[21] Productive assets refer to land, companies, and other financial holdings. Although land tenure patterns in the region are still highly skewed, the low percentage of the population now living in the rural sector, and the small share that agriculture contributes to regional GDP, suggest that the main bottleneck stems from concentrated ownership patterns of other productive assets. For example, in all four countries in Table 2.1, despite the implementation of ambitious reform packages based on liberalization, privatization, and deregulation, long-standing oligopolistic ownership patterns have prevailed. The degree of concentration is such that, on average, three to six firms still account for as much as 70 percent of market share in the most dynamic sectors of these economies.[22] While all four countries now have formal antitrust legislation on the books, enforcement has clearly lagged.

The causal link between these continued patterns of asset concentration and regressive income distribution is the following: For the larger and more globally integrated companies in the region, a dynamic process of microeconomic restructuring is under way, based on intra-industry trade, increasing specialization, rapid productivity gains, and the professionalization of technical and managerial networks. These top conglomerates have further consolidated their market position in the 1990s, but in ways that are capital-intensive and offer limited employment opportunities outside of the higher-skilled niches of the labor market. The remaining mass of productive sector firms are mostly small and medium-sized ventures that traditionally have produced nontradable goods for the domestic market and provided the main impetus for the expansion of less-skilled employment. Although in other regions, such as East Asia, these smaller enterprises have been an integral part of a competitive production strategy—from the provision of supply flexibility to the innovation of products, labor practices, and worker skills—the lack of know-how and financial resources has made it much more difficult for this second group of Latin American firms to adapt to new levels of competition. It is this increasing heterogeneity of the region's productive structure, and the compression of income shares within this burgeoning lower tier of smaller, weaker firms, that has perpetuated higher levels of inequality in the 1990s.

It could be argued that the contradictory dynamic just described, where dynamism and innovation have gone hand in hand with stagnation and regressive income returns, is simply a new fact of economic life for all countries operating within a fully integrated global economy. Although Latin America's struggle with income inequality is not unique on this count, the data suggest that the region's disproportionately higher international ranking on regressive distribution stems from major deficiencies in human capital formation. For example, the evidence on educational investments and achievement shows that, while Latin America actually spends more on education than East Asia (3.7 percent of regional GDP versus 3.4 percent), the average Latin worker is no better educated today than the average East Asian worker was in 1970.[23] These dramatic qualitative differences reflect East Asia's educational emphasis on universal school access and job skill acquisition, policies that have reaped much higher income returns. For example, the annual growth of per capita GDP in East Asia averaged 6.7 percent from 1980 to 1992, versus –0.5 percent for Latin America over the same time period.[24]

With an average educational level of just 5.2 years as recently as 1995, Latin America's shallow human asset base and poor skill acquisition have placed its adult working population at a startling disadvantage. This unfavorable lag reflects, first, the extent to which Latin America's educational systems have failed to forge dynamic links between schools and labor markets under a trade-driven economic model that demands increasingly higher skills and, second, the insidious ways in which cumulative human capital inequalities have compounded in the 1990s—like daily rates on a high-interest loan—as the demands for higher work skills are quickly outpacing the capacity of the educational system to meet the supply. In reference to these trends, Nora Lustig and Ruthanne Deutsch warn that in the absence of a more competitive approach and at current rates of per capita growth, "it could take close to 60 years to over two centuries, depending on the country, to completely eradicate poverty as measured by the proportion of individuals living below $2 per day."[25]

The FTAA: Breaking Through the Regional Impasse?

This final section explores the ways in which economic asymmetry and the kinds of adjustment stress reviewed above have converged to slow the expansion of hemispheric integration. The United States, for instance, had announced on behalf of its NAFTA partners at the 1994 Miami summit that Chile would be the first candidate for NAFTA entry, but those negotiations completely stalled until the outgoing Clinton team finally revived them in December 2000. The current U.S. trade representative, Robert Zoellick, has succeeded in keeping these negotiations alive. However, the eight-year delay in making good on this promise has not been lost on the Chileans.

While the Mercosur customs union has expanded by negotiating "associate status" free trade agreements with Bolivia and Chile, its members are still struggling with compliance and enforcement of basic liberalization initiatives and have fallen behind schedule in the further reduction of barriers in areas like services and government procurement. In the run-up to Argentina's 2001 debt default, the economic team frantically raised trade tariffs unilaterally and even leveraged new taxes on exports in hopes of quelling the financial imbalances. As Mercosur falters in the aftermath of severe crises and bailouts in Argentina, Brazil, and Uruguay, the passage of the TPA and revival of debate about advancing the FTAA negotiations could be welcome signs of relief. Nevertheless, the kinds of distributional politics and collective action dilemmas that have arisen within NAFTA, Mercosur, and at the FTAA negotiating table will still require more conscious effort and credible policy solutions; if the past decade has shown us anything, it is that these problems will not dissipate under the thrust of "freer trade." They are part and parcel of the liberalization process, and their mitigation will require constructive public policy interventions.

NAFTA

In the case of NAFTA, where huge asymmetries exist between Canada, the United States, and Mexico, economic integration theory tells us that the larger, wealthier, and more open states should expect to undergo marginal adjustments upon entering a free trade agreement. In turn, Mexico, as the smaller, poorer, and more highly protected economy, should expect to undergo a more sweeping and costly adjustment in the short term but to achieve considerable dynamic gains in the medium to long term.[26] From this theory, it would seem safe to presume that distributional conflict in the NAFTA era would be more pronounced in Mexico, and less so in Canada and the United States. Yet, even though Canadian and U.S. tariffs were already well below 5 percent prior to the launching of NAFTA, all three countries have experienced intense distributional conflicts that, in turn, worked to thwart NAFTA's expansion.

As discussed earlier, political conflicts over NAFTA expansion in Canada and the United States have stemmed from (1) the need to uphold labor standards and worker rights and (2) the need to tighten guidelines and enforce compliance procedures that would guarantee stronger environmental protection. However, the fact that organized labor in Canada and the United States has been vociferous in opposing NAFTA's expansion suggests that deeper distributional cleavages are at work here. Despite an impressive recovery from the 1990–1991 international recession, and the aura of economic boom that surrounded the North American bloc during the 1990s, over this same period average family incomes and disparities in income equality in Canada and the United States have continued to rise.[27]

In the United States, although weekly inflation-adjusted earnings for those with wages below that earned by 90 percent of the workforce rose by 1.6 percent in 1997, in general, wages at the bottom are still far lower than a decade ago.[28] Trade economists remain sorely divided over the extent to which wage and distributional erosion in these developed countries can be attributed to increased competition from trade, especially when one of the trade partners, Mexico, is a developing country with an abundance of cheap unskilled labor. For the purposes of this argument, and without diminishing the importance of this unresolved debate, direct causation between NAFTA and income losses in Canada and the United States is doubtful given that trade with Mexico amounts to less than 1 percent of each country's GDP.

In light of its dominant economic weight and leadership role in the hemisphere, the persistence of anti-free-trade attitudes in the United States warrants further attention, since this now constitutes a main bottleneck in the pursuit of the FTAA. Two main forces appear to be at work here. First, although total reported job losses related to NAFTA have not surpassed 200,000 since the agreement's implementation on January 1, 1994, versus the more than two million jobs created each year in the U.S. economy,[29] even this limited labor market stress has been exacerbated by insufficient adjustment support. The heavy reliance on market forces to assist workers in transition prompted former AFL-CIO president George Meany to declare U.S. labor adjustment support programs the equivalent of "burial insurance."[30] To its credit, the U.S. Congress took this criticism to heart and passed a TPA bill that broke significant new ground for workers. The TPA created "a program of subsidized health insurance, in addition to other job training benefits for Americans who lose their jobs because of foreign competition."[31]

Second, underpinning today's long-term patterns of income erosion and short-term labor market disruptions in the United States is an increasingly unequal human asset structure not unlike that of the Latin American cases explored in the previous section. As recently as 1989, for example, just 14 percent of the U.S. workforce held a college degree, while 40 percent had graduated from high school.[32] Although the "wage penalty" for not attending college in the United States had hit 60 percent by 1979, college grads earned as much as 140 percent more than those without a college degree by 1995. These data reflect the dynamic effects of rapid technological change and modernization of the U.S. workplace over the past two decades, as well as the extent to which the U.S. education system has fallen behind in increasing the quality and opportunities for improving human capital skills.[33] As absolute (growth) and relative (distributional) losses in income position continue to accumulate in the context of a sustained expansion of the U.S. economy, opposition to "free trade" has become a convenient, if misplaced, scapegoat for expressing dismay about much larger distributional challenges and public policy failures in the United States.

As compelling as these political obstacles in the United States appear to be, it helps to remember that a powerful business-government alliance triumphed over similarly difficult obstacles and secured the

NAFTA vote in 1993. Yet neither the Clinton administration nor the U.S. private sector showed similar determination in pursuing the FTAA. Why? NAFTA was designed as an inclusive arrangement in principle; in practice, the structural logic of intra-industry specialization and cross-border trade that encouraged the North American private sector to support NAFTA is simply not as strong when it comes to the FTAA. Other Latin reformers are pursuing similar strategies of intra-industry specialization with neighboring trade partners, as in the case of Mercosur, which helps explain why business-government coalitions in the United States and within Argentina and Brazil have not pushed harder for a broad regional initiative—a point I return to below.

In Mexico the pattern of adjustment under NAFTA has conformed more closely with the dictates of economic integration theory: Distributional stress has indeed been acute for those workers and producers who lack the skills and resources to participate successfully in a more competitive export-oriented industrial model.[34] But as NAFTA approaches its first decade, Mexico's dynamic gains from increased integration with the North American bloc are indisputable. Mexico's total trade (exports plus imports) since 1990 is around 60 percent higher than it was for all of the 1980s, while its trade with the United States has jumped by more than 400 percent since 1986. Similarly, the country's total stock of FDI has now surpassed $50 billion since the announcement of the NAFTA negotiations in 1990, compared to $23 billion for the decade that began in 1980. As Mexico has now become the United States' third most important trading partner and its largest coproducer in the processing of intermediate inputs for shipment back to the U.S. market, U.S.-Mexican cross-border production is moving into more advanced sectors (aerospace equipment, medical devices, semiconductors), which represent a higher-skill, higher-wage, higher-productivity track.

Whereas distributional conflict has divided the perceived "winners" and "losers" in the United States to the extent that further free trade initiatives have been highly contentious, in Mexico steep adjustment costs have worked to undermine the country's commitment to the FTAA, but not its allegiance to NAFTA. For the past decade, despite widespread job displacement, wage compression, and persistent income inequality, the majority of Mexican voters have consistently opted for a market model that more credibly offers to preserve the consumer surplus (in this case, low inflation, cheaper prices, and broader access to higher-quality goods). Since the 1994 peso crisis, voters have supported those candidates who represent a shift to a more competitive approach where public policy actively promotes educational opportunity, job creation, and income gains.[35] It was the failure of the ruling Partido Revolucionario Institucional (PRI, Institutional Revolutionary Party) to deliver quickly enough on such issues that led to its first presidential loss in 71 years. The election of President Vicente Fox on the Partido Acción Nacional (PAN, National Action Party) ticket in July 2000 reflects the voters' preference for the consolidation of Mexico's outward trade strategy under NAFTA before signing on to a full hemispheric accord.[36]

Similar go-slow or "status quo" preferences have been voiced by broad segments of the Mexican private sector. Mexico's buoyant trade and investment trends in the 1990s largely reflected the extent to which economic exchange with the United States has accelerated within, rather than across, industries (e.g., autos, telecommunications, and electrical machinery). This explosion of intra-industry trade is such that the top 20 U.S. imports from and exports to Mexico now flow across the border within the same manufacturing subsectors.[37] It is this increased opportunity for intra-industry specialization and rapid advances in competitiveness that prompted U.S. and Mexican producers to lobby so aggressively for an agreement like NAFTA that would further facilitate these dynamic gains. And the quest to consolidate these gains has fueled strong private sector preferences for delaying the negotiation of the FTAA.[38] For those smaller, weaker Mexican producers who are still watching this intra-industry boom from the sidelines, the propensity has been to push, not for protectionism, but for the kinds of public policies that would promote their incorporation into this more competitive model of production.

Mercosur

Like Mexico, the Mercosur member nations have pursued subregional integration as an extension of earlier unilateral liberalization measures implemented in the context of macroeconomic stabilization programs and as part of their long-term efforts at microeconomic restructuring. Because Argentina and Brazil represent more than 95 percent of Mercosur's combined GDP (approximately $1 trillion), to speak of Mercosur is to speak of these two dominant countries. Argentina and Brazil began their integration process even before the stabilization-related unilateral trade liberalization measures of the late 1980s. Since the launching of the Mercosur customs union on January 1, 1995, the Common External Tariff (CET) now averages 17 percent, and 80 percent of internal trade covered by the agreement has been liberalized.

Despite these advances, Mercosur is still riddled with numerous exceptions. Major sectors, such as automobile manufacturing, have yet to be incorporated into the agreement, and the capital goods, informatics, and telecommunications sectors are still exempted from the CET. Similar to NAFTA, Mercosur trade rapidly expanded in the 1990s under the impetus of intra-industry specialization and cross-border production,[39] while distributional cleavages within the Mercosur countries have been akin to those witnessed in Mexico. But in contrast to NAFTA, and even prior to the 2001–2002 economic meltdown in the Southern Cone region, major differences in economic strategy between Argentina and Brazil have complicated the implementation process, as each country has continued to act out national preferences in a subregional context.

Distributional conflict in both countries has centered on the widening gap between those skilled workers and producers who have successfully positioned themselves within the globalized sectors of the economy and those who are still struggling to survive within an increasingly competitive domestic market. Although neither Argentine nor Brazilian policymakers have yet to articulate a role for trade liberalization as part of a broader development strategy,[40] the economic agents involved in the expansion of intra-industry trade and specialized production within Mercosur have quickly come to define it for them. It is this contingent that has been most enthusiastic about accelerating the integration time line within Mercosur. This, however, is where the continuities within Mercosur stop, as preferences for markedly different adjustment strategies have divided Argentine and Brazilian policymakers in their attempts to implement the goals of Mercosur.

In Argentina, where a market-oriented approach to economic management prevailed from 1991 to 2001, domestic politics converged in favor of a liberal model that promises to preserve the consumer surplus. Even when faced with double-digit unemployment levels in the wake of the 1995 tequila shock, voters stood by candidates who espoused fine-tuning the market model, rather than returning to protectionism.[41] Such was the lesson with the October 1999 election of centrist presidential candidate Fernando de la Rúa. At the subregional level, these consumer preferences rendered Argentina the more cautious defender of Mercosur's commitment to a liberal trade regime. The shocking turn of events in Argentina since 2001—including De la Rúa's resignation, the implosion of the economy, and abandonment of the currency board and fixed exchange rate—has distracted policymakers from this commitment to free trade. Despite these setbacks, it is likely that Argentina will follow the trade policy cues of Brazil, its most important partner.

Brazil, it seems, is still sitting on the fence with regard to the FTAA. Policymakers and the private sector have displayed a determined preference for a competitive approach to trade liberalization and regional integration, as well as a willingness to resort to old protectionist remedies, as entire industries are now feeling the pinch from market reform. Such measures have included the use of various fiscal and financial incentives to promote industrial exports and foster the expansion of integrated intra-industry production networks. Brazil's trade strategy, however, has conformed to GATT/WTO guidelines. Its macroeconomic strategy, in distinct contrast to Argentina's hands-off approach under the currency board from 1991 to 2001, has consisted of a more flexible exchange rate regime and the use of capital controls to protect against the volatility of short-term capital movements.[42] These marked differences in economic strategy contributed to the wild swings in current account balance between the two countries in the 1990s, fueling tensions within Mercosur even under the best of economic times.

Even prior to the 40 percent devaluation of the real in January 1999, adjustment stress in Brazil had been exacerbated by the country's comparatively low levels of per capita GDP and educational achievement, as well as its much later start in launching market reforms.[43] As a result, voters have been ambivalent, at best, about the deepening of Mercosur's liberalization targets. Public opinion supports Brazil's integration goals, but with the caveat that any further liberalization will be carried out gradually and under the umbrella of an active state policy.[44] In light of conflicting distributional demands within Brazil, and the lack of consensus between Argentina and Brazil on economic strategy and the pace of liberalization, the Mercosur bloc—and its private sector in particular—has yet to display more than lukewarm enthusiasm for the negotiation of an FTAA. With the onset of recession in the entire Western Hemisphere since 2001, and a renewed propensity toward protectionism on the part of the U.S. Congress since the September 11 terrorist attacks, this nonchalance may be a foreclosed option. The Southern Cone's own political and economic crises, and the virtual stalling of Mercosur, mean that the FTAA is the only truly viable option for pulling out of this slump. With TPA in hand, this is now the focal point for the hemispheric integration process.

The FTAA

At face value, the uncertainty that has enshrouded the FTAA process since its inception has stemmed from procedural disputes between the United States and its Latin trade partners over how to approach the FTAA negotiations. On a deeper level, the process has been bogged down by the same distributional strains that have worked to slow the expansion and deepening of integration initiatives at the domestic level in the countries examined here—as evidenced by the "Battle of Seattle," the determination of well-organized social protesters to shut down the December 1999 WTO ministerial meeting in Seattle.[45] Just as politicians and policymakers in Argentina, Brazil, Mexico, and the United States have been hard pressed to maximize the benefits of trade integration while minimizing the political risks and adjustment costs on the home front, the potential for asymmetrical outcomes between regional groupings has posed further collective action problems. While econometric evidence points to the full multilateral liberalization of Western Hemisphere trade as the most optimal strategy for increasing widespread welfare gains, differences in size and income disparities have worked to shape short-term outcomes that are clearly suboptimal.

The conflicts and asymmetries that have divided the NAFTA and Mercosur blocs are a prime case in point. Because of the sheer economic weight of NAFTA ($7.4 trillion GDP) and Mercosur ($1 trillion GDP) in the Western Hemisphere and the dominant role that the United States and Brazil play, respectively, within each of these blocs, the collaboration of these two main players will be essential for the successful completion of a hemispheric free trade accord. But despite robust evidence showing that Brazil's strongest welfare gains lie, first, at the level of multilateral liberalization and, second, in closer integration with the U.S. economy,[46] complicated collective action problems have also relegated Brazil to its third-best option, Mercosur. At least three main factors have worked to convince Brazilian decisionmakers that, whatever the projected benefits from an accelerated multilateral liberalization timetable that includes the United States, these would still not be sufficient to outweigh the domestic political costs.

First is the question of tariff reductions and improved mutual market access between North and South. Because the average U.S. tariff on Latin American imports is just 3–4 percent, the burden of tariff reduction falls most heavily on the Latin side. This, combined with the fact that Latin American countries now buy the bulk of each other's products, means that increased U.S. access to Latin American markets will place some Latin exporters, and especially Brazil, at a competitive disadvantage in their own region. A second divisive factor is the differing liberalization priorities taken by the United States and Brazil. As a highly competitive service-based economy, the United States is most concerned with legal issues that reflect this status, for example, government procurement and intellectual property rights. In contrast, as more closed and industrial-based economies, Brazil and the remainder of the non-NAFTA countries in the hemisphere are still concerned with sectoral issues that most often hinge on tariff reductions and increased market access.

Third, and perhaps the main reason why Brazil never lined up for possible NAFTA accession, are the fundamental differences in each country's approach to political economic management. While longstanding tensions in the U.S.–Brazilian trade relationship initially eased in the wake of Brazil's commercial opening, the country's continued affinities for managed trade and state-led development symbolize a level of intervention that surpasses the tastes of most U.S. policymakers. To the chagrin of the entire region, the U.S. Congress has responded by raising import barriers on a wide range of Brazilian products (shoes, sugar, textiles, steel, soya beans, citrus fruits) since the advent of the Bush administration—tariffs now estimated to cost Brazil some $5 billion annually in trade revenues.[47] The economic fallout from U.S. trade remedies has been such that Brazilian policymakers no longer have the luxury of hedging on their commitment to reduce export subsidies (e.g., tax breaks and preferential exchange rates) that violate the spirit of free trade. Even though Brazil's October 2002 election showed that domestic political responses are moving in a more protectionist direction, the liberalization advances achieved thus far are too formidable to reverse.

Conclusion

In 2000, political leaders in the Western Hemisphere agreed to make "concrete progress" toward the creation of the FTAA and to draw up a schedule for intensive negotiating sessions. At the April 2001 Quebec City summit this goal was further advanced: The FTAA's 2005 completion date was reconfirmed; a rough draft agreement is now in circulation and, in the name of transparency, has been posted on the Internet; and, although still quite contentious, civil society's participation—including the incorporation of concerns long expressed by labor and environmental interests—is now firmly embedded in the FTAA process. However, the ultimate completion of the FTAA is still tied to three key matters.

First, at the domestic level, more must be done to ameliorate the distributional strains that have come to constitute a main bottleneck for the FTAA. Second, at the subregional level, politicians and economic policy makers must reconfirm that there is a sound political economic rationale for the FTAA. The data reviewed in this chapter suggest that the rise of regionalism in the Western Hemisphere has fostered a pattern of trade creation and welfare gains, and the evidence is encouraging for further trade and investment dynamism under the FTAA. Third, Brazil and the United States—the two hegemonic leaders of the Western Hemisphere—must work harder to bridge the gap between trade preferences and policy practices. The multilateral planners of the Santiago summit were prescient in assigning Brazil and the United States joint responsibility for chairing the final stages of the FTAA negotiations from 2003 to 2005; Canada's turnaround at the NAFTA negotiating table, as well as its constructive role in carrying the FTAA process forward in the absence of strong U.S. leadership, has shown that the apparent distance between the United States and Brazil could be bridged as the incentives for hemispheric integration continue to stack up against the disincentives.[48]

Notes

The author thanks Thomas O'Keefe, Scott Otteman, and José Manuel Salazar for their helpful comments on earlier drafts. Thanks also to John Hipp for compiling Table 2.1.

1. See, for example, Jeffrey J. Schott and Gary C. Hufbauer, "Whither the Free Trade Area of the Americas," *The World Economy* 22, no. 6 (1999): 765–782; and Jeff Hornbeck, "A Free Trade Area of the Americas: Status of Negotiations and Major Policy Issues," Congressional Research Service Report for Congress, 27 March 2002.

2. José M. Salazar-Xirinachs and José Tavares de Araujo, "The Free Trade Area of the Americas: A Latin American Perspective," *The World*

Economy 22, no. 6 (1999): 783–797; Richard Feinberg, "A Vision for the Americas," *Financial Times*, 7 August 2002, 11.

3. See Richard Feinberg and Robin Rosenberg, "The Quebec City Summit: Tear Gas, Trade, and Democracy," *North-South Center Update*, 13 May 2001.

4. David Firestone, "Senate Approves Bill to Give Bush Trade Authority," *New York Times*, 2 August 2002, A1.

5. Apart from Canada and the United States, the four Latin American countries on which successful hemispheric integration will most depend are Argentina, Brazil, Chile, and Mexico. See Raúl Hinojosa-Ojeda, Jeffrey Lewis, and Sherman Robinson, "Convergence and Divergence Between NAFTA, Chile, and Mercosur," Integration and Regional Programs Department, Working Paper Series 219 (Washington, D.C.: Inter-American Development Bank, 1997).

6. Juan Luis Londoño and Miguel Székely, *Distributional Surprises After a Decade of Reforms: Latin America in the Nineties* (Washington, D.C.: Inter-American Development Bank, 1997).

7. These five main subregional schemes in the Western Hemisphere include NAFTA between Canada, Mexico, and the United States, implemented on 1 January 1994; Mercosur, a customs union that comprises Argentina, Brazil, Paraguay, Uruguay, and two associate members—Bolivia and Chile—implemented on 1 January 1995; the Andean Community, a renovated customs union from the 1960s, comprising Bolivia, Ecuador, Colombia, Peru, and Venezuela; the Central American Common Market (CACM), also renovated from the 1960s; and the Caribbean Common Market (CARICOM), revived from the 1970s.

8. See Robert Lawrence, *Regionalism, Multilateralism, and Deeper Integration* (Washington, D.C.: Brookings Institution, 1996), 67–75.

9. Jagdish Bhagwati and Anne O. Krueger, *The Dangerous Drift to Preferential Trade Agreements* (Washington, D.C.: American Enterprise Institute, 1995).

10. All dollar amounts are U.S. dollars unless otherwise noted.

11. These figures are cited from the trade statistics database of the Inter-American Development Bank.

12. These figures are cited from the ECLAC (Economic Commission on Latin America and the Caribbean) website: [www.eclac.org].

13. ECLAC/CEPAL, "Sixth Ministerial Trade Meeting," *CEPAL News* 20, no. 4 (2001): 2.

14. The "Washington Consensus" refers to the general agreement among U.S. government officials, international and lending agencies, and mainstream economists that free markets and a reduced role of the state in economic affairs are the foundations of sustained growth in the developing world. For further information, see John Williamson, ed., *Latin American Adjustment: How Much Has Happened?* (Washington, D.C.: Institute for International Economics, 1990).

15. ECLAC/CEPAL, "Macroeconomic Performance in 1997," *CEPAL News* 18, no. 2 (1998): 1–3.

16. These figures are cited from the ECLAC database: [www.eclac.org].

17. Manuel Pastor and Carol Wise, "A Long View on the Mexican Political Economy," in *Mexico's Politics and Society in Transition,* ed. Joseph S. Tulchin and Andrew Selee (Boulder: Lynne Rienner, 2002), 179–213.

18. SECOFI, "Mexico: Program of Industrial Policy and International Trade" (Mexico City, May 1996).

19. Pedro da Motta Veiga, "Brazil's Strategy for Trade Liberalization and Economic Integration in the Western Hemisphere," in *Integrating the Hemisphere,* ed. Ana Julia Jatar and Sidney Weintraub (Washington, D.C.: Inter-American Dialogue, 1997), 197–207.

20. Londoño and Székely, *Distributional Surprises,* 17.

21. Nancy Birdsall and Juan Luis Londoño, "Asset Inequality Matters: An Assessment of the World Bank's Approach to Poverty Reduction," *American Economic Review* 87, no. 2 (1997): 32–37.

22. Werner Baer and William Maloney, "Neoliberalism and Income Distribution in Latin America," *World Development* 25, no. 3 (1997), 320.

23. Birdsall and Londoño, "Asset Inequality Matters."

24. Barbara Stallings, "The New International Context of Development," in *Global Change, Regional Response: The New International Context of Development,* ed. Barbara Stallings (New York: Cambridge University Press, 1995), 349–387.

25. Nora Lustig and Ruthanne Deutsch, *The Inter-American Development Bank and Poverty Reduction* (Washington, D.C.: Inter-American Development Bank, 1997), 3–4.

26. Roberto Bouzas and Jaime Ros, "The North-South Variety of Economic Integration," in *Economic Integration in the Western Hemisphere,* ed. Roberto Bouzas and Jaime Ros (Notre Dame, Ind.: University of Notre Dame Press, 1994), 1–45.

27. Louis Uchitelle, "6 Years in the Plus Column for the U.S. Economy," *New York Times,* 12 March 1997, D1; Howard Schneider, "Despite Booming Economy, Some Canadians See Little Benefit," *Washington Post,* 11 June 1998, A32; Peter Passell, "Benefits Dwindle Along with Wages for the Unskilled," *New York Times,* 14 June 1998, A1.

28. Jacob Schlesinger, "Wages for Low-Paid Workers Rose in 1997," *Wall Street Journal,* 23 March 1999, A2.

29. Sidney Weintraub, *NAFTA at Three* (Washington, D.C.: Center for Strategic and International Studies, 1997).

30. Cited in I. M. Destler, *Renewing Fast-Track Legislation* (Washington, D.C.: Institute for International Economics, 1997), 46.

31. Alison Mitchell, "Bush Hails Vote in House Backing Trade Legislation," *New York Times,* 28 July 2002, A1.

32. William Cline, *Trade and Income Distribution* (Washington, D.C.: Institute for International Economics, 1997), 23–26.

33. Daniel McMurrer and Isabel Sawhill, *Getting Ahead: Economic and Social Mobility in America* (Washington, D.C.: The Urban Institute, 1998), 39–44.

34. Manuel Pastor and Carol Wise, "Mexican-Style Neoliberalism: State

Policy and Distributional Stress," in *The Post-NAFTA Political Economy: Mexico and the Western Hemisphere,* ed. Carol Wise (University Park: Pennsylvania State University Press, 1998), 77–81.

35. Author's interview with Ricardo Pascoe, Fundación para la Democracia, Mexico City, 26 August 1997. See Michael Tangeman, "Factoring in the Cardenas Comeback," *Institutional Investor,* July 1997, 21–22.

36. Carol Wise, "Politics Unhinged: Market Reforms as a Catalyst for Mexico's Democratic Transition," in *Post-Stabilization Politics in Latin America: Competition, Transition, Collapse,* ed. Carol Wise and Riordan Roett, with Guadalupe Paz (Washington, D.C.: Brookings Institution Press, 2003).

37. Weintraub, *NAFTA at Three,* 34–38.

38. Luis Rubio, "Mexico, NAFTA, and the Pacific Basin," in *Cooperation or Rivalry?* ed. Shoji Nishijima and Peter Smith (Boulder: Westview, 1996), 86–88.

39. By 1997, over 30 percent of Argentine exports were destined for the Brazilian market, some 45 percent of which were manufactured goods; Brazil's exports to Argentina accounted for 13 percent of its total trade that same year, 80 percent of which were manufactured goods in the same sectors that Argentina exported to Brazil.

40. Daniel Chudnovsky, Andrés López, and Fernando Porta, "New Foreign Direct Investment in Argentina," in *Foreign Direct Investment in Latin America,* ed. Manuel Agosin (Washington, D.C.: Inter-American Development Bank, 1995), 39–104; Wilson Suzigan and Annibal Villela, *Industrial Policy in Brazil* (Campinas, Brazil: Universidade Estadual de Campinas, 1997).

41. Manuel Pastor and Carol Wise, "The Politics of Second-Generation Reform," *Journal of Democracy* 10, no. 3 (1999): 34–48.

42. María Beatriz Nofal, "Why Is There Scant Progress in the Consolidation and Deepening of Mercosur?" *Mercosur Journal* 8 (1997), 12–17.

43. Rudiger Dornbusch, "Brazil's Incomplete Stabilization and Reform," *Mercosur Journal* 8 (1997): 20–37.

44. Suzigan and Villela, *Industrial Policy in Brazil.*

45. For a full account of the Seattle fiasco, see William Finnegan, "After Seattle," *New Yorker,* 17 April 2000, 40–51.

46. Refik Erzan and Alexander Yeats, "U.S.–Latin American Free Trade Areas," in *The Premise and the Promise: Free Trade in the Americas,* ed. Silvia Saborio (Washington, D.C.: Overseas Development Council, 1992), 126–128.

47. Moisés Naím, "Bush's Responsibility to Brazil," *Financial Times,* 1 September 2002, 11.

48. Donald MacKay, "Challenges Confronting the Free Trade Area of the Americas" (Ottawa: Canadian Foundation for the Americas [FOCAL], June 2002), available at: [www.focal.ca].

The New Security Agenda for the Americas: Focus on "Insecurity"

Margaret Daly Hayes

Four realities shape the current international political and economic environment: (1) Democracy, despite its considerable practical difficulties, is still viewed as the most desired form of government; (2) a liberal, open-market economic model, with its attendant requirement for more efficient and competitive production, is acknowledged as the best option for achieving long-term growth and development; (3) regional and global integration, in response to the globalization of transactions, is under way; and (4) more efficient and effective governance is necessary to ensure achievement of democracy, the open economic model, and regional and global integration. To recognize these global realities is not to say that there is universal approval of them—there is not. The September 11, 2001, attack on the United States by Islamic fundamentalists was in no small measure a reaction against these global trends. Many parties of the left in Latin America argue for a return to "better times" of earlier decades. Nevertheless, nations must carry out their business in the climate today's realities produce, as well as responding to pressures to address them. In the case of Argentina, for example, candidate Eduardo Duhalde called for a return to pre-convertibility and pre–open market policies before donning the presidential sash in January 2002. As President Duhalde, however, he quickly assumed a different approach.

In responding to today's global realities, the countries of Latin America and the Caribbean have undergone a series of dramatic, often wrenching, and still incomplete political and economic transformations over the past two decades. The implications of these changes for the contemporary security environment in the Americas are profound.

Today's global environment places primary emphasis on economic well-being, or economic "security," and Latin Americans historically have believed that economic development is the principal guarantor of long-term security. This belief has been behind their interactions in the inter-American community since the origins of the Pan American Union, and it is no less important today. Consequently, economic stabilization and restructuring to cope with the competitive world economy as well as expanded trade relations and regional integration have received high-priority attention in most countries in the region.

The devastating economic crises of the 1980s led to some positive changes in the region's economies, including not only integration with the global economy but also dynamic regional integration, highlighted by the success of the North American Free Trade Agreement (NAFTA) and the evolution of regional markets in the Southern Cone (Mercosur), in Central America (Central American Common Market), and, to a lesser extent, in Caribbean and Andean countries. The economic transformation brought growth, but it also exacerbated income inequalities and produced record levels of unemployment, which are associated with greater violence, unprecedented population movements within and among countries, and deep frustration with governments that have failed to address adequately the many problems confronting Latin societies.

Beginning in the early 1980s, the region began a gradual transition from military government to elected civilian leadership. The transfer of presidential power in Chile in 1989 marked the passing of the last overtly military government in the hemisphere. However, the political transition to more democratic, effective representation and governance has been slow and frustrating and remains incomplete in most countries of the region. Even the English-speaking Caribbean countries, confident of their democratic history and origins, are concerned about the apparent inability of their governments to deliver the desired results of democratic government: liberty, security, and a better quality of life.

Most Latin American countries have begun to consider mechanisms for stronger, more effective exercise of civilian leadership in defense and security matters—subjects that for decades have been abdicated to the armed forces. Furthermore, both the long experience with authoritarian governments and the more recent experience with international peace initiatives, focused on Central America in the 1980s and on Peru and Ecuador in the mid-1990s, have contributed to reconsideration of Latin American countries' long-standing reluctance to take a position on the nature of neighboring governments. Nations of the Southern Cone acted decisively when dissident elements of the Paraguayan armed forces sought to overthrow its democratically elected government; the community of nations was not prepared to intervene in Peru's electoral process, however, despite widespread belief that irregularities and restrictions on free expression were rampant. Expanding awareness of the intractable nature of the drug scourge and its penetration of one country after another has heightened a desire for cross-national collaboration. Concern over democratic stability has led to evolving regional and subregional dialogues on economic integration, democracy, and defense and security cooperation.

The Organization of American States (OAS) has played a key role in this arena. Beginning with its 1991 Santiago de Chile "Commitment to Democracy" statement, followed by the Managua declaration in 1994 and the Declaration on Confidence and Security Building Measures in 1995, the OAS has expanded its own diplomatic dialogue to include issues of security and security cooperation, as well as transparency in defense spending and arms control. The Committee on Hemispheric Security, established in 1995 as a standing element of the OAS, has focused regional attention on the security concerns of small island states, problems of education for security, transparency in arms acquisitions, and peacekeeping. More recently, in response to the September 2001 terrorist attacks in the United States, the OAS has begun to focus on hemispheric collaboration in the fight against global terrorism. Brazil and Argentina took the lead in calling on the OAS to invoke the Inter-American Treaty of Reciprocal Assistance (TIAR) in the aftermath of the September 11 attacks.[1]

On another front, in July 1995 ministers of defense in the hemisphere gathered for the first time, at the invitation of U.S. secretary of defense William Perry, to discuss modes of security cooperation. In his closing remarks, Perry summarized the conclusions reached by the 34 defense ministers. In what are now known as the six "Williamsburg principles,"[2] defense ministers agreed to do the following:

- Uphold the promise of the Santiago agreement[3] that the preservation of democracy is the basis for ensuring mutual security.
- Acknowledge that military and security forces play a critical role in supporting and defending the legitimate interests of sovereign democratic states.
- Affirm the commitments made in Miami and Managua that the

armed forces should be subordinate to democratically controlled authority, act within the bounds of national constitutions, and respect human rights through training and practice.
- Increase transparency in defense matters through exchanges of information, through reporting on defense expenditures, and by greater civilian-military dialogue.
- Set as a goal for the hemisphere the resolution of outstanding disputes by negotiated settlement and widespread adoption of confidence-building measures, all of this in a time frame consistent with the pace of hemispheric economic integration, and recognize that the development of economic security profoundly affects defense security and vice versa.
- Promote greater defense cooperation in support of voluntary participation in United Nations–sanctioned peacekeeping operations, and cooperate in a supportive role in the fight against narcoterrorism.

Since the Williamsburg meeting, the ministers have met in Argentina in 1996, in Colombia in 1998, in Brazil in 2000, and in Chile in 2002.

Latin American Security Concerns

What constitutes *security*? Security is largely a state of mind. It is a feeling of well-being, a sense of predictability, a confidence in the absence of threat. It is much easier to perceive the lack of security than its presence. Security also involves much more than defense of territory or sovereignty against external threats. Indeed, today nations most often promote their security through a variety of political, economic, and social policies applied in both domestic and international arenas. Complex interrelationships exist between international pressures and national responses and among the political, economic, and social realms within a nation.

National power or capability is dependent on three pillars: (1) the capacity of political leadership, (2) strength of the economy, and (3) social cohesion and capabilities of the citizenry.[4] Each of these dimensions of the nation-state affects the other and is affected by events both internal and external to the nation. In the end, national security depends on the successful integration and balancing of these forces, and it necessarily involves far more than defense and the armed forces.

Nevertheless, as Clausewitz famously wrote, "war is the continuation of politics by other means," and it is predominantly in the political arena—but not exclusively there—that the nation-state uses its armed forces as extensions of its political efforts to influence its environment and to effect security in the classic sense of territorial protection. However, today's armed forces are also often tasked to perform missions that affect their nation's economy (most provide critical skills training to troops, logistical support to remote villages on the frontier, protection of economic interests in the nation's exclusive economic zone [EEZ]) or social welfare in general (health clinics, disaster response, and medical evacuation, for example). And the circle of interdependence continues: The capability of the military depends on the social and economic strength of the nation (Are the troops literate? Can the country maintain its forces' equipment?) and on the quality of political leadership and oversight provided at the national level.

Although the concept of security may be subjective, Latin Americans are quite clear about the principal threats to the security and well-being of their societies:

- Poverty and lack of economic growth.
- Drug trafficking and related violence and criminal activities.
- Social unrest and urban criminality caused by poverty, income inequality, and lack of educational opportunities.
- Organized crime, including arms trafficking and money laundering.
- Political and economic instability—often transmitted from outside the country—and illegal migration.
- International terrorism.
- Natural and environmental disasters.
- Corruption.[5]

These concerns affect each of the three realms that determine national power, and they occur at five different levels relevant to Latin America now and in coming years: the global, regional, national, local, and personal levels. Security threats at each of these levels are customarily addressed by different institutions—the armed forces, a national police, or local law enforcement—and often by more than one. The sorting out of responsibilities, requirements for integration, interagency collaboration, and demand for resources constitute some of the greatest challenges for Latin American security decisionmaking today.

Security at the Global Level

Global security concerns refer to the external political and economic environments that directly influence conditions in Latin America. The global ideological conflict that drove security policies in Latin America ended with the Cold War, although remnants of ideological conflicts still drive some internal wars. Today, the fluctuations of the global economy and the resultant fluctuations in trade and investment are the global events that affect most Latin American countries. Dramatic events like the September 11, 2001, terrorist attacks only exacerbate these trends by affecting the attitudes of international investors and slowing capital flows. Because of their sensitivity to the international environment, the larger Latin American nations have begun to define a commitment to promoting international stability. For example, former Chilean undersecretary of the navy Pablo Cabrera has argued that Chile, as a trading nation dependent on the viability and predictability of the global economy, has an interest in and obligation to contribute to global economic and political stability. Argentina's commitment to international peacekeeping also is based on its perception that global events have an impact at home and that Argentina has a role to play on the international scene.

Although little that happens in Latin America now—except perhaps a major regional economic crisis, such as a contagion effect from the 2001–2002 Argentine meltdown—has a critical impact on global political or economic stability, countries in the region, especially those in the Southern Cone, increasingly see a need to participate in, as well as to buffer themselves from, the global environment. They address this need by their presence in international political and economic forums and by military participation in international peacekeeping activities.

Regional and Cross-Border Security

Latin America's regional security concerns have changed over the last two decades. Confidence-building efforts by the OAS and regional trade integration have contributed to the now positive regional security environment. Military threats from a neighbor are no longer the primary security concern of most nations; rather, cooperative political, economic, and military activities predominate. Indeed, military cooperation in the region is at an all-time high.

For example, Brazil and Argentina have declared officially that they no longer entertain a hypothesis of conflict with each other. The armies, navies, and air forces of various countries, and in various combinations (Brazil and Argentina; Argentina, Brazil, and Uruguay; and Chile and Argentina), regularly conduct multinational, cooperative exercises. Annual joint staff talks are held between Chile and Peru and between Argentina and Chile, and student exchanges among war colleges and at the command and staff level are common throughout the region. Chile and Argentina recently agreed to collaborate in the development of a joint frigate project in which ships for both navies will be outfitted at Chile's Talcahuano shipyard, and Ecuador's navy is seeking a similar arrangement with Peru and its shipyard. In 1999, Chile's entire Naval War College paid a visit to its Argentine counterpart for the first time in history.[6] On many levels the practical cooperation between militaries in some operations—search and rescue, air traffic control, and disaster response, among others—surpasses diplomatic cooperation. Although some border issues remain unresolved, most have been decided satisfactorily. Nonetheless, countries in the region do worry about the impact that events in neighboring states may have on their political, economic, and social stability. Argentina's economic crisis has sent thousands of Bolivian and Paraguayan migrants back home, increasing unemployment and eliminating critical remittances, paralleling the impact the U.S. recession has had on remittances from both Mexican and Central American workers in this country.

Cross-border security concerns in general focus on transnational criminal activities, such as narcotrafficking—Colombia's neighbors have reinforced their borders against both narcotrafficking and guerrilla activities—illegal arms trafficking, money-laundering, smuggling of commercial goods and commodities, and illegal migration caused by severe economic conditions in neighboring countries. These regional security concerns are usually addressed by nonmilitary institutions—the national police, immigration agencies, and others—but often the scope and scale of illegal activities are so far beyond local authorities' capabilities that the armed forces must assist. That assistance may take the form of logistics support to police who have no way to get to distant sites, intelligence support, training (the Colombian air force had to teach the national police how to fly helicopters because the police force had no training capability of its own when it first acquired helicopters), and other types of collaborative efforts. Uruguay mobilized its army, just as England and Spain did, to round up and burn carcasses of livestock exposed to hoof and mouth disease and later to inoculate the remaining herd. In some cases, local authorities have been so corrupt or inept that the armed forces have been asked to assume responsibility for their functions; this is explained by the fact that across Latin America the armed forces—despite some obvious weaknesses—are regarded as more honorable than most other institutions of national society. In Paraguay and Ecuador, for example, the military forces have been asked to assume responsibility for customs control because local police are regarded as too corrupt and poorly trained to be effective.

National Security

National, or internal, security concerns refer to a broad set of issues ranging from terrorism (a concern in Argentina and in Colombia) to internal insurgencies, like those of the Shining Path (Sendero Luminoso) in Peru or of Colombia's Revolutionary Armed Forces (FARC) and National Liberation Army (ELN), to organized criminal activities and corruption. These internal security concerns encompass threats that originate both domestically (corruption, crime, and insurgency) and internationally (organized crime, arms trafficking, narcotrafficking, and money laundering). In the aftermath of September 11, 2001, Argentina, Brazil, and Paraguay are concerned that the activities of Islamic groups operating in their shared border area not contribute to a contagion of radical fundamentalist activities targeted at groups and governments in the region.

Exacerbating perceptions of internal insecurity is the Latin American (and Caribbean) preoccupation with the weakness and incapacity of democratic political and economic institutions, which have failed to contribute to greater social mobility and income equality. Such institutional security concerns—perhaps better stated as concern for institutional fragility—are widespread, as reflected in the troublingly low opinions that most Latin Americans have for government and politicians in general. Recent polling suggests that those low opinions may extend to democracy itself.[7]

While the better-off economies are less worried about the future of their democracies, Colombia, Venezuela, Ecuador, Peru, and Paraguay all have fallen short of achieving stable governance. Poor government performance by the historically dominant parties in Venezuela led to the overwhelming popular election of Hugo Chávez, the antiestablishment candidate. Ecuador's inability to resolve political and economic problems helped fracture the political system into myriad political parties organized around individuals or narrow interests that seldom, if ever, reach consensus decisions. That state of affairs in turn bred frustration among the peasants and military officers serving among them and led to a coup attempt in January 2000. Institutionalized corruption is entrenched in many countries, and local leaders do not seem able or willing to change this culture. A financial crisis brought down Argentina's government at the end of 2001, but the continued crisis in 2002 was exacerbated by an absence of political leadership. Polls in both Brazil and Uruguay favor antiestablishment candidates by a wide margin. The result of this accumulation of ineffective government is a pervasive sense of frustration and insecurity that is manifested in nearly every Latin American poll that asks about satisfaction with government or expectations about the future.[8]

Local and Personal Security

Institutional incapacity contributes to internal instability—economic unrest and illegal migrations—which gives rise to local and personal insecurity. Latin American and Caribbean expressions of concern about local and street violence are profound, widespread, and growing. Indeed, personal security concerns receive priority ranking in most countries of the region and are particularly acute in Colombia, El Salvador, Brazil, and several of the Caribbean islands.

A study conducted for the Inter-American Development Bank (IDB) noted that "in Latin America violence is widespread and has immense costs. . . . [The level of violence] is five times greater in this region than in the rest of the world."[9] Authors reported that violence against goods and people represents the destruction or transfer of resources equal to nearly 14.2 percent of the Latin American gross domestic product. Human capital losses are equivalent to all expenditures on primary education, while capital losses total more than half of all private investment in the region. The transfer of resources from victims to thieves is greater than the sum total distributive effect of all public finance policies.[10]

Urban vandalism, organized crime, youth mobs, high levels of unemployment, and poor police response (whether from incompetence or incapacity to deal with the volume of criminal activities) all affect the climate of personal security. High levels of local violence and feelings of personal insecurity exacerbate concerns over institutional fragility—many citizens fear that their governments are incapable of responding to local crises. As noted in the IDB study, when citizens do not have confidence in the police or in the judicial system, they are more likely to take justice into their own hands.

Security, Defense, and the
Evolving Roles of the Armed Forces

The proliferation of security concerns at all levels of national and international life and obvious institutional failures to cope with them has led to a new focus on the obligations of the state and on the roles of civilians and the military in designing and executing national security strategies. It has also demanded a more critical examination of the policy, resources, and institutional requirements for more effective security at all levels. Because a principal obstacle to effective governance in the past was the notable absence of civilian engagement in the direction of the armed forces and the lack of clear boundaries between civilian and military responsibilities, Latin American countries have begun their examination of policy with the armed forces.[11]

Latin American leaders are beginning to sort out the complexities and overlap of these different security environments and to devise strategies to address them. In particular, they have begun to consider, debate, and define broad national security policies, more focused defense policies, and specific roles and missions for the armed forces and security forces; they have also begun to give attention to the resources—both people and money—needed to support those roles and missions.[12] This process has advanced furthest in the Southern Cone, where several countries—most notably Chile and Argentina—have taken significant steps to define national security frameworks.[13]

In 1994 President Eduardo Frei of Chile asked Minister of Defense Edmundo Pérez Yoma to oversee the preparation of a national defense book *(Libro de Defensa Nacional de Chile)*, which was published in 1997. Around the same time, Eduardo Vaca, chairman of the Defense Commission of the Argentine Senate, organized a series of informal dinners and conferences on defense issues, which were held between 1995 and 1998. In both Chile and Argentina, active duty and retired military personnel, politicians, and academics gathered to discuss defense issues. The Argentine Defense Ministry Joint Staff assumed responsibility for the policy document (after Senator Vaca was incapacitated by a stroke), and the Argentine National Defense White Paper *(Libro Blanco de la Defensa Nacional)* was published in 1999. Brazil's president issued a national strategy paper in 1998. Uruguay published its defense white paper in 1999, and Bolivia and several other countries have documents under way. In 2002, Chile and Argentina both reviewed their defense policies and the laws that accompany them to ensure that they remain responsive to contemporary requirements.

Both the Chilean and Argentine ministers of defense noted in the introductions to their countries' respective publications that the white papers were the first such documents in the entire history of their countries. The papers represent the first effort by civilians to put their mark on the national security issue. For the civilian governments, the white papers serve several purposes: to let citizens know that defense is a subject for national discussion and a responsibility for all, to provide transparency in defense matters, and to air pending political questions. The documents provide an opportunity to recount broad security interests in the global, regional, and national arenas; to restate the implications of existing legislation for the roles and missions of the armed forces; and to consider the relationships between the military and national police. In a democracy, the papers argue, defense is a concern for the entire nation, not just the armed forces.[14] In fact, the Argentine paper stipulates that the nation's congress *must be* the author of and party ultimately responsible for defense law. The riots that preceded the fall of the Fernando de la Rúa government in December 2001 and the turmoil of 2002 demonstrated that the Argentine armed forces accepted their new legal responsibilities. Long the arbiters of Argentine politics in the twentieth century, the military remained in barracks while the police handled the rioters. There were civilian appeals for military action to "restore order," make no mistake, but the armed forces leadership said they would act "only when commanded to do so by law of Congress." Thus, they demonstrated their clear understanding of the armed forces' new objective role in Argentine society.[15]

Roles and Missions Issues

Because of their organizational strength, numbers, and discipline, Latin American armed forces are called on to deal with a growing number of causes of insecurity in the region. They often respond reluctantly, for, like militaries around the world, they see these "nontraditional" activities as detracting from their primary missions. Only a few countries— Argentina, Chile, and Brazil—have both the wherewithal and the national mandate to participate in global presence activities. In Bolivia and several Central American countries, the armed forces are prepared to participate in limited out-of-area activities, which entail costs but have the benefit of exposing the forces to international standards of humanitarian and operational comportment. Most other countries' armed forces would welcome the opportunity to participate abroad but are occupied at home or are constitutionally precluded from participating in activities outside their borders.

Nearly every country recognizes that the armed forces' primary responsibility is to defend the nation from external threats, as set forth in classical definitions of national security. Defense of sovereignty and national integrity is to be accomplished primarily through dissuasion, reinforcing the principles of nonaggression subscribed to in regional and international charters. The Argentine white paper, for example, stipulates that "the principal or primary mission of the Military Instrument is to act in a dissuasive manner by using its resources in an effective way such as to permanently protect and guarantee the vital interests of the Nation from externally originated aggression."[16] The armed forces are responsible too for contributing to peace operations in the region— and even outside it, depending on national decisions to participate in such operations—and to a variety of other activities in support of national development or other agencies, such as the police, customs authorities, and others.[17]

Clearly, the new white papers confirm the broad and overlapping range of roles for the armed forces. Unfortunately, equally close scrutiny has not been given to the roles, missions, organization, equipping, and education and training of national and local police forces. Because of the persistent bureaucratic weaknesses of these institutions and of institutions responsible for policymaking and oversight—both legislatures and ministries need strengthened capabilities for policy design and oversight—little has been done to coordinate activities. Given the vacuum of civilian leadership or operational capability, that function too often falls to the armed forces, thereby perpetuating the perception that they demand to be in charge, whereas they often are simply responding to the need for the kind of capabilities they possess.

Resources for Security

Neither the national nor international authorities pay enough attention to the critical levels of security concern in most Latin American countries. Spending on the armed forces is studied at aggregate levels, but good statistics on the adequacy of spending on police forces have not been compiled (it can safely be ventured, however, that such spending is far too little). The poorly trained, poorly equipped, and even more poorly compensated police forces of the region are overwhelmed by local violence, corrupted by local criminals, or involved themselves in violence. In 1995, the governor of the State of Rio de Janeiro was obliged to bring in the army to end violence in Rio's slums for precisely these reasons.[18] Both the World Bank and the IDB are investing in institutional reforms, with a small but very important portion of lending focused on improving the administration of justice. However, very little new money is targeted at developing the quality of law enforcement itself. The bulk of law enforcement efforts falls on local authorities who have neither the resources nor the institutional and leadership capacity to effect the required profound changes needed to quell violence and restore local citizens' perception of security in their neighborhoods.

Military spending in the region is at an all-time low. The sharp downward trend in military spending that began in the early 1980s with the onset of the debt crisis, and the subsequent overall downsizing of central governments, flattened out at about $1.2 billion[19] for Central American and Caribbean countries and $18 billion for all of South America, half of which was spent by Brazil.[20] In the same time frame, total armed forces declined from 500,000 in Central America to 209,000 (in 1995). In South America, forces have fallen from 1.1 million to slightly over 900,000.

Table 3.1 provides figures for 2001–2002 on military spending in South America.[21] Most countries spend less than 2 percent of their gross domestic product on defense. Per capita, no citizen pays more than $150 a year for the services of the national armed forces; in many countries the figure is far less. For most countries, 75 to 80 percent of the defense budget is devoted to salaries. Given that the armed forces are held in fairly high esteem in most countries of the region, such spending probably represents good value. More worrisome is that the spending per individual in the armed forces is very low, which raises serious questions about the adequacy of their preparation, equipment, or training. Over time, some Latin American countries may have to rethink the size of their standing forces and may need to consider converting to a better-paid, volunteer force.

Moreover, the operational readiness rate for most forces—especially the air force—is quite low in many countries. The long history of low budgets has resulted in inadequate logistical support, as well as anti-

Table 3.1   Assessing the Burden of Security and Defense Spending, Various Countries, 2001–2002

	Population (millions)	GDP (U.S.$ billions)	GDP Per Capita (U.S.$)	Defense Spending as Percentage of GDP	Defense Spending Per Capita (U.S.$)	Defense Spending Per Person in the Forces (U.S.$)
Argentina	37.5	282.8	7,541	1.7	128.00	68,474
Australia	19.3	399.0	20,674	2.0	404.15	154,150
Bolivia	8.4	9.4	1,119	1.4	15.48	4,127
Brazil	171.0	1,131.0	6,614	1.6	104.68	62,239
Canada	29.5	644.0	21,831	1.2	264.41	131,980
Chile	15.4	87.0	5,649	3.3	188.31	33,143
Colombia	43.7	81.0	1,854	2.6	48.05	13,291
Costa Rica	3.7	11.3	3,054	1.8	53.51	23,571
Dominican Republic	8.6	13.6	1,581	0.8	13.26	4,653
Ecuador	12.8	20.0	1,563	1.6	25.00	5,378
El Salvador	6.3	10.6	1,683	1.6	27.14	10,179
Guatemala	12.2	14.8	1,213	1.0	12.70	4,936
Haiti	7.7	3.9	506	1.3	6.49	9,434
Honduras	6.6	5.8	879	1.6	14.39	11,446
Italy	57.9	1,100.0	18,998	2.0	379.97	87,789
Mexico	100.5	554.0	5,512	1.0	52.74	27,494
Nicaragua	5.2	3.1	596	0.8	5.00	1,625
Panama	2.9	9.5	3,276	1.3	42.41	6,613
Paraguay	5.6	9.5	1,696	1.3	21.96	6,613
Peru	26.1	66.0	2,529	1.3	33.64	8,780
Spain	39.2	569.0	14,515	1.3	186.22	43,963
Sweden	8.9	230.0	25,843	2.3	584.27	98,672
United Kingdom	58.9	1,400.0	23,769	2.6	626.49	173,688
United States	275.6	9,200.0	33,382	3.0	999.64	201,713
Uruguay	3.4	14.1	4,147	2.6	107.06	15,230
Venezuela	24.6	91.0	3,699	1.5	57.11	17,072

Sources: GDP per capita: author's calculations; all other figures: International Institute for Strategic Studies, *The Strategic Balance, 2001–2002* (London: IISS, October 2001).

quated equipment, for which it is difficult and costly to acquire spare parts. Once economies are stabilized and growth is on track again, spending for new, supportable equipment will need to increase. That process may also force a sharp rationalization of inventories, permitting forces to "do more with less." It will not necessarily trigger an "arms race" in the region. In many countries the armed forces have already begun to undertake the kind of administrative and organizational reforms that will transform the defense sector in the new century. It is a secret too well kept that the armed forces in a number of countries have accomplished more reform of the state than any other segment of the public sector.

Conclusion

Security concerns in Latin America and the Caribbean today are not about the armed forces. Fragile though they are, the region's democracies have succeeded in establishing the fact of military subordination to civilian authority. Personal security is the primary concern of most Latin Americans (most Latin American countries have a rich experience with terrorism—the result of past internal wars—and with the kidnappings and ransoms that often accompany today's political conflicts), followed by internal security concerns (drug trafficking, money laundering, arms trafficking, illegal migration, and politically motivated violence) and concern about the fragility and corruption of domestic democratic institutions. Citizens of the region worry also that external events, such as market fluctuations or ethnic or religious hostilities, and now the reluctance to travel that has resulted from the September 11, 2001, events, may compromise their long-awaited hopes for national growth and development by discouraging new investment in their countries.

In most countries, the armed forces are held in relatively high esteem and civil-military relations are "okay."[22] The armed forces of the region have undergone important transformations. Although the extent of change varies from country to country, the broad trends are clear. They suggest a future with smaller, more mobile, and better-educated forces (officers increasingly have bachelor's and advanced degrees); deepening professionalism; and increasing integration with the civilian community through education and community involvement. An immediate challenge for public policy is better integrating local and national police and military activities so that these forces can cope more effectively with the serious security challenges confronting their countries. Given the levels of insecurity and the nature of these challenges, Latin American countries are not spending too much on security and defense. If anything, they are spending too little. They need to give more serious attention to how effectively they are spending these scarce resources.

Civilian leadership in the security arena is evolving slowly. The exercise of developing defense white papers has begun to clarify the roles and responsibilities of civilian leaders, legislatures, and public opinion in defining security and defense policy. Ministries and legislative committees need to be further strengthened and more resources need to be allocated to police forces and to justice administrations before security can be assured. In the end, Latin American and Caribbean security is profoundly dependent on the development of more effective institutions at the regional, national, and local levels of government; on their greater capacity for interagency cooperation; on the provision of adequate—that is, more—resources targeted at providing security at all levels of society; and, finally, on a more inclusive vision of the spectrum of security concerns, as perceived by citizens.

The insecurity that characterizes Latin America and the Caribbean countries at the outset of the twenty-first century must be addressed principally by Latin American governments, politicians, public and private institutions, and citizens. No outside actor, no matter how well intentioned, can effect the profound changes needed if the political will to effect change is not present.

That said, several U.S. agencies are involved in the region in various ways at different levels of government. The U.S. Agency for International Development (USAID), the Department of Justice, the Treasury Department (through its Bureau of Alcohol, Tobacco, and Firearms), and the Department of State's International Narcotics and Law Enforcement and Public Diplomacy Bureaus, as well as the Coast Guard, the Defense Department, the U.S. Southern Command, and others, are all engaged with Latin American and Caribbean countries in an effort to promote security by shaping attitudes and developing institutional capabilities. By far, the major focus of most of these agencies has been on Colombia and the counternarcotics effort (which extends beyond Colombia), and now—post–September 11—on counterterrorism.

Little of that effort, however, is effectively coordinated with the initiatives of other donors—like the international financial institutions (the World Bank and the IDB), the European Union, the United Nations, and the OAS. Whereas the United States is the principal donor for those programs aimed at countering drug trafficking, the international financial institutions are the major players in funding judicial and administrative reforms that may affect local and personal security. U.S. program planners need to be more cognizant of these international initiatives. While recognizing that it is even more difficult to coordinate across international bureaucracies than among national agencies (and that is already difficult), too often good projects and economies of scale are not realized because of the failure to achieve synergy. A donors' conference mandated to coordinate programs other than counternarcotics might facilitate more effective and efficient cooperation in these other security matters.

The weight of U.S. involvement in the security arena often falls too heavily on the military-to-military engagement carried out by the U.S. Southern Command. Although the Southern Command's forward-looking security cooperation efforts are helping to develop military capabilities in a number of useful areas (disaster response, military justice, crisis coordination, and humanitarian assistance, for example), a more robust vision for *civilian* engagement needs to be formulated.[23] As one minister of defense complained, "there is lots of money for the military, but my problem is in developing civilians able to work with the military and there is not enough money for this." The Southern Command should not be—nor does it seek to be—the lead U.S. agency sponsoring civilian-led interagency security coordination. But too often civilian agencies will not deal with the military, thus perpetuating a vicious circle in Latin American countries where good examples of civilian and military cooperation are rare.

In implementing a long-term vision, the United States should focus on strengthening all Latin American security institutions, not just the armed forces, and on improving those institutions responsible for overseeing security institutions. The problems of individual countries—which so readily spill across borders, as with drug trafficking—cannot be solved quickly or easily. Some ongoing projects in which the United States is involved, the biannual defense ministerial meetings, for example, should help strengthen regional and subregional civilian defense and security coordination. In addition, the United States should strongly support education in law enforcement and administration of justice, as well as follow up on promising ongoing initiatives to strengthen legislative capabilities and controller and inspector general functions. In general, the United States needs to focus on the full spectrum of civilian responsibilities in the security arena. In this realm, the U.S. policy community has a task only slightly less daunting than that facing its Latin American and Caribbean counterparts. For their part, Latin American academics and politicians need to focus on their own governments' weaknesses and on finding solutions to those weaknesses. Resolving the insecurity that Latin American and Caribbean countries perceive, however, requires a long-term vision as well as the political will to effect changes.

Notes

1. This occurred only shortly after Mexican president Vicente Fox had announced (prior to the September 11 attacks) his country's intention to withdraw from the treaty, calling it outdated and obsolete. The Inter-American Treaty of Reciprocal Assistance, known as the Rio treaty, is a collective security agreement that dates back to 1947 and calls for signatories to consider an attack against other nations in the region by an outside party an attack against all countries in the region.

2. The 1995 defense ministerial meeting took place in Williamsburg, Virginia. U.S. Department of Defense, First Conference of Ministers of Defense of the Americas, 24–26 July 1995 [www.state.gov/t/pm/rls/othr/rd/1991_1995/6434.htm]. For subsequent defense ministerial meetings, also see [www.state.gov/t/pm/csbm/amer/rd/dma/].

3. The Santiago agreement is the 1991 OAS general assembly declaration committing the member countries to support democratic government in the hemisphere.

4. The classic-realist conception of national power comprises four elements: political, economic, psychosocial, and military power. I see military power and capability as wholly dependent on social, economic, and political capabilities of the nation. Indeed, one reason for the military's divorce from the rest of society may be attributed to the erroneous premises of the classic-realist model, which remains part of the lexicon of most military schools in the United States and in Latin America.

5. This list of security threats is derived from an informal poll of students from the Center for Hemispheric Defense Studies (CHDS) at the National Defense University in Washington, D.C., conducted in October 1999. The themes have been reiterated across 16 classes and over 800 participants in our program.

6. It is worth noting that the commander of the Chilean Naval War College and the director of studies of the Argentine school met and became friends at the U.S. Naval Command College in Newport, Rhode Island. Both remained for a second year of study as scholars in the Center for War Gaming Studies, a program that has subsequently been terminated.

7. See *Latinobarómetro* surveys of Latin American political opinions, 1996 to 2002 [www.latinobarometro.org]. For Brazil, see "Maioria dos jovens é indiferente à democracia," *O Estado de São Paulo*, 14 May 2000, A9.

8. Ibid.

9. Juan Luis Londoño and Rodrigo Guerrero, "Violencia en América

Latina: Epidemiología y costos," Office of the Chief Economist's Research Network, Working Paper R-375 (Washington, D.C.: Inter-American Development Bank, 1999), 3. This paper can be obtained online on the IDB Web page at: [www.iadb.org].

10. Ibid.

11. This is the subject of a growing literature by Latin American scholars. See Ernesto López, "Latin America: Objective and Subjective Control Revisited," in *Civil-Military Relations in Latin America: New Analytical Perspectives,* ed. David Pion-Berlin (Chapel Hill: University of North Carolina Press, 2001), 88–107.

12. This is a substantial change from an earlier period when discussion of national security issues was the exclusive purview of the armed forces. According to former Colombian defense minister Rafael Pardo, "The identification of the military establishment with the concept of national security on the one hand and the military's monopoly in generating a vision of the subject on the other have created an aversion among Latin American intellectuals for dealing with themes associated with security. There were no alternatives posed to the conventional wisdom. The ideological differences between communism and anticommunism imposed a profound division, which in turn promoted unanimity and absence of debate about the concepts of security. Anyone who disagreed with the official view ran the risk of being classified as antipatriotic; a fool *(idiota útil)* or an ingenue." Rafael Pardo Rueda, *Nueva Seguridad para América Latina* (Bogotá: Universidad Nacional de Colombia, 1999, 26).

13. See Herbert Huser, *Argentina's Civil-Military Relations: Changing Patterns in a Democratic Society* (Washington, D.C.: National Defense University Press, 2002), which details Argentina's experience in redefining civilian-military relations, building a defense ministry, and crafting new legislation to govern the armed forces.

14. The concept that defines defense as a public good has been the subject of CHDS-sponsored conferences in Bolivia, Guatemala, Guyana, and Paraguay.

15. Margaret Daly Hayes, "Foreword," in Huser, *Argentina's Civil-Military Relations.*

16. *Argentina: Libro Blanco de la Defensa Nacional* (Buenos Aires: Government of Argentina, 1999), 9–81; available online at: [www.defensenet. ser2000.org.ar/Archivo/libro-argentina/defa-indice.htm].

17. Chile's army, for example, is the official mapping agency for the country. It conducts research, often in conjunction with universities; assists in the development of remote areas; provides tools and explosives for the mining industry; maintains the database of weapons registry; develops road-building projects in remote areas; provides specialized support for disaster response; instructs in civil defense; contributes to environmental control (especially in reforestation); offers instruction in national history and geography; and contributes specialized training useful in the civilian economy. Chile's navy subsumes the functions that in the United States fall to the U.S. Coast Guard, including patrol of the Exclusive Economic Zone, maritime pollution control, maintenance of buoys and hydrographic and meteorological services, medical services in remote regions, community and humanitarian support in remote

areas and ports, and so forth. The air force assists in hospital rescue and triage during disasters, supports civil aviation, and conducts space and meteorological research. Both Ecuador and Paraguay have assigned their armed forces responsibility for customs because civilian institutions were too corrupt and poorly managed to fulfill their duties. Guatemala is contemplating assigning its armed forces responsibilities for protection of its pre-Columbian archaeological heritage.

18. See Col. William W. Mendel (Ret.), "Operation Rio: Taking Back the Streets," *Military Review* 77, no. 3 (May–June 1997).

19. All dollar amounts are U.S. dollars unless otherwise noted.

20. Figures are from the U.S. Arms Control and Disarmament Agency (ACDA), *World Military Expenditures and Arms Transfers 1998*, available at the State Department website: [www.state.gov/www/global/arms/bureau_ac/wmeat98/wmeat98.html].

21. Latin American defense expenditure data are notoriously difficult to compare because different countries include different items in their defense budgets. Colombia's defense spending includes funds for the national police. Chile's defense budget includes expenditures from copper export revenues. Some countries include spending for pensions while others do not. Equipment purchases are often accounted for outside the budget. The UN's Economic Commission for Latin America and the Caribbean (ECLAC) has undertaken a project to align defense budget and expenditure presentations for Argentina and Chile; that effort may lead to a standardization of budget and expenditures presentations across the region. See ECLAC, "Metodología estandarizada para la medición de los gastos de defensa" (Santiago, Chile: ECLAC, November 2001).

22. This was a conclusion of the Third Conference of Senior Defense Institutions (superior war colleges) held in Buenos Aires, Argentina, in 1999. The conference was sponsored by the Inter-American Defense Board and the U.S. Southern Command and hosted by the Argentine Ministry of Defense.

23. This of course is the raison d'être of the organization for which I work, and it has been enormously successful in supporting a growing cadre of civilians active in and interested in defense and security matters. However, demand for help today far outpaces our meager resources, and there remains much to do.

U.S. Policy Toward Latin America: A View from the South

Roberto Russell

For almost two centuries, U.S. policy toward Latin America has provoked differing opinions. Indeed, for the United States, the very value of the relationship has always been somewhat dubious. Defenders and detractors of the "Western Hemisphere idea" have been equally vocal in expressing their conflicting positions: Some underscore the possibilities that Latin America offers for the United States, whereas others emphasize the irrelevance—even the "inconvenience"—of maintaining ties with nations in the South.[1]

As is well known, the U.S.–Latin America relationship has been characterized by a growing asymmetry of power (favoring the United States), generally accompanied by a strong asymmetry of interests. Global issues that have infiltrated Latin America have tended to determine the level of U.S. interest in the region, and the policies the United States has adopted have been essentially reactive in nature. For example, the Alliance for Progress promoted by the Kennedy administration at the beginning of the 1960s was a direct response to the Cuban revolution, founded on the fear that "other Cubas" would materialize in the hemisphere. More recently, former U.S. president George Bush's 1990 Enterprise for the Americas, which called for a hemisphere-wide free trade system, and its 1994 successor, the Summit of the Americas—at which the parties agreed to complete negotiations for a Free Trade Area of the Americas (FTAA) by 2005—were the expressions of a new U.S. trade policy that assigned regionalism a strategic role in promoting the economic interests of the United States as a previous step toward multilateral negotiation.[2]

Because of their fundamentally reactive nature, the few U.S. initiatives of regional or subregional reach have been negatively affected by the course of global events unrelated to Latin America or by the weight of more concrete and immediate domestic interests, or they may simply have faded away at the same rate as the threats that motivated them in the first place. For example, the Alliance for Progress lost its momentum when Washington understood that Fidel Castro's capacity to export his revolution to the rest of the region was very limited. Domestic interests in the United States have also imposed serious obstacles to the creation of an FTAA within the specified time frame. As expected, the weakening or impasse of these regional initiatives provoked frustration, disillusionment, and a déja-vu sensation of lost opportunity, followed invariably by proposals—generally unfulfilled—about what the United States should or should not do in the region.

U.S. Interest in Latin America

U.S. interest in Latin America has historically been concentrated on large or nearby nations and concerned with those topics that are perceived, according to the era, as threats to U.S. national security or to the well-being of U.S. citizens. In short, U.S. interest in the region adheres to a pattern that can be summarized in a few words: size, proximity, and level of perceived threat.[3] Mexico, therefore, has always captured more attention than Brazil or Guatemala. Chile under the government of the Unidad Popular in the 1970s, Nicaragua and El Salvador in the 1980s, and Colombia in the 1990s achieved a prominent place on Washington's regional agenda only because of their potential threat to U.S. security.

More recently, Argentina has suffered the direct consequences of the new policy introduced by the George W. Bush administration regarding rescuing emerging nations in situations of economic crisis. Geared toward promoting a more prudent use of International Monetary Fund (IMF) resources, this new vision holds that the international community should not always direct large-scale financing to countries that cannot resolve important domestic problems. To its misfortune, Argentina went from being a favored example of successful economic reforms promoted by the United States in Latin America during the 1990s to a test case of this new policy. After having supported important aid packages to Argentina through the multilateral credit organizations, in December 2001 the U.S. government decided to oppose the

IMF's distribution of a previously agreed on disbursement of $1.26 billion.[4] Washington's reasoning was threefold: that the costs for U.S. interests would be small; that the markets were already considering the cessation of payments and a devaluation inevitable for Argentina; and that there would be no contagion effect on other emerging nations—more specifically on neighboring countries of the Southern Cone.[5]

However, when the latter assumption was proven wrong by events in Uruguay and Brazil, the United States was forced to reassess its initial stance on foreign assistance to emerging markets in crisis, and it granted Uruguay a $1.5 billion emergency loan to avoid financial meltdown. Soon after, the IMF announced a $30 billion loan to Brazil over a 15-month period, despite the political uncertainty surrounding the 2002 presidential elections and its negative impact on investor confidence. Somewhat of a reversal from the initial position of the U.S. Treasury, Washington was now sending a new message: Countries with sound economic policies suffering from the effects of external factors, such as contagion from Argentina's crisis, deserve financial support from the international community. Once again, the threat of contagion to the rest of Latin America, coupled with the perception that the effects of such a crisis might reach as far as the United States, forced a reevaluation of the U.S. position on foreign aid.

Nothing indicates that the basis for defining U.S. interest in the region—size, proximity, and perceived level of threat—is likely to change substantially in the near future. As Joseph Tulchin remarked, "New technologies and new global issues have altered our sense of distance; nevertheless, the same rules appear to apply today as they have for the past 200 years."[6] In principle, this conclusion—with which most analysts in the United States and Latin America agree—is correct. It is based on powerful empirical evidence, and it stems from a more complete understanding of the U.S. foreign policy process toward Latin America than the one that prevailed 20 or 30 years ago. Such knowledge is not limited to academic spheres; it also extends to the political and economic elite. The sporadic nature of U.S. policy vis-à-vis Latin America, the intricacies of bureaucratic politics, the role of Congress in frustrating or impeding initiatives of the executive branch, the appreciation that almost all politics is local—to paraphrase Tip O'Neill, former Speaker of the U.S. House of Representatives—all contribute to integrate the vision of Latin American elites toward the United States.

At the same time, this better understanding of the U.S. policy process has made more evident the place Latin America as a whole, each of its subregions, and each of its nations hold in the priority ranking of U.S. foreign policy. No attentive observer was surprised by President Clinton's state of the union address in 2000, in which the only Latin American country mentioned was Colombia. After soliciting congressional approval for a strong two-year economic package "to help this country win the fight against narcotraffickers," he underscored the importance of the Colombian situation "for the long-term stability of [the United States], and for what happens in Latin America."[7] The lack of reference to the entire Latin American region did not provoke anxiety, but it did reinforce at least two perceptions: Priorities lay elsewhere and, except for Colombia—or, more precisely, the question of drug trafficking—no Latin American issue is serious enough to keep Washington awake at night. In the aftermath of the September 11, 2001, terrorist attacks on New York and Washington, it is not surprising to Latin Americans that U.S. foreign policy has focused primarily on relations with Europe, Russia, China, India, and the Arab world.

These sharper analytical tools for understanding U.S.–Latin American relations—in particular the U.S. decisionmaking process—generally are used to interpret the immediate facets of regional relations and their short- and medium-term outlooks. For example, at the end of the Clinton administration, many analysts believed that the relationship between the United States and Latin America would be spiraling downward at the dawn of the twenty-first century and the millennium, falling from the heights reached in the early 1990s. Europe's centrality for the United States, the impasse of the FTAA, the ups and downs of the democratization and integration processes in Latin America, and the persistence of unilateral policies and arrogant U.S. attitudes, among other important factors, seemed to support this position.

After President George W. Bush took office, however, the prevailing opinions tipped the balance toward the opposite direction. President Bush himself, readopting the Western Hemisphere idea in its purest sense, stated: "Some people look south and see problems. That is not the case with me. I look south and I see opportunity and potential. Our future cannot be separated from the future of our neighbors in Canada and Latin America."[8] Imbued in the same spirit, most analysts—many of whom then fed the lines of pessimism—concluded that the Bush administration would pay greater attention to Latin America than the Clinton administration had. These views were short-lived.

Following the September 11 terrorist attacks, the view that Latin America is of low priority for U.S. interests quickly resurfaced as the predominant political and academic stance. For instance, Latin America specialist Peter Hakim stated soon after the terrorist attacks that "for better or worse, Latin America—which before September 11 was considered among the White House's highest priorities—will be profoundly affected by United States actions in the coming months."[9] Sharing similar fears, Jorge Domínguez argued, "The only Latin Americanist of the Bush administration, Bush himself, is now too busy to pay attention to Latin America, and there are not many others in his administration who care about the rest of the hemisphere."[10] Paul Kennedy stated, "Intensified diplomatic and political efforts in Central Asia and the Persian Gulf will inevitably lead to less time being given to Latin America and Africa. To govern is to choose."[11]

By mid-2002, however, the outlook on U.S. policy toward Latin America took a more optimistic turn. The financial assistance offered to Brazil and Uruguay in August of that year was, of course, an important reason for such a change. Perhaps even more significant, however, was congressional passage—also in August 2002—of trade promotion authority (TPA), which grants the U.S. administration greater ability to negotiate trade agreements with other nations or regions and therefore, in the case of the Western Hemisphere, to move forward with FTAA negotiations.[12] Thus, within a short period of ten years, perceptions about the future of inter-American relations have shifted from positive to negative prospects five different times.

The emphasis on the current dynamics of U.S.–Latin American relations holds a hidden danger: One may lose sight of the relationship's historical evolution and its longer-term tendencies. An examination of the whole picture would yield the following conclusion: Latin America has grown in importance to the United States since the mid-1980s for political-strategic and economic reasons. Four closely related factors support this conclusion: (1) the democratization of Latin America; (2) the opening of the region to the world economy; (3) the new economic regionalism in the United States and Latin America; and (4) the cultural changes under way since the 1980s, particularly in Latin America, which facilitate inter-American cooperation. These factors are strongly correlated with a contextual variable (the end of the Cold War) and a structural variable (the process of globalization, in its broadest sense); they favor the development of a policy agenda that demonstrates heretofore unseen levels of convergence.

In effect, the U.S. policy agenda and priorities largely reflect those of Latin America:

- Strengthen democracy, political freedom, good governance, the rule of law, and respect for human rights.
- Combat the menace of the illegal drug trade, crime, and terrorism, and meet new challenges such as environmental degradation and sustainable development.
- Promote economic integration through an open and fair trade policy.
- Reduce poverty through growth and job creation, and improve health and education systems.

These key goals, as Howard Wiarda suggests, "enjoy support from Latin America as well as from mainstreams of U.S. foreign policy, ending the conflict that has raged, for the last 40 years, between the United States and Latin America over the U.S. agenda and policy priorities."[13]

The United States and the Democratization Process in Latin America

Since the end of the Cold War, the United States has actively promoted democracy throughout the world. Before then, strategic considerations stemming from the East–West rivalry had led U.S. governments to systematically subordinate this objective to others that were perceived as more valuable—containing communism, for example. Certainly this conflict of interests is (and will continue to be) present in U.S. foreign policy. As with the promotion of human rights, the U.S. commitment to democracy cannot avoid double standards. The United States played a decisive role in impeding the breakdown of the democratization process in Venezuela (1992), Guatemala (1993), Paraguay (1996 and 1999), and Ecuador (2000). However, its commitment to the defense of democracy was ambiguous during political crises in Peru (1992), Haiti (1991–1994), and Venezuela (2002). In Peru, achieving stability for the country and its government, whose cooperation in the war on drugs was essential for Washington, was at least as important an objective as the quality of Peruvian democracy. In Haiti, it was the worsening condition of Haitian refugees that finally pushed the Clinton administration to adopt a hard line and force Haiti's military and civilian supporters to restore deposed president Jean Bertrand Aristide to power.[14] Previously, as Richard Bloomfield underscores, "the Bush administration was divided internally as to whether it would be in the U.S. interest for Aristide to be returned to power. This ambivalence was reflected in a half-hearted policy, in which the rhetoric from the State Department was not matched by deeds."[15]

The ambivalence of U.S. policy toward Peru and Haiti did not cause wonder or unease in Latin America. The majority of Latin American countries had behaved similarly and therefore were not in any condition to cast the first stone. For Brazil and Chile, for example, maintaining Peru's stability was rated higher than addressing the violation of democratic institutions during the *fujimorazo*. In the case of Haiti, the larger countries of the region—with the exception of Argentina—opposed presenting the problem to the United Nations Security Council for fear that, once it had extended its jurisdiction to such an issue as democracy, the organization would find an excuse to intervene in the domestic affairs of those nations.

During the April 2002 political crisis in Venezuela, the Bush administration did not initially condemn the anti-Chávez coup; rather, it adopted an acquiescent stance on the displacement of a government it had strong reservations about. Once again, the United States was not alone in its position. As Chávez himself noted in his first speech after his release, the only countries in the region that immediately condemned the coup were Brazil, Chile, Guatemala, and Mexico.[16] After the initial decisions made by those who fleetingly took power—to shut down the congress, abolish the constitution, arbitrarily detain individuals—and Chávez's return to the presidency, Colin Powell summarized the U.S. position in an address to the Organization of American States (OAS) as follows: "Democracies do not remain democracies for long if elected leaders use undemocratic methods. And defending democracy by resorting to undemocratic means destroys democracy."[17]

The strong position the United States took regarding Venezuela (in 1992), Guatemala, Paraguay, and Ecuador was not surprising either, given that in these four countries the objective of defending democracy did not conflict with other goals of equal or greater importance. In fact, the mix of active commitment and ambivalence produced opposing interpretations of the scope of U.S. intentions to defend and promote democracy in Latin America. Those who focused on Peru, Haiti, and Venezuela (in 2002) concluded that the glass was still half empty. To the contrary, those who highlighted Venezuela, Guatemala, Paraguay, and

Ecuador saw the glass as half full. Again, an analysis limited to a particular moment cannot settle the question. To avoid getting sidetracked in this debate, it is necessary to observe the trajectory and intent of U.S. policy, as well as the democratization process in Latin America.

U.S. commitment to the defense and promotion of democracy in Latin America is much stronger than it used to be, and that commitment is here to stay.[18] It is an important facet of U.S. foreign policy that has bipartisan consensus and support from bureaucrats, businesses and investors, and numerous social forces with ties to the region. This is so for two main reasons. First, democratic consolidation in Latin America is an objective that coincides with and reinforces the values system of the United States and its political and economic interests. It strengthens stability in the region, more strongly guarantees continuity of the market-oriented economic policies adopted in the 1990s, and facilitates business as it promotes greater transparency and accountability than authoritarian regimes do.[19] As Jorge Domínguez argues, "In Latin America's present and likely future circumstances, democracy is good for markets, although it had not always been so in the past."[20]

Second, the United States is no longer involved in any competition for global power that demands unconditional loyalty in its areas of influence. It competes economically in Latin America with countries that are part of its privileged system of alliances and that do not hold out alternative political models to the region, such as fascism and communism. On the contrary, the strengthening of democracy is a flag that these other nations also wave.

Latin America clearly perceives these two circumstances. Great strides have been made since the not-too-distant past when Latin American dictators sought—and many times received—the blessing of the United States in exchange for certain favors. Both the democratic and nondemocratic sectors of Latin America know this. For the latter, the current U.S. position acts as a deterrent either when it contains them—something that we do not see—or when it forces them to back down, as happened in Ecuador in January 2000. The Clinton administration warned Ecuador's military and political leaders that a military overthrow would leave the country "more isolated than Cuba," which prompted armed forces chief General Carlos Mendoza on January 22 to dissolve the junta that had toppled President Jamil Mahuad only three hours earlier and hand power to Vice President Gustavo Noboa.[21]

Certainly, the strengthened U.S. commitment to the defense and promotion of democracy is not absolute in nature, as demonstrated during the Venezuelan crisis in April 2002. In this specific case, the Bush administration adopted a wait-and-see attitude and even seemed willing, at least initially, to justify Chávez's ouster. In the post–September 11 context it is likely that Washington will be less scrupulous when carrying out its commitments toward the defense of human rights and democracy around the world. As John Lewis Gaddis states, "[The United States will] have to define [its] allies more in terms of shared interests, and less in terms of shared values."[22] Nonetheless, on balance, the events of the last decade leave room for optimism: The current U.S. commitment to democracy in Latin America is much more genuine and firm than during the Cold War years.

For their part, Latin American nations have demonstrated varying levels of commitment to the defense and promotion of democracy; statements and policies in defense of democracy vie with reluctant, suspicious attitudes.[23] Despite these differences, some important steps have been taken to build an inter-American regime of democracy defense that is not merely formal. Among these steps, the historic Resolution 1080 on representative democracy and the Inter-American Democratic Charter stand out. The former, approved during the twenty-first general assembly of the OAS in Santiago, Chile, in June 1991, recognized an automatic safeguard regarding situations of "sudden or irregular interruption" in the democratic process in any OAS nation.[24] The Inter-American Democratic Charter was approved in Lima on September 11, 2001, during a special session of the OAS General Assembly. In addition to strengthening diplomatic sanctions measures for cases in which democratic order is altered or interrupted, the charter also established a collective commitment to help preserve democracy when it is usurped by an illegitimate government or when democratic order is greatly altered by a democratically elected government that develops clear antidemocratic tendencies.[25] This last instrument was applied for the first time in April 2002 in response to the political crisis in Venezuela and was one of the factors that contributed to President Chávez's return to power. Ironically, his government had on various occasions expressed opposition to the inclusion of clauses addressing the defense of democracy in the inter-American system, arguing that they violate the principle of self-determination of individual nations.

Some countries, such as the members of Mercosur, also signed important agreements with the purpose of defending democracy at the subregional level. For example, the "democracy clause" approved in June 1998 by Argentina, Brazil, Paraguay, and Uruguay, together with

Bolivia and Chile, states that "in the case of a breakdown of democratic order in a Member State," the other states are able to suspend that country's rights "to participate in the various bodies created by the respective integration processes," and even "the rights and obligations emerging from these processes."[26]

This interest in establishing safeguards for democracy through an inter-American regime or through specific, limited agreements comes from the justifiable unease in the Americas about a process that has already endured much turbulence and come perilously close to failure in more than one country.[27] Nevertheless, the setbacks to democratization have been fairly modest in Latin America, compared with setbacks elsewhere. Although there is no definitive set of prerequisites for democracy, it is clear that the democratization process that began in the 1970s around the world has been more solid in countries (1) where there has been prior experience with democratic practices; (2) that are in a region where liberal democratic values have a historical stronghold or a tendency to take root, and in which all or the majority of the largest nations have made significant advances toward the consolidation of democracy; (3) that seek integration with the West; and (4) that are in a region in which the strategic interests of the countries for whom the region is an area of influence are defined democratically.[28]

All or at least some of these prerequisites are met in Latin America. Accenting the breakdowns, though they are undoubtedly serious, hampers a full appreciation of the advances of a process that moves at different speeds, that has unknown scope and force, that is encouraged by a favorable external political context, that has helped erase negative agenda topics with Washington, and that introduced positive qualitative changes in intraregional relations.[29] The most significant case was the signing of nuclear agreements between Argentina and Brazil, which ended several decades of mutual suspicion and opened the path for both countries to cooperation with the international security system.[30]

In the early twenty-first century, unlike in the twentieth, it is unlikely that democracy in Latin America will have to contend seriously with other forms of government capable of competing with and replacing it. As noted above, there do not appear to be alternative political models available, nor are there significant external forces to promote and sustain them. Thus, it is quite probable that democratic "formality" will last even in nations mired in endemic violence (Colombia), in those where new political leadership has risen out of the ashes of former "formal" democracies (Venezuela), in those where laws were manipulated to permit an incumbent president's candidacy for another term (Peru), in those in which military power is once again behind the throne (Ecuador), or in those suffering a profound political, economic, and social crisis (Argentina).[31] It is interesting to note that Argentina is undergoing one of its gravest and most intense crises without democracy coming into question. In the words of Natalio Botana: "Nobody, for now, questions out loud the legitimacy of the democratic Republic. What is, in fact, being questioned is who represents this legitimacy, not its constitutional principle. This is small consolation in the midst of the disaster."[32]

Indeed, the central question is not whether electoral democracy can stay in place but whether liberal democracy can be effectively consolidated in Latin America. Doing so calls for a frontal attack on the enormous "illiberal"—as Fareed Zakaria terms it—flank of Latin American political systems. That is, simply stated, guaranteeing that there is rule of law and good governance, that the separation of powers is respected, and that the basic liberties of liberal constitutionalism, such as freedom of speech, religious assembly, and property are preserved.[33]

Unlike what happened during the construction process of today's consolidated democracies such as the United States and Great Britain, the challenge for Latin America in the twenty-first century is not only to limit the "tyranny of the majorities" and to take governmental action in order to guarantee civil liberties. Equally important is the need to strengthen state capacity to provide public goods in basic areas such as justice, security, and education, which state reforms initiated at the end of the 1980s did not do. It will also be necessary to fight the illiberal side of the Latin American market through public policies that favor a greater diffusion of private economic power.

In the 1990s, the United States emphasized the defense of democracy—that is, ensuring survival of democratic procedures (especially free and fair elections) and thwarting authoritarian attempts to seize power—more than its promotion. This policy orientation, more reactive than active, was not the product of narrow-mindedness, mere stupidity, or lack of interest. Rather, the United States concentrated on the most obvious threats to the democratization process and consequently played a fundamentally dissuasive or corrective role. In the twenty-first century, without losing sight of the defense of democracy, it should invert its priorities and cooperate with Latin America in the promotion of democracy—that is, in making Latin American political systems (and markets) less illiberal and its governments more effective, transparent, accessible, and responsible. The majority of Latin Americans would welcome this kind of intervention in the region.

Economic Liberalization and New Regionalism

The United States and Latin America have entered the twenty-first century with a predominantly positive economic agenda. Economic changes produced in the region during the 1990s paved the way for new opportunities for the United States and other foreign partners. At the same time, both parties modified their traditional positions vis-à-vis regional trade agreements. For the United States, regionalism became a natural and indispensable complement to the two other trade strategies it had employed since the end of World War II—unilateralism and multilateralism; the latter, however, is still the principal axis of U.S. trade policy because the nation's international economic relationships are so broadly diversified.

Two trade policy considerations decisively influenced the emphasis given to regionalism by successive U.S. administrations since the mid-1980s. First, the United States worried that European and Asian trade blocs would discriminate against it when it seemed possible that the Uruguay Round negotiations might fail. In this context, the United States saw regionalism as an insurance policy against an eventual rise in European and Asian protectionism, as well as a way to pressure other nations to commit to multilateral trade negotiations.[34] Second, the multilateral agenda has become increasingly complex, now including elements that traditionally pertained to the domestic sphere, such as protection of intellectual property, competitive policies, and labor and environmental standards. This situation has pushed many countries, within the framework of increasing global integration, to develop negotiations at regional or subregional levels with the purpose of making advances that would be very difficult to achieve at the multilateral level. Thus, for the United States, as for other important nations, regionalism has acquired strategic value for consolidating the global agenda of deepening integration because it is viewed as a first step toward multilateral negotiations.[35]

Aside from trade considerations, the United States also has a security interest at stake. As Stuart E. Eizenstat, former undersecretary for economic, business, and agricultural affairs, stated: "The trade agreements of the post–Cold War era will be equivalent to the security pacts of the Cold War—binding nations together in a virtuous circle of mutual prosperity and providing the new frontline of defense against instability. A more integrated and more prosperous world will be a more peaceful world—a world more hospitable to American interests and ideals."[36]

Latin America, for its part, abandoned the state-controlled, defensive orientation that had historically marked its integration processes and adopted a more dynamic, offensive, flexible, and pragmatic stance. The initial strategy was a logical derivation of the import-substitution industrialization model. Faced with increasingly narrow national markets, integration seemed to be a key instrument for maintaining and deepening that model on a regional or subregional scale, though always under the auspices of protectionism and active state participation.[37]

The second orientation was closely linked to structural reform policies and economic openings that have paved the way for Latin America's new international insertion. Less rhetorical than in the past, this regionalism shows concrete advances that are reflected in a growing level of intraregional interdependence, integration of infrastructure and energy installations (such as bridges and pipelines), and political cooperation. As in other parts of the world, regionalism in Latin America combines negative incentives, such as lowering or avoiding discrimination costs in third markets,[38] with positive ones—improving the individual bargaining power of each country and gaining access to the markets of trade partners, as well as those of other nations; locking in reform policies; gaining more credibility for domestic and foreign policies; and increasing economic efficiency and competitiveness by reassigning resources to activities with comparative and competitive advantages.[39]

The varied integration mechanisms being used in Latin America have important differences that reflect a diverse continent. However, Latin American integration contains an important set of common characteristics: (1) It is a priority goal in the foreign policy agenda of all the countries; (2) it tries to strengthen commercial, financial, and investment ties with the principal centers of economic power in the world; and (3) it is seen as compatible with the world trade order.

For the first time in inter-American history, this move from a closed regionalism to an open one has generated authentic economic convergences between the United States and Latin America. This is not a minor point, if one recalls that Latin American economic positions were characterized by their high level of divergence from the United States and that Latin American regionalism generated considerable unease in

Washington, given that it was historically defined as a tool to counter-balance U.S. power in the region.

The current convergences do not imply a harmony of interests between the United States and Latin America, nor has Latin America renounced using regional or subregional strategies as policy instruments to strengthen its bargaining power vis-à-vis external actors such as the United States and the European Union. An illustrative example is the First Conference of South American Presidents convened by Brazilian president Fernando Henrique Cardoso, which was designed to create a new space in which to discuss issues of mutual interest to the nations of the subregion.[40] Nor will the United States abandon its unilateral strategy to promote its own interests by using its abundant capabilities in economic diplomacy.[41]

There are important divisions over the scope of a future preferential trade agreement in the hemisphere, how to put it into practice, and how to deal with asymmetries. Mexico, for example, has not had much interest in extending NAFTA because it has already taken advantage of its entry into the U.S. market, and Central American and Caribbean countries still have a strong interest in maintaining arrangements that assure them trade concessions. Argentina, Chile, and Uruguay have shown great interest in the FTAA, while Brazil has been more reserved. According to Riordan Roett, "Brazil will continue to defend an autonomous position in trade negotiations and will carry the day in the Southern Cone, using Mercosur as a cover for its own ambitious international agenda."[42] As with democracy, the agenda is complex and will require much effort that will proceed in fits and starts. These difficulties, however, are natural in an intense relationship that is moving away from one marked by distrust and even hostility. Current differences are no longer defined ideologically; they stem from the parties' authentic interests.

It should also be noted that the impasse of the FTAA has not impeded market forces from moving easily in the Western Hemisphere. U.S. exports to Latin America almost tripled between 1990 and 1997. By the mid-1990s, the United States had sent 11 times more goods to Latin American nations than to China, twice as many as to Japan, and the same amount as to the European Union. Even excluding Mexico, the South and Central American nations were nearly as relevant as Japan to U.S. exporters. Similarly, their sales to Mercosur were twice those to Australia, while Argentina and Chile were more important markets for the United States than countries the size and importance of India and

Russia.[43] Latin America received approximately one-fifth of U.S. for-eign direct investment; capital stock from the United States in the region was greater than that in Canada, double the amount of that in the newly industrialized countries (including China), and triple the amount of that in Japan.[44]

These data show that the links between the United States and Latin America are sturdy and growing, strong enough to act as a countervail-ing force against protectionist positions and to ensure continued U.S. economic interest in the region in the twenty-first century. Moreover, Latin America is the region in the world where the United States can firmly exercise its leadership and power to promote its strategic vision of regionalism and multilateralism as complementary notions. This vision is widely shared in Latin America, where the idea prevails that free trade agreements should be an intermediate step toward greater lib-eralization of global trade.[45] Although the process will not always be smooth and may proceed in a partial and ad hoc fashion, it is reasonable to predict that hemispheric regionalism will make the glass appear more than half full in the twenty-first century. The social forces in favor of it are much more powerful, though perhaps less visible and resonant, than those that oppose it.

Cultural Changes

Over 30 years ago, Gordon Connell-Smith concluded that "since 1945, the global as well as hemispheric environments have been unfavorable to the Inter-American system. . . . Simplifying, the United States has considered the Inter-American system as an instrument to reinforce its own policy; Latin American nations as a means to persuade the United States to modify that policy."[46] From the same era, in the preface of his book about cultural factors, Samuel Shapiro wrote the following about the future of inter-American relations: "If a blowup is coming, few storms in recent history will have been so widely forecast."[47]

These works reflected the reigning pessimism regarding the prospects for U.S.–Latin American relations. Expectations of better times, which had been generated at the beginning of the 1960s with the launch of the Alliance for Progress, dissipated rapidly. That initiative, meant "to transform the 1960s into a decade of democratic progress," according to President Kennedy himself, did not meet any of its ambi-tious initial goals.[48] Later, the U.S. intervention in Santo Domingo in

1965 revived old fears concerning U.S. unilateralism and cooled the Latin American desire to cooperate with Washington.[49]

Instead of advancing toward common objectives, the United States and Latin America soon divided. In May 1969, through the Special Commission for Latin American Coordination, the nations of the region united to adopt the Viña del Mar agreement, which, among other important principles, avowed that the United States should accept "as legitimate and irreversible the appearance of a growing continental nationalism that pursues the affirmation of the Latin American personality with its own ideas, values, and organizational systems."[50]

An inspiring slogan—"liberation or dependence"—captured the historical choice of the moment for many people. For others, the relationship with the United States was reason for distrust and fear. The social sectors that supported stronger inter-American ties were in the minority. In the United States, things were not very different. At the beginning of the 1960s Washington abandoned the idea of a "special relationship" with Latin America. The coup de grace was President Nixon's decision in August 1971 to implement a 10 percent tax on all imports into the U.S. market; no Latin American countries, not even Mexico, were exempt.[51] Not only did U.S. interest in the region diminish significantly, but those who maintained an interest in Latin America defined it under a negative lens: The Cold War hawks worried about the spread of communism, and the developmentalists worried about the threat of poverty.[52]

Philosophies and interests played an equal role in separating the two parts of the hemisphere. The inter-American system's political organizations were under scrutiny, and some were even rejected. Voices raised in unison argued to disregard the OAS and the Tratado Interamericano de Asistencia Recíproca (TIAR, Inter-American Treaty of Reciprocal Assistance) and to structure the "authentic Latin American unit" on different bases.[53] In a well-remembered speech, the Argentine delegate to the third general assembly of the OAS, held in Lima in 1973 to revise the TIAR, maintained: "The Latin American system has not worked in the sense of the Latin American revolution. On the contrary, the majority of times it resulted in an obstacle in relation to the isolated efforts of some of the continent's governments to overcome the Balkanization of the Americas, product of imperialist diplomacy and ultimate result of foreign hegemony in Latin America."[54] In the late 1970s and early 1980s, the role the Reagan administration assigned to right-wing dictatorships in the fight against the "evil empire"; the unilateral U.S. policies toward El Salvador and Nicaragua, which were repudiated by the entire region; and the inefficiency of the OAS and TIAR in halting the war between the British and the Argentines in the Falklands (Islas Malvinas) revived a climate of suspicion and eliminated the possibility of developing some type of collective hemispheric action.

A combination of *fortuna*, necessity, and conviction turned the situation around beginning in the mid-1980s. The U.S. policy favoring democracy, which had been put on the back burner since the end of the 1960s, was returned to the front burner by none other than Ronald Reagan during his second presidential term. The military occupation of the Falklands in April 1982 by Argentina, at that time the most faithful ally the United States had in Latin America, was an important event in this change of position. The military action carried out under Argentina's General Leopoldo Galtieri, which proceeded despite the opposition of the U.S. president, heightened doubts in Washington about the pertinence of a policy that put so much stock in Latin American armed forces. The Falklands debacle undermined the military's credibility and opened the door for the United States to play a considerable role in the Latin American transition to democracy.

Meanwhile, the genuine revaluing of democracy in almost the entire region facilitated a close relationship between U.S. officials and democratic political and social forces in Latin America. The United States, an ally of right-wing dictatorships in the 1960s and 1970s, became an important—in some cases indispensable—partner in reaching a shared objective. In the 1990s the need for external safeguards to protect each nation's democratic process made progress in the inter-American system possible, whereas it had previously been unimaginable; collective action in support of democracy softened the classic rigidity of the nonintervention principle.[55] The first steps were taken toward inter-American multilateral cooperation to fight corruption, drug trafficking, and terrorism.[56] These new mechanisms are embedded within a process in which states voluntarily compromise their sovereignty and therefore will quite likely endure and evolve throughout the twenty-first century.[57]

In addition, the end of the Cold War shrank the space for ideological debates in Latin America and reduced its menu of external choices, making way for the adoption of more pragmatic attitudes that facilitated greater rapprochement between U.S. and Latin American positions. The weakening of the theoretical assumptions on which much of Latin

America and other underdeveloped nations' claims had been based vis-à-vis the nations of the North also helped close the ideological gap between the United States and the region. The confrontational positions of the 1960s and 1970s were abandoned and replaced by formulas that favored negotiation and cooperation.

Simultaneously, the structural crisis of the inward-oriented model in Latin America, together with the worldwide collapse of socialist regimes, discredited statist models. It was possible, therefore, in the 1990s to put into practice in almost the entire region—although with varying degrees of depth and ease—the pool of theoretical and empirical ideas about market utility, which had been dominant in industrial nations in the 1970s and 1980s.[58] The adoption of a market economy doctrine had its apostles from its inception and an ever-growing legion of converts who adhered to the new ideas—though not without criticism—as much out of necessity as conviction. Though still timidly, and with some vacillation, Latin Americans began to discuss and adapt this pool of "imported" ideas to regional requirements they did not address, such as the need to adequately regulate the functioning of the market economy or to develop aggressive social policies to alleviate the undesired effects of economic liberalization.[59] It is likely that over the course of the twenty-first century, politicians and academics on both sides will exponentially increase their exchange of ideas based on a common epistemology, a shared language, and—although still difficult to grasp—a common cultural tradition rooted in the basic values of the West. The goal should be to develop new ideas and proposals that will help formulate policies that address key concerns, such as mitigating the negative effects of market economics on income distribution, redefining the state's regulatory role, improving human development, and increasing productivity levels and competitiveness in Latin America.

As for international security issues, the end of the Cold War and the democratization process in Latin America made it possible to introduce important innovations in defense doctrines and threat perceptions, as well as new roles for the armed forces; these new approaches are founded on conceptions and assumptions distinct from those that historically sustained hemispheric and intraregional security. Such conceptual revision regarding security allowed the notions of cooperative security, confidence building, defense policy transparency, and civilian control of the armed forces to become basic elements of regional security in the 1990s and beyond. In addition, beginning in 1995—for the first time—

Latin America and the United States institutionalized periodic meetings of the defense ministers of the Western Hemisphere to exchange opinions about issues of defense, security, and, more specifically, the role of the armed forces in the post–Cold War era.

Finally, the growing exchange of university students between the United States and Latin America has enormous potential to influence the future of the relationship. An ever-larger number of U.S. university students choose to travel to countries like Argentina, Chile, or Mexico on study-abroad programs, and the number of Latin American students pursuing graduate studies in the United States also is growing rapidly. Moreover, according to a report by the U.S.-based Modern Language Association, in the year 2000 more than 657,000 undergraduate students chose to take Spanish classes, a substantial increase over the 179,000 students who did so in 1960.[60]

The point is not to present a rosy picture or suggest a future without conflict. That liberal ideas are not widespread among the masses, that the neoliberal market economy has not reduced poverty and economic marginalization, and that the economic policies adopted in the 1990s have displaced numerous preexisting social safety nets are realities that underscore the uncertainty lying ahead. This situation could lead to the rise of new populist or authoritarian expressions that once again wave the flags of nationalism and anti-imperialism, as well as to stronger and broader anti-globalization movements, all of which could be directed against the United States.

Many analysts point to these and other realities to illustrate the unclear nature of the region's future and, more specifically, of the future of inter-American relations. Two factors, however, are significant in thinking about the long term: First, the cultural changes produced over the last 15 years have brought the popularity of the concept of the Western Hemisphere to a historical peak;[61] second, as a result there is fertile ground for redefining inter-American relations on the basis of regional convergences.

Conclusion

We have entered the twenty-first century with an "unusually solid foundation" for pursuing the long-range goals shared by Latin America and the United States.[62] In practice the micro and immediate interests of the multiple actors in this increasingly dense relationship differ in substantial aspects, which will produce (and explain) impasses and agitation. Such interests separate Latin America from the United States on certain issues, such as the unilateral certification process in the United States regarding the war against drugs or U.S. policy toward Cuba. On others—the vast majority—the division lines are drawn domestically as well as between different countries (as the NAFTA and FTAA negotiations have shown).

Thus, it is inappropriate to suppose that the United States can develop a linear and consistent policy toward the region. Nevertheless, basic policy orientations certainly can be—and have been—established. Latin America, for its part, is not an international actor; it is a region with disparate situations, and joint positions are unlikely to be formulated and translated into effective policies except, perhaps, at the subregional level, particularly when there is effective regional leadership or when a critical situation arises. In addition, it is clear that the U.S. position vis-à-vis the countries of the region, and vice versa, is and will continue to be strongly conditioned by geography. The currently fashionable "intermestic agenda," which includes such issues as immigration, narcotics, the environment, and border management, applies essentially to the United States' closest neighbors, especially Mexico and the Central American and Caribbean countries, and only to a much lesser extent to the nations of South America.[63] As Kenneth Maxwell recently argued:

> The U.S. is increasingly seeing a differentiated region to the south; in effect, a series of concentric circles of greater and lesser engagement and de facto integration. The inner circle is NAFTA. Beyond is what might be called the "greater NAFTA" (i.e. the Caribbean and Central America). Beyond that are the Andean countries (Colombia, Venezuela, Ecuador, Peru, and the special case of Chile). And over Mercosul there is more ambiguity, and over Brazil—with or without Mercosul—great uncertainty.[64]

Despite these differences between and within the nations of the Western Hemisphere, shared interests, problems, and objectives, as well as a growing convergence of political and economic philosophies, should serve to progressively place relations under a cooperative umbrella and give way to a new inter-American multilateral dynamic, one that is less dominated by Washington's decisive influence than in the past. Moving from a framework characterized by discord to one in which a spirit of cooperation prevails implies neither the end to nor future absence of conflicts between the parties. As Robert Keohane would say, without the specter of conflict or potential conflict, there is no need to cooperate.[65] Cooperation is a highly political process that requires the coordination of policies and implies the use of strategies that appeal as much to persuasion, the force of good examples, and rewards as to threats and punishment.[66]

With this vision in mind, more than 40 years ago Argentine president Arturo Frondizi developed a conceptual outline for U.S.–Latin American relations; this framework separated basic agreements in values and long-term goals from authentic differences in national interests. The purpose was to show that the latter did not—or at least should not—touch on fundamental questions that would constitute the permanent basis of the link. For example, Frondizi argued that existing differences between the United States and the majority of Latin American countries over how to deal with the Cuban revolution were essentially methodological in nature, not of substance.[67] Conditions at that time did not facilitate advancement in the direction Frondizi proposed. Current conditions, on the contrary, suggest that inter-American relations will probably take shape in a slow, incremental manner and with different rhythms and sequences, within a pattern similar to that which characterizes relations between the United States and Canada or the European Union. In these relationships, there is a basic level of agreement that moderates the differences in interests typical of all dense and complex relations.

The erection of this new social macro-structure, whose pillars would be a common values system, democracy, the free market, and open regionalism, should be the ordering axis of U.S. policy toward the region in the twenty-first century. In the design and implementation of such a general policy, U.S. policymakers will need to call on great reserves of attention, dedication, and will, given the characteristics of the current situation. At the same time, the United States must avoid falling into the "imperial temptation" of imposing its interests solely through coercion or force. Should this occur, the undisputed hegemony the United States today enjoys in Latin America will once again face numerous expressions of opposition and resistance.

The Challenges to Democratization in Latin America

The democratization process in Latin America will continue to experience ups and downs, largely because of the highly inequitable social situation—the region has the most unequal distribution of income in the world—and the insufficient grounding of liberal democratic values in the political culture. The United States cannot determine the course of this process—that depends on domestic factors—but it can use its influence to promote democracy and prevent its rupture.

U.S. policymakers should keep in mind that the process of democratization in Latin America will not necessarily produce political systems identical to that of the United States or reduce differences in interests. On the contrary, by facilitating the expression of diverse demands by numerous and varied social actors, the democratization process will make certain objectives promoted by Washington more difficult to attain.

Furthermore, the greater pluralism of Latin American societies will complicate not only the management of the differences between parties but also that of foreign policy making in Latin America. Because foreign policy in Latin American countries will be developed in more open and participatory societies, it will exhibit some of the traits that typify the U.S. foreign policy formulation and implementation process. Simply stated, the more democratic the process, the more influence civil society wields in the formulation and execution of foreign policy.

U.S. policymakers should resist the temptation to "satanize" certain Latin American political figures, especially when they come to government through free and fair elections, as in the case of Hugo Chávez in Venezuela. It is better to gain their progressive incorporation into democratic politics than to besiege them. Experience shows that cooptation is usually a more fruitful strategy than isolation and systematic punishment. However, the United States should be prepared to condemn swiftly, and if necessary sanction, when the rules of the electoral process are broken, as happened in Peru, or when civil liberties are systematically violated.

Finally, U.S. policymakers should consider that advances toward greater democratization in Latin America will depend on the capacity of the nations to reduce poverty and inequality. Based on enlightened self-interest, the United States should cooperate with the countries of the region to bring solutions to the social problems that transcend what has been called *la pensée unique* and to circumvent certain technocratic rigidities of multilateral economic and financial organizations.[68] Improving the level and distribution of education is indispensable to helping reverse this situation. It is important that the United States maintain and deepen through bilateral and multilateral channels—for example, the OAS and the Inter-American Development Bank—its strong support of the hemispheric commitment made at the 1998 Second Summit of the Americas in Santiago, Chile, to improve education in the region. Improving education would serve several worthwhile purposes: It would promote equal opportunity, reinforce the values of democracy, and prepare Latin American citizens for the twenty-first century global economy.

The Future of Hemispheric Integration

With or without the FTAA, Latin America and the United States will have close and very intense economic relations. Unlike other goals in the inter-American agenda, the success of a hemispheric trade agreement will depend more on U.S. actions than on Latin American domestic factors. As Albert Fishlow says, "Inevitably, the evolution of a Free Trade Area of the Americas becomes the critical test of U.S. policy toward the region."[69]

The action or inaction of the United States will determine the course of hemispheric integration and condition the trade policies of Latin America, as well as those of other extraregional actors vis-à-vis the region. There is no doubt, for example, that the signing of the Interregional Framework Agreement for Cooperation between the European Community and Mercosur in 1995 was largely a response by Brussels to the 1994 commitment in Miami to establish a free trade zone in the Americas by 2005. European policy mixed an offensive component—participating in a subregional market with great prospects for growth—with a defensive one—avoiding the exclusion of the European Union from that market by acting before the creation of the FTAA. At the same time, the evolution of the intraregional Mercosur agenda has depended in large part on the level of third-party pressure, particularly from the United States and, to a lesser degree, the European Union, to involve Mercosur members in preferential trade agreements. Increased pressure produced defensive advances in Mercosur, whereas decreased pressure provoked backslides or at least stagnation. Likewise, the lack of U.S. fast-track negotiating authority before 2002 led Argentina to abandon its initial ambition to enter NAFTA after Chile, and, at that point in time, pushed Chile closer to Mercosur.

The process of hemispheric integration is complex, given that its course is subject to numerous factors inside and outside the Western Hemisphere.[70] Looking beyond the FTAA, however, it is very likely that in the early decades of the twenty-first century the United States and Latin America will form a free trade area of hemispheric reach. This process will be accompanied by other free trade agreements within Latin America, as well as between groups of countries in the region with the European Union and other extraregional actors; the future of those arrangements will depend on the depth and scope of the hemispheric agreement. In any case, these trade agreements will not be defined as projects strategically opposed to the United States in a classic realist sense. They will be complementary to, not competitive with, the hemispheric agreement and consistent with the principles and rules of the World Trade Organization. The fear expressed in some U.S. academic and governmental circles that the United States will be confronted by a united South America, led by a Brazil avid for world power, is exaggerated as well as anachronistic.

Latin America—particularly South America—will continue to seek diversification in its foreign relations or, conceptually reminiscent of the 1970s, to reduce dependence on only one actor. The aforementioned narrowing of the gap in philosophies may cloak this factor from many people's eyes. Nonetheless, it will be present in the twenty-first century because it is a structural trait of Latin American foreign policy that will be expressed in a wide variety of international ties and affiliations.

Approaching the Inter-American Agenda

The growing complexity of the inter-American agenda will require the development of new policy instruments. Using the terms of Stanley Hoffmann, most of the issues that make up that agenda are questions of "world order" and thus require world order policies, that is, policies that are based (or should be based) on a set of principles, norms, and procedures designed to deal with problems or threats that cannot be resolved or attacked by any one state, no matter how powerful.[71] The very nature of items on the inter-American agenda—from defense of human rights to democracy to the fight against drug trafficking and terrorism—calls for multilateral cooperation.

In this context, unilateral U.S. policies will be both unproductive and a source of resentment, as were the policies regarding certification of commitment to the war on drugs and the imposition of sanctions against Cuba. Latin America, for its part, should make a greater international commitment and assume more responsibility than it has in the past; it must confront its problems, relinquishing passive, complaining, and prim attitudes that merely encourage U.S. unilateralism. In this new type of diplomatic exercise, Latin America should keep in mind that U.S. involvement in the region will be greater than in the twentieth century, even in South America; that the nature and scope of that involvement will depend largely on the position that Latin American countries themselves adopt; and, finally, that Washington will look favorably on the region if it strives to solve a significant portion of the important challenges that will arise in the Western Hemisphere in this new century.

Notes

1. The "Western Hemisphere idea" calls for the nations of the American continent to integrate and cooperate with each other on a foundation of common values and goals.

2. See Roberto Bouzas, "Las perspectivas del Mercosur: Desafíos, escenarios y alternativas para la próxima década," *Documento de Trabajo de FLACSO,* August 1999, 4–5.

3. This pattern, obviously, is not peculiar to the United States. Brazil, for example, has always been more interested in Argentina than in Mexico or Bolivia.

4. All dollar amounts are in U.S. dollars, unless otherwise noted.

5. See Deborah Norden and Roberto Russell, *The United States and Argentina: Changing Relations in a Changing World* (New York and London: Routledge, 2002), 128.

6. Joseph S. Tulchin, "Reflections on Hemispheric Relations in the 21st Century," *Journal of Interamerican Studies and World Affairs* 39, no. 1 (Spring 1997): 36.

7. William J. Clinton, "State of the Union Address," Washington, D.C., 27 January 2000; available on the web from the Federal News Service, Inc.

8. George W. Bush, State Department address, informational cable from the Argentine Embassy in Washington, D.C., 28 February 2001. Author's translation from Spanish to English.

9. As quoted in Carlos Blanco, "Another Hundred Years of Solitude? Latin America After September 11," *Harvard International Review* 24, no. 1 (Spring 2002), 80.

10. Ibid.

11. Paul Kennedy, "Maintaining American Power: From Injury to Recovery," in *The Age of Terror: America and the World After September 11,* ed. Strobe Talbott and Nayan Chanda (New York: Basic Books, 2002), 58.

12. See, for example, Richard Feinberg, "A Vision for the Americas," *Financial Times,* 7 August 2002, 11.

13. Howard J. Wiarda, "Consensus Found, Consensus Lost: Disjunctures in US Policy Toward Latin America at the Turn of the Century," *Journal of Interamerican Studies and World Affairs* 39, no. 1 (Spring 1997): 14.

14. See Richard Bloomfield, "Making the Western Hemisphere Safe for Democracy? The OAS Defense of Democracy Regime," *Washington Quarterly* 17, no. 2 (Spring 1994): 157–169.

15. Ibid., 159.

16. See J. J. Aznárez, "Malestar en Venezuela por la visita del embajador de España al presidente golpista," *El País* (Madrid), 19 April 2002: [www.elpais.es/].

17. Colin L. Powell, Remarks to the Special Session of the General Assembly of the Organization of American States, Washington, D.C., 18 April 2002; available at [www.state.gov/secretary/]. The United States, Spain, and El Salvador have been perceived in Venezuelan government circles as the countries that most sympathized with the brief presidency of Pedro Carmona.

18. Regarding the weakness of the commitment during the years of the Cold War, see, among others, Gordon Connell-Smith, *Sistema Inter-Americano* (Mexico City: Fondo de Cultura Económica, 1961), 43–48.

19. A consolidated democracy is a necessary, but not sufficient, condition to control corruption, as the cases of Tangentopolis in Italy, Germany under Kohl, and France under Mitterrand have demonstrated. In these situations, long periods in power seem to have been the key factor in explaining the growth in corruption. See Natalio R. Botana, "La corrupción en la mira," *La Nación*, Sección Opinión, 17 February 2000, 15 [www.lanacion.com.ar].

20. Jorge Domínguez, "Technopols: Ideas and Leaders in Freeing Politics and Markets in Latin America in the 1990s," in *Technopols: Freeing Politics and Markets in Latin America in the 1990s,* ed. Jorge Domínguez (University Park: Pennsylvania State University Press, 1997), 5.

21. See Alejandra Pataro, "Mensaje de conciliación del nuevo gobierno de Ecuador," *Clarín,* 24 January 2000, 22 [http://old.clarin.com/diario/]; and John Lancaster, "U.S. Sees Democracy Wane in Latin America," *Washington Post,* 30 January 2000, A21.

22. John Lewis Gaddis, "And Now This: Lessons from the Old Era for the New One," in Talbott and Chanda, *The Age of Terror,* 19–20.

23. For details on these differences of opinion, see Bloomfield, "Making the Western Hemisphere Safe," 162–167.

24. In December 1992, the general assembly, during the XVI Período Extraordinario de Sesiones, adopted the so-called Washington protocol, which allowed the suspension of a nation in which a democratically elected government had been overthrown by force from participation in the deliberations and decisions of all bodies of the organization until democracy had been reestablished.

25. See Hugo de Zela, "La Carta Democrática Interamericana," *Archivos del Presente* 7, no. 25 (2001): 97–109.

26. On 25 July 1996, in the Argentine province of San Luis, Mercosur had adopted a preliminary *compromiso democrático* (democratic commitment), which established that any interruption of the constitutional order in the countries that form Mercosur or in Mercosur's associated countries constitutes an unacceptable obstacle to the continuation of the process of integration.

27. For some analysts, democracy has already failed in Peru and Ecuador.

See, for example, Mario Vargas Llosa, "Fujimorazo en Ecuador," *La Nación Line,* Sección Opinión, 12 February 2000, available at: [www.lanacion.com.ar].

28. For a similar argument, see Thomas Carothers, "Democracy Without Illusions," *Foreign Affairs* 76, no. 1 (January–February 1997): 85–99.

29. On this topic, see Roberto Russell, "Democratization and Its Qualitative Impact on Argentine Foreign Policy," *Documento de Trabajo del ISEN*, December 1998; and Andrew Hurrell, "Security in Latin America," *International Affairs* 74, no. 3 (July 1998).

30. See Julio César Carasales, *De rivales a socios: El proceso de cooperación nuclear entre Argentina y Brasil* (Buenos Aires: ISEN/Grupo Editorial Latinoamericano, 1997).

31. Note that most of the countries mentioned form part of Andean Latin America. For many years, analysts of the region have pointed out that there are two Latin Americas with distinct realities: the northern—from Mexico to Panama—and the southern. The southern part has begun to be divided as well, into the Andes and the Southern Cone. In the 1990s, the Andean region was the greatest focus of anxiety in the hemisphere. See Juan Tokatlián, "Sudamérica está partida en dos," *Clarín,* 11 January 2000, 9.

32. Natalio R. Botana, "¡Que se vayan! ¿Y después?" *La Nación,* Sección Opinión, 7 February 2002, 17 [www.lanacion.com.ar].

33. Fareed Zakaria, "The Rise of Illiberal Democracy," *Foreign Affairs* 76, no. 6 (November–December 1997): 22.

34. See Javier Corrales and Richard E. Feinberg, "Regimes of Cooperation in the Western Hemisphere: Power, Interests, and Intellectual Traditions," *International Studies Quarterly* 43, no. 1 (March 1999): 16.

35. For more details, see Bouzas, "Las perspectivas del Mercosur," 7.

36. Stuart E. Eizenstat, "Our Future Trade Agenda," remarks before the House of Representatives International Relations Subcommittee, Washington, D.C., 24 September 1997.

37. Heraldo Muñoz, *Política internacional de los nuevos tiempos* (Santiago, Chile: Los Andes, 1996), 102.

38. Negotiations between the United States, Canada, and Mexico to create NAFTA were one of the main reasons for the rapid formation of Mercosur.

39. Muñoz, *Política internacional*, 119.

40. Andrés Oppenheimer, "Brasil: De gigante dormido a líder económico regional," *La Nación*, Sección Exterior, 4 April 2000, 5 [www.lanacion.com.ar].

41. See Benjamin Cohen, "¿Gulliver o lilliputiense? Los Estados Unidos en la economía mundial de hoy," in *Globalización y regionalismo en las relaciones internacionales de Estados Unidos,* ed. Roberto Bouzas and Roberto Russell (Buenos Aires: ISEN/Grupo Editorial Latinoamericano, 1996), 55.

42. Riordan Roett, "United States Policy, the Fate of the FTAA and Mercosur" (paper presented at the Asociación de Bancos de la Argentina annual meeting, Buenos Aires, 7 July 1999), 26; published in Spanish as "La política estadounidense, el futuro del ALCA y del Mercosur," in *El futuro del Mercosur,* ed. Felipe de la Balze (Buenos Aires: ABA-CARI, 2002), 115–137.

43. See Gustavo Svarzman, "La Argentina y el Mercosur ante el proceso

de integración hemisférica," *Boletín Informativo Techint* (July–September 1998): 40.

44. Ibid., 41.

45. For more details, see Bouzas, "Las perspectivas del Mercosur," 24.

46. Connell-Smith, *Sistema Inter-Americano*, 41–43.

47. Samuel Shapiro, "Preface," in *Cultural Factors in Inter-American Relations,* ed. Samuel Shapiro (Notre Dame: University of Notre Dame, 1968), x.

48. John F. Kennedy, White House address, 13 March 1961, in Juan A. Lanús, *De Chapultepec al Beagle* (Buenos Aires: Emecé, 1984), 202.

49. See Joseph S. Tulchin, *La Argentina y los Estados Unidos: Historia de una desconfianza* (Buenos Aires: Planeta, 1990), 233.

50. The complete text of this document can be found in Gregorio Selser, *De la CECLA a la MECLA o la diplomacia de la zanahoria* (Buenos Aires: Carlos Samonta, 1972).

51. On the impact of this measure in Mexico, see Mario Ojeda, *Alcances y límites de la política exterior mexicana* (Mexico City: El Colegio de México, 1976), 175.

52. See Corrales and Feinberg, "Regimes of Cooperation," 19, 22.

53. See, for example, Alfredo Carella, *La Argentina y el pluralismo en el sistema inter-americano* (San Miguel de Tucumán, Argentina: Instituto de Estudios Políticos y Económicos para la Integración Latinoamericana, 1973), 80.

54. Cited in Lanús, *De Chapultepec al Beagle*, 168.

55. On this topic, its difficulties and perspectives, see Muñoz, *Política internacional,* 36–58.

56. Among them are the signature of the Inter-American Convention against Corruption (Convención Inter-Americana contra la Corrupción, Caracas, March 1996), the creation of the Inter-American Committee against Terrorism (Comité Inter-Americano contra el Terrorismo, Guatemala, June 1999), and the Multilateral Evaluation Mechanism (Mecanismo de Evaluación Multilateral) to evaluate the efforts of the OAS member states in the fight against drugs (Montevideo, October 1999).

57. About different ways in which states have compromised their sovereignty, see Stephen Krasner, *Sovereignty: Organized Hypocrisy* (Princeton: Princeton University Press, 1999).

58. Domínguez, "Technopols," 26, 27.

59. Ibid., 45.

60. See Andrés Oppenheimer, "Estados Unidos mirará más hacia el sur," *La Nación,* Sección Exterior, 14 March 2000, 4 [www.lanacion.com.ar].

61. Other periods when the Western Hemisphere concept was popular were 1889–1906 and 1933–1954. See Corrales and Feinberg, "Regimes of Cooperation."

62. Jeffrey Davidow, "U.S. Policy Toward Latin America and the Caribbean: Building upon a Solid Foundation," remarks by the assistant secretary of state at the Miami Conference on the Caribbean and Latin America, Miami, Florida, 9 December 1996, 1.

63. See Abraham F. Lowenthal, "United States–Latin American Relations

at the Century's Turn: Managing the 'Intermestic' Agenda," in *The United States and the Americas: A Twenty-First Century View,* ed. Albert Fishlow and James Jones (New York: Norton, 1999), 110.

64. Kenneth R. Maxwell, "Latin America: Back to the Past?" *Folha de São Paulo,* 7 April 2002: [www.cfr.org/]. "Mercosul" is the Portuguese equivalent of "Mercosur."

65. See Robert O. Keohane, *After Hegemony: Cooperation and Discord in the World Political Economy* (Princeton: Princeton University Press, 1984), 54.

66. Ibid., 53.

67. This approach was used by several Latin American governments in the 1980s to explain the differing opinions in the United States and Latin America on how to solve the foreign debt problem in the region.

68. *La pensée unique* is a French expression that was widely used in the 1990s to criticize the neoliberal ideology, and particularly those who sustain that there are no alternative economic avenues than those defended by neoliberalism.

69. Albert Fishlow, "The Foreign Policy Challenge for the United States," in Fishlow and Jones, *The United States and the Americas,* 203.

70. Regarding these factors see, among others, Scott Otteman, "The United States and Latin America & the Caribbean: Cooperation or Conflict in the New WTO Trade Round?," paper prepared for a conference on "Trade and Development in the Americas," organized by the Andean Development Corporation, the Organization of American States, and the Inter-American Dialogue, Washington, D.C., 9 September 1999.

71. Stanley Hoffmann, *Primacy or World Order: American Foreign Policy Since the Cold War* (New York: McGraw-Hill, 1980), 189–193.

5

Canada's New Opening to Latin America

Charles F. Doran

Within a three-year period, Canada will have hosted preparatory talks for the Free Trade Area of the Americas (FTAA), a meeting of the hemispheric heads of state, a meeting of the Pan American Games, several Team Canada visits of businesspeople to Latin American countries, and numerous exchange visits between its head of government and foreign minister and their Latin American counterparts. In addition, one of Canada's most delicate foreign policy problems involves a Caribbean government. During the 1990s Canada also became a full member of the Organization of American States (OAS) and participated actively in the restoration of democracy to Haiti. What has caused Canada's upsurge of interest in hemispheric involvement?

Canada has long held a place for Latin America in its foreign commercial and trade policy. In the 1880s the Royal Bank of Canada, then known as the Merchant's Bank of Halifax, established branches in Bermuda and Trinidad. Mining and agricultural interests set up operations in Chile, Brazil, and Argentina. West Indian sugar played a role in nineteenth-century Canadian tariff policy. Since the 1850s—well before Canadian confederation in 1867—large numbers of Canadian tourists have visited the warm Caribbean during the winter months.[1]

Nevertheless, it cannot be said that Canada had paid a lot of attention explicitly to Latin America in its foreign policy until lately, or that Latin America had taken great notice of Canada. As recently as the 1980s Canada had made very few annual foreign policy pronouncements regarding individual Latin American countries or the region as a whole.[2]

Canada's growing interest in Latin America in the 1990s is symbolized perhaps most strikingly by the country's full official participation in the OAS, although several other developments further signal the new demarche toward Latin America: Canada's continuing interest in Central America, its active role in restoring the Aristide government in Haiti, its alternating hot and cold diplomacy toward Cuba, its involvement in the North American Free Trade Agreement (NAFTA), and its open support for and leadership in negotiations for the Free Trade Area of the Americas (FTAA). What caused this sudden spate of interest in Latin America in the last decade of the twentieth century?

Canada's Changing Foreign Policy Priorities

At least three explanations for the recent revolution in Canadian statecraft stand out. The first is a post–Cold War reordering of foreign policy priorities, in particular a shift from traditional security issues and the East–West confrontation to a new emphasis on trade and commercial opportunities. Second is the loosening of ties between Canada and Europe, stemming primarily from a more "inward looking" Europe, as well as from a greater focus on domestic issues and regional economic opportunities on the part of Canada. Finally, Canada's new emphasis on multilateralizing its trade relations within the hemisphere has moved economic focus beyond its NAFTA partners—the United States and Mexico—to the rest of the continent.

Reordered Priorities After the Cold War

With the end of the Cold War, Canada, like other Western nations, has faced a reordering of its foreign policy priorities away from the East–West confrontation. Never so committed to the East–West confrontation as some of its allies, Canada reoriented its security policies and expenditures away from conventional military strength, stressing peacekeeping and humanitarian intervention. It sought a new emphasis on trade policy and commercial initiative, featuring so-called Team Canada visits of businesspeople and government officials, led by the prime minister, to various growth centers such as China, Southeast Asia, and Latin America. It agonized over a revised set of rules for the Canadian International Development Agency (CIDA), questioning whether grants and loans to transition governments in formerly communist Central Europe should receive priority over those to traditional recipients in developing countries. In short, the end of the Cold War shook the making and implementation of Canadian foreign policy to its roots.

This new thinking presented an opportunity to reassess Latin America as a priority. Likewise, the restructuring that took place in some of the foreign affairs bureaucracies gave new status to Latin American assignments inside the Department of Foreign Affairs and International Trade (DFAIT).[3] Resources that might not otherwise have been allocated to foreign policy matters involving Latin America became accessible at the end of the Cold War. Although the peace dividend was minimal, changes in the rate of growth of spending began to favor a shift from the East–West preoccupation toward a more "southerly" foreign affairs strategy.

Loosened Ties Between Canada and Europe

Over time the linkages between Canada and Europe have become more distant. Historically, Canada had been close to France through the Québec association and other ties, and so close to Britain that only recently had its constitution transferred from Westminster and its head of state obtained legitimation from the mythical Queen of Canada (that is, the Queen of Great Britain). Not only is the physical distance between Halifax and London less than that between Halifax and Vancouver, but there is probably more local news from London in the Halifax newspapers than there is local news about Vancouver. So in terms of *mentalité*, Canada, or much of Canada, has in the past thought European as much as it has thought North American.

But changes in the relationship between Canada and Europe have profoundly affected the prospect of a new opening to Latin America. Europe has become much more internally preoccupied ("inward looking," in the language of some analysts). One measure is the level of intra-European trade and investment as a ratio of total European trade and investment. Much more trade occurs within Europe than between Europe and its other trading partners, including Canada. With the enlargement of European institutions, that ratio of intra-European to external trade has grown.

At the same time, the tendency toward trade diversion has become more pronounced. Trade that normally would go to Canada—if, for example, it is the world's low-cost producer of an item—may be diverted to a member of the European Union (EU) because of nontariff barriers. As the EU becomes larger—and its members more diverse in terms of their industrial structure and more unequal in income—trade diversion becomes greater. Trading partners like Canada increasingly become frozen out of the export competition with Europe.

Europe is not anti-Canadian, but its internal political focus tends to complement the relative negative impact that its trade policies are having on Canadian–European relations. As it tries to deepen its political institutions, it shows less interest in its external ties, a shift that is felt first at the margin by smaller actors such as Canada.

Canada's decision to withdraw its troops from Germany, while remaining a full member of the North Atlantic Treaty Organization, has further distanced Canada from Europe. Although Canada was an early participant in Balkan peacekeeping on the ground, where its positive presence was crucial, some believe that Canada's withdrawal of its conventional presence from European soil overshadows its participation in the peacekeeping mission. More self-sufficient militarily, Europe feels less responsive to overtures of any kind from Canada.

And Canada, for reasons of its own internal politics, preoccupations, and makeup, is also distancing itself from Europe. The constitutional issue involving Québec forecloses a number of opportunities for better relations with France, for example. Immigration both to Québec and to the rest of the country has made Canada less European in its composition, and thus in its political affinities. George Grant's *Lament for a Nation*, which addresses the erosion of British values in central Canada, looks almost archaic today, given the evident invasion of new Canadians from all parts of the globe. Immigration and the constitutional issue have changed Canada's perspective toward Europe.

Moreover, trade within North America has affected Canada's external relations in much the same way that trade within Europe has affected those of the EU countries; it has made the Canadian business community, for example, less interested in Europe. With 85 percent of its trade conducted with the United States, Canada naturally prizes its relationship with the United States above all others. Pioneering in content and provision, both the Canada–U.S. Free Trade Agreement and its successor, NAFTA, have focused Canada's attention closer to home. For commercial and trade reasons that exactly mirror the situation in Europe, Canada has distanced itself from Britain and the European continent.

In sum, the old interaction, if not the cordiality, between Europe and Canada has broken down. Getting a hearing in Europe today is much harder for Canada than it was even a decade ago. The upshot is that as the Atlantic widens, Canada looks elsewhere for new friends and lucrative interactions. Starting from a very small base of contacts, Canada–Latin American relations are beginning to blossom.

New Emphasis on Multilateral, Hemispheric Trade Relations

The Liberal Party government of Jean Chrétien adopted a different style of foreign policy toward the United States, and therefore toward the world, which accounts for Canada's new interest in an opening to Latin America. In the words of former foreign affairs minister Lloyd Axworthy:

> We . . . seek out a different model of hemispheric co-operation, based on multilateral principles designed to promote systems where there is some chance of balancing various interests and ensuring more freedom of action by individual countries in the Hemisphere to choose their form of political and economic development. One way that we have proposed that Canada could specifically help would be to open up new trade opportunities with smaller countries in the Caribbean and Central America, especially in terms of access for their manufactured goods such as textiles.[4]

What the Liberal government was proposing, in contrast to the policies of its Conservative predecessor, was to try to multilateralize trade relations within the hemisphere beyond Mexico and the United States.

It could be argued that with so much trade with the United States, very little is left for other countries. Yet absolute size of trade volumes must be kept in mind. In terms of value, Canada's trade and investment with the United States exceeds that of all of Latin America's trade and investment involving the United States. Considering this large volume and value of trade, a significant increase in trade with Latin America is possible within the context of the overall Canadian trade budget, notwithstanding Canada's primary commitment to NAFTA.

In addition, Canada recognizes the growth potential of Latin American economies and the mutual propensity to establish "like-thinking" trade and commercial relationships between Québecois and Latin American counterparts. Canada feels more welcome in Latin America than in, for example, some Asian countries, where its firms often believed they received second- or third-rate opportunities while the first-rate deals went to local firms. In Latin America, Canadian firms feel more confident and are able to compete on an equal footing with local businesses.

For all of these reasons, then, a new opening toward Latin America is plausible for Canada. At the dawn of the twenty-first century, Canada's orientation toward Latin America has changed. Foremost among the foreign policy initiatives that reflect those changes in orientation is Canada's historic decision to enter the OAS.

Canadian Membership in the OAS

To understand why Canada finally exchanged its observer status in the OAS for full membership in January 1990, one must first ask why Canada for so long remained the only country in the Americas not to elect full membership. The answer reveals a great deal about the politics that underlies the Canadian role in the hemisphere.

Although never acknowledged in official pronouncements, the main reason Canada did not seek full membership in the OAS for so long is that it feared being caught between some U.S. policy it could not support and some Latin American demands for Canadian opposition to that U.S. policy that Canada would find painful. In other words, Canada does not want to get squeezed between its new friends in Latin America and its old friend the United States. Moreover, Ottawa feared that many of its own citizens might side with the Latin American country or countries involved, thus putting even greater pressure on the government to diverge from U.S. policy. Worse, Canada believed that although any hemispheric issue dividing it and the United States might be small, the costs of siding with Latin America might be large: The loss of U.S. goodwill stemming from discord over a hemispheric issue could jeopardize bilateral matters involving the two North American partners.

The 1990 decision of the Mulroney government (1984–1993) to opt for full membership in the OAS therefore came as a surprise. Significantly, it was a Conservative Party government in Ottawa that elected to join the OAS, a government that had built up a huge store of goodwill with its conservative Republican counterparts in the United States. Not long after its decision to take a full role in the OAS, the Mulroney government did face a crisis almost exactly as envisioned.

Justifying intervention for the first time in its fight against drug trafficking, the U.S. administration of George H. W. Bush (1989–1993) invaded Panama in December 1989 in a bold move against General Manuel Noriega. Canada did the predictable. Even though Canadian prime minister Brian Mulroney had earlier strongly supported U.S. policy in Panama, Canada joined the majority in the OAS who mildly criticized that policy.[5] Critics could not chastise Canada for a lack of boldness. Canada, so soon into its new tenure, did not smudge its record with abstention or a challenge to the OAS majority. Its posture was bound to disappoint some of its allies, notably the United States, because Mulroney had supported U.S. policy earlier. But the Canadian OAS decision had sufficiently been foreshadowed. As things turned out, few governments in the OAS thought ill of Canada for either of its stands regarding the Noriega situation. Indeed, Canada proved wrong the critics who thought that it could not muster the delicate diplomacy expected in its new role.

Early in its OAS tenure, Canada was quietly put on notice by both Brazil and Mexico that an activist role would not be appreciated. The logic here was clear. Activism could easily lead to support for military intervention in the domestic affairs of a member on humanitarian or other grounds. Interventions were not unheard of, of course, but the OAS had consistently opposed such intervention. Thus, Canada was politely encouraged to restrain its idealism and foreign policy proclivities. But even though Canada was cautioned against taking too energetic a role in the OAS, it did not disappoint its citizens who wanted it to have a prominent voice in the organization. On two matters Canada could not be silenced.

First, Canada would always speak out strongly on behalf of democracy, which altered the tone of dialogue within the OAS. Former foreign minister Barbara McDougall used uncompromising language to denounce the breach of democratic practice in Peru, calling Fujimori's conduct "unconstitutional, illegal, and unacceptable."[6] Canada supported vigorously the OAS resolution that demanded a return to democracy in Peru. Challenging custom in the OAS, Canada even hinted at introducing a resolution that would develop a program of sanctions.[7] Canada was likewise tough and explicit in opposition to the coup in Haiti.

Second, Canada would take a strong stand on human rights. It backed the OAS resolution expressing concern about the human rights situation in Haiti, and it continued to take a leadership position on human rights issues throughout the decade. Canada attempted to balance this assertiveness on human rights by advocating greater foreign assistance; higher shares of the operating costs for the richer members;

and reform of the Inter-American Defense Board, which absorbed such a large share of OAS budgets. Canada also insisted that OAS members pay their financial dues to the organization.

In short, Canada's admission to the OAS was marked by tough talk and some action. Those who expected a sharp split between U.S. and Canadian policy were disappointed. Yet Canada pressed its own agenda on democracy and human rights in its own way. Latin American governments that feared a bumptious Canada in the OAS discovered instead an experienced club member.

If Canada can be faulted at all for its first decade of participation in the OAS, it would be for its inability to elicit much interest in environmental matters. Although the OAS has no independent resources to encourage environmental protection, and Canadian activism on the environmental front could rouse the ire of some members that believe environmental protection to be strictly a domestic political issue, Canada might nonetheless have exercised more environmental leadership than it did. By not stepping forward with creative ideas about how rich and poor countries might acknowledge their common environmental destiny and work together toward sustainable development, Canada may have missed an important opportunity to do good on behalf of the hemisphere.

Canada's Role in Haiti

Canada's involvement with Haiti epitomizes its new engagement in Western Hemispheric matters. The French link to Haiti might have been expected to evoke some response from Canada to the overthrow of a democratic regime on the island; moreover, a small Haitian population in Montreal very effectively lobbied the federal government for action to support the ousted Aristide government. However, the values that shaped Canada's decision to assist Aristide, the mode of government involvement, the nature of coordination with other governments, and the interaction between domestic politics and foreign policy all suggest an increasing Canadian commitment to the Western Hemisphere.

"We cannot sit idly by while military thugs impose their rule of terror at will," said Christine Stewart, secretary of state for Latin America and Africa, a new post in the DFAIT.[8] Canada observed gross human rights violations in Haiti and saw a democratically elected government overturned. It lamented the continuing poverty in the poorest country in the Americas. It also disregarded racial difference in both insisting on a common standard of governmental behavior and offering its assistance to a population it regarded as oppressed. If these reactions reflect North American values, then Canada is undoubtedly acting as a liberal North American polity.

Shortly after the ouster of Jean-Bertrand Aristide by General Raoul Cedras on September 30, 1991, Canada took part in the general OAS pledge to oppose "sudden or irregular interruption" of democratically elected governments in the hemisphere. But Canada went further. It lobbied Washington to become active through diplomacy and to back the Carter initiative by the threat of force, if necessary, to restore the legitimately elected government. When its own OAS mission failed, Canada did not stop trying to support Aristide. Even when rumors of questionable behavior on the part of Aristide himself threatened to undermine political support in the United States and elsewhere in the hemisphere for his return to power, the Mulroney government ultimately persuaded Washington to become more actively and directly involved.

Canada was impressive in terms of follow-up as well. It provided substantial and immediate foreign assistance. The Chrétien government responded to U.S. president Clinton's call to replace American peacekeepers with Canadians. Exploiting its French advantage, Canada trained a 600-man police force that was organized to replace the brutal and corrupt force recruited by Cedras. Perhaps Canada's largest commitment, however, was to monitor elections in Haiti.[9] In 1990 and again in 1995 Québec's principal elections officers headed the joint OAS–United Nations electoral observation mission in Haiti and the electoral component of the International Civil Mission to Haiti. Elections Canada, the nonprofit organization responsible for conducting elections and educating voters in Canada, and the Ontario electoral officer helped with the legislative elections. The Canadian International Development Agency provided funding and personnel. Monitoring of human rights and elections is now carried out simultaneously. Clearly, the effort to supervise fair and comprehensive elections is a task to which Canada is committed and from which Haiti has benefited.

On the other hand, Canada, like the United States—and perhaps unlike most of Latin America, which tends to be more realistic—was capable also of delusion and pious hope. Canada truly believed that the intervention in Haiti could alter the course of its politics and development. However, lasting political and economic change has been slow to emerge. As of 1999, when the last Canadian and American troops were winding down their missions to Haiti, the Legislative Palace lay empty, the government of Rene Preval had been accused of mismanagement and of bypassing the parliament in naming a new prime minister, foreign assistance either was not distributed or was misused, and only 5 percent of the registered voters had participated in the 1997 local elections. Democracy has not blossomed in Haiti. The old ways—corruption, cronyism, and dictatorial action—continue. Greater freedom of speech and some relief from human rights abuses are perhaps the sole legacy of the intervention.

Canadian Relations with Brazil

Since the advent of civilian government in Brazil in 1985, relations between Canada and Brazil have warmed and matured. Despite NAFTA's importance to Canada, Canada in 1995 was exporting more goods and services to Brazil than to Mexico. And despite the international financial crises of the 1980s, Canadian investment has steadily increased in Brazil and Canadian banks have returned to that country. Brascan, a large Canadian multinational firm, for example, provides electricity, telephones, water, and gas to several major cities in Brazil. Other long-established Canadian firms there include ALCAN, NorTel, and Moore Business Forms.

Canada and Brazil have coordinated multilateral trade negotiations, most notably in the Uruguay Round, notwithstanding their initial divergence of views. The two countries worked together at the Miami summit on human rights issues and the strengthening of democracy.[10] Likewise, Brazil and Canada have collaborated in the Organization for Economic Cooperation and Development (OECD) in the effort to secure Brazil's participation in some OECD committees.[11]

In the important area of nuclear nonproliferation, Canada and Brazil have interacted considerably. Canada, which is one of the original signatories to the nonproliferation treaty and which voluntarily relinquished the acquisition of nuclear weapons, advocates a nonproliferation policy that is superficially similar to that of Brazil. Brazil, however, has been a long-standing critic of the nuclear nonproliferation treaty, although it observes the treaty's basic provisions. In export policies, too, Canada, an exporter of the CANDU nuclear reactor, must take care to observe the letter and spirit of the nonproliferation agreement.

Hence, Brazil and Canada are bound to communicate regarding the future terms and application of nonproliferation policy in the Western Hemisphere.

It appears that Prime Minister Chrétien and former Brazilian president Fernando Henrique Cardoso (1995–2002) adopted hemispheric policies that are congruent and mutually supportive.[12] Despite the turbulence of the Brazilian economy and its struggle with inflation, Canada continues to be a significant trading partner and provider of capital. Both governments seem to regard the Canadian–Brazilian relationship as a kind of positive long-term investment in an uncertain world.

Canada's Cuba Connection

For analysts of Canadian–Western Hemispheric relations, Canada's policy on Cuba reveals much about the purpose, complexities, contradictions, and capacities of Canadian foreign policy. Beneath the surface of these diplomatic relations lies a much more dynamic set of initiatives and concerns, not all of them consistent, than may be apparent to the casual student of Canadian foreign affairs.

Following the communist revolution in Cuba and the failed Bay of Pigs intervention, only Canada and Mexico among countries in the Western Hemisphere refused to break relations with the government of Fidel Castro. Regardless of whether a Conservative government was in power in Ottawa, as was true in 1961, or a Liberal government, balance-of-power politics suited Canada in its relations with Cuba. But the power that was being balanced was the United States, with Cuba the pawn in the game played between Ottawa and Washington. This was not how Ottawa expressed the policy, even to itself, but the format was transparent. The fact that the strategy employed was balance of power did not controvert substantive Canadian interests in trade and investment and Canadian political concerns about the Castro regime.

As a kind of reification of Mitchell Sharp's so-called third option of trade diversification away from the United States in 1968, Canada's Cuba policy suited the Trudeau government well. Because the United States was trying to isolate Cuba politically and economically to bring pressure on the regime, and Canadian trade and commercial relations so visibly departed from the U.S. strategy, Canada's Cuba connection fit admirably into the third option. In practice, however, the small value and volume of trade with Cuba did little other than symbolically reduce the concentration of Canadian trade with the United States.

However, when other Western Hemisphere governments put pressure on Cuba in 1978 because of its involvement in Angola, the Trudeau government did so as well, making Cuba ineligible for Canadian development assistance.[13] Ottawa used peculiar rationalization to justify what was overtly a move to force Cuba out of Africa. Canadians did not really want to admit that they were pressuring Cuba to alter its foreign policy. This about-face in Canadian policy became problematic in 1993, when the Mulroney government sought to allow Canadian churches to assist Cuba in its effort to counter the disease optic neuritis but found it no longer had the internal legal or political support for such foreign aid. Moreover, policy in the Canadian International Development Agency, in the Department of External Affairs (now DFAIT), and in the Prime Minister's Office conflicted on these issues.

Set against these policy shifts was Canada's characterization of its relations with Cuba as "correct but cordial."[14] The phrase summarized well the two aspects of Canadian policy toward Cuba: Canada disapproved of Castro's human rights record and denial of democratic procedure, and it sought to erode that regime through constructive engagement. Constructive engagement also furthered Canada's trade and investment interests in Cuba, in contrast to Washington's containment strategy.

Helms-Burton Legislation

Within the larger framework of Canada–Cuba relations is a smaller, more volatile issue that reflects all of the larger debates condensed and made more politically explosive. After the Castro government shot down over international waters two unarmed civilian aircraft that allegedly had been dropping propaganda leaflets on Cuban territory, the U.S. government on March 12, 1996, enacted Helms-Burton legislation as a punitive response. The measure was designed to tighten the commercial vise around Cuba by penalizing those who did business with Castro. Because of their presence and visibility, firms in Canada were penalized first in this clearly extraterritorial legislation, but Mexican and European interests were affected as well.

This legislation influenced U.S.–Canada relations in two ways. First, it highlighted the difference in strategic initiative between the approaches taken by Canada and by the United States to alter the nature of the Castro regime.[15] Second, it shifted the focus from tension between Cuba and its neighbors to tension between Canada and the United States. Though the Castro regime could scarcely claim credit for this dubious achievement, the resulting strain between the two stalwart allies must have been cause for some glee in Havana.

As a result of that strain, the Chrétien government attempted to establish a more cordial relationship with the Castro government. Doing so had two linked purposes. First, it served to show the world how different U.S. and Canadian foreign policy allegedly was. Because it was different, the foreign policy of Chrétien and Axworthy was highly popular at home. Reportedly, letters to the Canadian Foreign Ministry ran four out of five in favor of heavy criticism of Helms-Burton and in support of constructive engagement with Cuba. How could the Foreign Ministry not exploit such a political opportunity?

There was, however, a second, important piece to the puzzle. The Helms-Burton legislation was calculated to punish firms that took over and operated property that had previously been expropriated by the Castro regime, chief among them the nickel mines owned and operated by Sherritt, a Canadian firm. As to ownership of such property, here again U.S. and Canadian law diverged. Should expropriated property be resold without proper compensation to the previous owner? Such questions were hidden in the tumult of the debate.

Helms-Burton allowed U.S. citizens to sue Canadian firms on the matter of expropriation in U.S. courts. This was the issue that alarmed Canadian business. Canadian firms worried most of all that the U.S. government might take their U.S. holdings hostage. But Helms-Burton was mischievous in another way: It denied the officers and families of targeted Canadian and other firms entry into the United States. This provision outraged Canadians.

Of course, the Helms-Burton affair was even more complex politically, and each of the players knew all of its dimensions. The legislation was timed to put pressure on the Chrétien government to alter its "pro-Cuban" policies just before the U.S. national election. Strongly in favor of the legislation were Cubans in Florida who had fled the Castro regime or been expelled, and Florida was a key electoral state (how key Canada was soon to learn in the 2000 U.S. presidential election). Republican strategists in Congress therefore put President Clinton's feet to the fire. Clinton did not like the legislation, but he had to support it or risk losing Florida in the election. The Chrétien government was aware that Clinton did not like the legislation, but because it could not get at the Republican proponents directly, it did so indirectly by criticizing the Clinton administration's official support for Helms-Burton. Everyone knew the truth behind the official statements of each government.

Two further tactics underscored the complexities of the situation. Canada sought international support for its policies within the hemisphere from Jamaica, Dominica, and Trinidad and Tobago. It also obtained an OAS resolution that condemned U.S. policy as expressed in the Helms-Burton legislation. Canada and the EU talked about lodging a formal complaint before the World Trade Organization (WTO), but the EU came to its own terms with U.S. policy and the complaint was not lodged.

Meanwhile, the Clinton government employed subtle footwork as well. Clinton postponed implementation of the law without attempting to reverse its passage, a task that Canada knew was impossible in a Republican-controlled Congress. By failing to implement the legislation, the Clinton administration became less vulnerable to foreign criticism.

In the end, as often happens in Canada–U.S. relations, the sparring partners settled for a draw. The United States implied that it would not implement the hated legislation, while Canada hinted that it would stop trying so visibly to get a reversal, thus embarrassing the Clinton administration less. Both governments knew there were many other issues on the bargaining table, and Helms-Burton was becoming a liability for both Ottawa and Washington.

Final Steps

In the 1998–1999 interval, the Chrétien government held out to Cuba the inducement that Canada would pursue Cuba's inclusion in the OAS and possibly other organizations and events such as the Summit of the Americas, at which the creation of the FTAA would be discussed.[16] Canada also tried to be generous with its foreign assistance and by encouraging trade and foreign investment flows to Cuba. Chrétien went out of his way to meet with Castro and to visit Cuba.

Testing the value of constructive engagement in 1999, the Chrétien government quietly tried to prevent, on human rights grounds, the incarceration of several Cubans. Castro refused to consider clemency. From Cuba's perspective, Canada's pleas amounted to unwarranted meddling into Cuba's domestic affairs. The Chrétien government then invoked a policy of "northern ice": It cut off some aid and otherwise sought to distance itself from Castro.

In sum, two conclusions can be drawn about Canada's foreign policy toward Castro. The Canadian policy of constructive engagement and the U.S. policy of containment look suspiciously similar at different times in the evolution of policy implementation, whatever their respective intentions or justifications. And the Canadian policy, like the U.S. policy, so far has yielded few specific results with respect to Cuba's human rights conduct or a shift toward democracy. Whatever opening toward a freer market in Cuba or relaxation of authoritarian rule has occurred—and the degree thereof may be debated—that shift seems to have taken place independent of specific policy initiatives adopted by any government seeking to influence Cuba overtly and directly. However unattractive communism is, there may be value in using indirect and low-visibility processes to transform it, processes that best exploit communism's own abundant internal contradictions.

Canada as Advocate: The Chilean Example

An important question is whether Canada can perform as advocate for Latin American interests within the hemisphere, especially in the North American context. Is such advocacy in the interests of other countries in the hemisphere? Do they need that advocacy, and will they benefit from it? Will such advocacy be in Canada's interest? Moreover, does Canada have the capacity—the diplomatic skill and access to other governments—to become Latin America's advocate? How are the governments that are being lobbied likely to respond?

An excellent case study of the possibilities and limits of Canadian advocacy for Latin American interests is the effort to gain access to NAFTA for Chile. Although Chile ranks only about twenty-fifth among countries in terms of volume of trade with Canada, some of that trade is very important for each country. Canada exports forestry and mining machinery and wheat to Chile, while Chile exports high-end wine and fruit to Canada. Often Canada has a trade deficit on current account with Chile, underscoring the value to Chile of the Canadian market. Capital inflows to Chile from Canada also help determine the deficit on Canada's current account with Chile.

But Canada's interest in Chile as a NAFTA partner goes beyond trade and investment. Chile is a strongly free market–oriented economy. Its restoration of democracy is likewise exemplary. Chile is the kind of country with which Canada would like to increase its political, cultural, and commercial ties. Chile is also in many ways a natural partner for the NAFTA countries, despite the comparatively small size of its economy and the great geographic distance between Chile and North America. As Canada seeks to diffuse its trade linkages, Chile might well be able to assist in the endeavor.

In advocating a greater role for Chile in the North American marketplace, Canada and Chile had two choices. They could simply attempt to enhance their own bilateral trade ties and those between each of them and others, or they could seek to enroll Chile in NAFTA and promote multilateral ties. They chose the latter option. How did this attempt at advocacy fit the interests of Chile, Canada, and the other NAFTA trading partners?

Chile could hardly complain. Canada was acting as an intermediary with NAFTA on behalf of its interests. Chile recognized that if NAFTA was good for Mexico, it could be even better for Chile. But how could Chile overcome all the natural obstacles to accession, the most daunting of which was its own insignificance to U.S. trading interests? Perhaps Canada could not help, but surely its efforts could not hurt, either.

The United States was not opposed to Chile's entry; indeed, it was well-disposed to Chile as a country and as a market. The problem was that the United States would need to get both houses of Congress to back Chile's entry into NAFTA. To do that, the U.S. administration needed fast-track negotiating authority—that is, a provision that members of Congress would be precluded from adding meaningless riders to the agreement, thus slowing its passage. The real problem for the proponents of Chilean entry was that Chile and Chilean commercial interests were too small to trigger the powerful lobbying machinery from business necessary to gain the passage of fast-track legislation. If Chilean entry had been supplemented by the entry of Mercosur (the Common Market of the South), for example, Chile would have been in a much stronger position to gain admission to NAFTA. But Chile was isolated and alone—all the more reason it needed the good services of Canada.

Strategically, Canada took the line that Chile faced two scenarios for trade liberalization and that Canada could persuade Chile to opt for the one more in the interests of the United States. Initially, Chile had opted for a bilateral deal between itself and other NAFTA countries.

U.S. business interests frowned on these deals, however, because, like economists, they saw these arrangements as "balkanizing" the world trading system. Thus, Canada suggested to Washington, Chile should take the more multilateral route, and Canada could be counted on to bring Chile to that view.

What were the limits of Canada's diplomacy? Canada has no votes in the U.S. Congress and could not help President Clinton round up votes for the passage of fast-track legislation. No matter how well Canada understood the situation in the U.S. Congress, then, it could neither help the U.S. president with his domestic political problems nor amplify Chile's weight as an important trading partner for the United States. Moreover, President Patricio Aylwin Azócar of Chile had already made clear to Washington his ultimate willingness to become a member of NAFTA. So Canada was not able to deliver to Washington, or to Mexico City for that matter, anything that these countries could not themselves effect.

In the end, Canada could not assist Chile in gaining entry to NAFTA because President Clinton could not secure the votes necessary for fast-track negotiating authority. This failure, however, did not mean Canada's role as advocate was a failure. Canada succeeded in convincing the U.S. president that Chilean entry into NAFTA was desirable and made clear to the United States how strongly it supported that entry. Moreover, Canada for a time channeled negotiations toward a multilateral trade solution.

Although NAFTA entry for Chile failed for the time being (but surely not in the longer term, especially considering the 2002 passage of Trade Promotion Authority [TPA], the new term replacing "fast-track"), Chile forged bilateral trade ties with both Mexico and Canada but not with the United States. Even here Canada had some impact in that the terms of these bilateral deals were compatible with the terms of Chile's future NAFTA entry. Thus, it is reasonable to conclude that Canada might well usefully act as lawyer for other Latin American interests in North America, especially vis-à-vis the United States, if U.S. domestic political circumstances are at all favorable.[17]

More than any other country in the Western Hemisphere, Canada has felt the pressure of events following September 11 stemming from relations with the United States. First, the content of those relations changed as security issues began to replace some of the commonplace trade and environmental matters on the bargaining agenda. Second, the focus of relations changed as the advantage of geographic proximity to the United States became a vulnerability in terms of the effort to strengthen security procedures at the border and at airports. Canada found very difficult the task of trying to move the security perimeter from the 49th parallel and the border with Alaska to one that would include all of Canada and the United States.

Post–September 11 consequences for Canada involve three possibilities: (1) Canada and the United States will become more distant from each other; (2) Canada, the United States, and Mexico will become more integrated in security terms but also more separate from the remainder of the Western Hemisphere; and (3) Canada and the United States will learn to enhance security against terrorism without significantly impacting upon trade and commercial relations with the rest of the hemisphere. Events have not determined which of these outcomes will prevail. But the third of the options is likely to become a goal toward which the United States and Canada will work. Eventually, a restoration of the importance of trade and commerce relative to security will ease the pressure on Canada and will improve economic relations throughout the Western Hemisphere.

The Strategic Complexity of Western Hemispheric Trade Liberalization

Mexico has forever shattered the ritualistic hesitation of the developing country to negotiate equally and directly with the rich, industrialized country. NAFTA is a symbol of the vision and courage of the Mexican technocratic and business elite, demonstrating that opening an economy on the basis of equivalent tariff and nontariff reductions is the path to developmental prosperity. But for Canada, as for the other parties to NAFTA, the next steps are not so clear.[18] This section explores some of the options for Canada as it enters the twenty-first century.

Deepening NAFTA Arrangements

Despite its encompassing and innovative nature, NAFTA has some unfinished business. On one side, the architects of NAFTA would be well advised to revisit one provision of the agreement before it is too late. In the rush to use NAFTA as a lever against the EU's foot-dragging on agricultural reform in the WTO, NAFTA architects pushed through a far-reaching reduction of tariffs on maize (corn) production in the North

American countries. Mexico is historically a maize producer—so much so that traditional religion idolized the crop's societal role—but Mexico has very little comparative advantage in terms of soil, water, or capital in the production of maize. NAFTA tariff reductions are therefore likely to devastate the livelihoods of some 30 million Mexican peasants. Driven out of subsistence and marginal commercial maize agriculture, these peasants will probably migrate to Mexico City's ever-growing slums; or, if the rate of economic growth there slows, this multitude of displaced peasantry may converge on the U.S. border. Inasmuch as the United States already turns back to Mexico an estimated 1.5 million undocumented Mexican workers annually, this new influx of people could virtually overwhelm the capacity of the U.S. customs and immigration services to deal humanely and systematically with desperate would-be immigrants. It is time to revise the NAFTA statutes, not by canceling the tariff reductions on maize but by stretching out their effects so that change can be managed more effectively.

In the longer run, however, more significant NAFTA reform must deal with the further deepening and strengthening of reform.[19] One reason is that many barriers exist to the free flow of goods, services, capital, and people, hindering productive and distributive efficiency. For example, the lack of common standards—a metric system, for example—across these countries means that the United States needs to accelerate internal change in this area. The lack of congruent health, legal, and accounting systems for investment and trade matters continues to frustrate investors and often presents opportunities to conceal trade impediments under some other rubric. The insufficiency of mechanisms for trade dispute resolution means that 5 percent of the NAFTA trade not covered by these mechanisms now accounts for 90 percent of the disputes.

But another reason for deepening NAFTA arrangements, as Canada well knows, is that the opportunity for rapid change in trade liberalization is greatest when the number of actors involved is minimal. Decisions are likely to be reached faster and at a higher level of trade significance than when negotiations among many members with diverse interests and conflicting goals dilute outcomes to the lowest common denominator. If Canada and its NAFTA partners want greater trade and commercial efficiency with a minimum of bureaucratic superstructure, now is the time to pursue a far more energetic approach to reform inside NAFTA itself. The liberalization payoff is likely to be greatest here relative to the political effort expended.

Forging a Free Trade Area of the Americas

Parallel to the deepening of NAFTA should be the widening of trade liberalization within the Western Hemisphere. NAFTA alone, despite the benefits it has conveyed, will increasingly display a downside— namely, trade diversion and what might be termed investment diversion. These forms of economic inefficiency are most likely to be felt sharply among nearby and economically similar countries in Latin America. Brazil, for example, has experienced a relative loss of U.S. investment because much of that investment has been diverted toward Mexico. Even though Argentina and Chile may be the lowest-cost producers in the hemisphere of some agricultural commodities and some manufactured goods, once again Mexico may have been targeted for new production because of NAFTA. Barring offsetting global trade liberalization, the only way to abate trade and investment diversion within the hemisphere is for all of the hemispheric countries to form a single trade arrangement.

Whether the trade negotiations are conducted multilaterally among countries in the hemisphere or primarily between NAFTA and Mercosur makes very little difference. In practice, the large established trade groupings will probably reveal some group preferences. The important point is that states not partner to either grouping need to be part of the hemisphere-wide negotiations.

But from Canada's perspective, the true challenge for the FTAA will be crafting its purpose. Against the backdrop of other ongoing trade negotiations, the FTAA must find a unique purpose. Merely encompassing the countries of the hemisphere, or merely linking NAFTA and Mercosur (although this would be no mean feat), will be insufficient. The FTAA must establish itself at the forefront of trade negotiations in the way that NAFTA has done.

There are two outstanding ways to achieve this distinctiveness. First, the FTAA could focus on some aspect of trade liberalization especially relevant to the society, legal systems, culture, or politics of the entire region; among other focuses might be the legalisms of competition policy, financial services reform that would finally break down barriers between industries, the fuller pursuit of intellectual property rights, and truly imaginative work toward resolving issues concerning environmental protection or trade conflicts. A final possibility could be a much more encompassing regime for trade dispute resolution. Whatever the focus, it must be original and broadly based to be of interest to all members of the Western Hemisphere, including the largest members. This message Canada will convey.

Second, the FTAA might embark on a project not undertaken by other trade liberalization efforts, indeed, rejected by those projects: namely, investment liberalization. Since the rejection of the Multilateral Investment Agreement (MLA) in Paris in 1998, the matter of investment liberalization has been allowed to languish. Yet Canada has deep and unqualified interests in an investment pact that unlike the MLA would, for example, help safeguard Canada's concern about a U.S. cultural invasion through publications, movies, and the news media without undermining international trade and investment regimes. Canada may pursue this agenda in FTAA councils.

In short, Canada and other countries in the Western Hemisphere that want to be competitive in world markets need to pay heed to the idea of an FTAA. The task is to decide how best to craft such a large agreement for such a multifaceted set of countries within a single region.

Linking Region and Globe

Canada will be in the forefront of the effort to link the Western Hemisphere with the global trading system. However committed Canada is to innovative North American and Western Hemispheric schemes for trade liberalization, at heart Canada believes in multilateral arrangements that span the globe. As the fourth largest trading power in the world after the EU, the United States, and Japan, Canada cares about trade liberalization inside the Western Hemisphere and worldwide. But Canada will always seek to make the more regional agreements compatible with the commitment to global enterprise.

Conclusion

Canada's new opening to the Western Hemisphere has several origins, but that entry is visible, genuine, and enduring. Canada is politically and economically part of the Western Hemisphere, and it is here to stay. However, no overriding doctrine or perspective summarizing Canadian statecraft within the hemisphere can realistically be put forward. Better for explaining Canada's statecraft is an analytic approach that starts from the bottom in policy terms and works its way upward. Canada's Western Hemisphere policy is certainly the sum of its parts, yet to understand that statecraft in its totality, one must start with the parts and gradually move toward the whole in all dimensions—political, economic, security, and cultural—country by country. Canada is, at last, a fully committed member of the Western Hemisphere.

Notes

1. Graeme S. Mount, "The Canadian Presbyterian Mission to Trinidad, 1868–1912," *Revista/Review Interamericana* 7, no. 1 (Spring 1977): 30–45; Sahadeo Basdeo, "Caribecan: A Continuum in Canada–Commonwealth–Caribbean Economic Relations," *Canadian Foreign Policy* 1, no. 2 (Spring 1993): 56–57; and George E. Eaton, "Canada-Sugar and the Commonwealth Caribbean," *Caribbean Quarterly* 19 (March 1972): 72–74.

2. Robin Winks, "Canada and the Three Americas: Her Hemispheric Role," in *Friends So Different: Essays on Canada and the United States in the 1980s*, ed. Lansing Lamont and J. Duncan Edmonds (Ottawa: Americas Society–University of Ottawa, 1989), 253.

3. Christine Stewart, "Making a Difference: Canada in Latin America and Africa," *Canadian Foreign Policy* 2, no. 2 (Fall 1994): 1–5.

4. Lloyd Axworthy, "Canadian Foreign Policy: A Liberal Party Perspective," *Canadian Foreign Policy* 1, no. 1 (Winter 1992–1993): 8.

5. Peter McKenna, "How Is Canada Doing in the OAS?" *Canadian Foreign Policy* 1, no. 2 (Spring 1993): 81–98.

6. Barbara McDougall, "Canada and the New Internationalism," *Canadian Foreign Policy* 1, no. 1 (Winter 1992–1993): 2–3.

7. Stewart, "Making a Difference."

8. Ibid., 3.

9. J. Taylor Wentges, "Third Generation Electoral Observation and the OAS-UN International Civil Mission to Haiti," *Canadian Foreign Policy* 4, no. 3 (Winter 1997): 51–63.

10. Nestor Forster, "The Brazilian Position at the Cartagena Ministerial," statement issued by the Brazilian embassy in Ottawa, June 1996, 1–7.

11. Carmen Sorger and William A. Dymond, "Sisyphus Ascendant? Brazilian Foreign Policy for the Coming Century," *Canadian Foreign Policy* 4, no. 3 (Winter 1997): 37–49.

12. Speech by Prime Minister Chrétien at a luncheon hosted by President Cardoso of Brazil, Brasília, 27 January 1995.

13. John M. Kirk, "In Search of a Canadian Policy Towards Cuba," *Canadian Foreign Policy* 2, no. 2 (Fall 1994): 78.

14. Charlotte Montgomery, "Canada Seeks to Thaw Frost in U.S.–Cuban Relationship," *Toronto Globe and Mail*, 14 April 1990, A7.

15. Peter McKenna, "Helms-Burton: Up Close and Personal," *Canadian Foreign Policy* 4, no. 3 (Winter 1997): 7–20.

16. Jean Daudelin, "Between Cuba and a Hard Place: Another Bout of

U.S. Extraterritoriality," *Canadian Foreign Policy* 2, no. 3 (Winter 1994–1995): 119–121.

17. James Rochlin, "Markets, Democracy and Security in Latin America," in *Canada Among Nations 1995: Democracy and Foreign Policy,* ed. Maxwell A. Cameron and Maureen Appel Molot (Ottawa: Carleton University Press, 1995), 145–164.

18. For the historical discussion of these complexities inside polities, see Charles F. Doran, "The Trade and Political Party Flip-Flop," in *The NAFTA Puzzle,* ed. Charles F. Doran and Gregory Marchildon (Boulder: Westview, 1994), 1–8.

19. Charles F. Doran, "When Building North America, Deepen Before Widening," in *A New North America,* ed. Charles F. Doran and Alvin Paul Drischler (Westport, Conn.: Praeger, 1996), 65–90.

Part 2

Changing Ties with International Actors

6

The Role of International Financial Institutions

Rosa Alonso i Terme

Latin America is a microcosm of the developing world. It contains some of the most impressive success stories of the past few decades, some countries with per capita incomes comparable to those in sub-Saharan Africa, and a great majority of countries struggling in between. To ask what the international financial institutions can and should do for Latin America in the new century is to pose the wider question of what should be the role of these institutions in the developing world as a whole.[1] This chapter will thus focus on the likely and desirable evolution of the international financial institutions—the International Monetary Fund (IMF) and the World Bank—in a broader sense, but will also try to distill what that evolution means for Latin America.

There has recently been an enormous amount of debate about the need to reform the IMF and the World Bank. This debate, fueled by critics from diverse ideological perspectives, has been catalyzed by the increased frequency of financial crises in the past decade. In Joseph Stiglitz's words: "When a single car has an accident on the road, one is inclined to blame the driver or his car; when there are dozens of accidents at the same spot, however, the presumption changes. It is likely that something is wrong with the design of the road. The fact that there have been, by some reckonings, financial crises in 100 countries in the past quarter-century suggests that there are systematic problems."[2]

These observations reflect the consensus that the current international financial architecture can and should be improved. There is much less consensus, however, on just how deeply flawed the current architecture is, what its weaknesses are, and what exactly is required to reform it. This chapter will argue that the ultimate goal of reform meas-

117

ures for the international financial and development architecture should be the preservation of the existing liberal international economy while making sure it serves the purpose of enhancing equity and poverty-reduction.

Namely, the main goal of the Bretton Woods institutions in the twenty-first century should be to further the existing liberal international economy while correcting its less desirable features, thus making its functioning smoother and increasing its legitimacy. Open market economies are the best system to organize productive resources, to generate long-term growth and poverty-reduction, and possibly even to foster liberal democratic systems.[3] However, unless the existing international financial architecture and the policies of developed and emerging market countries improve, the impressive gains of the liberal international economy established in the past 50 years may be rolled back by those who see all their failures while failing to see their benefits.[4]

In Latin America, the international financial institutions will have a crucial role to play in ensuring that the economic reforms introduced in the aftermath of the 1980s debt crisis are consolidated and deepened. In the coming century, the World Bank will be increasingly less involved with the good performers, which will gain increasing access to international capital markets; in these countries, the IMF will foster transparency and strengthened financial sector and banking regulation and supervision while continuing to provide a safety net in the event of financial crises. In the case of poor performers, the World Bank will play a crucial role when reform efforts take hold, through program and sectoral adjustment lending and through the provision of training and technical assistance for capacity-building. In the absence of sufficient reform effort, however, there is an increasing determination not to lend. Finally, there is the possibility that the World Bank will be used increasingly to supplement the role of the International Monetary Fund through fast-disbursing programmatic lending in times of balance-of-payments crises.

The International Monetary Fund

This section argues that the main role of the IMF in the new century will be to diminish the frequency of crises, their duration, and their cost through strengthened crisis prevention and crisis management mechanisms. It also argues that the IMF should increasingly delegate the role of long-term lending for structural adjustment purposes to the World Bank.

Crisis Prevention

Emphasis on crisis prevention is essential. Even in the best of circumstances, financial crises are enormously costly, bailout packages are a highly regressive type of public expenditure, and financial contagion can easily occur.[5] The IMF is thus devoting a great deal of effort to help prevent the occurrence of financial crises. It is doing so by focusing on three sets of measures: First, it is continuing to encourage member countries to pursue the types of macroeconomic policies and structural and institutional reforms that diminish the likelihood of capital outflows; second, it is encouraging member countries to increase the public availability of economic and financial information and to strengthen their financial systems; and, third, it is introducing some reforms in its own lending policies.

The best recipe for crisis prevention is good policy—witness Chile's weathering the financial crises of the 1990s practically unscathed. Argentina's 2001 debacle makes this point forcefully, as it clearly resulted from domestic policy and institutional failures, including inconsistent macro- and microeconomic policies and a lax fiscal policy partly due to a poorly designed system of intergovernmental fiscal relations. In particular, the combination of a superfixed exchange rate and labor market rigidity leading to an increasingly overvalued real exchange rate with a rising budget deficit caused growing current account deficits and rapidly mounting foreign debt, ultimately undermining investor confidence. Most non-Argentine critics of the role of the IMF in the crisis blame the fund for supporting bad policies for too long; namely, they criticize it for being too "soft" on bad policies, not too "harsh" as the more common critique goes.[6] In the future, the IMF will likely be tougher in its assessment of whether the quality of a country's policies and institutions is good enough to warrant its support—at least in countries without great geopolitical import. This approach is already evident in the fund's handling of the Argentina crisis and is strongly supported by its new management.[7]

The availability of comprehensive economic and financial information is key to reducing the risk of sudden changes of sentiment in financial markets. For financial markets adequately to assess risk and make appropriate lending decisions, they need comprehensive and reliable information. If this information is not publicly available, financial markets are likely to overlend only to reduce suddenly their exposure as previously concealed information becomes known. Publicizing up-to-date, accurate, and comprehensive economic and financial information has thus been recognized as crucial to diminishing the risk of financial crises, particularly since the Mexican and Asian crises.

In this area, the IMF should play a key role by establishing standards on the information that governments ought to make available and by helping to publicize this information. In addition to public sector information, there should be improvements in the information required from the private sector, which should be encouraged to adopt sound accounting practices and appropriate standards of disclosure to investors, financial institutions, and official agencies. It was this view that led to the creation of the IMF's special data dissemination standard (SDDS), a system that, after a two-year trial period, is now in operation. The SDDS is a standard of good practice in the dissemination of economic and financial data to which IMF member countries subscribe on a voluntary basis.[8] The SDDS is intended for use mainly by countries that either have or seek access to international financial markets, to signal their commitment to the provision of timely and comprehensive data.

Moreover, in a world of high capital mobility and volatile short-term capital flows, the strength of a country's banking and financial system is crucial to its ability to withstand economic recessions and, particularly, sudden reversals in capital flows. As a result, the IMF is increasingly encouraging emerging countries to strengthen their financial market and banking regulation and supervision by, for example, adopting international standards in various areas. Standards both provide emerging countries with information on the measures they need to take to strengthen their financial and banking systems and give them an incentive to do so.

The IMF has recognized 11 different areas and associated standards as "useful for the operational work of the Fund and the World Bank" and, by extension, for capital markets to be able to monitor the evolution of economic and financial policies of countries in a reliable and timely manner.[9] As part of these sets of standards, the IMF has developed a "Code of Good Practices on Fiscal Transparency" and, in cooperation with the Bank for International Settlements, a similar "Code on the Transparency of Monetary and Financial Policies."[10] The IMF has also recognized standards developed by other organizations in related areas.[11] At the moment, the fund only prepares reports summarizing observance of these standards at the request of member countries and the reports are publicly accessible through the Web.[12] Although it would be very useful to have reports on the status of compliance of all countries in all eleven areas, it is unrealistic to expect countries with weak transparency and information standards to allow the IMF to assess their performance. Therefore, the current situation of voluntary assessment is probably the best that can be reasonably expected in the foreseeable future.

As capital accounts become more open, sudden reversals in capital flows are becoming increasingly frequent. The IMF will continue to advise countries to implement the types of macroeconomic, structural, and institutional policies that make them least vulnerable to such reversals. In the aftermath of the Argentina crisis, a key piece of this advice will be cautioning against the risks of fixed exchange rate systems in the context of open capital markets. The risks and costs of fixed exchange rates are particularly high in the case of pegs between commodity-dependent economies—like Argentina—and industrialized economies, like the United States, since they are likely to have highly asynchronic economic cycles requiring divergent monetary policies. Moreover, as the Argentina case has shown, when a fixed exchange rate system is accompanied by an overregulated labor market, the costs of loss of monetary and exchange rate autonomy in times of recession can be unbearably high in terms of foregone growth and unemployment. As a result of the Argentina debacle, the IMF will likely be more forthright in its advice against fixed exchange rates, particularly in the circumstances just mentioned.

Moreover, as the Asian financial crisis has painfully demonstrated, there is a great need for caution in the speed and sequencing of capital account liberalization. In March 1999, as the IMF's executive board reviewed member countries' experience in the use of capital controls, directors noted that "in countries most seriously affected by crisis, liberalization had been poorly sequenced or inadequately supported by economic policies, financial regulation and oversight."[13] As a consequence, directors recognized that "controls over inflows, particularly those designed to influence their composition, might be justifiable."[14] The IMF is right to point out the link between financial crises, poor sequencing, and weak regulation and supervision of financial markets and banking systems, and it should be more forceful in its advice in this area. In particular, it should strongly discourage member countries from adopting any measures that would lead to perverse incentives, such as the liberalization of short-term before long-term capital inflows. In countries that wish to liberalize their financial systems but have a weak banking system, poor supervision, or inadequate accounting and auditing standards, and where a culture of implicit guarantees exists, the IMF should advise caution.[15] In particular, it should advise either postponing liberalization of short-term capital inflows or establishing a tax on short-term capital inflows, as Chile did. This tax should apply to short-term borrowing by all domestic entities, including banks and corporations.

The IMF should also strengthen its surveillance process. IMF surveillance currently takes place yearly under the so-called Article IV consultation with each member on the state of its economy.[16] The frequency of surveillance of (consultation with) countries that face potential trouble should be stepped up. In addition to increasing the frequency of surveillance missions, incentives for national authorities to heed Article IV recommendations might be improved. The only way to strengthen the incentives for nonprogram countries—that is, countries not subject to conditionality—to take Article IV recommendations seriously, however, is by making these reports candid, reliable, and public.

Some progress has already been made on this front in recent years. The IMF has been releasing public information notices on Article IV consultations for 80 percent of member countries; 50 countries have agreed to participate in the Article IV pilot project on the publication of its consultation reports; and letters of intent are being released for about 80 percent of requests for fund resources or reviews of programs. Member governments should make a great effort, however, to guard against using the publicity of reports to justify a lack of candor in them. If the publication of IMF reports increasingly means that the reports do not sufficiently address economies' weaknesses, their publication will have undermined rather than strengthened the IMF's role as a provider of reliable information. Of course there is a risk that financial markets may overreact to the weaknesses pointed out in a report, but that risk is well worth taking.

Crisis Management

During times of financial crisis, the IMF already plays and will increasingly need to play three roles: crisis lender ("lender of last resort"), crisis manager, and crisis container for the rest of the international system. From the time the IMF was established, one of its main functions has been "to give confidence to members by making the general resources of the Fund temporarily available to them under adequate safeguards, thus providing them with opportunity to correct maladjustments in their balance of payments without resorting to measures destructive of national or international prosperity."[17] In other words, the IMF is to provide resources to countries facing balance-of-payments problems to avoid the dramatic reductions in standards of living necessary during the classical gold standard era—measures destructive of national prosperity—or the "beggar-thy-neighbor policies" adopted during the interwar period—measures destructive of international prosperity.

When the IMF was established in 1944, its resources were assumed to be sufficient to stabilize any balance-of-payments crisis. In today's world of high capital mobility, however, the IMF's resources are insufficient to achieve its goal. To improve its function as lender of last resort, at the end of 1997 the IMF established the Supplemental Reserve Facility (SRF), which can make short-term loans in large amounts (above usual quota limits) at penalty rates to countries in crisis.[18]

It is important to recognize, however, that even with increased resources, an IMF program can hope to stabilize a balance-of-payments crisis only if it catalyzes the return of private capital flows.[19] This will happen only if financial markets believe the economic package supported by the IMF program is credible—that is, that the reforms it contains are adequate to address the country's weaknesses and that its government is capable of and committed to its implementation. Therefore, the credibility of reforms that are part of an IMF program is crucial to the long-run effectiveness of the institution.

IMF lending can be viewed in game theoretical terms. If member states cooperate, then lending operates on technical grounds, the institution preserves its credibility, it can appropriately fulfill its function, and everybody is better off. However, if some countries start breaching the cooperative agreement to provide politically motivated lending to their preferred countries, every country has an incentive to do the same. Although this may bring some short-term gains to individual member states, it winds up destroying the long-term credibility of the institution's signaling effect, and therefore its ability to mitigate and contain financial crises, which is in nobody's long-term interest.[20] The incentives to use the signaling effect of an IMF program to lure back capital flows has been particularly strong in the 1990s with its myriad financial crises. As a result, noncooperative outcomes have increased over the past decade—most egregiously, but not exclusively, regarding Russia.[21]

In sum, one of the least discussed but most significant weaknesses of the current international financial architecture has nothing to do with the institutions themselves but rather with how they are being used by its larger shareholders. If this change does not take place, however, none of the technical/institutional reforms being put forward have a real chance of improving the actual working of international financial institutions.

The IMF already plays, and increasingly needs to play, the role of crisis manager, a role it assumed during the debt crisis of the 1980s. Under the Brady Plan,[22] IMF financing was not made available to indebted countries until they had reached an agreement with private creditors and a critical mass of financing was available from private banks. This approach was appropriate when the creditors were mainly banks and when the country at stake did not have market access. Currently, a large portion of debt is held by thousands of bondholders, and modifications to bond contracts can only be made by unanimity. This allows a minority of bondholders, for instance, to block a majority-supported restructuring agreement with the borrowing country.[23] As a result, debt workout processes are exceedingly ad-hoc, time-consuming, and costly to both creditors and debtors.

Over the 1990s, there has been an increasing recognition that the absence of appropriate tools for efficient debt workouts was as a problem, and the 2001 Argentina crisis has made the issue particularly pressing. Moreover, bailing in the private sector is essential to minimize moral hazard and reduce the burden on public budgets of highly regressive bailout packages.[24] A number of proposals to address this shortcoming have recently been put forward. The most ambitious and soundest plan has been proposed by IMF first deputy managing director Anne Krueger (2002).[25] Krueger's plan closely mirrors the features of domestic bankruptcy proceedings in private sector insolvencies for sovereign debtors. It calls for the creation of an international legal framework on sovereign bonds that would allow a qualified majority of a sovereign's creditors to approve a restructuring agreement and make the decision binding on the minority. This provision would be accompanied by three other features: a stay on creditor litigation after the suspension of payments, mechanisms to protect creditor interests during the stay, and the provision of seniority for fresh financing by private credit. The whole process would be overseen by the IMF.[26]

Other proposals focus on reforms to encourage debt rollovers. Willem Buiter and Anne Sibert have proposed that a clause providing for a universal debt rollover option with penalty be added to all foreign-currency denominated loans and credits.[27] Richard Haas and Robert Litan have suggested that IMF programs should require creditors in foreign currency to automatically suffer some loss of their principal when their debt matures and is not rolled over or extended. They argue that this approach would have the double virtue of discouraging sudden outflows of maturing debt when countries can least afford it and of leading to higher interest rates for borrowers with opaque or poorly capitalized balance sheets, which would better reflect the risk of not getting repaid.[28]

Stanley Fischer, on the other hand, argues that such radical reforms would have the opposite effect from what they intend. In his view, a formalization of the requirement that banks or any sort of creditors would always be forced to share in the financing of IMF programs would be destabilizing to the international system, since "creditors would have a greater incentive to rush for the exits at the mere hint of a crisis."[29] Fischer, instead, echoes a report issued by the G-10 in the wake of the 1994–1995 Mexican crisis, which proposed that bond contracts should be modified to make it easier to reschedule payments. Majority voting and clauses on collective representation, Fischer argues, would greatly facilitate decisionmaking in the event of a crisis, but they should be introduced by bond-issuers on a voluntary basis.

The position of George W. Bush's administration seems closest to Fischer's. The administration proposes "a market-oriented approach" to the sovereign debt-restructuring process, according to which new contingency clauses would be incorporated into debt contracts on a voluntary basis. These clauses would include supermajority decisionmaking by creditors (to replace unanimity), a process by which a sovereign would initiate a restructuring or rescheduling, including a standstill period, and a description of how creditors would engage with borrowers.[30] An intermediary position between that of Anne Krueger and the Bush administration is that of Barry Eichengreen, who proposes that because no country would be willing to be the first to take these measures, the IMF could play a role in coordinating their introduction in emerging market countries.[31]

In April 2002, the Group of Seven adopted a twin-track approach to sovereign debt restructuring. The first track goes along the lines of the Bush-Fischer proposal of encouraging the introduction of contingency clauses in new debt contracts. The second track follows Anne Krueger's plan of considering "approaches to sovereign debt restructuring that may require new international treaties, changes in national legislation or amendments to the articles of agreement of the IMF." Although this decision has been hailed as "genuine progress,"[32] it falls well short both of Krueger's plan and of what is needed. As long as it is up to individual countries to decide on a decentralized manner to start introducing these clauses, the reputational risk of being perceived by financial markets as looking for easy ways to default would be too great and the ensuing increases in borrowing costs too hefty. Therefore, I would tend to agree with Fred Bergsten that "I can't see countries leaping forth to sign up for this."[33] The role of an international institution in coordinating the introduction of contingency clauses and ensuring a common deal across legal systems is essential.[34] Unless the second track of the G-7 plan gels around an international legal framework along the lines described by Anne Krueger, progress in making sovereign debt workouts more manageable is highly unlikely.

Crisis Containment

The third function the IMF plays once crises unravel is that of crisis containment. It is precisely on this function that the new contingent credit lines (CCLs) introduced in April 1999 are predicated. Financing under this facility is available under the principle of lender of last resort, namely, as short-term loans available at penalty rates (though lower than under the SRF). The goal of these credit lines is to supplement the reserves of countries "that are not at risk of an external payments crisis of their own making, but may be vulnerable to contagion."[35] For a country to be eligible for access to a CCL, it must (1) follow sound economic and financial policies; (2) be making progress toward adherence to internationally accepted standards (including subscription to the IMF's SDDS; compliance with the Basle Core Principles of Banking Supervision, the IMF-designed code on fiscal transparency; and use of the IMF-designed code on transparency in monetary and financial policies); (3) have constructive relations with private creditors; and (4) have an IMF-endorsed macroeconomic and structural program.[36] Countries would prequalify for assistance and a significant amount of the credit line would be available automatically, with the remainder of the CCL becoming available subject to certain conditions. The fact that a significant amount would be available immediately and without conditions would speed up the process and increase the effectiveness of the mechanism.

One problem with the contingent credit lines, however, is that downgrading (dequalifying a member country with previously "good" policies) could itself set off a crisis. This is why a better option would be lending at higher rates to countries that are less qualified, and at lower rates to more qualified countries, along a qualification continuum. For the system to discourage contagion, the country classification provided by the IMF would need to be viewed as credible by financial markets. Once again, therefore, credibility is crucial.

Long-Term Lending

Since the debt crisis of the 1980s, the IMF has increasingly played a role in long-term lending for structural adjustment purposes. The Latin American countries that went to the IMF for help in the 1980s did not have just short-term balance-of-payments problems; rather, they needed to overhaul their whole development strategy. IMF conditionality changed accordingly. Until the debt crisis, conditionality had focused on limits on domestic or bank financing of budget deficits, growth in money supply targets, and floors on foreign exchange reserves, which are the types of variables that ought to be monitored when aiming at the restoration of macroeconomic stability in the midst of a short-term balance-of-payments crisis. In the 1980s and 1990s, however, conditionality became more focused on achieving long-term growth and thus featured budget deficit targets and structural issues such as privatization, trade liberalization, and tax and civil service reforms.

Except for tax reform, however, the IMF never developed sufficient expertise to deal efficiently in these issue areas, which are areas of expertise of the World Bank. Given these constraints, U.S. Treasury secretary Lawrence Summers proposed in late 1999 that the international financial institutions return to their original goals: The IMF should focus on balance-of-payments crises and short-term macroeconomic stabilization lending, and the World Bank should work on structural adjustment and long-term development issues. This has been increasingly the case for the fund. The IMF has again become more focused on its traditional core areas of macroeconomic policies, structural reforms in related areas (such as exchange rate and tax policy), fiscal management and transparency, and tax and customs administration.[37]

Two other changes in the IMF's long-term lending policy are its increased poverty focus and bottom-up approach. The IMF's long-term lending has—like the World Bank's—become more explicitly aimed at poverty reduction. As a consequence, the fund's former long-term, concessional lending facility ESAF (Enhanced Structural Adjustment Facility) has been replaced by the Poverty Reduction and Growth Facility (PRGF). The new facility has a clear mandate to integrate the objectives of poverty reduction and growth generation in low-income countries. A key implication of this new poverty-reduction focus is that although traditional macroeconomic constraints need to continue to be taken into account, macroeconomic frameworks should also reflect the financing needs of poverty-reduction strategies developed by member countries. This implies the setting of poverty-reduction targets and indicators, an elaboration and costing of sectoral and other strategies to achieve these goals, and, to the extent possible, the elaboration of a macroeconomic framework reflecting the resulting financing needs.[38]

It is the World Bank, however, that has the staff and the technical expertise to develop and cost sectoral strategies together with client countries. The IMF, therefore, should work closely with the World Bank to ensure that the macroeconomic frameworks of client countries reflect the financing needs of their poverty-reduction strategies. Achieving this result will entail much-improved coordination in-country between statistical agencies, line ministries, finance ministries, and central banks and, in Washington, between the IMF and the World Bank. Unless this improved cooperation is achieved, the "bottom-up" approach to macroeconomic frameworks will remain in the realm of intentions.

The Role of the World Bank: Knowledge, Participation, and Conditionality

This section argues that the World Bank of the twenty-first century should focus on policy-based lending, particularly structural and sectoral adjustment reform, based on strong, credible conditionality. Its main goal should be to strengthen the hand of reformers in countries that are moving in the right direction but do not yet have access to international capital markets. The Bank should also focus its training and technical assistance on strong performers. Strengthening institutional capacity by spreading technical knowledge among policymaking elites and civil servants works when there is a will to reform; when that will is absent, however, knowing the right policies and implementation techniques is not enough.

Fostering Knowledge and Education

There is a strong case for arguing that a key role of the World Bank in the future should be to provide development knowledge.[39] The most enthusiastic advocates of the "knowledge bank" argue that because development knowledge has implications for the global public good, there is a rationale for coordinating international resources to fund its provision.[40] Moreover, because linking global and local knowledge is key to its relevance to development and because there are important synergies to "bundling" development research and development lending, the World Bank is uniquely well placed for focusing on the creation and diffusion of development knowledge. However, fostering development is about much more than addressing lack of knowledge and weak capacity for implementation—it is about incentives and politics. As Joseph Stiglitz observes: "Successful development requires not only addressing these technical issues, but a transformation that puts educational and political development at its center. . . . The focus of the Bank will be on capacity-building and consensus-building: helping the country develop the capacity (including think tanks and research institutions) to formulate its own development strategy and democratic institutions to arrive at a national consensus about those strategies."[41]

Stiglitz makes two different points. The first is that development is partially a problem of lack of capacity, of knowledge. The second point, however, is that reaching a national consensus on development policies that work is not only a technical but also a political issue, one that requires an educated population and democratic institutions. Indeed, lack of progress in development is not caused mainly by lack of knowledge about the right policies to implement, but by lack of incentives and political will on the part of governing elites to implement good policies. When the policymaking process is not democratic and the distribution of power in a society is very unequal—as is often the case in developing countries—the political system is captured by elites who knowingly implement economic policies that redistribute income in their favor but that are both antipoor and inimical to economic development. These policies—whether they be a bloated civil service that employs the upper-middle classes without providing needed services, marketing boards that bleed the rural poor in Africa, or commercial protection favoring the urban middle classes in Latin America—can hardly be changed by narrowing the so-called knowledge gap or by ensuring the spread of scientific reasoning.

The single best policy the World Bank can implement to address this problem and thereby encourage economic development, an equitable distribution of income, and political democratization, is to foster education. Indeed, education, particularly at the primary and secondary levels, is the type of public expenditure with the highest social returns, and an educated population is one of the best antidotes to rent-seeking behavior by governing elites. Moreover, the distribution of educational assets is a key factor in determining income distribution. The highly unequal distribution of education in Latin America has been found to be the main reason why the region's income inequality is so much higher than East Asia's.[42] Finally, and perhaps most importantly, in the long run fostering education is key to developing conditionality from below. Indeed, the most efficient and legitimate way to hold governments accountable for the quality of their policies is the control exercised by their own citizens, an ability that is strongly contingent on the population's educational level. Therefore, encouraging adequate levels of equitable and efficient education expenditure and well-designed educational sector policies should remain at the core of the World Bank's role as a development lender.

Increasing Participation and Building Conditionality in Low-Income Countries

As the second part of Stiglitz's statement acknowledges, economic policy is a highly political issue. Ensuring the implementation of policies favorable to economic development requires taking into account the interests of the majority of the population, which is most efficiently done through democratic political processes. The current president of the World Bank has often emphasized the importance of democracy for economic development.[43] But should the World Bank address such thorny issues as political democracy? And if so, how? It is hard to imagine having World Bank funding depend on overt political conditionality; most member states would probably refuse to allow such interference in their internal affairs.

The recent emphasis of the World Bank on fostering participatory processes in its programs, however, is one good way to maximize the input of civil society in World Bank programs in nondemocratic and democratic societies alike. The World Bank has increasingly incorporated the participation of local communities in the selection, design, and execution of its projects, recognizing the positive impact of community involvement on project costs, relevance, and sustainability, as well as the importance of the psychological effect of participation on the "empowerment" of poor people. At a macro level, countries benefiting from debt relief provided under the Highly Indebted Poor Countries (HIPC) Initiative are required to elaborate a poverty-reduction strategy in a participatory manner. This requirement has led to a "process revolution" in the approach of the World Bank to lending—conditionality is now supposed to come not from "above" (i.e., the World Bank), but from "below" (from communities participating in the elaboration of poverty-reduction strategies).[44] In Latin America, where civil society is already highly active and well-organized, this participatory approach can also have the effect of further strengthening and leveraging the influence of nongovernmental and community-based organizations as well as other civil society organizations, fostering the formation of pro-poor coalitions, and bolstering democratic practices.

The Continuing Role of Conditionality for Middle-Income Countries

With increasing capital mobility, there is decreasing rationale for the World Bank to fund specific projects, particularly in middle-income countries. In these countries, projects that are worth financing should be able to find funds in international capital markets. The World Bank should thus wind down its role as a provider of financing for projects and instead focus its resources on fostering the adoption of good development and poverty-reducing policies through program and sectoral lending based on conditionality. Indeed, one of the most important roles played by international financial institutions to this day is strengthening the hand of reformers by providing them with financing and a seal of approval for their programs. A centerpiece of this process is conditionality.

Conditionality, however, has been criticized on several grounds.[45] First, some argue that it poses a problem of inconsistency in timing, in that countries may agree to reforms to get funding and then renege on them. This problem is easily solved, however, by lengthening the duration of programs and backloading disbursements—that is, making payments later in the life of the program. Moreover, if reforms are viewed as necessary by private capital markets, rolling them back will reduce capital market access. Also, after reforms have been in place for some time, it becomes much harder to roll them back, particularly in the case of "second generation" reforms such as the introduction of a value-added tax or a reduction in the number of civil servants.

Second, it is argued that a break-off in lending does not occur very often and, thus, the threat of it lacks credibility. It is true that there is a culture of lending at the Bank, and a similar ethos exists at the IMF, according to which individuals and departments are rewarded if programs are successful, in the misleading sense of "not interrupted." This situation, together with the increasing politicization of lending, puts enormous pressure on staff to continue with programs even when objective conditions would advise otherwise. The solution, however, is strengthening—not weakening or phasing out—conditionality. If the IMF and the World Bank's seal of approval for borrowing countries' economic policies is to be credible, conditionality must be viewed as appropriate and lending decisions as technical. This in turn requires a credible break-off threat if conditionality is not satisfactorily fulfilled.

Paul Collier and Jan Willem Gunning question the timing of lending imposed by conditionality. They argue that, currently, aid flows rapidly in the early stages of policy reform and tapers out as policy improves. In effect, "donors are targeting their aid flows on poor policy environments in the hope of inducing reform, withdrawing aid once policy reaches a satisfactory level."[46] And why not? Indeed, the World Bank should focus its aid on countries that, although they cannot yet borrow freely from capital markets, are making a sustained and serious attempt at reform. A tapering-in of aid at that point is key to strengthening the hand of reformers within that country, providing the needed technical assistance just when policymakers are actually ready to listen, and signaling to other official donors and to financial markets that the country in case is a serious reformer. Once policies and institutions reach a satisfactory level, aid *should* taper out as the country gains access to private capital flows as has been the case in Chile.

As an alternative to conditionality, Christopher Gilbert, Andrew Powell, and David Vines argue that "in countries with good growth experience and a favorable policy environment, the Bank will lend more heavily . . . [whereas] countries with poorer policy environments will receive proportionately more advice."[47] What they propose, then, is classifying countries as "good performers" and "bad performers" and focusing lending on the first and technical assistance and training on the second. This means, however, particularly for middle-income countries, that the Bank should focus on lending to countries that do not need its money—middle-income countries with good growth experience and a favorable policy environment already have access to private capital markets—and direct its policy advice to countries that are in no position to listen. Moreover, calling governments "good" or "bad" is not useful. On the one hand, doing so would have the perverse consequence of leaving completely in the cold some of the world's poorest countries, which may be making reasonable progress but do not yet qualify as having "good growth experience and a favorable policy environment."[48] On the other hand, it would not allow the punishment of good performers who backtrack until too late in the game, when they finally slip into the category of "bad" countries.

In my view, it is crucial for international financial institutions to focus on program- and sector-based lending, with strengthened conditionality, so that they can best perform their role as catalysts for reform in borrowing countries and providers of a credible seal of approval for reforming governments in world financial markets, as well as vis-à-vis bilateral donors. Programmatic lending, however, should not be used as a supplement to IMF lending in balance-of-payments crises, since the type of long-term programs and reforms it aims to support are intrinsically at odds with the fast-disbursing schedules imposed by crises.[49] Moreover, there is a danger that if World Bank lending becomes increasingly focused on supporting middle-income countries during balance-of-payments crises (as was the case in Latin America in the 1990s), borrowing by low-income countries will be crowded out.

Conclusion: The Implications for Latin America

The international financial institutions have a crucial role to play in sustaining and deepening the structural adjustment reforms that were initiated in Latin America after the debt crisis of the 1980s. In the case of good performers such as Chile and Mexico, the World Bank should be progressively less involved in lending as these countries become able to borrow in international financial markets. The World Bank, however, may continue to be involved in sectoral programs, particularly in the areas of education, health, and poverty alleviation, where the need for a fair amount of reforms remains. The Bank should also liberally assist these countries with capacity-building assistance when needed. Finally, it is key that neither institution be misused for political purposes by their largest shareholders. If these institutions came to be perceived as aiming to rescue investors from rich countries and to support the foreign policy objectives of their large shareholders instead of fostering global growth, development, and poverty-reduction, their credibility would be destroyed.[50]

The IMF should prod good performers to increase the transparency and availability of their public- and private-sector financial data and to adopt and abide by international standards in accounting practices, banking regulation and supervision, and other related areas. The strengthening of banking and financial-sector regulation is vital for Latin America because the region of the world with the highest level of income inequality can hardly allow itself to indulge in the most regressive type of government expenditure—financial bailout packages. The IMF should also be more forthcoming in encouraging Latin American countries with weak financial systems—the large majority—to be cautious in the sequencing of capital account liberalization, and it ought to recommend the adoption of taxes on short-term capital inflows to countries that wish to proceed with capital account liberalization despite weak banking systems. The strengthened presence of the IMF as crisis lender, crisis manager, and crisis container will also help reduce the risk and alleviate the costs of financial crises in Latin America when they do occur. It will continue to provide a much-needed safety net in this world of high capital mobility and volatile capital flows.

In the case of poorer performers, such as Ecuador, Venezuela, or Haiti, the World Bank and the IMF should get involved only when the government is willing to implement a critical mass of economic reforms. In these cases, the Bank should focus on structural and sectoral adjustment lending. Training and technical assistance should equally be provided only when there is enough will to reform, lest the advice fall on deaf ears. The IMF is likely to become involved with poor performers when their policies eventually cause a serious crisis and the will to reform steadies. It should be wary, however, of intervening to rescue poor reformers, even if they are considered too large to fail, such as Brazil and, more recently, Argentina, unless their reform efforts are deemed sufficient to address their economies' underlying weaknesses.

Although financial crises will continue to hit the region in the coming years, the frequency of crises and the ability of governments to weather them will vary significantly between good and poor perform-ers. As the contrast between the 1994–1995 Mexican peso crisis and the 2001–2002 Argentine crisis shows, financial market volatility can be weathered and growth restored relatively quickly with internation-al support in countries with fundamentally sound macroeconomic policies—as was the case of Mexico in 1994. On the other hand, coun-tries with important macroeconomic disequilibria—like Argentina with its budget deficit, unsustainable peg, and rigid labor market—will find it much harder both to summon support from international financial insti-tutions or bilateral donors like the United States and to restore growth.

What are the key reforms that the international financial institutions will be fostering in the Latin America of the twenty-first century? For poor reformers, the emphasis will be on the adoption of first-generation reforms, or what has become known as the "Washington consensus." These countries will be encouraged to deregulate their economies, pri-vatize, liberalize trade, and achieve macroeconomic stabilization. As many now acknowledge, however, these reforms are necessary but insufficient for sustained and equitable economic development. A liber-al economy, low budget deficits, and low inflation can indeed coexist with an unchanging comparative advantage in raw materials and agri-cultural products that yields highly unstable growth, an unequal distri-bution of income, and little progress on economic development or poverty reduction.

As the World Bank has increasingly emphasized, economic devel-opment and poverty reduction also require a second generation of reforms. These include strengthening the rule of law and institution-building and focusing the role of the state on the provision of education, health services, infrastructure, and social safety nets. Although most Latin American countries have made a great deal of progress in the implementation of first-generation reforms, they still have a long way to go in implementing second-generation reforms. Among these reforms, Latin American countries crucially need a sufficiently high tax-to-GDP ratio to provide resources for much-needed public expendi-ture (particularly in some of the region's poorest countries such as Guatemala); tax reforms that shift the weight from regressive indirect taxes toward direct taxation; civil service reforms that reduce the weight of the wage bill on the budget; higher and more efficient expen-diture on education, particularly at the primary and secondary levels; more and better expenditure on health care, mainly on preventive health care and primary health assistance in rural areas; and stronger, better-designed, and more focused social safety nets for the transitionally vulnerable and poverty-alleviation programs for the chronically poor. These reforms, together with strengthened rule of law and institutional capacity, are the key to sustaining and deepening Latin America's economic reforms. Moreover, the "process revolution" of increased participation in the elaboration of poverty-reduction strategies needs to result in a "content revolution" (i.e., to result in more pro-poor policies and outcomes). Unless this second generation of reforms is forcefully implemented, Latin American countries will continue to depend heavily on their traditional primary-sector products, with all of the attending consequences. Unstable growth, a highly inequitable distribution of the product of growth, and a sense that current policies are not yielding the expected results in terms of economic development or poverty reduction could well conspire to produce a rollback of the market-oriented reforms that were so hard to implement. International financial institutions can and should play a fundamental role in avoiding this scenario.

Notes

1. Although the Inter-American Development Bank plays an important role in multilateral lending and development policy in the region, its rationale as a regional development bank places it outside the scope of this chapter.
2. Joseph Stiglitz, "The World Bank at the Millennium," *Economic Journal* 109, no. 459 (November 1999): F584.
3. As Lipset argued and Barro has shown empirically, there is a strong positive correlation between economic prosperity and democratization. Seymour M. Lipset, "Some Social Requisites of Democracy: Economic Development and Political Legitimacy," *American Political Science Review* 53, no. 1 (March 1959): 69–105; Robert J. Barro, *Determinants of Economic Growth* (Cambridge: MIT Press, 1998).
4. Although international financial institutions have traditionally directed their advice to developing countries, they are increasingly speaking out against developed country protectionism. On the IMF management's criticism of the new U.S. farm bill and tariffs on steel imports, see "IMF's Deputy Head Criticises US Tariffs on Steel Imports," *Financial Times*, 15 May 2002, 2; and Horst Köhler, "The Monterrey Consensus and Beyond: Moving from Vision to Action," introductory remarks at the International Conference on Financing for Development, Monterrey, Mexico, 21 March 2002, available at: [www.imf.org]. On the potentially highly disruptive effect of U.S. protectionism on the international liberal economy, see Susan A. Aaronson, "George W. Bush, Protectionist," *The International Economy* 14, no. 1 (Winter 2002): 54–62.

5. One can look at bailout packages as retroactive subsidies to overly risky investment by domestic business and banking elites and foreign investors.

6. See, for instance, C. David Finch, "Cry for Argentina," *The International Economy* 16, no. 2 (Spring 2002): 26–28; and Martin Feldstein, "Argentina's Fall," *Foreign Affairs* 81, no. 2 (March/April 2002): 8–14.

7. See an interview with Anne Krueger, first deputy managing director of the IMF, in Alan Beattie, "Top Lieutenant Allays Fears over Her Role After Baptism of Fire," *Financial Times*, 20 April 2002, 8.

8. As of May 2002, there were 50 subscribers. See [http://dsbb.imf.org].

9. These areas are data, fiscal transparency, monetary and financial transparency, banking supervision, securities, insurance, payments systems, corporate governance, accounting, auditing and insolvency, and creditor rights.

10. The Code of Good Practices on Fiscal Transparency and the Code on the Transparency of Monetary and Financial Policies are available at: [www.imf.org].

11. For instance, in the banking area, the Basle Committee on Banking Supervision has developed "Core Principles for Effective Banking Supervision," which serve as a basic reference and minimum standard for supervisory authorities. In the area of securities, the IMF has recognized the "Objectives and Principles of Securities Regulation" developed by the International Organization of Securities Commission to improve securities market regulation and disclosure standards. In accounting, the IMF-recognized standards are those of the International Accounting Standards Committee, which are aimed at achieving uniformity in international accounting practices, while, in auditing, the standards are those established by the International Federation of Accountants. There is also a World Bank–led initiative to harmonize domestic bankruptcy laws and, in the area of corporate governance, the Organization for Economic Cooperation and Development (OECD) has developed a set of principles of corporate governance.

12. Reports on the Observance of Standards and Codes can be found at: [www.imf.org].

13. International Monetary Fund, *IMF Survey* 28 (supplement, September 1999): 4.

14. Ibid.

15. See Barry Eichengreen, *Toward a New International Financial Architecture* (Washington, D.C.: Institute for International Economics, 1999), 51–55.

16. Article IV of the IMF's *Articles of Agreement* outlines the organization's member countries' obligations regarding exchange arrangements, the purpose being to facilitate global financial and economic stability. The *Articles of Agreement* were adopted at the United Nations Monetary and Financial Conference, Bretton Woods, New Hampshire, 22 July 1944; they entered into force 27 December 1945. The IMF Articles of Agreement can be accessed at: [www.imf.org].

17. "Article IV: Obligations Regarding Exchange Arrangements," *Articles of Agreement.*

18. SRF loans have been made to Korea, Russia, Brazil, and Argentina.

19. There is empirical evidence that IMF programs do tend to have this effect. Nadeem Ul Haque and Mohsin S. Khan, "Do IMF-Supported Programs Work? A Survey of the Cross-Country Empirical Evidence," IMF Institute Working Paper Series 98/169 (Washington, D.C.: IMF Institute, December 1998).

20. There is some empirical evidence that financial markets can distinguish between "good" and "bad" IMF programs. A recent study finds that IMF programs enhance market access for borrowers with "intermediate" credit, presumably due to the additional commitments that the program entails. The study also finds, however, that this effect is not found for either borrowers with very poor credit—where politically motivated lending would fall—or borrowers with very good credit—who are presumably able to commit to reform in the absence of IMF programs. Barry J. Eichengreen and Ashoka Mody, "Bail-Ins, Bailouts, and Borrowing Costs," *IMF Staff Papers* 47, Special Issue, IMF Annual Research Conference (2001): 157.

21. It is understandable that countries may wish to lend for political-military reasons. This lending, however, should take place either as bilateral aid or as multilateral aid, but outside the framework of the international financial institutions. Using these institutions for politically motivated lending risks ruining their technical reputation and preventing them from playing their intended role in the long run.

22. The plan was put forth by U.S. Treasury secretary Nicholas Brady to deal with the Latin American debt crisis. Previous proposals (like the Baker Plan) had only granted debt rescheduling while the Brady Plan acknowledged the need for debt relief. The Brady Plan proposed exchanging old debt for new long-term debt with a lower face value. Conversion ratios and the exact characteristics of the new debt instruments were to be negotiated on a case-by-case basis between debtor countries and their creditors.

23. Even worse, so-called vulture funds routinely take advantage of this situation by buying discounted debt of troubled companies and then suing for full repayment. This situation also affects sovereign debt, with highly indebted poor countries having had to pay the vulture funds in full to avoid being taken to court by them. See Rosemary Bennet, "Chancellor Plans Treasury Crackdown on 'Vulture Funds,'" *Financial Times*, 6 May 2002, 2.

24. For an opposing view, see Steven Hanke, "The Great Argentine Train Robbery," *The International Economy* 16, no. 2 (Spring 2002): 18–21.

25. Anne Krueger, *A New Approach to Sovereign Debt Restructuring* (Washington, D.C.: International Monetary Fund, 2002).

26. Two similar but less ambitious proposals, including a "broker" role for the IMF, had been put forth by Jeffrey Sachs and Martin Feldstein. Sachs proposes to have the IMF take as its new model the bankruptcy court as it functions under chapter 11 of the U.S. bankruptcy code. In cases of sovereign debt, Sachs argues, the main function of the IMF should be "to provide a forum to which all of a country's creditors are brought for a comprehensive, across the board settlement." Jeffrey Sachs, "Beyond Bretton Woods: A New Blueprint," *The Economist*, 1 October 1994, 27. Martin Feldstein also proposes that the

IMF should act as an "honest broker—or a convener or a deal maker—between debtors and creditors." In Feldstein's view, however, this should be the IMF's main role, rather than lending, which he opposes on the grounds of moral hazard. Martin Feldstein, "No New Architecture," *The International Economy* 13, no. 5 (September–October 1999): 32–35.

27. Willem H. Buiter and Anne Sibert, "UDROP: A Small Contribution to the New International Financial Architecture," CEPR Discussion Paper 2138 (London: Centre for Economic Policy Research, 1999).

28. Richard Haas and Robert Litan, "Globalization and Its Discontents," *Foreign Affairs* 77, no. 3 (May–June 1998): 2–6.

29. Stanley Fischer, "IMF as Lender of Last Resort," *Central Banking* 9 (February 1999): 34–35.

30. Martin Wolf, "Debt to the World," *Financial Times*, 24 April 2002, 16.

31. Eichengreen, *Toward a New International Financial Architecture*, 15–16.

32. Wolf, "Debt to the World."

33. Alan Beattie and Raymond Colitt, "US Scorns IMF Plan for Bankrupt Governments," *Financial Times*, 6 April 2002, 7.

34. Another IMF decision goes in the direction indicated by Fischer and Eichengreen. The IMF has decided to lend to countries that are in payment arrears to private creditors holding securitized debt, provided that they pursue appropriate policies and make good faith efforts to cooperate with the creditors. This reform is designed to force private lenders to be more willing to negotiate favorable terms during debt workouts.

35. *The IMF's Contingent Credit Lines: A Factsheet* (Washington, D.C.: International Monetary Fund, June 2001), available at: [www.imf.org].

36. An interesting characteristic of the CCLs is the IMF's implicit recognition that a country may have solid practices on transparency and follow good macroeconomic and financial policies and yet be unable to resist contagion from unstable international capital markets.

37. *The IMF's Poverty Reduction and Growth Facility (PRGF): A Factsheet* (Washington, D.C.: International Monetary Fund, March 2001), available at: [www.imf.org].

38. Traditionally, macroeconomic frameworks have been elaborated with a top-down macroeconomic approach, to achieve specific growth, inflation, and balance-of-payments objectives. Overall resource envelopes have been taken as given and funds are allocated to various ministries according to historical criteria rather than reflecting sectoral strategies and their financing needs.

39. See, for example, James Wolfensohn's 1996 address at the annual meetings of the World Bank and IMF, Washington, D.C., 1 October 1996, available at: [www.worldbank.org]; and World Bank, *The 1998 World Development Report: Knowledge for Development* (Washington, D.C.: World Bank, 1998).

40. See Inge Kaul, Isabelle Grunberg, and Marc Stern, eds., *Global Public Goods: International Cooperation in the 21st Century* (New York and Oxford: Oxford University Press [for the United Nations Development Programme], 1999); in particular, Joseph Stiglitz, "Knowledge as a Global Public Good," 308–326.

41. Stiglitz, "World Bank at the Millennium," 587, 591.

42. Juan Luis Londoño and Miguel Székely, *Distributional Surprises After a Decade of Reforms: Latin America in the Nineties* (Washington, D.C.: Inter-American Development Bank, 1997).

43. See, for example, James D. Wolfensohn, "Coalitions for Change" (president's address to the board of governors, World Bank Group, Washington, D.C., 28 September 1999), available at: [www.worldbank.org].

44. HIPC countries in Latin America comprise Bolivia, Guyana, Honduras, and Nicaragua. Bolivia led perhaps the most impressive participatory process, which built on an already-existing national dialogue. Through this participatory process, a comprehensive poverty-reduction strategy was elaborated and is now in the process of being implemented in a decentralized manner, with 70 percent of resources being executed at the municipal level.

45. Paul Collier and Jan Willem Gunning, "The IMF's Role in Structural Adjustment," *Economic Journal* 109, no. 459 (November 1999): F634–F651.

46. Ibid., F646. Collier and Gunning focus their argument on the IMF, but the rationale is the same for World Bank lending.

47. Christopher Gilbert, Andrew Powell, and David Vines, "Positioning the World Bank," *Economic Journal* 109, no. 459 (November 1999): F631.

48. Ibid.

49. There is also empirical evidence that World Bank lending does not have a positive effect on private lending, thus suggesting that it cannot usefully play the role of catalyst for the return of other capital flows during balance-of-payments crises. Graham Bird and Dane Rowlands, "World Bank Lending and Other Financial Flows: Is There a Connection?" *Journal of Development Studies* 37, no. 5 (June 2001): 83–103; and Dani Rodrik, "Why Is There Multilateral Lending?" (paper presented at the Annual World Bank Conference on Development Economics, World Bank, Washington, D.C., 1996).

50. To preserve a modicum of independence for both institutions, it is key that they be as financially autonomous as feasible. The recent proposal of U.S. Treasury secretary Paul O'Neill of making World Bank financing depend on grants would be highly deleterious to this objective, as it would make the World Bank dependent on U.S. congressional decisions for its very operation.

7

Human Rights and the Role of International Actors

Alison Brysk

As we enter a new millennium, the citizens of Latin America have ample grounds for both hope and despair. Hope, because the past century has brought a revolution in living conditions, democratic political systems, and the potential for self-determination. Despair, because progress in each area has been thwarted by inequalities of rights and resources. What role can international actors play in securing human rights in Latin America in the twenty-first century? What are the emerging sources of threat to human rights? And how do these changes in Latin America fit into an emerging system of global politics?

Human Rights: The New Consensus and Challenge

Human rights is an idea whose time has come. As the concept has developed since World War II, human rights means that no individual— regardless of identity, condition, or behavior—may be deprived of life, liberty, or physical integrity by state agents without due process of law, and that some forms of coercion (such as torture) are absolutely illegitimate.[1] By the waning years of the twentieth century, the notion of universal rights had become a global political referent.[2] Although widespread violations of fundamental human dignity continue and even diversify, the vocabulary of human rights is invoked to legitimize the exercise of power at all levels, from popular mobilization to regime legitimacy to international intervention.

This is especially true in the Western Hemisphere, where military authoritarianism robbed a continent of a generation of its citizens, frac-

141

tured fragile institutions of law and state accountability, distorted development models, and extorted substantial portions of the national patrimony. In the last two decades of the twentieth century, Latin American states mounted a variety of responses to these losses, among them domestic human rights trials of military rulers in Argentina, "truth commissions" in Chile and El Salvador, and police and judicial reform in Bolivia and Brazil. The Latin American experience helped stimulate the emergence of an international human rights regime, including the founding of a United Nations Working Group on Forced Disappearance and a dense regional network of nongovernmental organizations (NGOs) such as the Washington Office on Latin America. The region's highest institutional expression—the Organization of American States (OAS)—pledged to defend democracy throughout the hemisphere in 1991, endorsed an international convention on forced disappearance in 1994, and issued judgments of state accountability for human rights abuse against many of its own members through the Inter-American Human Rights Court. Most Latin Americans now seek human rights— not revolution—as redress for social wrongs. From voting booths in Mexico to courtrooms in Santiago, the dominant political program of the citizens of Latin America is to defend and extend their rights.

However, the third wave of democratization and its new norms and reforms have not resolved human rights problems in Latin America. Although incidences of state-sponsored massacres, assassinations, disappearances, and torture are much reduced, they have not been eradicated. Torture is still a regular feature of the Mexican judicial system, and thousands of Colombians are killed each year by that state's military, military-linked paramilitary gangs, and guerrilla forces. Unrepentant authoritarians still commit assassinations—a bishop in Guatemala and a vice president in Paraguay, for example—as well as kidnappings. In the Andean countries, Brazil, and Central America, recurrent urban protests and rural land takeovers are often met with deadly force and massive illicit detentions. Throughout the region, burgeoning crime and the collapse of policing have led to frequent extrajudicial killings of urban marginals, as well as extortive kidnappings by corrupt police. Amnesty International reports that in 2001, twenty countries in the Americas practiced torture, seven committed extrajudicial executions (481 police killings in São Paulo alone), and four continue to hold prisoners of conscience (Argentina, Cuba, Mexico, and Peru).[3]

In addition to these legacies of authoritarianism and deficits of emerging democracies, new threats have come from international actors and forces. International organizations and campaigns set up to defend political dissidents from state coercion are now challenged to address transnational threats such as border killings of migrants or abuses by private security forces contracted by multinational corporations. U.S. military aid sustains Colombia's bloody anti-insurgency campaign, as well as Mexican and Bolivian counternarcotics initiatives, which generate significant abuses. Even seemingly domestic forms of human rights abuse, such as poor prison conditions and riots (in Venezuela, Colombia, and Brazil), are closely linked to international patterns of economic adjustment. Therefore, the impact on human rights of international actors in Latin America in the twenty-first century must be evaluated, and we must go beyond the twentieth-century assumption that states threaten citizens while international actors rescue them.

Globalization: New Challenges and Opportunities

Who are the international actors and how do they act? Since the late twentieth century, Latin America has entered an era in which international politics is more connected, cosmopolitan, and communications-based. Analysts may debate the level, sources, impact, and even definition of globalization, but it is clear that the pace and weight of interactions across borders have increased.[4] In Latin America, this development has coincided with a general shift away from U.S. hegemony toward a blend of bilateral, multinational, and transnational influences.

Globalization is real, but it is not all one thing—and we must understand the many faces of globalization to analyze their impact on human rights in the hemisphere. The world system comprises shifting relationships among overlapping spheres of interstate, intermarket, and intersociety relations. In the interstate realm, states and some multilateral bodies exercise authority and seek security. In the sphere of markets, profit-seeking firms, individuals, international financial institutions, and sometimes states, engage in exchange motivated by self-interest. In the domain of civil society, religious, epistemic, and ethnic communities build and project identities through the transfer of information (and associated material resources) across borders.[5]

The contradictions within and among these forms of globalization make it a "double-edged sword" for human rights. While Latin America has arguably benefited more than any other region from the globalization of human rights law, institutions, and networks, economic globalization has hurt most Latin American societies.[6] With international support, Latin America has become much more tolerant of political dissidence. Yet the majority of Latin American protest movements are now inspired by opposition to free trade or economic adjustment policies or both; increasingly, those most vulnerable to state repression are what might be called economic dissidents.

The rise of new transnational threats and opportunities for human rights, alongside the traditional struggles of government and opposition, has created what might be called a citizenship gap. In a national political context, the citizenry—ideally—provides accountability for the exercise of state power in formal institutions and the public sphere. However, no comparable citizenry or citizenship role exists in private and transnational interactions with nonstate or multiple actors, even when the state is deeply implicated in the administration of these interactions—hence the citizenship gap.[7]

Thus, alongside the tens of millions of migrants and refugees who lose their rights when they leave their state, hundreds of millions of Latin Americans within their native borders also are people without a state—or "low-intensity citizens."[8] In the liberal worldview, economic exchange both requires and builds political openness, but there have been reversals of democratic trends under market pressures in all of the Andean countries. Even in the more institutionalized but fragile democracies of the Southern Cone and Mexico, the limitations of democratic transitions include ongoing military tutelage, weak judicial guarantees, and local-level enclaves of authoritarianism. Internal refugees often suffer a deflation of citizenship rights—like the estimated two million Colombians displaced by conflict in that country. Furthermore, formal democracy can be systematically overwhelmed by economic disparities that block full citizen participation, which means that important domains of economic decisionmaking are not subject to political control and democratic accountability. The result is a multilevel crisis of governance.

How can international actors close the citizenship gap and address the many layers of human rights violations in Latin America? For interstate interactions, threats to human rights come from state power, policing of borders, and interstate intervention. The pathways of change include construction of (1) international regimes to monitor and pressure states, (2) transnational coalitions to support nationalist resistance to interstate intervention, (3) transborder identities, and (4) state learning. In the economic sphere of international relations, challengers respond to market penetration with dual strategies: They seek greater accountability from multilateral financial institutions, multinational firms, and states, and they attempt to establish identity-based market niches (such as green marketing). As transnational civil sectors assume political roles, social movements also seek to shift the identities, agendas, and legitimacy of global civil society.[9]

International Actors' Responses to Human Rights Violations

Threats to human rights in Latin America today are a product of past, present, and future—the legacies of authoritarianism, barriers to constructing democracies, and distortions produced by globalization. International actors respond differently to each type of problem, and their roles will continue to evolve. Transnational social movements have mushroomed for human rights, environmental preservation, gender equity, and development, and state reform in these areas is more likely when NGOs provide pressure, resources, and policy models.[10] At the interstate level, observers now speak of both an international human rights regime and an inter-American human rights regime, centered in the OAS.[11] Although multilateral financial institutions and multinational corporations may exacerbate social tensions, international pressure points such as protest and consumer campaigns also provide the impetus for transnational social-movement influence.[12] In general, the roles of international actors in promoting human rights can be summarized as monitoring, promoting accountability, transferring resources, establishing institutions both domestic and international, intervening in crises, providing education, waging international campaigns, and promoting citizen empowerment.

Response to Violations Arising from Authoritarianism

The legacies of authoritarianism continue to haunt Latin America. Contrary to the predictions of advocates of reconciliation, the unfinished business of accountability for massive human rights violations will continue to emerge as a political issue for at least another generation. Because most of these violations were state-sponsored, the role of international actors has been to provide information and monitoring, promote the establishment of international norms and institutions, and transfer resources to local NGOs and democratizing governments.

A new role is the use of transnational litigation to promote accountability, as in the case of Pinochet and the prosecution of Argentine military officers under parallel Spanish initiatives. Moreover, the Alien Torts Act has been revived to promote civil suits by U.S.-resident victims against Latin American repressors, with judgments issued against Argentine, Guatemalan, and Chilean military officers. In such cases, transnational coalitions of NGOs generally pressure Northern states to prosecute, a course that may be reinforced by the recent creation of an international criminal court mandating universal jurisdiction for torture, disappearance, and genocide. International pressure may also foster greater domestic accountability—the international prosecution of Pinochet has inspired new cases within Chile, while international aid has underwritten a truth commission in Peru.

Response to Violations
Arising from Incomplete Democratization

Similar international actors play a different set of largely supportive roles in the construction of new democracies. Once again, state action (or negligence) is the main source and target of human rights activity. Many Latin American states lack the trained personnel and legal and physical infrastructure to exercise legitimate coercion in the administration of justice, while others lack the monopoly of force and political will. In the latter scenario, international intervention by the United States and the United Nations has played a useful role in demobilizing abusive militaries and irregular forces and establishing legitimate police in El Salvador, but such intervention has been less successful in Haiti and Nicaragua.

The United States, the United Nations, and foreign NGOs have committed resources to improve the administration of justice throughout the region. International pressure has produced dramatic improvements in selected cases in amenable states, such as the release of Mexico's most well-known political prisoners in response to OAS decisions: two rural environmentalists and a dissident military officer. More structural improvement in legal systems and policing has been highly uneven, however. Brazil has convicted military police for a 1992 prison massacre. Aid programs appear to have improved the administration of justice in Bolivia but have been unavailing in Colombia.

Response to Violations Arising from Globalization

In terms of the interstate dimension of globalization, cross-border human rights violations are generally less severe in Latin America than in other regions with higher levels of interstate military conflict and historically hostile borders, yet Latin Americans do suffer the human rights impact of migration and intervention. The economic disparities and political persecutions that fuel migration will continue well into the future, demonstrating the interdependence of threats to social and civil rights. Hundreds of migrants die each year crossing the U.S.–Mexico border, most of them from causes within the range of state responsibility, from shootings by state agents to persecution in unsafe conditions to exploitation by private border guides; by contrast, 450 Germans were killed fleeing East Germany during the more than 30 years that the Berlin Wall stood. Caribbean refugees in the hundreds suffer similar fates on the high seas. Once they arrive in the United States, many migrants experience illegitimate detention, abusive prison conditions, and denial of health care by government policies and agents. There are similar patterns of persecution of Bolivian migrants in Argentina and the Haitian migrants in the Dominican Republic. In the United States, domestic NGOs monitor and litigate the rights of migrants, but both the target state and large sectors of the host civil society resist their efforts—ever more since the post–September 11 reframing of migration as a security threat.

Direct military intervention and its attendant abuses by the regional hegemon has abated tremendously in Latin America, and it is unlikely that an increasingly isolationist U.S. public will countenance a regular or significant U.S. military presence in Latin America in the future. Furthermore, no extrahemispheric power has the motive or means to intervene. Nevertheless, the United States continues to support indirect and covert interventions in pursuit of "stability" and the management of transnational flows such as drug trafficking. U.S. military aid, equipment, and advisers flow mainly to the Andean region to suppress drug production, processing, and transport. In Colombia (as earlier in Peru), drug interdiction efforts are intermingled with counterinsurgency campaigns. This indirect intervention results in both direct abuses by U.S. advisers and DEA agents and more serious and widespread violations by U.S.–funded and U.S.–advised national forces. These abuses include torture, kidnapping, illegitimate imprisonment, and even murder. Credible reports link the provision of hundreds of millions of dollars in

U.S. aid to Colombian military abuses and bloody paramilitary campaigns, responsible for the majority of the 4,000 Colombian civilians murdered in 2001. Although local, U.S., and transnational NGOs monitor these activities, there is little transnational accountability or multilateral institutionalization in this area.[13] Drug production and trafficking—inspired primarily by market forces—demonstrate another facet of the interdependence between social and political factors, as well as the gap in governance of bilateral relations.

The globalization of market relationships also introduces new direct and indirect threats to human rights, both social and civil. Some of these threats are generated by international actors themselves, such as multinational corporations and multilateral financial institutions (as well as more diffuse market forces), and local civil societies and transnational networks together mobilize and monitor in opposition. As economic globalization takes hold more and more in Latin America, the potential for such abuses will grow, although increasing awareness of the situation may lead to preventive monitoring and restraint by those international economic actors who seek a more stable and educated workforce and improved public relations with consumers.

Some multinational corporations endanger the human rights of their employees and host communities through direct or subcontracted coercive labor suppression; life-threatening health and safety workplace conditions; workplace violations of free speech, assembly, and privacy; and suborning of local authorities. Guatemalan strikers against Del Monte have been assassinated, Colombian peasants kidnapped by oil companies' private security forces, Mexican border communities poisoned, and countless indignities visited on citizens of every other country in Latin America. In Ecuador, children as young as eight toil in the banana plantations of Chiquita, Del Monte, and Dole.[14] Mexican women working in some *maquiladoras* are forced to display menstrual pads to management to prove that they are not pregnant—a discriminatory condition of employment. Cross-border coalitions of human rights and labor groups have secured scattered reforms—such as reinstatement of fired union organizers in Mexico—through monitoring, protests, and appeals to the OAS and International Labour Organization (ILO). However, since some of the most abusive multinational corporations are based in Latin America or Southeast Asia, not in the United States, there are decreased opportunities for transnational accountability for labor rights via antisweatshop campaigns dependent on the threat of consumer boycotts.

In a more structural, indirect sense, multilateral financial institutions and market forces contribute to violations of social rights and threats to civil rights through the imposition of structural adjustment programs. Whether or not such programs are inevitable or ultimately beneficial, structural adjustment schemes and associated measures, such as currency devaluations, have the short-run effect of increasing inequality and unemployment while cutting social services. These deprivations of social rights have systematically increased the numbers and deepened the plight of social marginals, that is, urban shantytown dwellers, rural squatters, street children, and prostitutes. This newly enlarged underclass is subject to various threats to life and liberty, from shantytown police—who shoot to kill—to rural and urban vigilante groups. Police brutality against social marginals is especially pronounced in Argentina, Mexico, Brazil, Venezuela, Haiti, and the Dominican Republic. As Argentina descended into international economic crisis and rising poverty and displacement in 2001, police killed 266 criminal suspects and protesters.[15] In an environment of mounting crime, Latin America's poor and powerless are also increasingly victimized by illicit detentions (often combined with assault or torture) and horrendous prison conditions, exacerbated by overcrowding and high rates of preventive detention. International human rights campaigns have highlighted some especially egregious abuses and secured more state accountability, as was the case, for example, with trials for the massacre of street children in Brazil. But international NGOs have been slow to recognize and to be challenged to monitor these types of victims. Globalization of communications has enabled socially isolated groups such as squatters and prostitutes to form transnational peer networks, which may ultimately increase government responsiveness to their plight.

Finally, we must consider a new class of human rights threats that emanate from civil society and transnational private actors. Journalists in Latin America are being assassinated in record numbers by organized crime groups (often linked to corrupt politicians), especially in Mexico, Argentina, and Colombia. Guerrilla forces in Colombia have been both perpetrators and victims of human rights violations: One guerrilla group abducted an entire church full of civilians during Mass. In response to the epidemic of crime, neighbors have lynched criminal suspects in the Andes, Guatemala, and Mexico. Even some missionaries and development groups have occasionally been associated with abuses in areas that they administer or informally control. The growing underside of globalization is that civil, nonstate, and transnational actors now have an equal opportunity to violate human rights, and neither state nor global governance addresses these threats.

Conclusion

What are the implications of the emergence of a new generation of human rights problems for Latin America? First of all, it is clear that awareness and monitoring have improved far faster than institutions and behavior, and that international actors are more effective at promoting norms than at changing practices. Furthermore, international presence has been most effective for breaking down authoritarianism and least helpful in governing the problems associated with globalization. While discouraging in the short run, this pattern may match the so-called spiral model of human rights improvement noted by Thomas Risse, Stephen Ropp, and Kathryn Sikkink, which would predict further change through strengthened local human rights initiatives. In their model, human rights in Latin America is stuck between the phase of prescriptive status and the phase of rule-consistent behavior.[16] However, their model deals largely with transitions from abusive authoritarian regimes and does not treat emerging forms of human rights abuse that arise from changing social contexts.

The growing link between social and international contexts and abuses of rights of the person suggests that the state and civil society need to play a larger role in balancing market forces. At the same time, Latin American states need to be checked in their ability to violate political rights and strengthened in their ability to provide social rights and public order. Meanwhile, rights-seeking sectors of civil society must be nurtured and transnationalized to meet global threats. A disturbing trend in Latin America is the continuing threat to human rights monitors; in 2001, human rights advocates were assassinated in Colombia, Ecuador, Guatemala, Honduras, Mexico, and Nicaragua.[17] International actors seeking to support human rights must coordinate their activities among themselves and among various policy initiatives, and carefully evaluate the multiple impacts of any given measure on states, markets, and citizens. Aid packages and adjustment plans must also be evaluated for their human rights implications.

Finally, the emerging patterns of rights and repression bespeak a post–Cold War normalization of Latin America in which U.S. hegemony is no longer the sole influence on political outcomes. A broader range of international actors now operates in much the same manner in Latin America as elsewhere, and the citizenship gap created by strong markets and weak states is not a phenomenon restricted to Latin America. This means that the problems of Latin America are becoming more akin to the general problems of global governance—and that lessons and mechanisms that might ameliorate and manage these problems should be transferable beyond the boundaries of historical or cultural zones.

The challenge of securing human rights in Latin America in the new century means that international actors must continue to monitor, pressure, and even intervene in state-based abuses. But international actors must also transfer resources, establish new institutions, and promote the establishment of transnational civil society to govern the problems of globalization. Above all, it means that the new division of labor among actors must be matched by new forms of global decisionmaking and global rights.

Notes

1. Scholars and international organizations generally distinguish three sets of rights: civil and political rights (often labeled "rights of the person" or "rights to personal integrity"), social and economic rights, and "third-generation" collective rights, such as cultural rights. Historical understandings and international commitments concerning these sets of rights developed in this order. Most activists and many states concentrate on the first-generation rights of the person (life and liberty); one reason for this is that these are seen as basic rights that enable the pursuit of the other two kinds.

2. Jack Donnelly, "Human Rights: A New Standard of Civilization?" *International Affairs* 74, no. 1 (1998): 1–24.

3. *Amnesty International 2002 Report* (London: Amnesty International, 2002), available at: [http://www.amnesty.org].

4. David Held, Anthony G. McGrew, David Goldblatt, and Jonathan Perraton, *Global Transformations: Politics, Economics, and Culture* (Stanford: Stanford University Press, 1999).

5. Alison Brysk, *From Tribal Village to Global Village: Indian Rights and International Relations in Latin America* (Stanford: Stanford University Press, 2000), Chap. 1.

6. Alison Brysk, "Globalization: The Double-edged Sword," *NACLA Report on the Americas* 34, no. 1 (July–August 2000): 29–33.

7. Alison Brysk, ed., *Globalization and Human Rights* (Berkeley: University of California Press, 2002).

8. Richard Stahler-Sholk, "El Salvador's Negotiated Transition: From Low-Intensity Conflict to Low-Intensity Democracy," *Journal of Interamerican Studies and World Affairs* 36, no. 4 (Winter 1994): 1–59.

9. Brysk, *From Tribal Village to Global Village.*

10. Margaret Keck and Kathryn Sikkink, *Activists Beyond Borders* (Ithaca: Cornell University Press, 1998).

11. Susan Burgerman, *Moral Victories: How Activists Provoke Multilateral Action* (Ithaca: Cornell University Press, 2001).

12. Jonathan Fox and David L. Brown, *The Struggle for Accountability: The World Bank, NGOs and Grassroots Movements* (Cambridge: MIT Press, 1998).

13. Human Rights Watch, *The "Sixth Division": Military-Paramilitary Ties and U.S. Policy in Colombia* (New York: Human Rights Watch, 2001).

14. Human Rights Watch, *Annual Report 2002—Americas* (New York: Human Rights Watch, 2002), available at: [www.hrw.org/americas].

15. Ibid.

16. Thomas Risse, Stephen Ropp, and Kathryn Sikkink, eds., *The Power of Human Rights: International Norms and Domestic Change* (Cambridge: Cambridge University Press, 1999).

17. *Amnesty International 2002 Report.*

8

Latin America and the European Union: A Strategic Partnership?

Wolf Grabendorff

If indeed "the United States and Latin America have grown apart in recent decades,"[1] has Europe filled the void? The European Union (EU) did make a concerted effort, as did its individual member states, to construct a new relationship with Latin America over the past two decades. The second summit of heads of state from Latin America, the Caribbean, and the EU, which took place in Madrid in 2002, reaffirmed a new institutional relationship based on common values and positions between the two regions.[2]

Since the first biregional summit in Rio in 1999, the international profiles of Latin America and the EU have evolved quite differently. The Rio summit took place 15 years after the symbolic meeting of European and Central American foreign affairs ministers in San José, Costa Rica, which marked the beginning of a European political presence in the region and the first institutional talks between Latin America and the EU. The Rio summit, which demonstrated the firm commitment of two Western regions to play a part together in the redefinition of the international system, was seen as further evidence of the end of the Monroe doctrine. But did this meeting of 48 countries mark the beginning of a biregional strategic partnership? Mutual expectations (and, to some extent, fears) about the future of biregional relations are as asymmetric as European–Latin American relations have been in almost 20 years of close cooperation. Even so, no other two regions have such close and varied ties between them politically, economically, and culturally. The idea of holding a summit was originally conceived by Jacques Chirac, the French head of state, and José María Aznar, government leader of Spain; encouraged by democratic stability and suc-

153

cessful economic development in Latin America, they put forward their proposal for the summit in 1997. The countries in the region reacted to this initiative with enthusiasm, particularly the members of Mercosur.[3]

The conditions that prevailed during the planning of the first summit have since, without doubt, changed substantially. Fallout from a series of financial crises in Asia and Russia had a serious impact on Latin America, first by leading Brazil to recession and then by contributing to default in Argentina, conditions which in turn contributed to severe economic crises in most countries in the region. Risks to democratic stability in countries such as Argentina, Colombia, Ecuador, Paraguay, and Venezuela have emerged. Europe, for its part, has been involved in a war on its own borders, and the EU is struggling to adapt its internal structure to pave the way for inclusion of up to 12 new member states. These distortions in both regions' internal and external agendas are not just short-lived phenomena; they shape the image and perceptions of the two partners and deflate mutual estimates of the benefits involved, profoundly affecting any strategic alliance.

This scenario raises two questions: Will Europe continue to be Latin America's vital partner in political, economic, and cultural matters, as well as in development cooperation, and will Latin America remain a democratic and stable region with growing economic potential? The success of a strategic partnership as envisaged during the first summit—and stressed during the second summit—will depend mainly on the answers to these vital questions. Whether EU–Latin American ties will continue to strengthen in the twenty-first century and whether democracy and stability will prevail in Latin America are uncertain at best. Furthermore, the viability of a strategic alliance is threatened by the two regions' increasing vulnerability to internal and global developments.[4]

The Parallels in Development

Despite considerable differences in the levels of development of the two regions, some common political and economic characteristics are worth pointing out. Certain cultural traditions and values common to both Latin America and Europe, such as respect for human rights, democracy, and the market economy, have provided the right conditions for better relations between them for over a decade. The experiences of Europe and Latin America as the junior partners of the United States during the Cold War, and continuing close economic and security ties with the last remaining world power, have strengthened agreement on shared values inasmuch as those conditions created the need for both regions to pursue independent foreign policies in the post–Cold War international system.

The twentieth century is already seen as the century of integration. It is therefore hardly surprising that the only two world regions with significantly lasting experience of integration should fully appreciate their sense of identity and shared values. Europe and Latin America both see integration as a process that transcends purely economic considerations. Faced with the increasing challenges of globalization at the start of the twenty-first century, the small and medium-size countries of these regions (Brazil aside) view efforts to integrate as a way to minimize conflicts and enhance their international competitive edge, with the ultimate aim of achieving greater development and more favorable economic prospects. They see greater negotiating power and influence in the process of reshaping the world economic order as additional benefits of integration.

The fact that such benefits have been more obvious in Europe than in Latin America is understandable, given Europe's long experience with integration. That said, however, Mercosur's undeniable successes, in spite of its current stagnation, clearly reflect widespread belief in the European concept of integration as a suitable means to boost the South's interests within the international system.[5] By signing an interregional framework agreement with the EU in December 1995, Mercosur gained special status in biregional relations and the opportunity to become an associated partner of the EU.

Another important feature that the two regions have in common is the difficult process of democratization, or redemocratization, which occurred significantly later and in much less dramatic circumstances in Latin America than in Europe. Although current debate in Latin America still gives precedence to the opening up of the economy, the issue of a permanent solution to the direct and indirect consequences of authoritarian rule is still very much alive. Europe too still needs to consolidate democratic government, particularly in those societies that are now undergoing political and economic transformation and are preparing to become members of the European Union.

These similarities have facilitated the political dialogue over almost 20 years and undoubtedly provide a fruitful basis for biregional relations, but one should not underestimate the striking divergences in the two regions' policies and in their relations with third countries. The concept of national sovereignty illustrates this point: Both the Chilean government's position against Spain and Great Britain in the Pinochet case and the Rio Group's strong criticism of North Atlantic Treaty Organization (NATO) operations in Kosovo show that Latin America's understanding of sovereignty is far different from that of EU member states.[6]

Parallels in the regions' development also end when considering the relative positions of Latin American and European countries within the international system. On the Latin American side, diplomats and analysts often note that the region has not accepted the hierarchy of the international system on the terms established at the end of World War II; instead, Latin America has sought to change that hierarchy in its favor over the long term—a legitimate aspiration, given that in Latin America, North–South conflict has always been subordinate to East–West conflict. However, current European stances make it unlikely that substantial modifications in the international system could be facilitated through a strategic relationship between the EU and Latin America.

The Character of Biregional Relations

The idea of biregional relations was devised by the EU and initially took the form of "group-to-group dialogues," which have also been initiated with other partners such as members of the Association of Southeast Asian Nations (ASEAN) or the Gulf States.[7] Nevertheless, in Latin America's case, these forums for dialogue have a structure of their own because the EU holds regular talks not only with the region but also with its four subregions and two countries.

For the region as a whole, the EU has held annual meetings of foreign ministers of countries in the Rio Group since 1990; the Rio Group includes (since 1999) all Central and South American countries, Mexico, the Dominican Republic, and a representative for the Caribbean. There has been political dialogue at the subregional level with the Central American countries since 1984, the so-called San José process. Regular ministerial meetings are also held with the Andean Community (Comunidad Andina, or CAN) and with Mercosur, which take place alternately in the two subregions and in the country holding the EU presidency. In addition, the Caribbean countries are part of the APC (Africa,

Pacific, and Caribbean) Convention, which has its own forums for dialogue with the EU. The EU has specific mechanisms for bilateral talks with Chile and Mexico, which do not belong to any subregional body of Latin American integration (Chile, however, as an associate member of Mercosur, takes part in EU–Mercosur political dialogue at the ministerial level).

This complex and overlapping network for dialogue—Colombia, Mexico, Panama, and Venezuela also participate in the San José process as cooperating countries—is evidence of European efforts to meet the expectations of certain regional groups. It also acknowledges the impossibility of carrying out talks on economics and cooperation with each of the 33 Latin American and Caribbean countries.

Problems with the disparateness of the Latin American states became evident during the biregional summit in Rio de Janeiro: Common positions on political, economic, and cultural issues, which might have allowed workable relations with all the countries in the region, were not easily identified. Nonetheless, the summit provided the opportunity for biregional agreement on at least the priority issues— those in which both partners share common values—and the impetus for future action.[8] Just before the second summit in Madrid, the European Commission outlined its cooperation strategy in the biregional program 2002–2006.[9] The strategy document stresses the medium-term challenges for the region, dividing them into four categories: political, economic, social, and environmental. It also calls for national, bilateral, or multilateral responses to these challenges, but it does not follow the grand design for a global partnership and a common strategy for relations between the EU and Latin America, as proposed in the 2001 report by the European Parliament.[10]

In this context, experience has shown that the greatest difficulty in biregional relations lies in first reaching consensus within each region. The EU member states—which often find it difficult to agree on foreign policy, particularly on security issues—faced this dilemma during preparations for the Rio summit. During this period, agriculture was the major stumbling block, as it has been in other multilateral and bilateral discussions, as well as in the enlargement process. EU member states' failure to agree on the mandate to initiate talks with Mercosur about the creation of an interregional association blocked approval of the measure until the end of June 1999. Because the Mercosur countries had hoped for a fast-moving agenda for the talks to demonstrate to the United States that they were advancing with their EU partners ahead of the

Free Trade Area of the Americas (FTAA) talks with the United States and Canada, the belated commitment of the EU to arrive at the summit with a mandate for talks with Mercosur clouded any other vision of a strategic link.

The start of nontariff talks in November 1999 in Brussels, which addressed all issues related to norms and standards as well as export subsidy regimes on both sides and the pledge to begin more sensitive negotiations relating to tariffs in July 2001, was seen in Latin America as a resounding success of the summit, even though it had been obvious at the Rio meetings that common positions for the talks were still lacking. At any rate, the summit did strengthen the process of negotiating on both sides, at least to the point of reaching consensus about when negotiations would begin. The divergence of European and Latin American interests is also evident in the position of Germany versus that of France, and that of Argentina versus Brazil. While Germany believes that it can only advance in its industrial exports to Latin America if agricultural imports from there have easier access to the European market, it appears to be France's conviction that European farmers should be protected against Mercosur's competitive agricultural products. Argentina seems to have little objection to increased industrial imports from the EU, yet Brazil seeks to protect some of its infant industries from European competition and therefore seems to have less urge to conclude a free trade agreement with the EU. The implication is that talks are going to be long and drawn out, not just because the results of those talks need to be reconciled with those of the World Trade Organization (WTO) Doha Round but also because positions on both sides need to be harmonized.

So much uncertainty makes it difficult to predict a final date for signing the EU–Mercosur agreement, which in any event is unlikely to happen before 2005, when the FTAA hemispheric talks are expected to conclude. Nor will a final agreement mean that a free trade zone is established for all goods and services, because, as with all such agreements, transitional regimes must be allowed up to ten years to bring more sensitive goods into compliance with a tariff agreement; therefore, the negotiations may not achieve total success until 2015. Still, approximately 90 percent of all EU–Mercosur trade could be liberalized by about 2010.[11]

The vulnerability or precariousness of biregional relations is magnified because, unlike in traditional bilateral and multilateral relations, there are no established roles for the actors of either region. The

Europeans have instituted procedures to ensure cooperation between the European Commission and representatives of EU member states; because it has no comparable supranational bodies, however, Latin America lacks similar mechanisms. Those member states of the EU and the Rio Group that share long-standing and successful bilateral links are less interested than smaller countries with little or no association with the other region in widening the scope of biregional relations. Thus, interregional dialogue offers the chance to strengthen political and economic ties among all countries in both regions, which could produce results with favorable repercussions for EU–Latin American relations generally.

A clear advantage of the biregional approach is greater predictability in relations because the political situation in any one country affects biregional relations less than it does bilateral relations. Likewise, the need to harmonize political and economic interests in each of the regions helps to reduce conflicts between them. Although there has been no shortage of difficult subjects either within the interregional dialogue or subregionally, both sides have repeatedly highlighted the positive net result of relations over the last 20 years, mainly in the field of political dialogue.

The Successes of Political Dialogue

Essentially the oldest interregional forum, the San José process with Central America has often been described as a success story in European–Latin American relations. One reason for this outcome is that common EU policy in Central America, which foreign ministers Hans Dietrich Genscher of Germany and Claude Cheysson of France encouraged, posed very few difficulties for internal consensus. The European strategy of supporting Central American nations in their search for a regional solution to their serious security problems, which had worsened during the Cold War, had significant consequences: Latin American countries became more independent international actors through the Contadora Group and, subsequently, the Rio Group; in Europe, the positive experience of projecting a common stance toward a regional problem fostered the willingness to search for solutions to complicated challenges in the region, such as those posed now by Colombia and Cuba.

In addition to reducing conflicts in Central America, political dialogue with Europe has encouraged democratization efforts in many Latin American countries, fostered respect for human rights, and promoted regional and subregional integration projects. Political dialogue in recent years has concentrated less on national and regional topics and more on global issues.[12] This phenomenon has been particularly evident in the debates and outcomes of the Rio summit and, even more so, during the Madrid summit, which focused on the threat of terrorism, combating drug trafficking, conflict prevention, sustainable development, and the promotion and protection of human rights.[13] Thus, political dialogue helps Latin America find its place within the international system and, when decisions have to be taken, it encourages Europeans to consider various regional viewpoints on matters on the international agenda—in particular, the viewpoint of the South.

In contrast to Latin America's involvement in the inter-American system through the Organization of American States (OAS) and the hegemonic ambitions of the United States, participation in political dialogue with the EU has fostered a cooperative style in coordination of Latin American foreign policies. That capacity to coordinate at the intraregional level was amply demonstrated during intra–Latin American preparations for the June 1999 summit, both within the Rio Group and in the consultations between Latin Americans and Caribbeans. It would be hard to imagine that level of cooperation—or the intense efforts of the region to participate more actively in the international system—in the absence of the political dialogue with the EU.[14]

Although no political dialogue yet exists between the Rio Group and the United States (but first steps in this direction were taken during the second Americas summit in April 1998 in Santiago, Chile), the European example served as a model for the Rio Group for initiating conversations with ASEAN members, as well as with Russia and Japan. Talks between the EU and the Rio Group were somewhat pro forma until 1994, but in recent years meetings between foreign affairs ministers have shown a high degree of flexibility regarding subject matter, which demonstrates, among other things, increasing mutual trust.

Against this background, Latin America's and Europe's sense of common values has allowed discussion of extremely sensitive topics, such as the struggle against drug trafficking, which tend to cause rifts between consumer and producer countries. In 1998, the EU and the Rio Group established a special high-level, biregional dialogue mechanism to deal with the drug issue. The idea of shared responsibility on this subject, developed during the dialogue, is starting to be applied to the no less complex and controversial issue of environmental policy.

Although there is no doubt that there is still a long way to go toward clearly defining common stances on global problems and the challenge of globalization, it is also without doubt that some joint progress along this path was made at the summit in Rio de Janeiro. A group of senior officials was charged with the tasks of implementing the "priorities plan" and of organizing ad hoc consultations to coordinate EU and Latin American positions within the structure of the United Nations. This biregional group meets regularly between the summits; it includes Cuba, which otherwise has been left out of the formal EU dialogue.

Although not discounting the benefits of the dialogue with the EU, Latin Americans point to the obvious incongruity of successful political dialogue and less-than-satisfactory progress in economic relations with the EU. Not until logistical structural hitches are addressed and widely divergent interests among EU member states are reconciled, however, will the positive results in the political arena show up also in the area of economic relations.

The Asymmetry in Economic Relations

Biregional relations reflect not only growing cooperation but also growing competition between economic blocs, whose consolidation has impeded development of a multilateral trade system. There is no doubt that since 1994 the North American Free Trade Agreement (NAFTA) has spurred EU attempts to promote trade liberalization with its leading Latin American economic partners. Worries in the EU, emanating in particular from the business sector, that the extension of NAFTA or the adoption of the FTAA around 2005 could diminish European presence in emerging Latin American markets, led to the interregional framework agreement of the EU with Mercosur in 1995, as well as to the framework agreement with Chile in 1996. More recently, those worries led also to a very rapidly negotiated economic association, political coordination, and cooperation agreement with Mexico, which was signed in March 2000 in Lisbon.

Experience since Mexico's entry into NAFTA is a large part of the basis for concern: From 1994 to 1998, Mexico's trade with the EU was cut in half.[15] Given the increasing importance of NAFTA as an economic bloc, and Mexico's role in it, it was no surprise that the first EU free trade agreement in Latin America was reached with Mexico after only two years of negotiations. However, in contrast to the U.S. approach in Latin America, free trade negotiations concluded with Mexico and Chile and currently under way between the EU and Mercosur seek more than economic liberalization. Because the EU's general system of preferences (GSP) is designed to give tariff advantages to low-income countries, the more developed Latin American countries are in the process of "graduating" from the GSP system. Therefore, these initiatives reflect also the EU's need to improve market access for medium-income countries that, unlike those in Central America or the Andean Community, will no longer benefit from the EU's tariff preference system.

Although European exports to Latin America doubled (105 percent) between 1991 and 2002, the EU lost market share because the overall increase in Latin American imports reached 169 percent. Latin American exports to Europe during this period grew no more than 25 percent, an inauspicious figure for amicable trade relations.[16] For this reason, the Rio Group has been constantly criticizing not only European protectionism in the agricultural sector but also the EU's nontariff restrictions.[17] It is highly unlikely that these imbalances in trade will be resolved without the successful completion of the EU's Agenda 2000, which is linked to progressive reforms in the EU's common agricultural policy and a steady, substantial opening up of the agricultural products market until 2006. Unless these reforms are carried out expeditiously, Latin Americans warn, Latin America might strengthen its economic interdependence with the United States when a free trade area is established within the hemisphere.

It is sometimes argued that many Latin American countries want to use the EU negotiations to pressure the United States and force progress in the FTAA negotiations. The Mercosur countries, in particular, see the EU as a counterweight to U.S. influence and wish to keep negotiations parallel with both partners. As a strictly commercial matter, counterbalancing negotiations might make sense; negotiations with the EU, however, address political considerations as well, in that their aim is to create a partnership between like-minded integration processes that are already custom unions and want to develop a relationship that goes much beyond trade considerations.

Economic relations also embrace EU foreign direct investment (FDI), which has increased substantially in the last few years, spurred by privatizations, the regional integration process, and subsequent market expansion. In 1998, the EU toppled the United States from its leading position as FDI provider. In the 1990s almost 30 percent of total FDI flows to Latin America were from the EU; absolute figures increased eightfold between 1993 and 1999.[18] Considering that the emerging Latin American market is bigger than that of all the Eastern European and Mediterranean countries put together, European companies' investments in Latin America will very likely continue to grow, despite financial crises and negative growth experienced by many of the countries in Latin America since 1999 and uncertain future prospects for some of them.

The difficult path the EU has to follow to set up free trade with certain countries or integration schemes within Latin America is complicated by the simultaneous efforts both regions are making to open up their economies to third parties. On the Latin American side, Brazil—after making some progress on a free trade agreement between the Andean Community and Mercosur—signed a bilateral agreement in 1999 with the Andean Community because the other Mercosur members were unwilling to negotiate as a group. Preparations for the hemispheric FTAA are proceeding, but at a slower pace than originally intended because President Clinton was unable to obtain congressional approval for fast-track negotiating authority, which only his successor, George W. Bush, secured in July 2002 (now called Trade Promotion Authority, or TPA). The creation of a free trade area from Alaska to Tierra del Fuego by 2005, as originally envisaged, will now largely depend on Bush's success in overcoming the skeptical posture in Congress and public opinion about the merits of free trade in the hemisphere.

As for the EU, negotiations are under way for enlargement with 12 eastern and southern European countries, which are mostly exporters of agricultural products, and for an association agreement with the non-EU Mediterranean countries. In addition, in the context of the WTO Doha Round, both regions—the EU and Mercosur—will be involved in complex multilateral negotiations concerning the agricultural and service sectors. It is within this scenario that Mercosur, together with the United States, will likely make a stand against the EU's protectionist agricultural policy.[19] In terms of trade, then, it appears that an "association of interests" against the EU might coalesce.

Toward the Creation of an Atlantic Triangle?

The close ties between the United States and the EU within the transatlantic dialogue and between the United States and the Latin American countries in the inter-American system, as well as the strong biregional links between the EU and Latin America, have fueled countless debates and speculation about the possibility of an emerging transatlantic triangle.[20] In this context, perceptions about common values and close economic ties between partners dominated the agenda in the 1990s.

Klaus Kinkel, then German foreign minister, suggested at the EU–Rio Group ministerial meeting at Noordwijk that the three well-defined economic blocs—the EU, NAFTA, and Mercosur, and perhaps a South American Free Trade Area (SAFTA) evolving from the efforts to link up Mercosur with the Andean Community[21]—might combine to create a Trans-Atlantic Free Trade Area (TAFTA), which would enhance the economic potential of all three regions. Through TAFTA, South America could become the third political pillar of a more balanced transatlantic dialogue as the old dividing line between North and South shifts. In addition, such an alliance could help dispel the historic suspicion that has marked inter-American relations.

Latin America obviously wants to play a more active part in international relations, and it is not averse to using EU and U.S. competition for trade in Latin America to gain more bargaining power in negotiations with both. Latin America views better relations with Europe—including a strategic alliance—not as a move against the United States but as a step in the process of integrating into the world economy and redefining the international political agenda.

An argument against the establishment of a triangular relationship is the historic strategy of the United States: The United States prefers to maintain an institutional, economic, and security status quo with both Europe and Latin America, which allows it to play one of its partners against the other at any given moment for its own political or economic benefit. Consider, for example, that the United States and the EU initially stood together against Latin America on the subject of drugs and that there exists a U.S.–Latin American alliance of interests against the EU on the issue of agricultural protectionism.

A strategic alliance between the EU and Latin America would undoubtedly curb the U.S. tendency to play off one partner against the other, and it may stave off possible commercial conflicts. Nevertheless, strong political will from the Europeans would be required to build such an alliance, and Latin Americans would have to demonstrate a higher level of realism and efficiency in the management of biregional relations.[22] An efficient transatlantic triangle with shared values and clearly defined codes of conduct would unburden and simultaneously strengthen transatlantic relations and biregional relations between Europe and Latin America. The efficiency and strength of a triangular arrangement could be proved by concerted action on at least four fronts, none of which could be addressed successfully by any one or even two of the partners:

- Cuba: An Atlantic triangle could help pave the way for a nonviolent transition and for the country's political and economic reintegration into the international system.
- Drugs: The triangle could enforce the concept of shared responsibility in reducing supply as well as demand.
- Poverty reduction: The triangle could implement a package of measures nationally and internationally and increase available financial resources.
- Trade liberalization: An Atlantic triangle could foster compatibility between the trade regimes of NAFTA, Mercosur, and the EU.

The functioning of such a transatlantic triangle will depend a great deal on the smooth policy process between each of the partners on a bilateral/biregional basis. The inter-American and the transatlantic dialogues have already proved—in spite of all their shortcomings—their effectiveness, while the EU–Latin American strategic alliance is still under construction. Only if this new form of a biregional alliance proves to be stable and successful will the Atlantic triangle itself have a future.

A "Communication" from the European Commission in 1999,[23] which is considered to be the strategic blueprint for biregional relations at the beginning of the twenty-first century, identified the big challenges facing Latin America as the following: (1) consolidation of the democratic systems, (2) harmonious insertion into the world economy, and (3) strengthening of the regional integration processes. It is clear that these challenges could be applied almost equally to the EU as it expands to include up to 12 more member states. Progressive globalization, and the risks that this process entails, makes it possible and necessary for the EU to develop strategic alliances based on common interests and goals with other integration processes. Even though asymmetric relations with Latin America exist, and may continue to exist in some areas for many years to come, both regions have been drawing substantially closer in their perceptions of shared global challenges and responses to them. During the Rio summit in 1999, this vision facilitated consensus on a joint program of strategic alliance in the twenty-first century, which was endorsed at the summit in Madrid. The challenges and the strains of such an alliance between Latin America and Europe will certainly become even more evident by the time representatives of all 48 countries meet again at the third summit in Mexico in 2004.

Notes

1. Heraldo Muñoz, "Good-bye U.S.A.?" in *Latin America in the New International System,* ed. Joseph S. Tulchin and Ralph H. Espach (Boulder: Lynne Rienner, 2001), 89.
2. See European Union, "EU-LAC Common Values and Positions," Madrid, 17 May 2002, available at: [http://europa.eu.int].
3. *Mercosur* stands for Mercado Común del Sur, or Common Market of the South.
4. For the changes in the relationship between the two summits, see Susanne Gratius, "América Latina y Europa ante la cumbre de Madrid: Intereses, conflictos y expectativas," Serie Europa–América Latina 6 (Rio de Janeiro: Fundación Konrad Adenauer, 2002).
5. Dieter Benecke, "Relación entre la Unión Europea y el Mercosur," *Contribuciones* 1, no. 16 (Buenos Aires: CIEDLA, 1999): 7–17.
6. On the consequences of the Pinochet case for European-Chilean relations, see IRELA, "The Pinochet Case: A Test for European–Latin American Relations?" *IRELA Briefing* 9 (Madrid: IRELA, 1998). On the NATO Kosovo operations, see Rio Group, "Comunicado del Grupo de Río sobre Kosovo," *GRIO/SPT-99* (Mexico City, 25 March 1999).
7. Geoffrey Edwards and Elfriede Regelsberger, eds., *Europe's Global Links: The European Community and Interregional Cooperation* (London: Pinter, 1990).
8. See "Rio Joint Declaration" and "Action Plan" of the First Summit Between Latin America, the Caribbean, and the European Union, Rio de Janeiro, 28–29 June 1999, available at: [http://europa.eu.int]; and the "Communication from the Commission to the Council and the European Parliament: Follow-up to the First Summit Between Latin America, the Caribbean, and the European Union," Commission of the European Communities, Brussels, 31 October 2000, available at: [www.eurocaribbean. org].
9. See European Union, *European Commission: Latin America Regional Strategy Document* (Brussels: European Commission, 2002), available at: [http://europa.eu.int].

10. European Union, "EU/Latin America Relations," Report A5-0336/2001 (Brussels: Committee on Foreign Affairs, Human Rights, Common Security, and Defence Policy, European Parliament, 11 October 2001), available at: [http://europa.eu.int].

11. IRELA, *The Rio Summit: Towards a Strategic Partnership?* (Madrid: IRELA, 1999), 7–8.

12. Alain Rouquié, "Perspectivas inmediatas del diálogo Unión Europea–América Latina," in *Unión Europea–América Latina* (Bogotá, Colombia: Fundación Friedrich-Ebert, 1995), 101–107.

13. See European Union, "EU–Latin America and the Caribbean Summit" (Brussels: EU, 17 May 2002), available at: [http://europa.eu.int/].

14. Wolf Grabendorff, "El papel de América Latina en un nuevo orden internacional," in *El Estado en América Latina,* ed. Manfred Mols and Josef Thesing (Buenos Aires: CIEDLA, 1995), 451–476.

15. See IRELA, "Latin America and Europe: Beyond the Year 2000," *Dossier* 65 (Madrid: IRELA, 1998): 16.

16. Inter-American Development Bank, "Periodic Note on Integration," *Integration and Trade in the Americas: Special Issue on Latin American and Caribbean Economic Relations with the European Union* (Washington, D.C.: IADB, May 2002), 85.

17. Rio Group, "III reunión de alto nivel económico y comercial Grupo de Río–Unión Europea" (Brussels, 7 March 1995).

18. Inter-American Development Bank, *Integration and Trade in the Americas,* 22.

19. Agence Europe, *Bulletin Quotidien Europe* 7446 (16 April 1999): 9 (English version).

20. See Wolf Grabendorff and Riordan Roett, eds., *Latin America, Western Europe, and the United States: A New Atlantic Triangle?* (New York: Praeger, 1985); José Briceño Ruiz, "Strategic Regionalism and the Remaking of the Triangular Relation Between the USA, the European Union and Latin America," in *Journal of European Integration* 23, no. 2 (2001): 105–137; and Wolf Grabendorff, "El Triángulo Atlántico: ¿Una visión realista?" in *El Triángulo Atlántico: América Latina, Europa y los Estados Unidos en el sistema internacional cambiante,* ed. Klaus Bodemer, Wolf Grabendorff, Winfried Jung, and Josef Thesing (Sankt Augustin, Germany: Konrad Adenauer Stiftung, 2002), 375–392.

21. See the "Guayaquil Consensus on Integration, Security, and Infrastructure for Development," Second Meeting of the Presidents of South America, Guayaquil, Ecuador, 26–27 July 2002, available at the Summit of the Americas Information Network: [www.summit-americas.org].

22. Alberto van Klaveren commented on this subject some years ago in "Europa-Lateinamerika: Zwischen Illusion und Realismus auch nach 1992," *Zeitschrift für Lateinamerika-Wien* 43 (Vienna: ÖLAI, 1996): 7–35.

23. European Union, "Communication from the Commission to the Council, the European Parliament, and the Economic and Social Committee on a New European Union–Latin America Partnership on the Eve of the 21st Century" (Brussels: European Commission, 9 March 1999), available at: [http://europa.eu.int].

Part 3

Two Pivotal States

9

Mexico's Changing Domestic and International Dynamics

Russell Crandall

Different from the rest of Latin America and its North American counterparts, Mexico has always been a unique case in the Western Hemisphere. When, for example, countries throughout Latin America underwent transitions from authoritarian rule to democratic governance in the 1980s, Mexico stubbornly held on to its decades-long one-party system. Although many observers then believed that it was only a matter of time before Mexico became truly democratic, few hazarded an opinion on whether this process would be sudden or gradual, peaceful or violent.

With the historic defeat of the Institutional Revolutionary Party (PRI) and the election of National Action Party (PAN) candidate Vicente Fox Quesada in July 2000, however, Mexico might finally have made its first true shift toward consolidated democracy. That election strongly suggests that Mexico's continuing democratic transition will remain peaceful. It also signals that in many respects the transition is almost complete. Indeed, Mexico seems to have entered into a period of solid political and economic stability, fueled by political reforms implemented under Fox's predecessor, Ernesto Zedillo, and economic dynamism spurred by the North American Free Trade Agreement (NAFTA).

The government of Carlos Salinas de Gortari (1988–1994) attempted to modernize Mexico, but that experiment yielded disastrous consequences, both political and economic. Other attempts in modern times likewise failed. Although historical experience might suggest that the Fox administration should be greeted with a healthy dose of caution, Mexico now may be able to move from its status as a developing country—a position it has long held but always resented—to that of a developed country. As such, Mexico would be geared to promote more effective social welfare and economic development at home and promote international security abroad.

Mexico's road to development will accentuate its status as a North American nation, further distinguishing it from its Latin American counterparts. With the advent of NAFTA in 1994, Mexico almost irrevocably tied its future to integration—at this point still mostly economic—with its colossal neighbor to the north. Since then, both the United States and Mexico have made impressive gains in institutionalizing their bilateral relationship. In fact, the level of cooperation that exists between Washington and Mexico City on a variety of issues would have been unimaginable just a few years ago.

Thus, it would seem that Mexico's future lies in its ability to become a stable, reliable partner of the United States, as Canada already is. This "Canada-ization" of Mexico will serve to lock in a productive economic and political relationship with both of Mexico's northern neighbors, the United States and Canada. This is not to say that a normal Mexico would not disagree with the United States. Rather, this new Mexico would continue to disagree with the United States, but the disputes between the two countries would not be the disputes of the past; instead of focusing on the negative aspects of immigration and on drugs, U.S.–Mexican relations, like U.S.–Canadian relations, would concern collegial issues within the framework of trade and diplomacy.

Mexico's future development and continued integration into North America will depend on its ability to change the social, political, and economic climate within its own borders. Mexico has always wanted to be seen as a country that emerged from the developing to the developed world, but this image has been continually sullied by civil conflict, economic crises, and revelations of widespread corruption. Unlike other countries in which a strong military is viewed as the key to international respect, Mexico will be defined by its domestic development. This chapter looks at several key aspects of Mexico's domestic situation that will serve to promote its international standing, above all as an increasingly strong partner of the United States and an emerging regional player in the Western Hemisphere.

What is clear is that Mexico's development will require more than the invisible hand of the free market. To promote effective and lasting change and to ensure that a great many Mexicans benefit from the country's evolution and insertion into North America, Mexico will have to be proactive. This will be an enormous challenge: Mexico is still a politically, socially, and economically diverse and unequal country.

President Fox faces a unique opportunity to provide the dynamic leadership that Mexico desperately needs. While promoting reform in post-PRI Mexico might seem like a Herculean task, as the first two years of his administration have shown, some variables bolster Fox's efforts. Chief among these is the support and encouragement of the United States. For decades the United States prized stability over liberal democracy south of the border; it shied away from opening up the "black box" of the domestic Mexican system, afraid of what it would find. Today, however, there is a growing recognition that Mexico is a vital nation in the hemisphere and that its internal evolution matters. Indeed, the U.S.–Mexico relationship is more interdependent than ever, and that trend can only grow in the future, a reality that will lend crucial external support to Fox's reform efforts. In other words, the United States and Mexico are moving from a relationship of distant neighbors to a *relación especial*.[1]

Any examination of Mexico's prospects for modernity must start with the recognition that in many aspects Mexico is a poor country. Indigenous populations in the states of Chiapas and Guerrero suffer injustices and discrimination; the shantytown neighborhoods that surround industrial cities in the north lack water. Mexico must address these and other problems before a substantial proportion of its citizens can feel as though they are living in a developed country. Weak political institutions, corruption, and endemic inequality of income all are enormous obstacles that must be overcome, regardless of whether the current account balance is healthy or whether Moody's gives the country an investment-grade debt rating. We already know that Mexico can grow. But can it *develop*, a task that is altogether more complex and challenging? Neither NAFTA nor a strong U.S. economy can develop Mexico. Such collaborations and circumstances can help, but ultimately education, leadership, and solid institutions are the means to sustained and equitable growth. Even in the rosiest scenario, achieving those goals will take a very long time. Therefore, what Mexico does to promote the welfare of its citizenry is of utmost importance.

Mexico Crosses over the Abyss

"The next president of Mexico will be Vicente Fox Quesada." With those words in July 2000 President Ernesto Zedillo sealed Mexico's first national-level transition of power in modern times. Amazingly, only six years earlier, in 1994, Mexico was suffering through its own "year of living dangerously," when a currency devaluation, political assassinations—including that of PRI presidential candidate Luis Donaldo Colosio—and an indigenous uprising in Chiapas completely deflated enthusiasm about Mexico's prospects. Indeed, that long, tormented year revealed a nation that needed intensive care. In addition to enduring persistently high levels of corruption, poverty, and political repression, Mexico was teetering on the edge of economic collapse. In fact, without the successful infusion of around $50 billion[2] from the United States and multilateral financial agencies, there is no telling how deep Mexico's economy could have sunk.[3]

Thus, the economic and political situation Ernesto Zedillo faced when he took office in 1994 may have been even more daunting than what Fox faces today. Confidence in the country's economy was low, and the dirty laundry of over seven decades of single-party clientelistic rule was beginning to show. Yet, for reasons only historians will be able to comprehend fully, during the course of his six-year term Ernesto Zedillo was able to lead Mexico out of its political and economic malaise: He stabilized the economy and quickly returned the country to positive growth. Almost like Gorbachev in Russia, he took Mexico over the "democratic abyss" by implementing a number of laws that allowed for stronger electoral bodies and contested primary elections in the PRI.

In the course of this reform process, Zedillo was essentially falling on his own political sword to ensure that Mexico would undergo a smooth democratic transition. Although Zedillo's actions may have seemed traitorous to some of the hard-liners in the PRI, history may well judge him to be the Mexican president most responsible for Mexico's orderly and comprehensive transition to full democracy.[4] Such a legacy is all the more impressive in that Zedillo was an "accidental" president: Only after the PRI's favored candidate for president, Luis Donaldo Colosio, was murdered did Zedillo become the PRI nominee.

Promoting the Relación Especial with Uncle Sam

The foundation of Mexico's emergence in the Western Hemisphere will depend largely on its ability to foster and ultimately to institutionalize its relationship with the United States. Of course it is risky to place so much of its prosperity and legitimacy into this relationship, but today's global economy limits Mexico's options. Its relationship with the United States must remain primary. Fortunately, the United States also appears to want to cultivate this new relación especial.[5]

As longtime resident and former governor of Texas, George W. Bush feels at home with the NAFTA culture, and he is eager to promote it during his term as president. Albeit mostly symbolic, the first overseas trip President Bush made was to Mexico, whereas President Clinton failed to visit Mexico until his second term in office. Indeed, the Fox–Bush "cowboy summit" of February 2001 signaled that both sides are committed to going beyond a tradition of suspicion and scorn, so that they may promote bilateral solutions to what is fast becoming one of the most interdependent relationships in the world.

Bush's statement that he would support Mexico's efforts to suspend the annual drug certification process was the most stunning and potentially productive result of this preliminary meeting between the two leaders. Even more important was the U.S. reaction to a more radical proposal from Fox, to extend NAFTA beyond goods and services to labor: Although the United States did not immediately embrace the idea, it did not discount it, as it surely would have a few years earlier. In fact, in a politically courageous move, due to entrenched anti-immigrant sentiment within the Republican Party, the Bush administration has floated the idea of granting amnesty to potentially millions of undocumented Mexicans residing in the United States.

While any lasting immigration agreement has yet to be reached, it is clear that Washington is listening to Mexico and taking its ideas seriously, at least in part because of Mexico's growing status as a developed country, a trend Zedillo began and Fox must move forward. But despite these signs of cooperation and the optimism they engender, it is important to keep in mind that the improvement in the bilateral relationship has occurred against the backdrop of unprecedented economic growth in the United States, although the first two years of the Bush administration were marked by an economic slowdown and the war against terrorism. It is generally during times of economic stagnancy and crisis that relations are truly put to the test.

Only a few years ago many sectors of the U.S. economy were in poor shape and California was passing the anti-immigrant Proposition 187. The real test of the new relationship will come when the U.S. economy turns south and Mexican workers seem more like competition than valuable cheap labor. Both sides must invest heavily in their relationship today so that they can amass political reserves to call on when times become more difficult.

While the Fox administration is clearly betting its future on closer ties with the United States, it is clear that the United States is realizing that it too needs Mexico. Since the implementation of NAFTA, Mexico has become a giant Wal-Mart for the United States—a place that lays out just about every sort of good for a good price. Nor is the seemingly endless resource of cheap labor that Mexico provides for the U.S. labor market to be discounted. Despite NAFTA's benefits, the U.S.–Mexico relationship is quickly becoming more than one of economic convenience.[6]

A decades-long process of cultural integration has been taking place, only to be expedited by the advent of NAFTA in 1994. What this means for U.S. policymakers is clear: Mexico matters. Take, for example, the case in 1994 of then–Texas governor George W. Bush and his reputation for being more accepting of Mexican immigration than his counterpart, Pete Wilson of California. Though his stance certainly may spring from genuine conviction, its benefits have been undeniable: This more liberal position on Mexican immigration has paid strong political dividends for Bush. As the Latino population in the United States continues to grow—and a good proportion of those Latinos are tied to Mexico—the U.S. political system will increasingly incorporate strong ties with Mexico into its domestic political calculus.

With Fox in office, improving U.S.–Mexican ties is much easier above all because Mexico is better able to project an air of respectability and credibility. Persuading U.S. citizens that their future lies with more and better ties to Mexico is difficult when the images that emerge from the country are dominated by drugs, corruption, and guerrilla insurgencies. So far, Fox has been viewed as the antithesis of those stereotypes of Mexico. The Fox presidency is thus crucial: It represents a golden opportunity to solidify a strong relationship while the environment is favorable.

Mexico as the Honest Broker in the Western Hemisphere

An important corollary to the institutionalization of Mexico's relationship with the United States is the potential for Mexico to emerge as a credible regional foreign-policy player. Part of that potential is attributable to the ironic fact that throughout the Cold War Mexico stubbornly refused to toe Washington's anticommunist line. Instead, it used its oil resources and strong anti-American diplomatic rhetoric to champion itself as one of the leaders of the nonaligned movement. A certain amount of such behavior—especially Mexico's willingness to recognize nearly every political regime across the globe—was undoubtedly intended to deflect questions about Mexico's own, sometimes not very democratic actions, but whatever the motivation for nonalignment, Mexico now has some credibility as an honest broker on international issues.

On issues ranging from economic reform in Central America to drug trafficking and the peace process in Colombia, Mexico is increasingly well-positioned to serve as an objective intermediary between North America and Latin America. If Washington is wise, it will consult with Los Pinos (Mexico's presidential residence) on various issues before formulating policy, ensuring that U.S. initiatives toward Latin America will be seen as more multilateral than unilateral and thus deserving of support. One case in point concerns the annual drug certification process, whereby the U.S. government "certifies" whether drug-producing—or "source"—countries are cooperating in the war on drugs. The Bush administration has consulted with Mexico on that issue, and any effective solution these countries reach could easily be extended to other countries in the region that resent the annual ritual. But as already stated, before Mexico can begin designing grand plans about its relations with the United States or its role as a regional foreign policy power, it must first reform its domestic political, economic, and social institutions.

The Economy: Moving from Macro- to Microstabilization

What is perhaps most remarkable about Mexico's economic performance over the last several years is what has not happened. Unlike the situation in 1982 or 1994 when it was the epicenter of regional and international economic crises, Mexico has now emerged from those dark days with a reformed economy and sounder macroeconomic management. The key test for Mexico came after Brazilian monetary authorities devalued the real in January 1999. Many economic analysts expected that the so-called samba effect would claim Mexico as its first victim of economic contagion throughout the emerging markets. This did not happen. Thanks to a more sustainable exchange rate regime, a stronger banking sector, open trade, and more competitive industries, the Mexican economy of 1999 was in far better shape than the one that precipitated what is now called the first global economic crisis of the twenty-first century.

Indeed, Mexico's economic performance—and its ability to weather external shocks—has been nothing short of impressive. Gross domestic product has grown by an average of 5.1 percent over the past four years, and inflation that peaked at 52 percent in 1995 hovered in the single digits in 2002. The current account—which, along with the fixed (and overvalued, in real terms) exchange rate, caused so much damage in 1994—is in much better shape. The current-account deficit that Mexico is running should not be ignored, but at least it is being financed with more foreign direct investment than was previously the case, and with less of the volatile portfolio capital that ran for the exits in 1994. Moreover, a higher domestic savings rate (12 percent in 1994, 20 percent in 2000) has allowed Mexico to tap internal markets for its borrowing needs to finance a fiscal deficit that amounts to a manageable rate of less that 1 percent of GDP.[7] The floating exchange-rate system has cured one major headache of the Mexican authorities. Alarm bells may sound if the nominal exchange rate stubbornly clings to the rate of 10 pesos per U.S. dollar, which could spark even greater real appreciation and pressure the current-account balance; however, central bank authorities no longer fear a disruptive currency crisis provoked by massive capital flight.

Here too Zedillo laid the foundation for Mexico's economic growth and stability. It almost seems as though, after getting burned so many times, Zedillo's economic team was determined to do everything right so that no blame could be attached to it if Mexico were to suffer another catastrophic crisis.[8] Oil revenues are a poignant example: Unlike the oil shocks in the 1970s, when Mexico used windfall revenues to borrow even more money (which ultimately precipitated the debt crisis of 1982), Mexico used the recent surge in the price of oil to repay—three years early—$3 billion of debt to the International Monetary Fund. Conversely, when the price of oil was barely over $10 a barrel in 1997, Mexico's energy minister, Luis Téllez, cut spending to ensure that Mexico could operate under the new economic reality.

Although Mexico has been able to stabilize and institutionalize its macroeconomic climate in a remarkably short time, the now-famous aphorism reminds us that "no one lives in the macro economy." Healthy current-account balances and low external debt, for example, mean little to the average Mexican. With this in mind, let us turn now to some of the key challenges facing Fox as he continues his efforts to modernize and humanize the Mexican economy.

Broadening NAFTA

To say that the inauguration of NAFTA on January 1, 1994, has revolutionized the Mexican economy is an understatement. Mexico has become the United States' second largest trading partner, after Canada. Mexico's exports to the United States have doubled: An astounding 88 percent of Mexico's exports went to the United States in 1999 (see Table 9.1), a figure that alone justifies the claim that the nations are two of the most economically interdependent in the world. With tariffs scheduled to reach zero in both directions by 2009, the forecast is for this economic relationship—and in turn the Mexican economy's orientation around an export-led model—to deepen.

The rapid increase in the growth of the *maquiladora*-based part of the Mexican economy is one indication of the response to the United States' seemingly insatiable demand for goods produced in Mexico.[9] These manufacturing plants now produce about half of Mexico's exports, and the sector has grown some 20 percent a year since the inception of NAFTA.[10] But although the maquiladoras are certain to remain an engine of Mexican economic growth in the future, unfortunately they are not a panacea for development ills.

One concern is that only about 3 percent of the maquiladoras' inputs are locally produced, a figure that lowers the potential for back-

Table 9.1   Mexico's Main Trading Partners, 1999

Exports to	Percentage of Total	Imports from	Percentage of Total
United States	88.4	United States	74.3
Canada	1.7	Germany	3.5
Germany	1.5	Japan	3.3
Spain	0.7	South Korea	1.9
Japan	0.6	Canada	1.9

Source: Instituto Nacional de Estadística, Geografía e Informática (INEGI), Mexico City and the Economist Intelligence Unit (EIU), 9, as cited in "A Survey of Mexico," *The Economist,* 28 October 2000, 52.

ward links to other sectors. A much more pressing concern is that of the maquiladoras' role in promoting regional economic imbalances. NAFTA has induced "a giant sucking sound," not from Mexico to the United States but rather from southern to northern Mexico. With wages and job prospects significantly lower in the southern part of the country, an internal migration process has been under way for years, but the social and economic effects are just beginning to be known. What is well understood, however, is that the booming maquiladora-driven border cities do not possess adequate infrastructure for providing basic human services to these newly arrived residents.

The way that Fox responds to the social effects of Mexico's economic and social transformation will help determine the success of his administration. NAFTA is an irrevocable reality of Mexico's economy and society; how Mexico chooses to deal with that reality is an entirely different issue. In addition to an aggressive plan to humanize the conditions in which Mexico's workers labor to maintain the country's economic growth rate, the Fox administration will need to find ways to promote job creation in nonborder regions. With Fox's impressive track record for successful efforts of this type while he was governor in Guanajuato, there is hope that his national government will rise to the occasion. Fortunately, there are already signs that some maquiladora-structured manufacturers are moving south. For example, a Japanese cable car company hired 2,500 people in Chiapas, and manufacturing veterans in Guanajuato and Puebla are also gearing up to welcome maquiladoras.[11]

Tax Revenue and the Labor Market

While domestic savings has increased, tax revenue remains well short of what will be required to fund Fox's myriad social programs—greater spending on teachers and schools, for example, and an aggressive attack on absolute poverty. Raising tax revenue has never been an easy chore in Latin America. Profligate governments anywhere oftentimes waste the revenue, which in turn makes citizens and corporations hesitant to pay more. Mexico has been no exception, and its tax take is the lowest of the 29 members of the Organization for Economic Cooperation and Development. Excluding taxes on oil, tax revenue stands at 11 percent of GDP.

Fox's government hopes to increase this figure to around 16–17 percent, a tall order but an essential one. Simplifying the tax system and cracking down on evasion are the two strategies most likely to produce results, combined perhaps with a lower corporate tax rate.[12] Since official estimates put tax evasion in Mexico at around 30 percent, there is plenty of money for the government to target. The legitimacy Fox gains through his reputation as an honest no-nonsense businessperson should foster greater will to honor the tax code—Mexicans will be less inclined to evade taxes if they know their resources will not line the pockets of corrupt politicians. But Fox still faces the challenge of pushing controversial and always unpopular tax reform through a Congress without a clear majority and only weak backing from his own party.

Along with increasing tax revenue, a key element in Mexico's microeconomic reform process will be dealing with Mexico's corporatist labor legacy. Even after the death of union boss Fidel Velázquez, who for 53 years oiled the wheels between the PRI and labor, the Mexican labor system is still plagued by unrealistically high severance packages that discourage managers from hiring and firing, automatic promotions that increase costs without any connection to productivity, and closed shops that limit labor mobility. These rigidities put a severe strain on economic dynamism, especially in the small and medium-size business sector. Although various forms of workers' protection such as social security and the ability to organize should remain fundamental rights of Mexican workers, many observers feel that a strong dose of "modernization" should be administered, especially if Mexico is to compete effectively not just with countries such as Jamaica and Colombia but also with Indonesia, Thailand, and South Korea.

Whereas President Porfirio Díaz quipped at the end of the nineteenth century that Mexico was "so far from God and so close to the United States," in the twenty-first century Mexico is in one of the most enviable economic positions anywhere: It has unfettered access to the world's largest economy. But although "location, location, location" is clearly serving its economic interests right now, Mexico must realize also that its own economic performance is increasingly dependent on a single country. Yet Mexico's sacrifice of a certain degree of economic sovereignty does not in any way suggest that the economy would be stronger with more sovereignty. In fact, it might even be a relief to many Mexicans that Alan Greenspan is becoming more important to their nation's health than their own finance minister. Again, no matter what the level of economic interdependence or Mexico's NAFTA-driven growth rates, Fox's challenge to humanize the Mexican economy remains paramount.[13]

Authoritarian Enclaves, Chiapas, and Drugs

In addition to the economy, there are several other key issues that will require considerable attention from the Fox administration. These include the persistence of PRI-era political "authoritarian enclaves" at the regional and local level; the seemingly intractable standoff between the government and Zapatista rebels in the southern state of Chiapas; and the deleterious effects of Mexico's involvement in the international drug trade, including its cooperation with the United States. Each one of these issues represents a potential "poison pill" for the new government. In other words, any one of them could easily spin out of control, an occurrence that could seriously undermine the Fox administration's credibility.

Authoritarian Enclaves

Fox's victory in the 2000 presidential race signaled the beginning of the democratic era at the national level. Nonetheless, this unprecedented step forward in Mexico's political evolution does not address the absence of free and fair elections—and the continuation of old-style Mexican politics—at the subnational (i.e., local and regional) levels.[14] In other words, the continued move toward democratization and institutionalization at the national level—and the press attention normally focused on this level—does not necessarily guarantee a concomitant political evolution at the local and regional levels. The persistence of authoritarian enclaves continues to be a thorn in the side of Mexico's democratization. Such enclaves prevent democratic politics from reaching citizens at the levels that most directly affect their everyday lives— namely, the local and regional levels.

The former governor of the state of Yucatán, Víctor Cervera Pacheco (of the PRI), is one example. After an electoral scandal that exposed dirty tricks by the PRI-dominated election council, Cervera started to rail against "federal imperialism" and called for renewed respect for Yucatán's sovereign state rights. Vehicles sported bumper stickers stating "Yucatán, Free and Sovereign."[15] The very clear message Cervera was sending to Mexico City was that, while Mexico might be changing at the national level, there remains strong sentiment for "business as usual" in places such as Yucatán.

Mexican courts prevented Cervera from running for another term of office in Yucatán, suggesting that the Fox administration was having—

at least initially—success in reining in "renegade" governors. While the PRI suffered a setback in Yucatán (PAN candidate Patricio Patrón eventually won the election), the August 5, 2001, gubernatorial election of PRI candidate Manuel Andrade in the state of Tabasco suggests that the PRI has not completely vanished as a political force at the regional level, even if its national leadership remains in disarray. Whether regional PRI governors will cooperate with Fox's national reform process is still not clear, something that could help to make or break Fox's presidency.

Chiapas

In the heat of the 2000 presidential campaign Fox glibly said that he could solve the conflict in Chiapas in 15 minutes. He most likely regrets that dismissive tone, but the very fact that there is a fresh, non-PRI face in Los Pinos does provide hope that a lasting solution can be found for the situation in Chiapas—and for the entire issue of Mexico's indigenous peoples. Native Indians comprise 38 percent of the population in Chiapas, and their illiteracy and poverty rates are shamefully high. Furthermore, their political and economic rights have been ignored for centuries.[16]

However, these discouraging facts reveal only a fraction of the complexity of Chiapas and its peoples. To take one small example, the indigenous population is divided between Catholic and Protestant, which can rive unity like no other cultural difference. Also, Indian paramilitary groups—some linked to the PRI and others to landowner associations—cause havoc within a community that cannot afford such conflict among its own peoples. Despite all of this adversity, led by their inimitable leader Subcomandante Marcos, the Zapatista guerrillas have remained committed to their struggle since January 1994.

Peace talks between the government and the Zapatistas broke down in 1996 after the government failed to follow through on an indigenous rights accord agreed upon by the two sides. This legislation was back on the table in 2001, although a watered-down version that passed the Mexican Congress was quickly rejected by the Zapatista leadership as inadequate. It is far from certain whether a new agreement can be brokered that will satisfy both Congress and the Zapatistas; the extent to which President Fox pushes for future legislation will send a clear signal about the level of his commitment to ending the conflict.

The broader issue concerning the Zapatistas is that of political incorporation. That the Zapatistas have justifiable demands for political, economic, and social reform is undeniable; how the government and Zapatistas go about dealing with their demands will be the telling issue. In effect, a major test for the Fox administration will be the extent to which they can address the demands of indigenous groups such as the Zapatistas within the orthodox political system.

The case of Ecuador is illustrative. Over the past decade Ecuador has witnessed the political activation of its indigenous peoples, who comprise roughly half the population. While their demands are legitimate, like those of their counterparts in Chiapas, their methods of effecting political change have tended to remain outside the orthodox political system. Work stoppages, riots, and other disruptive acts demonstrate not just the frustration of Ecuador's indigenous peoples but also the firm belief that these methods are more effective than attempting to produce change within the political system. And while Ecuador's indigenous groups are probably right in thinking that they can gain more from anti-institutional forms of political behavior, the long-term damage done to Ecuador's political legitimacy is considerable. This could be the path for Chiapas unless measures are taken to ensure that the Zapatistas' voices are heard within the political system. The March 2001 Zapatista "caravan" from Chiapas to Mexico City, which heralded the arrival of Subcomandante Marcos in the nation's capital, was a step in this direction.[17]

Postrevolutionary Mexico was built on the idea that the vanquished Indians, after suffering ignominious defeat at the hands of the Spanish, would rise again. Thus, Chiapas and the Zapatistas' struggles represent Mexico's societal consciousness. That these peoples are struggling still serves as a wake-up call to many Mexicans. Despite all of the enthusiasm over the country's modernization, there are many (especially the indigenous) who continue to suffer, a reality that neither NAFTA nor the invisible hand of the free market can alter. In a sense, the Zapatistas are the sentinels, the canary in the coal mine for the Mexican psyche as it enters the twenty-first century: If the Zapatistas fail to thrive, so too will the social fabric of Mexican culture and society.

Drugs

The movie *Traffic* has brought home to many in the United States and across the world not just the acute absurdity of the U.S.-led war on drugs but also the extent to which drugs infect Mexican society. And have no doubt that Mexican society suffers from the cancer of drugs, not just in drug-related violence and corruption but increasingly in greater domestic consumption. But though the drug crisis is a tremendous problem, it also presents an excellent opportunity for successive government administrations to show that they are committed to leaving the practices of the past behind. Some encouraging developments have taken place recently: Drug seizures increased by 48 percent from 1999 to 2000, and extradition to the United States for drug crimes—once thought to be a flagrant violation of Mexico's sovereignty—is now standard procedure, a measure that is sure to strike fear in Mexican drug traffickers.

However, even to make a dent in the drug traffic, Mexico, so long suspicious of its northern neighbor's motives, will have to work with the United States. This is especially true because there is very little likelihood that the United States will significantly alter its demand that Mexico cooperate unconditionally in antidrug efforts. Once Mexico comes to terms with the United States' politically implacable devotion to cutting the drug supply, it will be better able to accommodate this tough stand, finding small victories and opportunities for cooperation when it can. Direct confrontation with the United States is not only counterproductive, it is not in Mexico's ultimate interests now that it recognizes the destruction the drug trade can visit on a country. George W. Bush's recent pronouncement that he will push to suspend temporarily the annual drug certification process—a ritual that infuriates Mexicans and other Latin Americans every twelve months—is one such example.[18] Indeed, partnership, not suspicion, must characterize the bilateral efforts against drug cultivation, demand, and distribution.

Conclusion

Mexico at the beginning of the twenty-first century is at a crossroads: It has made great strides in renouncing its nondemocratic legacy, but it still has not institutionalized its modern incarnation. In this sense, while Ernesto Zedillo will be remembered as the selfless martyr who placed his nation's welfare above personal political gain, it is now up to Fox to ensure that Mexico stays firmly grounded on the path toward social, political, and economic development. Mexico has shown that it can grow. Comprehensive and equitable development, however, is not so easily attainable, whether led by the Mexican state or delegated to the market economy.

There is no doubt that Mexico will continue to modernize. With NAFTA as the locomotive, Mexican business—indeed, Mexican society—will change rapidly in coming years. What is less certain, however, and what Fox must tackle as president, is ensuring that this modernization benefits all of society, not just those who own or work in maquiladoras. Fox's mission is much greater than that, and ultimately infinitely more important to Mexico. Expectations for Fox were incredibly high at the start of his administration, but the Mexican people must demand a lot from their new leader. They have waited decades for the United States to treat their country more like Canada, and it is now up to Fox to lead them to that destination.

Notes

1. Although the September 11, 2001, terrorist attacks in the United States steered the focus of U.S. foreign and security policy toward the war against terrorism, the strengthening of the U.S.–Mexico bilateral relationship continues, even if at a slower pace than was originally envisioned at the start of the Fox and George W. Bush administrations. The term *distant neighbors* was coined by Alan Riding in his excellent book, *Distant Neighbors: A Portrait of the Mexicans* (New York: Vintage, 1989).

2. All amounts are in U.S. dollars, unless otherwise noted.

3. For more on the 1994–1995 peso crisis and its aftermath, see Sebastian Edwards and Moisés Naím, eds., *Mexico 1994: Anatomy of an Emerging Markets Crisis* (Washington, D.C.: Brookings Institution Press, 1997); and Riordan Roett, ed., *The Mexican Peso Crisis: International Perspectives* (Boulder: Lynne Rienner, 1996).

4. See Riordan Roett and Russell Crandall, "Beyond Bad Press: Mexico's Quiet Revolution," *Christian Science Monitor*, 15 June 1998, 11.

5. See Denise Dresser, "Post-NAFTA Politics: Uneasy, Uncertain, Unpredictable," in *The Post-NAFTA Political Economy: Mexico and the Western Hemisphere*, ed. Carol Wise (University Park: Pennsylvania State University Press, 1998), 241–253.

6. Andrés Oppenheimer, "U.S. Parties Court Mexico," *Miami Herald*, 17 August 2000, A12.

7. "Putting 'Missed' Chances Behind," *Financial Times*, 14 December 2000, 5.

8. For more on Mexico's response to the 1997–1998 Asian economic crisis, see Riordan Roett and Russell Crandall, "The Global Economic Crisis,

Contagion, and Institutions: New Realities in Asia and Latin America," *International Political Science Review* 20 (July 1999): 271–283.

9. The *maquila* program was established by the Mexican government in the mid-1960s, and it allows duty-free capital equipment imports that are to be used in maquiladoras or in-bond industries. Maquiladoras pay duties only on the value-added in Mexico, and at least 80 percent of the assembly plant output must be reexported.

10. "Central States Dominate the Action," *Financial Times*, 14 December 2000, 3–4.

11. Ibid.

12. "A System That Needs Some Simplifying," *Financial Times*, 14 December 2000, 3.

13. For more on the challenges of "second-generation" reforms in Latin America and Mexico, see Carol Wise and Manuel Pastor, "The Politics of Second Generation Reform," *Journal of Democracy* 10, no. 3 (1999): 34–48.

14. For more on subnational politics, see Wayne A. Cornelius, Todd. A. Eisenstadt, and Jane Hindley, eds., *Subnational Politics and Democratization in Mexico* (La Jolla: University of California at San Diego, 1999).

15. Tim Weiner, "Mexico's New President Faces Pesky States' Rights Revolt," *New York Times*, 12 February 2001, A3.

16. "A Fresh Start for Chiapas," *The Economist*, 10 August 2000, 31–32.

17. "El Zapatour," *Semana* (Bogotá, Colombia), 19 March 2001.

18. Tim Weiner and Ginger Thompson, "Bush Gives Mexico Backing on Drive Against Narcotics," *New York Times*, 17 February 2001, A1.

Brazil's Role as a Regional Power

Riordan Roett

Efforts to assess Brazil's role in the international system are filtered through a general belief in the international community that the country should be a more important player in global affairs but is not. Although the Brazilian economy is large and vibrant—it was ranked eighth in the world before the January 1999 devaluation of its currency—the country's income distribution is among the worst in the world. Neither have the fruits of that large economy been distributed nor have they trickled down. The respected United Nations *Human Development Report 2002* ranks Brazil 73rd in the world (down from 58th in 1996) on the human development index,[1] which combines factors such as life expectancy at birth, adult literacy, and education levels to arrive at a ranking that indicates country standing in measures of social and economic accomplishment. It is difficult to imagine that a nation-state that fails to address the basic welfare needs of its population will be able to play a significant leadership role on the world scene.

The reasons are clear and simple. Low levels of education make it more difficult to add value to exports and to insert the country into the globalized economy. Poorly prepared workers find it difficult to adapt to new technologies in the workplace. Low levels of social development create the possibility for social unrest. And the consolidation of democracy and the creation of a strong and vibrant civil society are retarded by extreme levels of inequality and income distribution. Ultimately, failure to address social development needs will impede the creation of a more sophisticated economy and society and reduce the appeal of the country to direct foreign investment. In the short run, these issues can be overlooked—Brazil remains an attractive market for foreign investors—but at some point in this century, these issues will become increasingly salient. The longer the delay in addressing the development agenda, the greater the possibility that the catch-up period will prove to be long and difficult. This appraisal is supported by *The Global Competitiveness Report 2001–2002,* prepared by the World Economic Forum and Harvard University.[2] In it, Brazil is ranked 44th of 75 countries on the "Growth Competitiveness Ranking," which measures factors that contribute to a high rate of growth in GDP per capita. On the report's "Current Competitiveness Index Ranking," which seeks to measure the conditions that determine a nation's sustainable level of productivity, Brazil is ranked 30th of 75 countries.

The Brazilian military, although an important institution, is not a predominant player in national affairs today. Since the end of the authoritarian regime in 1985, the military has been reduced in size and a civilian minister of defense instated, which has reduced the direct influence of the armed forces commanders on government policy. On a per capita basis, Brazil's military budget was never large in comparison with that of some of its neighbors or other intermediate powers in the international system. The country has abandoned any plans to develop a nuclear capability and has embraced international safeguard arrangements. Thus, Brazil's international role will not be enhanced by superior military or weapons capabilities.

International affairs and foreign policy do not preoccupy Brazilian elites, with the exception of the foreign ministry, Itamarati. There is yet no real equivalent to the Council on Foreign Relations or the World Affairs Council, which play an important role in the United States. Argentina, Brazil's major interlocutor in the Southern Cone, has had a thriving foreign affairs council for some years.[3] Academics and journalists write what little is published on foreign policy. The Brazilian congress infrequently addresses international issues; it routinely approves without debate executive branch nominees for foreign posts. Although Brazil does participate in international peacekeeping initiatives, those activities are not viewed as a key component of the country's role in the world. There is certainly interest in having Brazil occupy a permanent seat on the United Nations (UN) Security Council, if there is a reorganization of that institution, but it is, again, primarily a preoccupation of a small number of foreign ministry strategists.

In spite of these limitations, foreign analysts and policymakers continue to be fascinated by Brazil's potential. In recent discussions of "big emerging markets" or of "pivotal states," Brazil is always included.[4]

The potential of Brazil—the belief that it will, someday, assume a more dynamic leadership role in global affairs—is a given. But at the opening of the new century, that potential remains unfulfilled. This chapter will discuss the reality of Brazil's international posture: that of an important, if flawed, regional leader. Given the importance of its economy to South America, and the single-minded dedication of its foreign ministry, which also serves as the country's trade ministry, Brazil has emerged in the last decade as a more dynamic actor in regional affairs. Whether or not this regional role is a stepping-stone to a larger international role in the twenty-first century remains to be seen.

Brazil's Role in World Affairs: The Old Perception and the End of the Dream

If this chapter were being written 30 years ago, the theme would be that of Brazil emergent.[5] The military regime that seized power in 1964 had begun to create an economic powerhouse, and the concept of *grandeza* (greatness) was widely used to describe Brazil's expanding role and expanding ambitions in world affairs.

Brazil also saw itself as a natural leader of the developing countries and began playing an imaginative role in Africa as colonialism ended. Concomitantly, the country's neighbors were intimidated by what they imagined to be a military-led Brazil on the march. As minor border disputes erupted, diplomatic hostility between Brazil's military rulers and similar dictators in neighboring countries became apparent.

The military regime made it clear that it would not follow the lead of the United States in world affairs, as some predecessor governments had done, but would seek to differentiate itself from Washington on a broad range of issues. The most vexing, of course, was the issue of human rights during the administration of U.S. president Jimmy Carter (1977–1981). The military regime brooked no criticism of the degradation of the Amazon Basin as it built roads and supported the development of major infrastructure projects, all related to the export-led drive to earn foreign exchange. Brazil's preoccupation with developing an independent arms industry and its involvement in the conflicts in the Middle East caused consternation among the industrial countries.

That golden era of grandeza ended abruptly in the early 1980s. It has not returned, nor will it do so in the foreseeable future. The ingredients of the demise of grandeza were simple—politics and economics. The growing pressures from civil society for an end to the dictatorship left little room for either grand schemes of geopolitics or a flourishing arms industry. And with the onset of the international debt crisis in 1982, the bubble burst in Brazil, financial flows ceased, and the implications of Brazil's fiscal deficits hit home.

The 1980s were a decade of political transition, which resulted in a weak and indecisive government under President José Sarney (1985–1990) and in desperate economic juggling, with the balls in the air usually crashing down on the government. Brazil tried a heterodox economic shock program, the Cruzado Plan, in 1986; it failed. In 1988 Brazil declared a unilateral moratorium on its international debt obligations, which accomplished nothing but an increase in the cost of borrowing in international markets. Criticism grew over the appalling devastation of the Amazon, but the government was helpless to stop it. The plight of Brazil's indigenous peoples was a matter of international concern, but the government's efforts to protect the remaining Indian tribes were lackluster. Ironically, as a result of the weakness of the Sarney government, the armed forces played an important role in propping up the faltering administration in Brasília.

Elections in late 1989 produced a young, unknown president, Fernando Collor de Mello, whose incompetent economic team botched a feeble effort to stop inflation and jump-start the economy with another heterodox program. Collor did begin the process of trade liberalization, which would become the cornerstone of the market-reform program that has emerged in the last few years in Brazil. And he should be given credit for continuing to support the one important foreign policy initiative of the Sarney government—the creation of a common market in South America, known as Mercosur.[6] Collor also presided over a symbolically important global environmental meeting in Rio de Janeiro, which, although dramatic, has resulted in little that is new in terms of policy.

The transitional government of President Itamar Franco (1992–1995), who assumed office after the impeachment of Collor on charges of corruption, had little interest in foreign affairs. The preeminent preoccupation was the internal economy, which suffered from decades of high inflation fiscal mismanagement. Franco's foreign minister, Fernando Henrique Cardoso, moved to the Finance Ministry in 1993 and recruited a group of young technocratic economists to draft a new shock program to control inflation and lay the groundwork for sustained economic growth. This time the program succeeded—for a while. The introduction of the Real Plan in 1993–1994 dramatically reduced inflation. Cardoso's election in late 1994 opened a window of opportunity for economic reform and for a renewed interest in foreign affairs.

The important component of that paradigm shift was the apparent success of the Real Plan. For the first time in decades, it seemed that Brazil had a competent economic and financial team with an appropriate strategy. The economic plan was accompanied by the commitment of the government to undertake the difficult task of revising the 1988 statist constitution to allow economic modernization to proceed and to attract foreign direct investment and portfolio capital to support the ambitious expansion program and to cover the current account deficit.

As an indication that Brazil was coming of age, the governments of the industrial world welcomed Cardoso, a highly presentable chief executive—unlike his immediate predecessor—and a distinguished academic. Cardoso cut an impressive figure at Buckingham Palace, the United Nations, and Camp David. However, although some progress was made on opening the economy during the first Cardoso administration (1995–1999), much remained to be done. The principal culprit continued to be the fiscal imbalances, combined with the apparent unwillingness of the country's political leadership in the congress to take the matter seriously. Brazil might have muddled through the remainder of the century using international capital flows to balance its budget, had the Thai baht not collapsed in July 1997 and the Russian government not declared a default on its debt in the summer of 1998. Contagion traveled quickly. By the autumn of 1998, the international financial institutions and the G-7 industrial countries were openly concerned that a crisis in Brazil would worsen the emerging-markets trauma then in full swing.

The year 1998 was also the one in which Cardoso would seek reelection for a second term. It was therefore a campaign year, and reforms came to a stop in Brasília. International speculators sensed that the Brazilian currency was vulnerable. It was clearly overvalued. Would investors, spooked by Asia and Russia, give Brazil the benefit of the doubt? As Cardoso sailed through a smooth election in October 1998, frantic efforts were under way in Washington, D.C., during and after the annual meetings of the World Bank and the International Monetary Fund, to provide a package of financial guarantees for Brazil that would allow the newly elected chief executive time to convince a recalcitrant congress to quickly approve a package of fiscal reforms. The congress instead went home for the holidays. In mid-January 1999 the real collapsed and was allowed to float. Under the deft management of Cardoso's economic team, the impact of the devaluation was contained within the year and the country experienced a continuation of low inflation and reasonable rates of growth. In late 2001 and 2002, a collapse of the Argentine economy again threatened to destabilize the Brazilian economic program, but the sound monetary policy in place appeared to have mitigated any sharp impact of the crisis in Argentina.

Brazil is still a big emerging market, and it probably remains a so-called pivotal state. But it is not a world player, nor will it have the capacity to be so without finally addressing the fiscal issue and the weighty concerns over social and economic inequality. What Brazil is now, and will remain for the foreseeable future, is a formidable regional actor in the Americas. In that capacity, it has proven to be effective and insightful.

Brazil's Emerging Regional Role in the Hemisphere

Before the 1980s, Brazil played a limited role in the international relations of the hemisphere. The only Portuguese-speaking state, it was viewed with suspicion by many of its neighbors. For a brief period in the nineteenth century Brazil became involved in the power politics of the region, but it did so with less focused interest than Chile, Peru, and Argentina.[7] With the onset of the twentieth century, Brazil aligned itself with the United States, which was more than happy to have a counterweight to a cranky and mean-spirited Argentina. The Brazilians reinforced their ties to the Americans with the opening of U.S. bases in the Brazilian northeast during World War II and the dispatch of a Brazilian military force to fight in Italy. In the postwar period, with important exceptions, Brazil was viewed as a quiescent partner of Washington in world affairs.

Nevertheless, the military years in Brazil marked a period of tension both with the United States and with Brazil's neighbors. As both Argentina and Brazil returned to weak civilian rule—in 1983 and 1985, respectively—their leaders were beset by similar problems. Weak economies, strong militaries, and rising social expectations forced both countries to seek to better manage tensions, reduce military budgets, and identify a new economic strategy. Tentative steps had been taken at the end of the military regime to create a rapprochement between the two countries, but it was the inauguration of democratic governments in both countries that legitimated a new approach to regional integration.

Mercosur

In July 1986, President José Sarney visited Argentina. He and Argentine president Raúl Alfonsín signed a 12-point protocol aimed at creating a regional common market in the Southern Cone by 1999, the Argentine–Brazilian Program for Integration and Economic Cooperation (PICAB). In December 1986, Alfonsín traveled to Brasília and the two heads of state initiated 20 economic agreements and finalized the general strategy that had been discussed in Buenos Aires. President Julio María Sanguinetti of Uruguay joined his colleagues at the Brasília meeting and indicated his country's strong interest in immediately joining the regional integration movement.

Brazil and Argentina signed the Treaty on Integration and Economic Cooperation in November 1988. The stated goal was to transform Argentina and Brazil into a customs union by 1999. The two initiatives—PICAB and the 1988 treaty—were highly significant. For the first time since independence, the two countries put aside mutual suspicions and committed themselves to a deepening of their relations, both economic and political. The initiatives, while historic, languished in the next few years as economic problems overwhelmed both fragile democratic governments.

The next important diplomatic step in the Southern Cone took place in early 1990. U.S. president George Bush had announced his Enterprise for the Americas Initiative in June 1990. Negotiations had opened to establish the North American Free Trade Agreement (NAFTA) between Mexico, the United States, and Canada. In that context, newly elected presidents in Brazil and Argentina—Collor de Mello and Carlos Menem respectively—negotiated and signed the Act of Buenos Aires on July 6, 1990, which sought to reignite the economic integration effort. The presidents decided to hasten the integration process and set December 31, 1994, as the new date for the creation of a common market. The act was the founding document for what would soon be known as Mercosur. The leaders also agreed to create a free trade zone by the end of 1995. In September 1990, nine working groups were formed to clear the way for progressive tariff reductions and to unify policy on matters ranging from weights and measures to agricultural and transport policies.

Regional policymakers at a meeting in February 1991 in Buenos Aires drafted the Southern Cone Common Market Treaty and reconfirmed the target date of December 31, 1994. The Treaty of Asunción was signed by the four regional leaders (Paraguay had by then joined the negotiations) on March 26, 1991, which formally launched the new initiative. The first summit meeting of the four presidents was held in Uruguay in December 1991.

Central to the future of Mercosur is the debate on whether the trade bloc should be broadened or deepened, or, in the words of Félix Peña, how to strike the right balance between broadening and deepening.[8] Broadening (the number of members) and deepening (building a more sophisticated institutional infrastructure including mechanisms for dispute resolution) remain critical policy questions. To date, two associate members, Bolivia and Chile, have joined the original four. Discussions are under way with Andean countries, although little progress has been reported. The deepening issue is more political. Brazil has resisted moving beyond a skeletal infrastructure and prefers the current process, in which all key decisions are taken at the presidential level. Uruguay and Argentina would like to move more quickly to consolidate the decisionmaking process and thereby routinize day-to-day decisionmaking.

In the aftermath of the Brazilian devaluation in January 1999, events did not favor Mercosur. However, the Argentine economic crisis, which not only brought an end to the peso's peg to the U.S. dollar but also resulted in the resignation of President Fernando de la Rúa and Economy Minister Domingo Cavallo, may present an opportunity for Brazil and Argentina to seek closer integration through Mercosur. Chile opted early on to open bilateral trade negotiations with the United States in lieu of full membership in Mercosur. The United States, despite continued interest in a Free Trade Area of the Americas, has floated the idea of bilateral talks between Washington and Montevideo and Buenos Aires. What direction Mercosur will follow is yet uncertain. As Roberto Bouzas stated, "Rather than making long lists of unfinished business, what Mercosur needs most is the re-creation of a sense of political understanding and shared interests."[9] The Argentine crisis may provide the incentives to work toward greater political and economic cooperation within Mercosur.

The Free Trade Area of the Americas

In late 1994, the first Summit of the Americas met in Miami, Florida, on the initiative of U.S. president Bill Clinton's White House. The preparations for that event set the stage for a new regional role for Brazil, that of principal antagonist of the United States in its efforts to create a free trade area in the Western Hemisphere by 2005. The Brazilian foreign ministry, the country's chief trade negotiator as well as lead diplomat, was perceived by the United States in the negotiations leading to the summit as an obstacle.[10] Brazil suggested that a "building block" approach was most appropriate—NAFTA in the north and Mercosur in the south. Only after further consolidation of both of those trade agreements, Brazil argued, would negotiations for a broader, hemispheric framework—the Free Trade Area of the Americas (FTAA)—be appropriate.

The United States, fearful of diluting the Clinton vision for a hemisphere-wide arrangement, lobbied strongly and carried the day, in theory. Brazil won many of its points in practice. Two important issues colored the debate. The first was the recent election of Cardoso as president of Brazil and the successful implementation of the Real Plan earlier in the year, which gave Brazil new bargaining chips in the hemispheric poker game. Brazil, for the first time since the era of grandeza, thought it had the clout to set forth the terms of the participation of the Southern Cone in which it was primus inter pares. But the Real Plan had not yet produced its intended effects, and the general perception in Washington was that Brazil was big but not worthy of a veto, certainly, or more than its appropriate share of say in the outcome of the negotiations.

The second factor, which occurred shortly after the summit, was the devastating Mexican devaluation of the peso in December 1994. That event introduced a note of political crisis into the future of the FTAA. It meant that the new Republican majorities in the U.S. Congress were wary of trade integration. On the other side of the aisle, the opponents of NAFTA, pushed by the newly resurgent AFL-CIO, balked at new trade initiatives. The convergence of those two trends precluded Congress from granting the president fast-track negotiating authority for new trade agreements. The Mexican devaluation gave Brazil more political space to pursue its own Southern Cone agenda—until it devalued the real in January 1999.

During the U.S. presidential campaign in 2000, both candidates—Al Gore and George W. Bush—defended a deepening of regional economic integration, with Bush the more forceful advocate. The election of Bush in November 2000, and the third Summit of the Americas in Quebec City in April 2001, reopened the discussions over integration strategies in the Americas. The United States, supported by Chile and

Argentina, wanted to conclude the negotiations for an FTAA by 2003; Brazil objected and held to the original 2005 date. The Brazilian argument carried the day. But the summit, principally ceremonial, did little to move the agenda forward. To the surprise of many observers, the Republican leadership in the House of Representatives won approval of Trade Promotion Authority (TPA)—the new term for fast-track negotiating authority—by one vote in December 2001. But the price was a series of concessions to protectionist interests in many product areas critical to Latin America (textiles and citrus fruits, among others). The reaction from the region, and especially Brazil, was immediate and negative. The final version of TPA was approved by both houses of Congress in August 2002. The final outcome favored the more protectionist version voted on in December 2001. Brazil's reaction was tepid. Foreign Minister Celso Lafer's comments following President George W. Bush's signing of the TPA expressed Brazilian skepticism: "FTAA negotiations were never going to be easy but with the wave of [U.S.] protectionism, we know they will be even more difficult."[11] In particular, Brazil remained skeptical about Bush's capacity to move quickly on trade negotiations, even with TPA, and Brazil reemphasized that the FTAA was an option, and Mercosur was its "destiny."

Regional Diplomacy

Regional economic integration is not the only area in which Brazil might play a significant leadership role in the new century. Regional diplomacy is a relatively new field of endeavor, but one with potential for Brazilian involvement. Given the historical antipathy on the part of Spanish America toward greater Brazilian involvement in the affairs of South America, Brazil remained aloof from its Spanish American neighbors until the early 1980s. Desultory talks on trade and economic integration included Brazil, of course, but because the stakes were low, so too was Brazil's commitment to the talks. With the onset of the debt crisis in 1982 and the gradual political liberalization in the region in the early and mid-1980s, however, Brazil began to demonstrate a greater proclivity for collective action.

Brazil actively participated in all of the regional efforts to reduce the burden of regional debt after Mexico defaulted in 1982 and credit lines and loans disappeared. In a more marginal way, Brazil joined the so-called support group for the Contadora Process, which aimed to seek a negotiated settlement to the conflict in Central America in the mid-

and late 1980s. In December 1986, Brazil hosted a meeting in Rio de Janeiro of the Group of Eight, which quickly became known as the Rio Group. It was composed of the support group and the four countries known as the Contadora Group. The foreign ministers of the Rio Group drafted a "Permanent Mechanism of Political Consultation and Cooperation" that eventually led to the creation of a permanent forum for the discussion of the entire agenda of multilateral concerns of the countries involved. Brazil assumed the role of secretary for the Rio Group and undertook a series of initiatives to resolve the debt crisis. Those efforts were an important element in the decision of the administration of President Bush in early 1989 to initiate a new program of debt reduction known as the Brady Plan.

Brazil has participated in other regional initiatives in recent years. The government of President Cardoso was a strong supporter of the "democratic clause" in Mercosur, which stipulates that membership in the regional bloc is open only to democratically elected governments. Paraguay threatened to disrupt that protocol during its national elections in 1998, when it was not clear that free and fair balloting would take place. Brasília spoke out clearly that the democratic protocol would be invoked if fair play were not permitted. In the border conflict between Ecuador and Peru, which erupted again in 1995, Brazil was one of the four "guarantors" of a 1940s cease-fire agreement. Along with Argentina, Chile, and the United States, Brasília actively sought to reinstate the cease-fire agreement and to urge the two protagonists to seek a permanent treaty settlement, which eventually occurred.

Brazil has been an active member of the annual Ibero-American summits, which bring together the heads of state of Latin America, Spain, and Portugal. This venue has been useful for restructuring relations between the region and Europe. The summit held in Rio de Janeiro in 1999 between the European Union (EU) and the heads of state of Latin America and the Caribbean was an important priority for Brazilian foreign policy. Latin American relations with the EU were formalized with the Rome Declaration of 1990, which institutionalized a European–Latin American dialogue. The administration of President Cardoso was a strong supporter of that dialogue. And in the boldest gesture of regional leadership to date, Brazil invited the heads of state of South America (North America—and therefore Mexico—was not included) to a summit in Brasília in late August 2000. The "Brasília Communiqué" adopted a "South American" approach to resolving conflicts and addressing important policy questions. It was the first such meeting in the history of the region. Brazil was clearly the convener and the driving force behind the summit.

Brazil has assumed an important leadership role in an area that had long been controversial in South America, nuclear weapons. During the Cold War, there was a great deal of concern about the spread of nuclear weapons to developing countries. In the early 1960s, Brazil proposed that Latin America be made a nuclear-free zone. Following the Cuban missile crisis in 1962, Brazil led a group of five Latin American presidents and again urged the United Nations to act. The UN General Assembly approved the concept of a nuclear-free Latin America in November 1963. The Treaty for the Prohibition of Nuclear Weapons in Latin America was signed in February 1967 in the Tlatelolco section of Mexico City (the treaty is known by that name). Although a majority of the countries in the region ratified the treaty, Argentina and Brazil did not. Argentina had signed but not ratified the document, whereas Brazil ratified the treaty but with the reservation that it would not enter into force until all other eligible states had ratified it (that is, Argentina). This issue became a point of contention in the Southern Cone and between the United States, Argentina, and Brazil.

During the military regime, a nuclear program was developed and the Brazilian arms industry grew to become the sixth largest exporter in the world. The Sarney government was too weak to confront the military establishment on either the nuclear program or the arms industry. To his credit, President Collor de Mello in 1990 closed down secret nuclear facilities and publicly endorsed the nonproliferation regime. In November 1990, Argentina and Brazil formally renounced the manufacture of nuclear weapons. Other measures followed, such as the dismantling of the Condor 2 ballistic missile project, the ratification of the Tlatelolco treaty, and the adherence to the Missile Technology Control Regime. Brazil has emerged as a leader in the efforts to slow down the arms race and to consolidate the region as a nuclear-free zone.

A final and important area in which Brazil must take the lead is the Amazon Valley. The Amazon holds an almost mystical fascination for Brazilians. Although it has been explored only intermittently, the region attracted worldwide attention in the nineteenth and twentieth centuries from botanists, anthropologists, adventure seekers, and European aristocrats. It was only after military intervention in 1964, however, that the Amazon achieved political and economic importance. A military regime that based its right to rule on the dual propositions of national security and national development saw the Amazon as relevant to both.

The regime had the financial resources to secure the area through emigration and settlement. It could also think about the integration of the region into Brazil. The building of the Transamazon Highway in the 1970s served all of those purposes. There were also strong domestic economic interests. The need for foreign exchange and the expanding international market for foodstuffs led inexorably to the introduction of agroindustry—large, mechanized farms that produced for export. Violence erupted when the large developers, responding to the beckon of opportunity, attempted to expel small landowners and squatters.

The Amazon also served as a safety valve for the poverty-ridden northeast region. Planners in Brasília saw the Amazon as an obvious area for internal migration, eliminating the possibility of large-scale social unrest in the northeast. As poor farmers moved in, they brought with them their traditional methods, foremost among them slash-and-burn agriculture. By the late 1970s the Amazon was ablaze. The rain forest and the woodlands began to disappear at an alarming rate. As the political transition began in Brazil in the early 1980s, environmental groups were growing in strength and receiving increased support from groups in the industrial countries, as well as from many governments. Scientists and ecologists became effective lobbyists, using Brazil as an example of how authoritarian regimes were damaging the global environment. At this point, another element was added to the equation, the indigenous populations of the region. Suddenly, Brazil was confronted with an international storm of protest over ecology, damage to the ozone layer, Indian rights, and the disappearance of the jungle fauna and flora.

During the Sarney administration, feeble efforts were made to respond to the criticism, without success. The murder of Chico Mendes, leader of a rubber tappers union in the state of Acre and recipient of the United Nations Global 500 ecology prize in 1987 for his pioneering work to preserve the Amazon, ignited a worldwide protest. U.S. senators, English prime minister Margaret Thatcher, and a host of other political leaders began to publicly criticize the Brazilian government for its insensitivity.

The Collor de Mello administration in 1990 took a proactive position. A number of Amazon defenders were appointed to important positions in the government. The new government actively supported plans for the UN Conference on Environment and Development—the Rio conference—in 1992. A principal outcome of the meeting in Rio de Janeiro was Agenda 21, an action plan for the 1990s and the twenty-first century, which elaborated strategies and proposed programs to halt and reverse the effects of environmental degradation.

President Cardoso's first administration continued to receive strong international condemnation and pressure to respond to such international concerns. In addition to the degradation of the Amazon Valley itself, the media reported a series of brutal murders of homeless peasants by local guns-for-hire, under the direction of the large landowners. The government's predicament has been made more apparent by the emergence of a strong movement of people without land (Movimento Sem Terra, or MST), which has marched on Brasília and has captured the interest of the international media.

The Amazon Valley is a dilemma for Brazil. While the government receives the brunt of the criticism for inaction, much of the region is in private hands. There is strong support for the landowners in the Brazilian congress. And the economic development goals of the country directly contradict the international demands for the protection of the region, its rich diversity, and its indigenous inhabitants. Although this is a problem with international implications, the regional dimension is important because the several countries that border the Amazon Valley are becoming increasingly concerned about spillover environmental contamination.[12]

The U.S. Perspective on Brazil's Future Global Role

Every four years the Chicago Council on Foreign Relations publishes a comprehensive analysis of *American Public Opinion and U.S. Foreign Policy*.[13] The 1999 report provides some useful data with which to conclude the analysis of Brazil's future role in world affairs. The survey includes the opinions of two groups of interviewees—"the public" and "the leaders"—in response to the question "Please tell me whether in your estimation the following countries will play a greater role or a lesser role in the next ten years than they do today (percentage)."[14] From the leaders, Brazil received a ranking of 64 percent, following in rank order the United States, China, and India, but ahead of Japan, Russia, and Germany. The public ranked Brazil seventh (21 percent) of the seven countries.

The interviewees were asked also whether or not the United States had a vital interest in each of 26 countries. With the leaders, Brazil ranked 11th—between South Korea and Iran. The public placed Brazil in 21st place, clustered with Indonesia and Turkey but after India. Finally, to gauge how the public perceives its various neighbors, allies, friends, and foes around the world, the public was asked to rate 25 countries on a "feeling barometer," ranging from 0 to 100 degrees. A warm feeling toward a country is defined as a temperature above 50 degrees, which is neutral. Interestingly, warm feelings persist for Brazil (56 percent—equivalent to Germany, but after Mexico and ahead of Japan), despite the low ranking on the vital interest list.

Another important benchmark in determining the evolving perceptions of Brazil in the United States was the publication in 2001 of an Independent Task Force Report of the Council on Foreign Relations on U.S. Policy Toward Brazil. The thrust of the report was stated in a cover letter to President Bush:

> Brazil, we believe, can and should be a crucial player with the United States in promoting economic reform and free trade, in sustaining democracy and open markets, and in combating narcotics, terrorism, and transregional crime. The United States cannot act alone in South America, and there is no better strategic partner than Brazil in tackling these problems. A realistic and sustained dialogue with Brazil is central to any successful U.S. policy in the Western Hemisphere. Brazil is the fulcrum. Brazil is too important to everything that is going to happen in South America for a policy of benign neglect.[15]

For Brazil, these findings represent both a challenge and an opportunity. Much remains to be done to convince the American public that Brazil is important to the United States or that it has an international role to play in the future. Among leaders, the spadework has been done. Brazil counts. The challenge is to work to expand the understanding among the U.S. public of Brazil's relevance to the United States and to world affairs. The opportunity is to build on the strong and positive impression held by the "leaders" to identify issue areas in which Brazil can exercise leadership. As argued earlier in this chapter, Brazil's assumption of a greater leadership role will require a higher level of perceived political stability and a comprehensive commitment to reducing inequality and directly addressing the issue of income distribution.

Conclusion: The Consolidation of Regional Leadership

There is no doubt that Brazil in the last two decades has emerged as a recognized leader in South America. Its regional role is secure. On a

wide range of important initiatives—nuclear proliferation, arms production, economic integration, diplomatic negotiations—the government
has broken with its past isolation and become a strong advocate of multilateral regionalism. But because of its size and economic weight, it is
viewed as a leader that often gets its way whether or not others agree
with its position. Under Fernando Henrique Cardoso, the leadership was
generally collegial, although its immediate neighbors in Mercosur complained about heavy-handed decisionmaking when Brazil's vital economic and industrial interests were at stake. Indeed, a long period of
tension and near-crisis followed the January 1999 devaluation of the
currency, but astute negotiations appear to have reduced the concerns
about the survival of Mercosur.

There remains a great deal of room for Brazil to broaden and
deepen its regional leadership role. While Brazil continues to insist
that Mercosur will be the pivot for that strategy, fissures have
appeared in that organization that have begun to raise doubts about its
long-term viability unless strong leadership emerges to refocus the
energies of the member countries and of the entity itself. Important
decisions need to be taken regarding deepening or widening. Tariff
reduction policies need to be coordinated and implemented. These and
many other matters have been pending for a decade. It is not clear
how influential Mercosur can be in the future without addressing this
pending agenda in the near future. To the degree that Mercosur recov-
ers its diplomatic initiative following the Argentine crisis of 2001–
2002, it will play a strategic role in concluding the FTAA negotiations
in 2005. Without Mercosur as a shield, Brazil will face a more difficult task in defending a South American—as opposed to a Brazilian—
position in the talks.

Does this situation necessarily indicate a greater global role for
Brazil in the near term? Not necessarily. As argued earlier in this
chapter, Brazil's need in the twenty-first century is to focus on fiscal
stability and social investment. Income distribution issues need to be
addressed. Basic human needs—education, health, and housing—
need to be addressed. As those issues yield to good governance in
the years ahead, Brazil will be ready to expect and to receive a
broader, more strategic role in whatever international system
emerges. In the meantime, its efforts at establishing a legitimate and
useful regional leadership role are widely recognized and increasingly valued.

Notes

1. United Nations Development Programme, *Human Development Report 2002* (New York: Oxford University Press, 2002).

2. Harvard University and the World Economic Forum, *The Global Competitiveness Report 2001–2002* (New York: Oxford University Press, 2002), 11.

3. It may be that the formation of the Brazilian Center of International Relations (CEBRI) will open an opportunity for a broader discussion of foreign affairs in Brazil. It is located in Rio de Janeiro and is headed by former foreign minister Luiz Felipe Lampreia. But the issue is whether or not an Itamarati-oriented CEBRI will be able to criticize and debate Brazilian foreign policy or merely endorse what is formulated in Brasília.

4. Jeffrey E. Garten, *The Big Ten: The Big Emerging Markets and How They Will Change Our Lives* (New York: Basic Books, 1997); Robert Chase, Emily Hill, and Paul Kennedy, eds., *The Pivotal States: A New Framework for U.S. Policy in the Developing World* (New York: Norton, 1999).

5. Indeed, one of my early essays on Brazil was entitled "Brazil Ascendant: International Relations and Geopolitics in the Late 20th Century," *Journal of International Affairs* 29 (1975): 139–154.

6. Mercosur (Mercado Común del Sur) is the most widely used acronym; however, it is also known as Mercosul, its Portuguese equivalent.

7. Robert N. Burr, *By Reason or Force: Chile and the Balancing of Power in South America, 1830–1905* (Berkeley: University of California Press, 1967).

8. Félix Peña, "Broadening and Deepening: Striking the Right Balance," in *Mercosur: Regional Integration, World Markets*, ed. Riordan Roett (Boulder: Lynne Rienner, 1999), 49–61.

9. "Another Blow to Mercosur," *The Economist*, 31 March 2001, 34.

10. Richard E. Feinberg, *Summitry in the Americas: A Progress Report* (Washington, D.C.: Institute for International Economics, 1997).

11. Raymond Colitt, "Brazilian Leader Urges U.S. to Lower Trade Barriers: Cardoso Rules Out Joining Americas Trade Agreement Unless Tariffs Are Cut," *Financial Times*, 7 August 2002, 1.

12. Larry Rohter, "Amazon Forest Is Still Burning, Despite Pledges," *New York Times*, 23 August 2002, 1.

13. John E. Rielly, ed., *American Public Opinion and U.S. Foreign Policy, 1999* (Chicago: Chicago Council on Foreign Relations, 1999).

14. Ibid., 10.

15. Council on Foreign Relations, cover letter to President George W. Bush, *Independent Task Force Report on U.S. Policy Toward Brazil* (New York: Council on Foreign Relations, January 2001).

Part 4

Conclusion

Latin America and the Western Hemisphere in the Age of Globalization

Russell Crandall

If this volume had been written a decade ago, the overriding theme would most likely have been democratization, as several Latin American countries were in the process of making the arduous and complex transition from authoritarian to democratic regimes. Today, however, most nations in the Western Hemisphere are democratic, if at least in the electoral sense. If the transition to democracy was Latin America's last great question of the twentieth century, what will be the question for the twenty-first century? If the themes of the chapters in this volume are any indication, it will be globalization. That we are increasingly discussing the "Western Hemisphere" and not just "North America" and "Latin America" is one more indicator of how interconnected the region has become. Unfortunately, this new reality does not ensure that Latin America's difficulties are behind it; rather, it means that Latin America must adapt to—and ultimately thrive in—these new global circumstances.

It goes without saying that the era of globalization has arrived in the Western Hemisphere. With the Cold War well over, and along with it the ideological clash between capitalism and communism, there is a broadening consensus in the international financial community surrounding the efficacy of free market economic principles in promoting economic growth. While critics on the right and left are constantly challenging this consensus, it has nonetheless been adopted by developing countries across the globe. Accelerating this ideological change have been the rapid advances in technology that have permitted capitalism to penetrate into corners of the developing world where up until recently it had never dared enter. The Western Hemisphere—and especially Latin

America—cannot ignore this trend. It is within this context that the chapters in this volume have addressed some of the region's most pressing social, political, and security issues.

The Era of Globalization

The era of globalization has also meant that actors such as international financial agents—or Wall Street—have gained an unprecedented importance and influence in what is the global game of capital flows.[1] A strong argument can be made that signals of support from Wall Street investment houses have become as important to a developing country's economic well-being as praise from the White House or the World Bank. For the Latin American countries this is of great significance, as their political, social, and economic welfare is now dependent on this relationship. The behavior of the United States and Canada is also of considerable importance because the era of globalization is a two-way street: The northern part of the Western Hemisphere must embrace and respect its southern counterparts.

Perhaps the present era of globalization—and the significant increase in financial power that it has given to private financial agents— can be characterized as *king capital*. Capital today is more fickle and ruthless than at any other point in history; new technology allows it to be transferred from one bank account to another—or one country to another—with a keyboard stroke. For many developing countries—or emerging markets—the advent of the era of king capital has made for a veritable survival of the fittest or, perhaps better said, survival of the most appealing to Wall Street.[2]

Within this new global context developing countries are still free to disregard the demands of international financial agents, the International Monetary Fund (IMF), or the U.S. Treasury, but there is a very high risk associated with such nonconformist behavior as it might result in the financial blacklisting of the country, which most likely would prevent the country from receiving future resources from these institutions. This reality is made even more sober by the fact that an extremely cozy relationship exists among the aforementioned global financial referees such as the IMF and Wall Street, meaning that offending one institution can very easily translate into even greater consequences.[3] The IMF's August 2002 decision to provide a multibillion-dollar financial assistance package to Brazil represents one more example of the tenuous relationship that Latin America has with the international financial community. Neighboring Argentina, the present black sheep of Wall Street and Washington due to its inability or reluctance to implement the requested economic reforms, could only dream of receiving such supportive treatment from international actors.

Concomitant with these rapid advances in technology that have driven the prominence of king capital, there have also been dramatic changes in public policy management around the world, above all in the emerging markets. While capital might be able to move from place to place faster than ever before, only effective governing practices and financial management can properly take advantage of the potentially significant opportunities that international capital can provide for a developing country. In other words, institutions matter.

Some have called this precarious balance between the amounts of capital that the international markets make available to a particular country and the ability of that country to utilize this capital effectively the *impossible trinity*. The impossible trinity is the quest for emerging markets to reconcile financial and economic integration and to strengthen state institutions, all the while maintaining sovereignty. The belief is that only once this impossible trinity is achieved can emerging countries be assured of more consistent, predictable patterns of capital flows and, more importantly, sustained economic, social, and political development. This new framework will set the context in which Latin America and the hemisphere as a whole will evolve in this new century.

The Limits of Globalization

While there is much to the notion of the impossible trinity, the chapters in this volume have demonstrated that the Western Hemisphere's challenges in the global world go well beyond just reconciling international and domestic political economy considerations. Rather, the Western Hemisphere today is a region that faces a plethora of strategic, social, political, and economic issues that will shape its evolution in this new century. Thus, globalization will the set the parameters for the Western Hemisphere, but this does not negate the pressing issues that have plagued many countries in the region for centuries. In fact, the new global reality will often make them more difficult to address. In this sense, it is vital that globalization's unparalleled ability to generate wealth for some does not distract states and individuals from attending to those in society who have not benefited from that wealth.

Latin America's current unimpressive economic performance has led many observers to talk of a "backlash" in the region against the "neoliberal" reforms implemented in the 1990s under the notorious "Washington Consensus." The logic is that the savage free market ideologies forced on the people of Latin America are now being rejected since they have been complete failures. The reality, however, is more complex than this and, fortunately, more optimistic.

To be sure, Latin America's experience with economic reform has been mixed, and a great number of citizens have not seen any improvement in the quality of their lives. Yet many Latin Americans understand that their inability to permanently do away with economic anemia and instability lies far deeper than any Washington Consensus tenet such as trade reform or privatization. Instead, Latin America's successful economic and social performance—and concomitant insertion into the world economy—rests on a foundation of civic and corporate probity and effective institutions that promote the rule of law.

Forrest Colburn's recent book on contemporary Latin America argues that Latin America has reached the "end of politics."[4] That is, the major ideological debates that characterized much of the twentieth century have been decided in favor of liberal democracy; yet according to Colburn, while Latin America might be at the end of politics in terms of the major issues of political organization, this does not mean that Latin America has done away with misery, public insecurity, and economic and political instability. With its position now at the end of politics, the pressing question for Latin America becomes "now what?"

The current situation in the region indicates that effective responses will not be easy to formulate or implement. Credible leadership is scarce and the region's political and economic elites have not adequately committed to addressing the political, social, and economic weaknesses. Perhaps Latin America was better during the era of "politics," when revolution and utopian ideals were seen as both desirable and achievable. Effective municipal governance, for example, might not be as passionate a topic as world revolution, but these are the types of reforms that the region desperately needs right now.

The contributors to this volume have laid out a number of the key issues confronting the region in the new century. These chapters can be seen as intellectual shots over the bow in the sense that they provide the frameworks within which change will take place in Latin America and the Western Hemisphere. While it is impossible to accurately predict the course that the region will take in this new century, we can be reasonably confident that the issues addressed in this volume will represent some of the most formidable obstacles—and potential opportunities— for all countries in the Western Hemisphere.

This process will not be smooth or linear. We do know that it will take place within the parameters of globalization. This reality is at once terrifying and inspiring: The Western Hemisphere knows that it must embrace this new era, but it is still unsure of exactly how to do it effectively. This irrevocable insertion into the global economy signifies the beginning of the modern understanding of the Western Hemisphere. Unfortunately, we are still unable to tell if this change represents unqualified good, but we can be sure that it represents a new set of exciting challenges and opportunities for the region. Strong leadership, effective government institutions, and active civic participation represent some of the key factors that will continue to define Latin America's place in the global community.

Notes

1. For an original analysis of the "mentality" of Wall Street analysts, see Javier Santiso, "Analysts Analyzed: A Socio-economic Approach to Financial and Emerging Markets," *International Political Science Review* 20, no. 3 (Summer 1999): 307–330.

2. These views were first put forth in Riordan Roett and Russell Crandall, "Confining Conditions: New Guidelines for Latin America's Leaders," *Harvard International Review* 21, no. 3 (Summer 1999): 64–67.

3. For more on the relationship among Wall Street, the IMF, and the U.S. Treasury, see Jagdish Bhagwati, "The Capital Myth," *Foreign Affairs* 77, no. 3 (May–June 1998): 7–12.

4. Forrest D. Colburn, *Latin America at the End of Politics* (Princeton: Princeton University Press, 2002).

Bibliography

Aaronson, Susan A. "George W. Bush, Protectionist." *The International Economy* 14, no. 1 (Winter 2002): 54–62.

Agence Europe. *Bulletin Quotidien Europe* 7446 (16 April 1999).

Amnesty International 2002 Report. London: Amnesty International, 2002.

"Another Blow to Mercosur." *The Economist*, 31 March 2001, 34.

Argentina: Libro Blanco de la Defensa Nacional. Buenos Aires: Government of Argentina, 1999.

Axworthy, Lloyd. "Canadian Foreign Policy: A Liberal Party Perspective." *Canadian Foreign Policy* 1, no. 1 (Winter 1992–1993): 1–8.

Aznárez, J. J. "Malestar en Venezuela por la visita del embajador de España al presidente golpista." *El País* (Madrid), 19 April 2002.

Baer, Werner, and William Maloney. "Neoliberalism and Income Distribution in Latin America." *World Development* 25, no. 3 (1997): 311–327.

Barro, Robert J. *Determinants of Economic Growth.* Cambridge: MIT Press, 1998.

Basdeo, Sahadeo. "Caribecan: A Continuum in Canada–Commonwealth–Caribbean Economic Relations." *Canadian Foreign Policy* 1, no. 2 (Spring 1993): 56–57.

Beattie, Alan. "Top Lieutenant Allays Fears over Her Role After Baptism of Fire." *Financial Times*, 20 April 2002, 8.

Beattie, Alan, and Raymond Colitt. "US Scorns IMF Plan for Bankrupt Governments." *Financial Times*, 6 April 2002, 7.

Benecke, Dieter. "Relación entre la Unión Europea y el Mercosur." *Contribuciones* 1, no. 16 (Buenos Aires: CIEDLA, 1999): 7–17.

Bennet, Rosemary. "Chancellor Plans Treasury Crackdown on 'Vulture Funds.'" *Financial Times*, 6 May 2002, 2.

Bhagwati, Jagdish. "The Capital Myth." *Foreign Affairs* 77, no. 3 (May–June 1998): 7–12.

Bhagwati, Jagdish, and Anne O. Krueger. *The Dangerous Drift to Preferential Trade Agreements.* Washington, D.C.: American Enterprise Institute, 1995.

Bird, Graham, and Dane Rowlands. "World Bank Lending and Other Financial

Flows: Is There a Connection?" *Journal of Development Studies* 37, no. 5 (June 2001): 83–103.

Birdsall, Nancy, and Luis Londoño. "Asset Inequality Matters: An Assessment of the World Bank's Approach to Poverty Reduction." *American Economic Review* 87, no. 2 (1997): 32–37.

Blanco, Carlos. "Another Hundred Years of Solitude? Latin America After September 11." *Harvard International Review* 24, no. 1 (Spring 2002): 79–80.

Bloomfield, Richard. "Making the Western Hemisphere Safe for Democracy? The OAS Defense of Democracy Regime." *Washington Quarterly* 17, no. 2 (Spring 1994): 157–169.

Botana, Natalio R. "La corrupción en la mira." *La Nación,* Sección Opinión, 17 February 2000, 15.

———. "¡Que se vayan! ¿Y después?" *La Nación,* Sección Opinión, 7 February 2002, 17.

Bouzas, Roberto. "Las perspectivas del Mercosur: Desafíos, escenarios y alternativas para la próxima década." *Documentos de Trabajo de FLACSO,* August 1999.

Bouzas, Roberto, and Jaime Ros. "The North-South Variety of Economic Integration: Issues and Prospects for Latin America." In *Economic Integration in the Western Hemisphere,* edited by Roberto Bouzas and Jaime Ros, 1–45. Notre Dame, Ind.: University of Notre Dame Press, 1994.

Briceño Ruiz, José. "Strategic Regionalism and the Remaking of the Triangular Relation between the USA, the European Union and Latin America." *Journal of European Integration* 23, no. 2 (2001): 105–137.

Brysk, Alison. *From Tribal Village to Global Village: Indian Rights and International Relations in Latin America.* Stanford: Stanford University Press, 2000.

———. "Globalization: The Double-edged Sword." *NACLA Report on the Americas* 34, no. 1 (July–August 2000): 29–33.

———, ed. *Globalization and Human Rights.* Berkeley: University of California Press, 2002.

Buiter, Willem H., and Anne Sibert. "UDROP: A Small Contribution to the New International Financial Architecture." CEPR Discussion Paper 2138. London: Centre for Economic Policy Research, 1999.

Burgerman, Susan. *Moral Victories: How Activists Provoke Multilateral Action.* Ithaca: Cornell University Press, 2001.

Burr, Robert N. *By Reason or Force: Chile and the Balancing of Power in South America, 1830–1905.* Berkeley: University of California Press, 1967.

Carasales, Julio César. *De rivales a socios: El proceso de cooperación nuclear entre Argentina y Brasil.* Buenos Aires: ISEN/Grupo Editorial Latinoamericano, 1997.

Carella, Alfredo. *La Argentina y el pluralismo en el sistema inter-Americano.* San Miguel de Tucumán, Argentina: Instituto de Estudios Políticos y Económicos para la Integración Latinoamericana, 1973.

Carothers, Thomas. "Democracy Without Illusions." *Foreign Affairs* 76, no. 1 (January–February 1997): 85–99.

"Central States Dominate the Action." *Financial Times,* 14 December 2000, 3–4.

"The CEO Presidency." *The Economist,* 21 June 2002, 34.

Chase, Robert, Emily Hill, and Paul Kennedy, eds. *The Pivotal States: A New Framework for U.S. Policy in the Developing World.* New York: Norton, 1999.

Chudnovsky, Daniel, Andrés López, and Fernando Porta. "New Foreign Direct Investment in Argentina: Privatization, the Domestic Market, and Regional Integration." In *Foreign Direct Investment in Latin America,* edited by Manuel Agosin, 39–104. Washington, D.C.: Inter-American Development Bank, 1995.

Cline, William. *Trade and Income Distribution.* Washington, D.C.: Institute for International Economics, 1997.

Cohen, Benjamin. "¿Gulliver o lilliputiense? Los Estados Unidos en la economía mundial de hoy." In *Globalización y regionalismo en las relaciones internacionales de Estados Unidos,* edited by Roberto Bouzas and Roberto Russell, 27–58. Buenos Aires: ISEN/Grupo Editorial Latinoamericano, 1996.

Colburn, Forrest D. *Latin America at the End of Politics.* Princeton: Princeton University Press, 2002.

Colitt, Raymond. "Brazilian Leader Urges U.S. to Lower Trade Barriers: Cardoso Rules Out Joining Americas Trade Agreement Unless Tariffs Are Cut." *Financial Times,* 7 August 2002, 1.

Collier, Paul, and Jan Willem Gunning. "The IMF's Role in Structural Adjustment." *Economic Journal* 109, no. 459 (November 1999): F634–F651.

Connell-Smith, Gordon. *Sistema Inter-Americano.* Mexico City: Fondo de Cultura Económica, 1961.

Cornelius, Wayne A., Todd A. Eisenstadt, and Jane Hindley, eds. *Subnational Politics and Democratization in Mexico.* La Jolla: University of California at San Diego, 1999.

Corrales, Javier, and Richard E. Feinberg. "Regimes of Cooperation in the Western Hemisphere: Power, Interests, and Intellectual Traditions." *International Studies Quarterly* 43, no. 1 (March 1999): 1–36.

Council on Foreign Relations. Cover letter to President George W. Bush, *Independent Task Force Report on U.S. Policy Toward Brazil.* New York: Council on Foreign Relations, January 2001.

Da Motta Veiga, Pedro. "Brazil's Strategy for Trade Liberalization and Economic Integration in the Western Hemisphere." In *Integrating the Hemisphere: Perspectives from Latin America and the Caribbean,* edited by Ana Julia Jatar and Sidney Weintraub, 197–207. Washington, D.C.: Inter-American Dialogue, 1997.

Daudelin, Jean. "Between Cuba and a Hard Place: Another Bout of U.S. Extraterritoriality." *Canadian Foreign Policy* 2, no. 3 (Winter 1994–1995): 119–121.

Davidow, Jeffrey. "U.S. Policy Toward Latin America and the Caribbean:

Building upon a Solid Foundation." Remarks by the assistant secretary of state at the Miami Conference on the Caribbean and Latin America, Miami, Florida, 9 December 1996. Published in *Dispatch Magazine* 7, no. 51 (16 December 1996).

Destler, I. M. *Renewing Fast-Track Legislation.* Washington, D.C.: Institute for International Economics, 1997.

De Zela, Hugo. "La Carta Democrática Interamericana." *Archivos del Presente* 7, no. 25 (2002): 97–109.

Domínguez, Jorge. "Technopols: Ideas and Leaders in Freeing Politics and Markets in Latin America in the 1990s." In *Technopols: Freeing Politics and Markets in Latin America in the 1990s,* edited by Jorge Domínguez, 1–49. University Park: Pennsylvania State University Press, 1997.

Donnelly, Jack. "Human Rights: A New Standard of Civilization?" *International Affairs* 74, no. 1 (1998): 1–24.

Doran, Charles F. "The Trade and Political Party Flip-Flop." In *The NAFTA Puzzle,* edited by Charles F. Doran and Gregory Marchildon, 1–8. Boulder: Westview, 1994.

———. "When Building North America, Deepen Before Widening." In *A New North America,* edited by Charles F. Doran and Alvin Paul Drischler, 65–90. Westport, Conn.: Praeger, 1996.

Dornbusch, Rudiger. "Brazil's Incomplete Stabilization and Reform." *Mercosur Journal* 8 (1997): 20–37.

Dresser, Denise. "Post-NAFTA Politics: Uneasy, Uncertain, Unpredictable." In *The Post-NAFTA Political Economy: Mexico and the Western Hemisphere,* edited by Carol Wise, 241–253. University Park: Pennsylvania State University Press, 1998.

Eaton, George E. "Canada-Sugar and the Commonwealth Caribbean." *Caribbean Quarterly* 19 (March 1972): 72–74.

ECLAC/CEPAL (Economic Commission for Latin America and the Caribbean). "Macroeconomic Performance in 1997." *CEPAL News* 18, no. 2 (1998): 1–3.

———. "Metodología estandarizada para la medición de los gastos de defensa." Santiago, Chile: ECLAC/CEPAL, November 2001.

———. "Sixth Ministerial Trade Meeting." *CEPAL News* 20, no. 4 (2001): 2.

Edwards, Geoffrey, and Elfriede Regelsberger, eds. *Europe's Global Links: The European Community and Interregional Cooperation.* London: Pinter, 1990.

Edwards, Sebastian, and Moisés Naím, eds. *Mexico 1994: Anatomy of an Emerging Markets Crisis.* Washington, D.C.: Brookings Institution Press, 1997.

Eichengreen, Barry. *Toward a New International Financial Architecture.* Washington, D.C.: Institute for International Economics, 1999.

Eichengreen, Barry, and Ashoka Mody. "Bail-Ins, Bailouts, and Borrowing Costs." *IMF Staff Papers* 47, Special Issue: IMF Annual Research Conference (2001): 155–187.

Erzan, Refik, and Alexander Yeats. "U.S.–Latin American Free Trade Areas: Some Empirical Evidence." In *The Premise and the Promise: Free Trade in the Americas,* edited by Silvia Saborio, 117–152. Washington, D.C.: Overseas Development Council, 1992.

European Union. "Action Plan." First Summit Between Latin America, the Caribbean, and the European Union. Rio de Janeiro, 28–29 June 1999.

————. "Communication from the Commission to the Council and the European Parliament: Follow-up to the First Summit Between Latin America, the Caribbean, and the European Union." Brussels: Commission of the European Communities, 31 October 2000.

————. "Communication from the Commission to the Council, the European Parliament, and the Economic and Social Committee on a New European Union–Latin America Partnership on the Eve of the 21st Century." Brussels: European Commission, 9 March 1999.

————. "EU-LAC Common Values and Positions." Madrid, 17 May 2002.

————. "EU–Latin America and the Caribbean Summit." Brussels: European Union, 17 May 2002.

————. "EU/Latin America Relations." Report A5-0336/2001. Brussels: Committee on Foreign Affairs, Human Rights, Common Security, and Defence Policy, European Parliament, 11 October 2001.

————. *European Commission: Latin America Regional Strategy Document.* Brussels: European Commission, 2002.

————. "Rio Joint Declaration." First Summit Between Latin America, the Caribbean, and the European Union. Rio de Janeiro, 28–29 June 1999.

Feinberg, Richard E. *Summitry in the Americas: A Progress Report.* Washington, D.C.: Institute for International Economics, 1997.

————. "A Vision for the Americas." *Financial Times,* 7 August 2002, 11.

Feinberg, Richard E., and Robin Rosenberg. "The Quebec City Summit: Tear Gas, Trade, and Democracy." *North-South Center Update,* 13 May 2001.

Feldstein, Martin. "Argentina's Fall." *Foreign Affairs* 81, no. 2 (March–April 2002): 8–14.

————. "No New Architecture." *The International Economy* 13, no. 5 (September–October 1999): 32–35.

Finch, C. David. "Cry for Argentina." *The International Economy* 16, no. 2 (Spring 2002): 26–28.

Finnegan, William. "After Seattle." *New Yorker,* 17 April 2000, 40–51.

Firestone, David. "Senate Approves Bill to Give Bush Trade Authority." *New York Times,* 2 August 2002, A1.

Fischer, Stanley. "IMF as Lender of Last Resort." *Central Banking* 9 (February 1999): 34–35.

Fishlow, Albert. "The Foreign Policy Challenge for the United States." In *The United States and the Americas: A Twenty-First Century View,* edited by Albert Fishlow and James Jones, 197–205. New York: Norton, 1999.

Fox, Jonathan, and David L. Brown. *The Struggle for Accountability: The World Bank, NGOs and Grassroots Movements.* Cambridge: MIT Press, 1998.

"A Fresh Start for Chiapas." *The Economist,* 10 August 2000, 31–32.

Gaddis, John Lewis. "And Now This: Lessons from the Old Era for the New One." In *The Age of Terror: America and the World After September 11,* edited by Strobe Talbott and Nayan Chanda. New York: Basic Books, 2002.

Garten, Jeffrey E. *The Big Ten: The Big Emerging Markets and How They Will Change Our Lives.* New York: Basic Books, 1997.

Gilbert, Christopher, Andrew Powell, and David Vines. "Positioning the World Bank." *Economic Journal* 109, no. 459 (November 1999): F598–F633.

Grabendorff, Wolf. "El papel de América Latina en un nuevo orden internacional." In *El Estado en América Latina,* edited by Manfred Mols and Josef Thesing, 451–476. Buenos Aires: CIEDLA, 1995.

———. "El Triángulo Atlántico: ¿Una visión realista?" In *El Triángulo Atlántico: América Latina, Europa y los Estados Unidos en el sistema internacional cambiante,* edited by Klaus Bodemer, Wolf Grabendorff, Winfried Jung, and Josef Thesing, 375–392. Sankt Augustin, Germany: Konrad Adenauer Stiftung, 2002.

Grabendorff, Wolf, and Riordan Roett, eds. *Latin America, Western Europe, and the United States: A New Atlantic Triangle?* New York: Praeger, 1985.

Gratius, Susanne. "América Latina y Europa ante la cumbre de Madrid: Intereses, conflictos y expectativas." Serie Europa–América Latina 6. Rio de Janeiro: Fundación Konrad Adenauer, 2002.

Hakim, Peter. "Two Ways to Go Global." *Foreign Affairs* 81, no. 1 (January–February 2002): 148–162.

———. "The Uneasy Americas." *Foreign Affairs* 80, no. 2 (March–April 2001): 46–61.

Hanke, Steven. "The Great Argentine Train Robbery." *The International Economy* 16, no. 2 (Spring 2002): 18–21.

Haque, Nadeem Ul, and Mohsin S. Khan. "Do IMF-Supported Programs Work? A Survey of the Cross-Country Empirical Evidence." IMF Institute Working Paper Series 98/169. Washington, D.C.: IMF Institute, December 1998.

Harvard University and the World Economic Forum. *The Global Competitiveness Report 2001–2002.* New York: Oxford University Press, 2002.

Hass, Richard, and Robert Litan. "Globalization and Its Discontents." *Foreign Affairs* 77, no. 3 (May–June 1998): 2–6.

Hayes, Margaret Daly. "Foreword." In *Argentina's Civil-Military Relations: Changing Patterns in a Democratic Society,* by Herbert Huser. Washington, D.C.: National Defense University Press, 2002.

Held, David, Anthony G. McGrew, David Goldblatt, and Jonathan Perraton. *Global Transformations: Politics, Economics, and Culture.* Stanford: Stanford University Press, 1999.

Hinojosa-Ojeda, Raúl, Jeffrey Lewis, and Sherman Robinson. "Convergence and Divergence Between NAFTA, Chile, and Mercosur." Integration and Regional Programs Department, Working Paper Series 219. Washington, D.C.: Inter-American Development Bank, 1997.

Hoffmann, Stanley. *Primacy or World Order: American Foreign Policy Since the Cold War.* New York: McGraw-Hill, 1980.

Hornbeck, Jeff. "A Free Trade Area of the Americas: Status of Negotiations and

Major Policy Issues." Congressional Research Service Report for Congress, 27 March 2002.

Human Rights Watch. *Annual Report 2002—Americas.* New York: Human Rights Watch, 2002.

———. *The "Sixth Division": Military-Paramilitary Ties and U.S. Policy in Colombia.* New York: Human Rights Watch, 2001.

Hurrell, Andrew. "Security in Latin America." *International Affairs* 74, no. 3 (July 1998).

Huser, Herbert. *Argentina's Civil-Military Relations: Changing Patterns in a Democratic Society.* Washington, D.C.: National Defense University Press, 2002.

"IMF's Deputy Head Criticises US Tariffs on Steel Imports." *Financial Times,* 15 May 2002, 2.

Inter-American Development Bank. "Periodic Note on Integration." *Integration and Trade in the Americas: Special Issue on Latin American and Caribbean Economic Relations with the European Union.* Washington, D.C., May 2002.

International Monetary Fund. *IMF Survey* 28 (supplement, September 1999): 4.

———. *The IMF's Contingent Credit Lines: A Factsheet.* June 2001.

———. *The IMF's Poverty Reduction and Growth Facility (PRGF): A Factsheet.* March 2001.

IRELA (Instituto de Relaciones Europeo–Latinoamericanas). "Latin America and Europe: Beyond the Year 2000." *Dossier* 65. Madrid: IRELA, 1998.

———. "The Pinochet Case: A Test for European–Latin American Relations?" *IRELA Briefing* 9. Madrid: IRELA, 1998.

———. *The Rio Summit: Towards a Strategic Partnership?* Madrid: IRELA, 1999.

Kaul, Inge, Isabelle Grunberg, and Marc Stern, eds. *Global Public Goods: International Cooperation in the 21st Century.* New York and Oxford: Oxford University Press (for the United Nations Development Programme), 1999.

Keck, Margaret, and Kathryn Sikkink. *Activists Beyond Borders.* Ithaca: Cornell University Press, 1998.

Kennedy, John F. White House address, 13 March 1961. In *De Chapultepec al Beagle,* by Juan A. Lanús. Buenos Aires: Emecé, 1984.

Kennedy, Paul. "Maintaining American Power: From Injury to Recovery." In *The Age of Terror: America and the World After September 11,* edited by Strobe Talbott and Nayan Chanda. New York: Basic Books, 2002.

Keohane, Robert O. *After Hegemony: Cooperation and Discord in the World Political Economy.* Princeton: Princeton University Press, 1984.

Kirk, John M. "In Search of a Canadian Policy Towards Cuba." *Canadian Foreign Policy* 2, no. 2 (Fall 1994): 73–84.

Köhler, Horst. "The Monterrey Consensus and Beyond: Moving from Vision to Action." Introductory remarks at the International Conference on Financing for Development, Monterrey, Mexico, 21 March 2002.

Krasner, Stephen. *Sovereignty: Organized Hypocrisy.* Princeton: Princeton University Press, 1999.

Krueger, Anne. *A New Approach to Sovereign Debt Restructuring.* Washington, D.C.: International Monetary Fund, 2002.

Lagos, Marta. "Public Opinion." In *Constructing Democratic Governance in Latin America,* edited by Jorge I. Domínguez and Michael Shifter. Washington, D.C: The Inter-American Dialogue, 2003.

Lancaster, John. "U.S. Sees Democracy Wane in Latin America." *Washington Post,* 30 January 2000, A21.

Lanús, Juan A. *De Chapultepec al Beagle.* Buenos Aires: Emecé, 1984.

Lawrence, Robert. *Regionalism, Multilateralism, and Deeper Integration.* Washington, D.C.: Brookings Institution Press, 1996.

Lipset, Seymour M. "Some Social Requisites of Democracy: Economic Development and Political Legitimacy." *American Political Science Review* 53, no. 1 (March 1959): 69–105.

Londoño, Juan Luis, and Rodrigo Guerrero. "Violencia en América Latina: Epidemiología y costos," Office of the Chief Economist's Research Network, Working Paper R-375. Washington, D.C.: Inter-American Development Bank, August 1999.

Londoño, Juan Luis, and Miguel Székely. *Distributional Surprises After a Decade of Reforms: Latin America in the Nineties.* Washington, D.C.: Inter-American Development Bank, 1997.

López, Ernesto. "Latin America: Objective and Subjective Control Revisited." In *Civil-Military Relations in Latin America: New Analytical Perspectives,* edited by David Pion-Berlin, 88–107. Chapel Hill: University of North Carolina Press, 2001.

Lowenthal, Abraham F. "United States–Latin American Relations at the Century's Turn: Managing the 'Intermestic' Agenda." In *The United States and the Americas: A Twenty-First Century View,* edited by Albert Fishlow and James Jones, 109–136. New York: Norton, 1999.

Lustig, Nora, and Ruthanne Deutsch. *The Inter-American Development Bank and Poverty Reduction.* Washington, D.C.: Inter-American Development Bank, 1997.

MacKay, Donald. "Challenges Confronting the Free Trade Area of the Americas." Ottawa: Canadian Foundation for the Americas (FOCAL), June 2002.

Mahon, James E., Jr., and Javier Corrales. "Pegged for Failure? Argentina's Crisis." *Current History* 101, no. 652 (February 2002): 72–75.

"Maioria dos jovens é indiferente à democracia." *O Estado de São Paulo,* 14 May 2000, A9.

Maxwell, Kenneth R. "Latin America: Back to the Past?" *Folha de São Paulo,* 7 April 2002.

McDougall, Barbara. "Canada and the New Internationalism." *Canadian Foreign Policy* 1, no. 1 (Winter 1992–1993): 1–3.

McKenna, Peter. "Helms-Burton: Up Close and Personal." *Canadian Foreign Policy* 4, no. 3 (Winter 1997): 7–20.

———. "How Is Canada Doing in the OAS?" *Canadian Foreign Policy* 1, no. 2 (Spring 1993): 81–98.

McMurrer, Daniel, and Isabel Sawhill. *Getting Ahead: Economic and Social Mobility in America.* Washington, D.C.: The Urban Institute, 1998.

Melville, Keith. "Coming to Terms with Terrorism." *Kettering Review* (Winter 2002): 48.

Mendel, William W. "Operation Rio: Taking Back the Streets." *Military Review* 77, no. 3 (May–June 1997).

Mitchell, Alison. "Bush Hails Vote in House Backing Trade Legislation." *New York Times,* 28 July 2002, A1.

Montgomery, Charlotte. "Canada Seeks to Thaw Frost in U.S.–Cuban Relationship." *Toronto Globe and Mail,* 14 April 1990, A7.

Mount, Graeme S. "The Canadian Presbyterian Mission to Trinidad, 1868–1912." *Revista/Review Interamericana* 7, no. 1 (Spring 1977): 30–45.

Muñoz, Heraldo. "Good-bye U.S.A.?" In *Latin America in the New International System,* edited by Joseph S. Tulchin and Ralph H. Espach, 73–90. Boulder: Lynne Rienner, 2001.

———. *Política internacional de los nuevos tiempos.* Santiago, Chile: Los Andes, 1996.

Naím, Moisés. "Bush's Responsibility to Brazil." *Financial Times,* 1 September 2002, 11.

———. "Even a Hegemon Needs Friends and Allies." *Financial Times,* 13 September 2001, 23.

Nofal, María Beatriz. "Why Is There Scant Progress in the Consolidation and Deepening of Mercosur?" *Mercosur Journal* 8 (1997): 12–17.

Norden, Deborah, and Roberto Russell. *The United States and Argentina: Changing Relations in a Changing World.* New York and London: Routledge, 2002.

Ojeda, Mario. *Alcances y límites de la política exterior mexicana.* Mexico City: El Colegio de México, 1976.

Oppenheimer, Andrés. "Brasil: De gigante dormido a líder económico regional." *La Nación,* Sección Exterior, 4 April 2000, 5.

———. "Estados Unidos mirará más hacia el sur." *La Nación,* Sección Exterior, 14 March 2000, 4.

———. "U.S. Parties Court Mexico." *Miami Herald,* 17 August 2000, A12.

Pardo Rueda, Rafael. *Nueva Seguridad para América Latina.* Bogotá: Universidad Nacional de Colombia, 1999.

Passell, Peter. "Benefits Dwindle Along with Wages for the Unskilled." *New York Times,* 14 June 1998, A1.

Pastor, Manuel, and Carol Wise. "Argentina: From Poster Child to Basket Case." *Foreign Affairs* 80, no. 6 (November–December 2001): 60–72.

———. "A Long View on the Mexican Political Economy." In *Mexico's Politics and Society in Transition,* edited by Joseph S. Tulchin and Andrew D. Selee, 179–213. Boulder: Lynne Rienner, 2002.

———. "Mexican-Style Neoliberalism: State Policy and Distributional Stress." In *The Post-NAFTA Political Economy: Mexico and the Western Hemisphere,* edited by Carol Wise, 41–81. University Park: Pennsylvania State University Press, 1998.

————. "The Politics of Second-Generation Reform." *Journal of Democracy* 10, no. 3 (July 1999): 34–48.

Pataro, Alejandra. "Mensaje de conciliación del nuevo gobierno de Ecuador." *Clarín,* 24 January 2000, 22.

Peña, Félix. "Broadening and Deepening: Striking the Right Balance." In *Mercosur: Regional Integration, World Markets,* edited by Riordan Roett, 49–61. Boulder: Lynne Rienner, 1999.

"Prioridades de Acción." *Documentos de la Cumbre Unión Europea–América Latina y el Caribe.* Rio de Janeiro, 29 June 1999.

"Putting 'Missed' Chances Behind." *Financial Times,* 14 December 2000, 5.

Riding, Alan. *Distant Neighbors: A Portrait of the Mexicans.* New York: Vintage, 1989.

Rielly, John E., ed. *American Public Opinion and U.S. Foreign Policy, 1999.* Chicago: Chicago Council on Foreign Relations, 1999.

Rio Group. "III reunión de alto nivel económico y comercial Grupo de Río–Unión Europea." Brussels, 7 March 1995.

————. "Comunicado del Grupo de Río sobre Kosovo." *GRIO/SPT-99.* Mexico City, 25 March 1999.

Risse, Thomas, Stephen Ropp, and Kathryn Sikkink, eds. *The Power of Human Rights: International Norms and Domestic Change.* Cambridge: Cambridge University Press, 1999.

Rochlin, James. "Markets, Democracy and Security in Latin America." In *Canada Among Nations 1995: Democracy and Foreign Policy,* edited by Maxwell A. Cameron and Maureen Appel Molot, 145–164. Ottawa: Carleton University Press, 1995.

Rodríguez, Miguel, and Barbara Kotschwar. "Latin America: Expanding Trade Opportunities." *SAIS Review* 17 (1997): 39–60.

Rodrik, Dani. "Why Is There Multilateral Lending?" Paper presented at the Annual World Bank Conference on Development Economics, World Bank, Washington, D.C., 1996.

Roett, Riordan. "Brazil Ascendant: International Relations and Geopolitics in the Late 20th Century." *Journal of International Affairs* 29 (1975): 139–154.

————. "United States Policy, the Fate of the FTAA and Mercosur." Paper presented at the Asociación de Bancos de la Argentina annual meeting, Buenos Aires, 7 July 1999. Published in Spanish as "La política estadounidense, el futuro del ALCA y del Mercosur." In *El futuro del Mercosur,* edited by Felipe de la Balze, 115–137. Buenos Aires: ABA-CARI, 2002.

————, ed. *The Mexican Peso Crisis: International Perspectives.* Boulder: Lynne Rienner, 1996.

Roett, Riordan, and Russell Crandall. "Beyond Bad Press: Mexico's Quiet Revolution." *Christian Science Monitor,* 15 June 1998, 11.

————. "Confining Conditions: New Guidelines for Latin America's Leaders." *Harvard International Review* 21, no. 3 (Summer 1999): 64–67.

————. "The Global Economic Crisis, Contagion, and Institutions: New

Realities in Asia and Latin America." *International Political Science Review* 20 (July 1999): 271–283.

Rohter, Larry. "Amazon Forest Is Still Burning, Despite Pledges." *New York Times,* 23 August 2002, 1.

Rouquié, Alain. "Perspectivas inmediatas del diálogo Unión Europea–América Latina." In *Unión Europea–América Latina,* 101–107. Bogotá, Colombia: Fundación Friedrich-Ebert, 1995.

Rubio, Luis. "Mexico, NAFTA, and the Pacific Basin." In *Cooperation or Rivalry?* edited by Shoji Nishijima and Peter Smith, 76–93. Boulder: Westview, 1996.

Russell, Roberto. "Democratization and Its Qualitative Impact on Argentine Foreign Policy." *Documento de Trabajo del ISEN,* December 1998.

Sachs, Jeffrey. "Beyond Bretton Woods: A New Blueprint." *The Economist,* 1 October 1994, 27.

Salazar-Xirinachs, José, and José Tavares de Araujo. "The Free Trade Area of the Americas: A Latin American Perspective." *The World Economy* 22, no. 6 (1999): 783–797.

Santiso, Javier. "Analysts Analyzed: A Socio-economic Approach to Financial and Emerging Markets." *International Political Science Review* 20, no. 3 (Summer 1999): 307–330.

Schlesinger, Jacob. "Wages for Low-Paid Workers Rose in 1997." *Wall Street Journal,* 23 March 1999, A2.

Schneider, Howard. "Despite Booming Economy, Some Canadians See Little Benefit." *Washington Post,* 11 June 1998, A32.

Schott, Jeffrey J., and Gary C. Hufbauer. "Whither the Free Trade Area of the Americas." *The World Economy* 22, no. 6 (1999): 765–782.

SECOFI (Secretaría de Comercio y Fomento Industrial). "Mexico: Program of Industrial Policy and International Trade." Mexico City, May 1996.

Selser, Gregorio. *De la CECLA a la MECLA o la diplomacia de la zanahoria.* Buenos Aires: Carlos Samonta, 1972.

Shapiro, Samuel. "Preface." In *Cultural Factors in Inter-American Relations,* edited by Samuel Shapiro, x. Notre Dame: University of Notre Dame Press, 1968.

Shifter, Michael. "Democracy in Venezuela, Unsettling as Ever." *Washington Post,* Outlook Section, 21 April 2002, B2.

———. "A Shaken Agenda: Bush and Latin America." *Current History* 101, no. 652 (February 2002): 51–57.

Smith, Peter. "Whither Hemispheric Integration?" *Business Economics,* July 1999, 41.

Sorger, Carmen, and William A. Dymond. "Sisyphus Ascendant? Brazilian Foreign Policy for the Coming Century." *Canadian Foreign Policy* 4, no. 3 (Winter 1997): 37–49.

Stahler-Sholk, Richard. "El Salvador's Negotiated Transition: From Low-Intensity Conflict to Low-Intensity Democracy." *Journal of Interamerican Studies and World Affairs* 36, no. 4 (Winter 1994): 1–59.

Stallings, Barbara. "The New International Context of Development." In

Global Change, Regional Response: The New International Context of Development, edited by Barbara Stallings, 349–387. New York: Cambridge University Press, 1995.

Stewart, Christine. "Making a Difference: Canada in Latin America and Africa." *Canadian Foreign Policy* 2, no. 2 (Fall 1994): 1–5.

Stiglitz, Joseph. "Knowledge as a Global Public Good." In *Global Public Goods: International Cooperation in the 21st Century*, edited by Inge Kaul, Isabelle Grunberg, and Marc Stern, 308–326. New York and Oxford: Oxford University Press (for the United Nations Development Programme), 1999.

———. "The World Bank at the Millennium." *Economic Journal* 109, no. 459 (November 1999): F577–F597.

Suzigan, Wilson, and Annibal Villela. *Industrial Policy in Brazil*. Campinas, Brazil: Universidade Estadual de Campinas, 1997.

Svarzman, Gustavo. "La Argentina y el Mercosur ante el proceso de integración hemisférica." *Boletín Informativo Techint* (July–September 1998): 40.

"A System That Needs Some Simplifying." *Financial Times*, 14 December 2000, 3.

Tangeman, Michael. "Factoring in the Cardenas Comeback." *Institutional Investor*, July 1997, 21–22.

Tokatlián, Juan. "Sudamérica está partida en dos." *Clarín*, 11 January 2000, 9.

Tulchin, Joseph S. *La Argentina y los Estados Unidos: Historia de una desconfianza*. Buenos Aires: Planeta, 1990.

———. "Reflections on Hemispheric Relations in the 21st Century." *Journal of Interamerican Studies and World Affairs* 39, no. 1 (Spring 1997): 33–43.

Tulchin, Joseph S., and Ralph H. Espach. "Latin America in the New International System: A Call for Strategic Thinking." In *Latin America in the New International System*, edited by Joseph S. Tulchin and Ralph H. Espach, 1–33. Boulder: Lynne Rienner, 2001.

Uchitelle, Louis. "6 Years in the Plus Column for the U.S. Economy." *New York Times*, 12 March 1997, D1.

United Nations Development Programme. *Human Development Report 2002*. New York: Oxford University Press, 2002.

U.S. Arms Control and Disarmament Agency (ACDA). *World Military Expenditures and Arms Transfers 1998*. Washington, D.C.: ACDA, 1998.

Vaky, Viron P., and Heraldo Muñoz. *The Future of the Organization of American States*. New York: The Twentieth Century Fund Press, 1993.

Van Klaveren, Alberto. "Europa-Lateinamerika: Zwischen Illusion und Realismus auch nach 1992." *Zeitschrift für Lateinamerika-Wein* 43 (Vienna: ÖLAI, 1996): 7–35.

Vargas Llosa, Mario. "Fujimorazo en Ecuador." *La Nación Line*, Sección Opinión, 12 February 2000.

Weiner, Tim. "Mexico's New President Faces Pesky States' Rights Revolt." *New York Times*, 12 February 2001, A3.

Weiner, Tim, and Ginger Thompson. "Bush Gives Mexico Backing on Drive Against Narcotics." *New York Times*, 17 February 2001, A1.

Weintraub, Sidney. *NAFTA at Three*. Washington, D.C.: Center for Strategic and International Studies, 1997.

Wentges, J. Taylor. "Third Generation Electoral Observation and the OAS-UN International Civil Mission to Haiti." *Canadian Foreign Policy* 4, no. 3 (Winter 1997): 51–63.

Wiarda, Howard J. "Consensus Found, Consensus Lost: Disjunctures in US Policy Toward Latin America at the Turn of the Century." *Journal of Interamerican Studies and World Affairs* 39, no. 1 (Spring 1997): 13–31.

Williamson, John, ed. *Latin American Adjustment: How Much Has Happened?* Washington, D.C.: Institute for International Economics, 1990.

Winks, Robin. "Canada and the Three Americas: Her Hemispheric Role." In *Friends So Different: Essays on Canada and the United States in the 1980s*, edited by Lansing Lamont and J. Duncan Edmonds, 251–261. Ottawa: Americas Society–University of Ottawa, 1989.

Wise, Carol. "Politics Unhinged: Market Reforms as a Catalyst for Mexico's Democratic Transition." In *Post-Stabilization Politics in Latin America: Competition, Transition, Collapse,* edited by Carol Wise and Riordan Roett, with Guadalupe Paz. Washington, D.C.: Brookings Institution Press, 2003.

Wolf, Martin. "Debt to the World." *Financial Times,* 24 April 2002, 16.

World Bank. *The 1998 World Development Report: Knowledge for Development*. Washington, D.C.: World Bank, 1998.

Zakaria, Fareed. "The Rise of Illiberal Democracy." *Foreign Affairs* 76, no. 6 (November–December 1997): 22–43.

"El Zapatour." *Semana* (Bogotá, Colombia), 19 March 2001.

The Contributors

Rosa Alonso i Terme is senior economist in the Economic Policy for Poverty Reduction Division (Attacking Poverty Program) of the World Bank Institute.

Alison Brysk is associate professor of political science at the University of California at Irvine.

Russell Crandall is MacArthur Assistant Professor of Political Science at Davidson College. He is also summer adjunct professor of Latin American studies at the Paul H. Nitze School of Advanced International Studies at Johns Hopkins University.

Charles F. Doran is Andrew W. Mellon Professor of International Relations and Director of the Center of Canadian Studies at the Paul H. Nitze School of Advanced International Studies at Johns Hopkins University.

Wolf Grabendorff is director of the Friedrich Ebert Foundation in Bogotá, Colombia. He is the former director of the Madrid-based Institute for European–Latin American Relations (IRELA).

Margaret Daly Hayes is director of the Center for Hemispheric Defense Studies at the National Defense University in Washington, D.C.

Guadalupe Paz is assistant director of the Western Hemisphere

Program at the Paul H. Nitze School of Advanced International Studies at Johns Hopkins University.

Riordan Roett is Sarita and Don Johnston Professor of Political Science and director of the Western Hemisphere Program at the Paul H. Nitze School of Advanced International Studies at Johns Hopkins University.

Roberto Russell is academic director at the Foreign Service Institute (ISEN) in Buenos Aires, Argentina. He is also director of the Master's Program in International Relations at Torcuato di Tella University.

Michael Shifter is vice president for policy and director of the Colombia and democratic governance programs at the Inter-American Dialogue.

Carol Wise is associate professor in the School of International Relations at the University of Southern California.

Index

Act of Buenos Aires (1990), 195
Africa, 191
Africa, Pacific, and Caribbean (APC)
    Convention, 157
Agency for International Development
    (USAID), 56
Agenda 21, 201–202
Agriculture, 163
ALCAN, 100
Alfonsín, Raúl, 195
Alien Torts Act, 146
Alliance for Progress, 61–62, 75
Amazon Basin, 191–192, 200
American Public Opinion and U.S.
    Foreign Policy (1999), 202
Andean Community (CAN), 38*n7*,
    87*n31*, 156, 163
Andrade, Manuel, 183
Angola, 102
Argentina: armed forces role, 50–52;
    Bolivian migrants to, 147; Brazilian
    relations, 32, 70, 194–195; crisis
    (2001), 124, 135; democratic formal-
    ity, 71; economic policy, 41; EU–
    Latin American relations, 158;
    exports, 40*n39;* Falklands war, 77;
    FDI in, 24; FTAA, 74; governance,
    49; growth rates, 24–25; human
    rights violations, 149; IMF role in
    financial crisis, 8, 62–63, 119, 121,
    211; income inequality, 33–34; infla-
    tion, 22; Islamic radical groups in,
    48; market reforms, 21; Mercosur,
    32; nuclear weapons, 70, 200; pris-
    oners of conscience, 142; regional
    security cooperation, 47, 69–70;
    September 11 events, 43; taxes and
    tariffs, 28; trade liberalization, 110;
    trials of military rulers, 142, 146;
    unemployment, 17, 24–25; U.S. rela-
    tions, 196; U.S. response to financial
    crisis in, 9, 62–63; World Bank/IMF
    role, 134
Argentine-Brazilian Program for
    Integration and Economic
    Cooperation (PICAB), 195
Aristide, Jean Bertrand, 67, 92, 98–99
Armed forces: civilian tasks of, 48,
    59*n17;* national security frame-
    works, 50–52, 56, 59*n12;* profes-
    sionalism in, 55; spending on,
    52–55; traditional views of, 59*n12*
ASEAN. *See* Association of Southeast
    Asian Nations
Asian financial crisis, 121, 154
Assassinations, 142
Asset concentration, 26
Association of Southeast Asian Nations
    (ASEAN), 156, 160
Atlantic triangle, 164–166
Authoritarianism, 145–146
Axworthy, Lloyd, 95, 103
Aylwin Azócar, Patricio, 107
Aznar, José María, 153

231

Balance of payments, 123, 127, 133
Bank for International Settlements, 120
Basle Core Principles of Banking
    Supervision, 126, 137*n11*
Battle of Seattle (1999), 35
Bergsten, Fred, 126
Bermuda: Canadian role in, 91
Biregional relations. *See* European–
    Latin American relations; Latin
    American–U.S. relations
Bolivia: antidrug campaign, 143; as
    HIPC country, 140*n44;* Mercosur
    membership, 196; migrants from, 47,
    147; military role in, 52; police/judi-
    cial reform, 142, 146; regional secu-
    rity cooperation, 70; U.S. trade rela-
    tions, 5
Bonds, 124–125
Botana, Natalio, 71
Bouzas, Roberto, 196
Brady, Nicholas, 138*n22*
Brady Plan, 124, 138*n22, 199
Brascan, 100
Brasília Communiqué (2000), 199
Brazil: Andean Community agreement
    with, 163; Argentine relations, 32,
    70, 194–195; Canadian relations, 97,
    100–101; Chilean relations,
    105–108; currency devaluation, 177,
    194, 196–197, 204; democracy in
    Peru, 67; development failures,
    189–190; environmental issues,
    191–192, 201; EU–Latin American
    relations, 158; exports, 40*n39;* FDI
    in, 24; foreign policy development,
    190; FTAA, 74; governance, 49;
    growth rates, 25–26; as hegemon, 5;
    human rights violations, 142–143,
    146; IMF rescue package (2002), 9,
    63, 65, 211; income inequality,
    33–34; inflation, 22; Islamic radical
    groups in, 48; market reforms, 22;
    Mercosur, 32, 34, 74; military role
    in, 53, 190; NAFTA membership,
    36; nuclear weapons, 70, 200;
    police/judicial reform, 142; regional
    diplomacy, 198–204; regional secu-
    rity cooperation, 47, 69–70;
    September 11 events, 43; social

agenda, 10; trade liberalization, 110;
    UN role for, 190; unemployment, 17;
    U.S. perspectives on, 202–203; U.S.
    relations, 62, 80, 191, 194, 196–198;
    Venezuela coup (2002), 67; violence,
    49; World Bank/IMF role, 134
Brazilian Center of International
    Relations (CEBRI), 205*n3*
Bretton Woods institutions, 118
Britain. *See* United Kingdom
Buiter, Willem, 125
Bush, George H. W.: Brady Plan, 199;
    Enterprise for the Americas
    Initiative, 18, 61, 195; Haiti, 67;
    Panama war, 96–97
Bush, George W.: Brazil, 203; debt
    restructuring, 125; drugs, 185; Latin
    America policy, 64–65; Mexican–
    U.S. relations, 9, 175–176; protec-
    tionism, 5; regional integration,
    197; trade promotion authority, 16,
    21, 163; Venezuela coup (2002),
    69

Cabrera, Pablo, 46
CACM. *See* Central America, Common
    Market
CAN. *See* Andean Community
Canada: Brazilian relations, 97,
    100–101; Chilean relations,
    105–108; Cuban policy, 6, 101–105;
    Department of Foreign Affairs and
    International Trade (DFAIT), 93, 98;
    European relations, 93–95; FTAA,
    37, 91, 110–111; Haitian role for,
    91–92, 97–99; hemispheric role of,
    6, 91; human rights, 97–98,
    104–105; as Latin American advo-
    cate, 6, 105–108; Latin American
    trade with, 95–96; Mexican rela-
    tions, 97; military role, 94; NAFTA
    expansion, 29; NAFTA role of,
    17–18, 92–93, 108–109; OAS role
    of, 6–7, 91–92, 96–99; Peruvian
    relations, 97; post–Cold War foreign
    policy, 92–96; trade liberalization,
    108–111
Canada-U.S. Free Trade Agreement
    (CUSFTA), 17

Canadian International Development
   Agency (CIDA), 92, 99
Canadian-U.S. relations: Cuba, 6,
   101–105; Panama war, 97; post–
   September 11, 107–108; trade,
   94–95
CANDU nuclear reactor, 100
Capacity-building, 134
Capital account liberalization, 134
Capital controls, 121–123
Capital flows, 46, 55, 134
Capital markets, 131–132, 210
Cardoso, Fernando Henrique: Amazon
   Basin, 202; Canadian-Brazilian rela-
   tions, 101; election of, 193, 197;
   Real Plan, 192–193, 197; regional
   role of Brazil, 74, 204; stability
   under, 10
Caribbean Common Market (CARI-
   COM), 38*n7*
Caribbean region, 49, 91, 147, 156
Carmona, Pedro, 86*n17*
Carter, Jimmy, 191
Castro, Fidel, 62, 101, 104–105
Cavallo, Domingo, 196
CCLs. *See* Contingent credit lines
Cedras, Raoul, 99
Central America: Common Market
   (CACM), 38*n7*, 42; EU relations, 53,
   159; international peace initiatives,
   42, 198; Rio Group membership for,
   156
Cervera Pacheco, Víctor, 182
Chávez, Hugo: election of, 48; return to
   power of, 69; U.S. attitude toward
   coup against, 7, 67; U.S. satanization
   of, 82
Cheysson, Claude, 159
Chiapas uprising, 174, 182–184
Chile: armed forces role, 50–51, 59*n17*;
   Brazilian relations, 105–108;
   Canadian relations, 105–108; crisis
   prevention, 119; democracy in Peru,
   67; EU relations, 157, 161–162; foreign investment in, 24; foreign trials
   of military officers, 146, 156; FTAA,
   74; market reforms, 22; Mercosur
   membership, 83, 196; military rule
   ended in, 42; NAFTA membership,

28, 83, 105–107; poverty, 2; regional
   security cooperation, 47, 70; taxes
   on capital inflows, 122; trade liberal-
   ization, 110; truth commissions, 142;
   U.S. relations, 62, 196; Venezuela
   coup (2002), 67; World Bank loans,
   133
China, 92
Chiquita Brands International, 148
Chirac, Jacques, 153
Chrétien, Jean, 95, 99, 101, 103
CIDA. *See* Canadian International
   Development Agency
Citizenship gap, 8, 144, 151
Civil service reforms, 135
Clausewitz, Carl von, 45
Clinton, Bill, 64, 103–104, 196–197
Clinton administration: Ecuador coup
   (2000), 68; fast-track authority, 15,
   107, 163; Haiti crises, 66; Helms-
   Burton legislation, 103–104;
   Mexican-U.S. relations, 175; trade
   agreements of, 18–19
Coast Guard, U.S., 56
Colburn, Forrest, 212
Collier, Paul, 132
Collor de Mello, Fernando, 192, 195,
   200–201
Colombia: anti-terrorism in, 4; democ-
   racy in, 70; governance in, 48; as
   hemispheric security problem, 6;
   human rights, 8, 142–143, 146–150;
   narcotrafficking, 47, 64; National
   Liberation Army, 48; Revolutionary
   Armed Forces, 48; U.S. relations, 5,
   62, 147; violence, 49
Colosio, Luis Donaldo, 174
Conditionality, 127, 130–133
Condor 2 missiles, 200
Conglomerates, 26–27
Connell-Smith, Gordon, 75
Contadora Group, 159, 198
Content revolution, 136
Contingent credit lines (CCLs),
   126–127, 139*n36*
Corn, 108–109
Corruption, 49, 86*n19*, 181
Council on Foreign Relations, 202–203
Crime, 6, 49, 149

Crisis containment, 126–127
Crisis management, 122–126
Crisis prevention, 119–122
Cruzado Plan, 192
Cuba: Atlantic triangle and, 165; Canadian-U.S. differences over, 6, 101–105; EU–Latin American talks on, 161; FTAA membership, 104; missile crisis (1962), 200; prisoners of conscience, 142; revolution in, 61; U.S.–Latin American policy differences over, 80, 84
Customs, 48, 60n17

Debt default, 192–193
Debt restructuring, 124–126, 131, 138n22
Defense, U.S. Department of, 56
Defense spending, 54fig, 60n21
De la Rúa, Fernando, 33–34, 51, 196
Del Monte Corp., 148
Democracy Charter, 7
Democratic formality, 70–71
Democratization: challenges to, 81–83; consolidation of, 71, 209; desirability of, 41; economic prosperity and, 136n3; EU–Latin American relations and, 155, 160; human rights violations and, 146; income inequality and, 82; Latin American attitudes toward, 69–71; OAS role, 7–8; prerequisites for, 70; subregional defense of, 69–70; U.S. promotion of, 66–69, 71–72; World Bank promotion of, 130–131
Deutsch, Ruthanne, 28
Díaz, Porfirio, 181
Dole Food Co., 148
Domínguez, Jorge, 65, 68
Dominica, 104
Dominican Republic, 75–76, 147, 156
Drugs: Atlantic triangle and, 165; certification, 177, 185; EU–Latin American discussions on, 160; human rights abuse and, 143; in Mexico, 143, 177, 184–185; Multilateral Evaluation Mechanism, 88n56; regional cooperation against, 47; as security problem, 6, 43; U.S.

agency focus on, 56; U.S.–Latin American policy differences over, 80, 84
Duhalde, Eduardo, 41

EAI. *See* Enterprise for the Americas Initiative
East Asia, 27, 130
Economic dissent, 144
Economic liberalism. *See* Market reform
Ecuador: coup (Jan. 2000), 1, 7, 49, 66–68; democratic formality, 71; governance in, 48; human rights violations, 148, 150; indigenous people of, 184; international peace initiatives, 42; military as customs control, 48, 60n17; Peru border conflict, 199; regional security cooperation, 47; U.S. trade relations, 5; World Bank/IMF role, 134
Education: exchange students, 79; income inequality and, 27–28, 130; levels in Latin American workers, 27–28; levels in the United States, 30; U.S. aid for improvement of, 82–83; as World Bank role, 129–130, 135
Eichengreen, Barry, 125, 139n34
Eizenstat, Stuart E., 72
Elections: Brazil (1994), 193, 197; Brazil (Oct. 2002), 36; Haiti (1997), 100; Mexico (2000), 32, 171, 173, 182; Paraguay (1998), 199; United States (1996), 103
Elections Canada, 99
El Salvador: human rights violations, 146; truth commissions, 142; U.S. policy, 62, 77; Venezuela coup (2002), 86n17; violence, 49
End of politics, 212
Enhanced Structural Adjustment Facility (ESAF), 128
Enterprise for the Americas Initiative (EAI), 18, 61, 195
Environmental protection, 16, 191–192, 201
EU. *See* European Union
European Commission, 157, 159, 165

European–Latin American relations: Atlantic triangle, 164–166; character of, 156–159, 166; democratization, 155, 160; divergence of interests, 153–154; drugs, 160; economic competition, 161–163; NAFTA and, 161; parallels in development, 154–156; political dialogue, 159–161

European Union (EU): Canadian relations, 93–94; Central American relations, 53, 159; Chilean relations, 157, 161–162; Colombian relations, 157; expansion of, 163; funding for security programs, 56; Helms-Burton legislation, 104; Latin American trade agreement with, 83; Madrid summit (2002), 10, 153, 157, 160; Mercosur relations, 155–158, 162; Mexican relations, 156–157, 161–162; Panamanian relations, 157; Rio summit (1999), 153, 157, 160–161, 166, 199; San José summit (1984), 153, 156; Venezuelan relations, 157

Exchange rates, 121

Exchange students, 79

Exclusive economic zones (EEZs), 45

Exports: from Europe, 162; growth rates, 20–21, 74; between Mercosur countries, 40*n39;* Mexican, 31

Extrajudicial killings, 142

Falklands war, 77

Fast-track authority; 15–16, 83, 106, 197. *See also* Trade Promotion Authority

FDI. *See* Foreign direct investment

Feldstein, Martin, 138*n26*

First Conference of South American Presidents, 74

Fischer, Stanley, 125–126, 139*n34*

Fishlow, Albert, 83

Foreign direct investment (FDI): from the EU, 163; increases in, 21; Latin American share, 75; market reform and, 22, 23*tab*

Fox Quesada, Vicente: Chiapas uprising, 183–184; economy of Mexico, 181; election of, 32, 171, 173, 182; leadership challenges of, 173, 175, 180, 185–186; Rio Treaty, 58*n1;* U.S.-Mexican relations, 9, 176

France, 93–94, 158

Franco, Itamar, 192

Free Trade Area of the Americas (FTAA): Argentine position, 198; Brazil-U.S. differences, 196–198; Brazilian position, 34–37; Canadian role, 37, 91, 110–111; Chilean position, 198; Cuban membership, 104; differences over, 15–16; EU–Latin American relations and, 161; EU-Mercosur relations and, 158, 161; motives for, 17–18; negotiating groups, 20–21; prospects for, 4–5, 17, 21; time-frame for completion of, 37, 61–62; U.S. action for, 83; U.S. obstacles to, 30

Frei, Eduardo, 50

Frondizi, Arturo, 81

FTAA. *See* Free Trade Area of the Americas

Fujimori, Alberto, 97

Fujimorazo, 67

Gaddis, John Lewis, 69

Galtieri, Gen. Leopoldo, 77

General Agreement on Tariffs and Trade (GATT), 18

Genscher, Hans Dietrich, 159

Germany, 94, 147, 158

Gilbert, Christopher, 132

Global Competitiveness Report 2001–2002 The, (World Economic Forum/Harvard University), 190

Globalization: desirability of, 41; era of, 210–211; human rights and, 143–145, 147–150; limits of, 211–213; twenty-first century problems, 1, 209

Gore, Al, 197

Governance, 41–42, 48–50

Grandeza, 191–192, 197

Grant, George, 94

Greenspan, Alan, 181

Group of Seven (G–7), 126, 193
Group of Ten (G–10), 125
Growth competitiveness, 190
Guatemala: democratic crises in, 7, 66–67; foreign trials of military officers, 146; human rights violations, 148, 150; military role in, 60*n17;* U.S. interest in, 62; Venezuela coup (2002), 67
Gulf States, 156
Gunning, Jan Willem, 132
Guyana, 140*n44*

Haas, Richard, 125
Haiti: Canadian role in, 91–92, 97–99; democratic crises in, 7, 66–67; human rights violations, 146; World Bank/IMF role, 134
Hakim, Peter, 10, 65
Health care, 135
Hegemony, 5, 160
Helms-Burton legislation, 102–104
Hemispheric integration: future of, 83–84
Hemispheric relations: Canadian policy, 6, 91, 95–96; defense ministers' meetings, 5; September 11 events and, 3
Highly Indebted Poor Countries (HIPC) Initiative, 131, 140*n44*
Hoffmann, Stanley, 11, 84
Honduras, 140*n44,* 150
Hoof and mouth disease, 47
Human Development Report 2002 (UN), 189
Human rights: authoritarianism and, 145–146; Canadian position, 97–98, 104–105; in Colombia, 8, 142–143, 146–150; democratization and violations of, 146; globalization and, 143–145, 147–150; in Haiti, 146; monitors, 150; multinational corporations and abuses of, 148; new consensus on, 141–142; poverty and violations of, 149; responses to violations of, 145–150; Spanish prosecution of violators of, 146, 156; spiral model of improvement in, 150; types of, 151*n1;* of workers, 16

IADB. *See* Inter-American Development Bank
Ibero-American summits, 199
IMF. *See* International Monetary Fund
Impossible trinity, 211
Income inequality: in Argentina, 33–34; asset concentration and, 26–27; in Brazil, 33–34, 189–190; democratization and, 82; education and, 27–28, 130; market reform and, 16; NAFTA and, 29–32
Inflation, 22
Information, 120
Integration. *See* Regional integration
Inter-American Committee against Terrorism, 88*n56*
Inter-American Convention against Corruption, 88*n56*
Inter-American Convention against Terrorism, 3–4
Inter-American Defense Board, 60*n22,* 98
Inter-American Democratic Charter, 69
Inter-American Development Bank (IADB), 49, 53, 83
Inter-American Treaty of Reciprocal Assistance (TIAR), 43, 58*n1,* 76–77
International Accounting Standards Committee, 137*n11*
International Labour Organization (ILO), 148
International Monetary Fund (IMF): Argentine financial crisis (2002), 8, 62–63, 119, 121, 211; Article IV, 122; balance-of-payments crises, 133; Brazil rescue package (2002), 9, 63, 65, 211; broker role for, 138*n26;* Code of Good Practices on Fiscal Transparency, 120, 126; Code on the Transparency of Monetary and Financial Policies, 120, 126; crisis containment, 126–127; crisis management, 122–126; crisis prevention, 119–122; debt restructuring, 124–125; Enhanced Structural Adjustment Facility, 128; future role for, 118–119; good vs. bad loans, 123–124, 138*n20;* Latin America role of, 134; long-term lending,

127–128; Mexican debt, 178; poverty, 128; reform of, 117–118; Supplemental Reserve Facility, 123; surveillance process, 122; World Bank cooperation with, 128

International Organization of Securities Commission, 137*n11*

Interregional Framework Agreement for Cooperation between the European Community and Mercosur (1995), 83

Investment liberalization, 111

Islamic radical groups, 48

Jamaica, 104

Japan, 160

Judicial reform, 142, 146

Justice, U.S. Department of, 56

Kennedy, John F., 75

Kennedy, Paul, 65

Keohane, Robert, 81

Kidnappings, 6

Kinkel, Klaus, 164

Kohl, Helmut, 86*n19*

Kosovo, 156

Krueger, Anne, 124–126

Labor unions, 148, 181, 197

Lafer, Celso, 198

Lament for a Nation (Grant), 94

Lampreia, Luiz Felipe, 205*n3*

Latin America: Canadian trade with, 95–96; EU view of challenges to, 165; heterogeneity in, 2–3, 82; lack of supranational bodies, 159; U.S. interest in, 62–66; World Bank role in, 133–136

Latin American–U.S. relations: asymmetry in, 3, 61; democratization process, 66–72; differences in goals, 75–76; exchange students, 79; intermestic agenda, 80; market economics and, 78; market reform and, 72–75; multilateralism in, 84–85; over Falklands war, 77; post–Cold War, 77–78; security issues, 78–79; terrorism, 3; U.S. disengagement, 9;

U.S. interest in, 62–66; U.S. policy agenda, 66

Lending, 130–133

Litan, Robert, 125

Low-intensity citizens, 144

Lustig, Nora, 28

Lynchings, 149

Mahuad, Jamil, 7, 68

Maize, 108–109

Malvinas, Islas, 77

Managua Declaration (1994), 43

Maquiladoras, 148, 179–180, 187*n9*

Marcos, Subcomandante, 183–184

Market reform: diversity of strategies for, 21–22; FDI and, 22, 23*tab;* income inequality and, 16; inflation, 22; results of, 2; U.S.–Latin American relations and, 72–75, 78

Maxwell, Kenneth, 80

McDougall, Barbara, 97

Meany, George, 30

Mendes, Chico, 201

Mendoza, Gen. Carlos, 68

Menem, Carlos, 195

Mercosur: Argentine-Brazilian integration, 32; Atlantic triangle and, 165; Bolivian membership, 196; Brazilian view of, 34, 74; Chilean membership, 83, 196; Common External Tariff, 33; creation of, 192, 195; democracy agreements, 69–70; EU relations, 155–158, 162; export growth, 20, 40*n39;* interregional framework agreement with EU, 155; membership of, 38*n7;* NAFTA as influence on, 87*n38;* Paraguayan membership, 196; successes of, 42; tariffs and, 195; trade agreements, 110; Uruguayan membership, 195–196; weakness of, 5, 28, 196, 204

Mexican-U.S. relations: bilateral trade agreement, 17; drugs, 143, 177, 184–185; migrants, 147; September 11 and, 9, 186*n1;* special nature of, 173–176; U.S. import taxes, 76; U.S. interest in, 62

Mexico: authoritarian enclaves,

182–183; Canadian relations, 97; Chiapas uprising, 174, 182–184; as developed country, 171–173; distributional conflicts, 31–32; drugs, 143, 177, 184–185; economy of, 177–181; EU relations, 156–157, 161–162; exports, 31; FDI in, 24; growth rates, 25; "honest broker" foreign policy, 176–177; human rights violations, 142, 146, 148–150; inflation, 22; market reforms, 21; NAFTA effect on, 9, 171, 179–180; NAFTA objectives of, 19, 74; oil revenues, 178; peso crisis (1994), 20, 125, 135, 197; prospects for, 185–186; regional imbalances, 180; regional integration commitment of, 172; Rio Group role of, 156; tariff reductions on maize, 108–109; trade liberalization, 108, 110; trading partners, 179*tab;* uniqueness of, 171; Venezuela coup (2002), 67; World Bank loans, 133

Migrants, 47, 147, 175

Missile Technology Control Regime, 200

Mitterand, François, 86*n19*

Modern Language Association, 79

Moore Business Forms, 100

Movimento Sem Terra (MST), 202

Mulroney, Brian, 96–97, 102

Multilateral Evaluation Mechanism, 88*56*

Multilateral Investment Agreement (MLA), 111

Multilateralism, 84–85

Multinational corporations, 148

Muñoz, Heraldo, 10

NAFTA. *See* North American Free Trade Agreement

Narcotics. *See* Drugs

National power, 44, 58*n4*

Native Americans, 183–184, 192, 201

Nicaragua, 77, 140*n44*, 146, 150

Nixon, Richard M., 76

Noboa, Gustavo, 68

Noriega, Gen. Manuel, 97

NorTel, 100

North American Free Trade Agreement (NAFTA): as aid to investment, 18; Argentine membership, 83; Atlantic triangle and, 165; Brazilian membership, 36; Canadian role in, 17–18, 92–93, 108–109; Chilean membership, 28, 83, 105–107; distributional conflicts from, 29–32; EU–Latin American relations and, 161; expansion of, 29; Mexican objectives, 19, 74; Mexico as effected by, 9, 171, 179–180; negotiations for, 195; successes of, 42

North Atlantic Treaty Organization (NATO), 156

Nuclear nonproliferation, 100, 200

OECD. *See* Organization for Economic Cooperation and Development

OAS. *See* Organization of American States

Oil, 178

O'Neill, Paul, 140*n50*

O'Neill, Tip, 63

Open economies, 41

Organization for Economic Cooperation and Development (OECD), 100, 137*n11*, 180

Organization of American States (OAS): as advocate for democracy, 7–8; Canadian role, 6–7, 91–92, 96–99; Committee on Hemispheric Security, 43; education, 83; funding for security programs, 56; human rights, 142, 148; Inter-American Democratic Charter, 69; Resolution 1080, 69; security issues, 43; terrorism, 3; U.S. hegemony in, 160

Organized crime, 149

Panama, 96–97, 157

Pan American Games, 91

Pan American Union, 42

Paraguay: democratic crises in, 7, 43, 66–67, 199; governance in, 48; Islamic radical groups in, 48; Mercosur membership, 196; military as customs control, 48, 60*n17;* regional security cooperation,

69–70; return of migrants to, 47
Paramilitaries, 183
Pardo Rueda, Rafael, 59*n12*
Patrón, Patricio, 183
Peace dividend, 93
Peña, Félix, 196
Pensée unique, la, 82, 89*n68*
Pérez Yoma, Edmundo, 50
Perry, William, 43
Peru: Canadian relations, 97; democratic crises in, 7, 66–67; democratic formality, 71; Ecuador border conflict, 199; governance in, 48; international peace initiatives, 42–43; prisoners of conscience, 142; regional security cooperation, 47; Shining Path guerrillas, 48; truth commissions, 146; U.S. trade relations, 5
Pinochet, Augusto, 147
Plan Colombia, 4
Police reform, 53, 142, 146
Political parties: Conservative (Canada), 96; Liberal (Canada), 95; Partido Acción Nacional (PAN, Mexico), 32, 171; Partido Revolucionario Institucional (PRI, Mexico), 32, 171, 181; Republican (U.S.), 175; Unidad Popular (Chile), 62
Politics, end of, 212
Portugal, 199
Poverty: Atlantic triangle and, 165; conditionality and, 130–131; human rights violations and, 149; IMF focus on, 128; in Mexico, 173; of native Americans, 183; persistence of, 2, 28; social safety nets and, 136
Poverty Reduction and Growth Facility (PRGF), 128
Powell, Andrew, 132
Powell, Colin, 4, 67
Preval, Rene, 100
Prisoners of conscience, 142
Prisons, 143
Process revolution, 131, 136
Proposition 187 (California), 175
Protectionism: agricultural, 164; in the EU, 162; international financial

institutions' view of, 136*n4;* in the U.S., 5, 198

Québec, 93–94

Reagan, Ronald, 76–77
Real Plan, 192–193, 197
Refugees, 144
Regional integration: desirability of, 41; EU–Latin American parallels in, 155; hemisphere-wide, 83–84; market reform and, 72–75, 78; Mexican commitment to, 172; strategies for, 197–198
Resolution 1080, 69
Rio Conference (1992), 192, 201
Rio Group, 7, 156, 159–160, 162, 199
Rio Treaty (TIAR), 43, 58*n1*, 76–77
Risse, Thomas, 150
Rome Declaration (1990), 199
Ropp, Stephen, 150
Royal Bank of Canada, 91
Russia, 124, 154, 160, 193

Sachs, Jeffrey, 138*n26*
Salinas de Gortari, Carlos, 171
Sanguinetti, Julio María, 195
San José process, 156–157, 159
Sarney, José, 192, 195, 200–201
SDDS. *See* Special data dissemination standard
Security: armed forces role in, 45, 50–55; definitions, 44; economic, 42; global, 46; international funding for, 56–57; local/personal, 49–50, 55; national, 48–49; regional/cross-border, 46–48; strategy papers for, 50–51; threats to, 45; trade and, 72–73; U.S.–Latin American relations over, 78–79; Williamsburg principles, 43–44
September 11 events: Canadian-U.S. relations after, 107–108; capital flow and, 46, 55; FTAA prospects and, 21; hemispheric relations and, 3; hemispheric response to, 43; Mexico-U.S. relations after, 9, 186*n1;* U.S. Latin America policy and, 65. *See also* Terrorism

Shapiro, Samuel, 75
Sharp, Mitchell, 101
Sherritt, 103
Shining Path, 48
Sibert, Anne, 125
Sikkink, Kathryn, 150
Social welfare, 45
South American Free Trade Area
    (SAFTA), 164
Southeast Asia, 92
Southern Command, U.S., 56–57,
    60*n23*
Southern Cone, 5, 50–52. *See also*
    Mercosur
Spain, 86*n17*, 146, 156, 199
Special Commission for Latin American
    Coordination, 76
Special data dissemination standard
    (SDDS), 120, 126
SRF. *See* Supplemental Reserve Facility
State, U.S. Department of, 56
Stewart, Christine, 97
Stiglitz, Joseph, 117, 129–130
Subsidies, 5
Summers, Lawrence, 127
Summit of the Americas: Miami (1994),
    7–8, 20, 61, 196; Québec (2001), 6,
    8, 37; Santiago (1998), 8, 160
Supplemental Reserve Facility (SRF),
    123, 138*n18*

Tariffs: in Argentina, 28; on Brazilian
    products, 36; on maize, 108–109;
    Mercosur and, 33, 195; on U.S.
    imports, 76. *See also* Taxes
Taxes: in Argentina, 28; in Chile, 122;
    in Mexico, 180–181; reform of, 127,
    135; on short-term capital inflows,
    134. *See also* Tariffs
Team Canada, 91
Téllez, Luis, 178
Terrorism, 3–4; 56. *See also* September
    11 events
Thailand, 193
Thatcher, Margaret, 201
TIAR. *See* Inter-American Treaty of
    Reciprocal Assistance
Tlatelolco Treaty (1967), 200
Torture, 142

TPA. *See* Trade Promotion Authority
Trade liberalization, 108–111, 165, 192
Trade Promotion Authority (TPA), 4,
    16, 28, 107, 163, 198. *See also* Fast-
    track authority
Transamazon Highway, 201
Trans-Atlantic Free Trade Area, 164
Treasury, U.S. Department of, 56
Treaty of Asunción (1991), 196
Treaty on Integration and Economic
    Cooperation (1988), 195
Trinidad and Tobago, 91, 104
Trudeau, Pierre Elliott, 101–102
Truth commissions, 142, 146
Tulchin, Joseph, 63

Unemployment, 17
Unilateralism, 84–85
United Kingdom (UK), 77, 93–94, 156
United Nations (UN): Conference on
    Environment and Development
    (1992), 192, 201; Economic
    Commission for Latin America and
    the Caribbean, 60*n21;* funding for
    security programs, 56; *Human
    Development Report 2002,* 189;
    Security Council, 190; Working
    Group on Forced Disappearance,
    142
United States: Argentine relations, 196;
    Brazilian relations, 62, 80, 191, 194,
    196–198; Canadian trade with, 94;
    Chilean relations, 62, 196;
    Colombian relations, 5, 62, 147; dis-
    tributional conflicts, 29–31; as hege-
    mon, 5, 160; migrants in, 147;
    Southern Command role, 56–57; tar-
    iffs on Brazilian imports, 36; trade
    strategies, 72; Uruguayan relations,
    196; Venezuela coup (2002), 86*n17*.
    See also Canadian-U.S. relations;
    Latin American–U.S. relations;
    Mexican–U.S. relations
Unit for the Promotion of Democracy, 7
Uribe, Alvaro, 6
Uruguay: FTAA, 74; governance, 49;
    hoof and mouth disease, 47;
    Mercosur membership, 195–196;
    regional security cooperation, 47,

69–70; U.S. loans to, 63, 65; U.S. relations, 196
Uruguay Round, 18–19, 100

Vaca, Eduardo, 50
Velásquez, Fidel, 181
Venezuela: coup (Apr. 2002), 1, 7, 67, 69, 86*n17;* democratic crises in, 66–67; democratic formality, 70; EU relations, 157; governance in, 48; prison conditions, 143; World Bank/IMF role, 134
Viña del Mar agreement, 76
Vines, David, 132
Violence, 49
Vulture funds, 138*n23*

Wages: erosion of, 29
Washington Consensus, 21, 38*n14,* 135, 212
Washington protocol, 86*n24*
Western Hemisphere concept, 79, 88*n61*
Wiarda, Howard, 66

Williamsburg principles, 43–44, 58*n2*
Wilson, Pete, 176
Wolfensohn, James D., 130
World Bank: conditionality, 130–133; direction of, 8; financing of, 140*n50;* funding for security programs, 56; future role of, 8, 128–129; IMF cooperation with, 128; as knowledge bank, 129–130; Latin America role of, 133–136; police reform, 53; reform of, 117–118
World Trade Organization (WTO): agricultural reform, 108; Doha Round, 158, 163; Helms-Burton legislation, 104; Seattle meeting (1999), 35; trade negotiations, 17

Yucatán, 182–183

Zakaria, Fareed, 71
Zapatistas, 182–184
Zedillo, Ernesto, 171, 173–175, 178, 185
Zoellick, Robert, 28

About the Book

Considering Latin America's emerging challenges and opportunities in the first decade of the twenty-first century, the authors examine key political, economic, and security concerns in the region. They focus both on the changing dynamics within the Western Hemisphere and on Latin America's evolving relationships with international actors and institutions.

Riordan Roett is Sarita and Don Johnston Professor of Political Science and director of the Western Hemisphere Program at the Paul H. Nitze School of Advanced International Studies (SAIS), Johns Hopkins University. **Guadalupe Paz** is assistant director of the SAIS Western Hemisphere Program.

WHERE YOU SEE YOURSELF

WHERE YOU SEE YOURSELF

YOURSELF

CLAIRE FORREST

Scholastic Press / New York

Library of Congress Cataloging-in-Publication Data

Names: Forrest, Claire (Young adult author), author.

Title: Where you see yourself / Claire Forrest.

Description: First edition. | New York : Scholastic Press, 2023. | Audience: Ages 12+ | Audience: Grades 10–12 | Summary: Effie Galanos' goals for her senior year include her navigating her way through her high school that is not really wheelchair-friendly, getting into the perfect college, and getting her crush Wilder to accompany her to the prom—but by spring she is beginning to see herself entirely differently.

Identifiers: LCCN 2022033818 (print) | LCCN 2022033819 (ebook) | ISBN 9781338813838 (hardcover) | ISBN 9781338813852 (ebook)

Subjects: LCSH: People with disabilities—Juvenile fiction. | High school seniors—Juvenile fiction. | Identity (Psychology)—Juvenile fiction. | Dating (Social customs)—Juvenile fiction. | Minneapolis (Minn.)—Juvenile fiction. | Bildungsromans. | CYAC: People with disabilities—Fiction. | High schools—Fiction. | Schools—Fiction. | Identity—Fiction. | Dating (Social customs)—Fiction. | Coming of age—Fiction. | BISAC: YOUNG ADULT FICTION / Disabilities & Special Needs | YOUNG ADULT FICTION / Coming of Age

Classification: LCC PZ7.1.F66266 Wh 2023 (print) | LCC PZ7.1.F66266 (ebook) | DDC 813.6 [Fic]—dc23/eng/20220830

LC record available at https://lccn.loc.gov/2022033818

LC ebook record available at https://lccn.loc.gov/2022033819

10 9 8 7 6 5 4 3 2 1   23 24 25 26 27

Printed in Italy   183

First edition, April 2023

Book design by Cassy Price

For Mom and Dad, who have never bet against me

SECTION I: FALL

CHAPTER ONE

I look up at the familiar brick building. At the newly cleaned metal door, and my blurry reflection in its surface.

I noticed the area around the flagpole has freshly potted plants. These are the type of things Mill City High School spends money on.

Behind the door, I hear the distinct rise and fall of chatter. I take the deepest breath I've taken all day, like they said to do on that guided meditation they played in health class once, and wait for it to rush over me.

You know, that *this is it* feeling.

I wait.

Focus.

Then I exhale long and slow like letting the air out of a balloon.

As I suspected.

It's the first day of my senior year of high school and I feel nothing.

I hit the door opener. The gears above the door rumble for a second in consideration before puttering out in a guttural whine. The door doesn't even try to open.

Yeah, I'm not gonna miss this place.

I go up to the door and grip the handle, yanking it open and slipping inside, letting the door hit me slightly as it closes.

Taking a look around, I see the scared freshmen with their too-cute outfits and too-big backpacks. I see the sophomore boys who grew a foot over the summer. I see the junior girls with stick-straight hair and leather tote bags for backpacks. And I see the other seniors wearing their yellow-and-black-tie-dye STOMP shirts.

It's only the first day, but I'm ready to move on from this place and on to something bigger. Something that gives me that *this is it* feeling.

In the meantime, *this* is it.

I head to my second locker. I've been testing each component of the two-locker system for the past three years, and on this, the first day of senior year, I'm proud to say I've nailed it.

The locker is one turn down a hallway and a few feet from the side door by the parking lot and within sight of the ramp that leads to the main hub of the school. Looking to my left, I see one unexpected cherry on top. Fellow senior Katie Hollins looks up shyly, her lips forming in a half-hearted smile. Perfect. A locker neighbor who is nice but not chatty.

Yep, nailed it.

I unzip my backpack and pull out my retractable locker shelf. When I can't get it quite even, Katie smiles sympathetically. "Oh, those are tricky."

She looks at me for permission and I nod. She helps me level it and snaps it into place.

I may not have all the excitement of my classmates, but that doesn't mean it won't be a good year.

The first bell rings and I launch into my perfectly executed routine:

1. Take the short ramp through the first-floor Commons. (Swerve around Abe Crawford and Sarah Smith, who unfortunately are still together after the summer, and are resuming their annoying habit of kissing in the middle of the ramp, like it's never occurred to them some people might have a hard time getting around them. Speaking of which, now seems like a good time to address the rumor that I once rammed into Abe's ankles mid-make-out on purpose. To which I say, prove it.)

2. Enjoy the ease of the long glide down the main Commons ramp into the North Wing. (A hall monitor inevitably thinks they're the first person to come up with the "Hey, slow down, you got a license for that thing?" joke, and I inevitably wonder what happened to them to make them so unfunny.)

3. Make a sharp right turn and barrel down the hallway as fast as I can. Looking up, I see there are no STOMP-shirted people around me. Figures, most seniors don't need every second of passing time to get to class.

I, however, manage to get to AP Lit only seconds before the final bell, skidding to a stop and getting into the seat Harper saved for me next to her.

"Hey," she says. Her short brunette hair covers the side of her face and eyes as she looks at her phone on the desk, savoring the last possible seconds before she has to turn it in. "You made it."

"Yeah," I huff. "No thanks to Abe and Sarah."

"Oh god. Swapping Spit Slope is still a thing? I'm sorry. I was hoping their relationship would bite the dust over the summer. You know, for your sake." She stands to walk her phone up to the basket in the front of the classroom where Mr. Andersen makes us store them during class time. "You should complain about them, like, to the administration. They can't block your access like that."

They don't have working door openers on half the entrances to this place, but yeah, sure, let's make Abe and Sarah the hill—or rather, ramp—that I die on.

Just as Harper returns to her seat, Cam plops down in the empty seat on the other side of me, her backpack making a satisfying *thunk* as she throws it to the floor. Today, she's wearing her green cat-eye glasses that make her red hair and green eyes pop.

I notice that both of them are wearing STOMP shirts.

Harper and I met in fifth grade when we were scrawny kids on the playground getting wood chips in our shoes at recess. I don't know life without her. We had a science class with Cam freshman year, and it was instantly like she was always a part of our friend group. Now I don't know life without her either.

"I got a locker all the way up on freaking third floor. I swear I had to pass through time and space to make it here," Cam explains, clearly annoyed.

"Sucks to suck," Harper says dryly. Harper is always the one to say exactly what she thinks.

"And I have two random sophomores as locker neighbors." Cam mouths "Hello" to me, the much more reserved of my two best friends.

"I have Katie Hollins and three freshmen," I say.

"How do you have four people?" Harper asks.

"My second locker," I reply, bracing myself for what I know is coming next.

"Ugh, you're so lucky." Harper stands, and holds out her hand. I drop my phone in her palm and she walks up to drop mine and Cam's into the basket.

Yep, just me, sitting on my throne of privilege.

The ding-ding-ding of morning announcements on the PA takes the pressure off wondering how to respond. Harper's comments sometimes make me feel like maybe she might never fully understand that those things don't exactly make me *feel* lucky.

"Hello, Mill City High School!" The voice of our assistant principal, Ms. Ross, fills the classroom. "A happy first-day-of-school greeting to you all, and especially to our freshman class!"

A low, loud boo rumbles through our classroom.

Mr. Andersen looks up from shuffling papers at his desk. "Be nice, guys," he warns. "You were them once, too."

Ms. Ross continues. "And of course, congratulations, seniors!" This time, a loud roar fills the room. Several boys bang their fists on their desks, which earns us another glare from Mr. Andersen.

"We know you all will accomplish great things this year as you soar toward opportunities, milestones, and personal progress."

Harper snorts a bit too loudly.

I may not be feeling super stoked about senior year, but judging by their matching shirts, apparently my friends and all my peers are.

Every year, the seniors at my high school sell these shirts in the school colors, emblazoned with the word SENIOR on the back and some secret acronym on the front. This year, it is STOMP.

If any of the underclassmen ask what the acronym stands for, the answer is the same every year: "We can't tell you."

Truth is, I don't think any of the seniors truly know. *Soaring Toward Opportunities, Milestones, Progress* was the official line fed to the administration, but everyone knows what it actually stands for is way more . . . sexual than that.

The idea behind the shirts is that the money raised is supposed to go to the Student Council's endowment fund, but seeing as I'm on the Student Council, I know the money goes directly toward a party fund for a select few popular seniors.

The whole concept is pointless and representative of senior year: None of us know what it is supposed to signify anyway.

"Do you know what it stands for?" I whisper.

"I heard Snatching—" Cam guesses.

"No, it's Slurping—" tries Harper.

Make it Shudder.

The announcements carry on. "And this seems like the opportune time to remind you that our first college-application workshop will be on September fifteenth."

"—Which, might I add, you are required to attend as part of my class," Mr. Andersen interjects.

Harper, of course, groans loudly, and I see Cam's shoulders slump a bit.

As for me, I wonder what it would be like to be so cavalier about the whole college thing. What would it be like to narrow your list simply by name alone, or because you just thought it would be cool to live there?

I open my planner and circle the date.

"And she's at it again with the lists!" Cam says.

"Yeah, seriously," Harper agrees. "You don't even need to go to the workshop. We both know you've had your list of schools to apply to since junior year."

Sophomore year, actually.

The rest of the day is pretty typical first-day stuff: reminders of the grading scale, warnings about turning homework in late. And, of course, there is a ton of talk from teachers across all six periods that this is our senior year. If we really get it together and work hard, who knows what could happen? We hold the keys, and our final year of high school is our oyster.

We just have to STOMP all over it, I guess.

As I reach my second locker, my hand goes for the lock, which I quickly realize is severed, hanging through the clasp. When I move the top part back in place, I see it's a clean, perfect cut. And then I notice the note taped to the door: *Unassigned locker. Please see main office to claim your things.*

Sure enough, inside the locker I see that I've been cleaned out from top to bottom. I slam the door so that it echoes through the empty hallway. Going down the ramp is a lot faster with no lovebirds blocking my way. I also pick up a lot of speed when I'm just plain pissed off.

I ride the elevator up to the second floor and open the door to the main office. There's no door opener, so I grip the handle and pull it down, but I don't give myself enough of an angle between the door and the doorframe. The door falls shut, leaving me wedged between.

The secretary looks up from her computer and stands up quickly. "Can I help you with the door?" she asks just as I squeeze my way through and the door shuts behind me.

"I got it," I huff, and look her in the eyes. "You cut the lock off my locker? I'm here to claim my stuff."

She lets out a *tsssk* sound.

Five minutes. Five minutes was all it would have taken to realize the locker was assigned to me, and would be properly logged by the end of the day. Instead, they called a janitor to get the metal cutter. They found a paper bag somewhere. They hauled all my stuff up here. That must've taken multiple people at least half an hour.

"Why?" I manage to get out.

"That locker wasn't assigned to your name," she says. "We can't have students storing items in lockers and not know the combination to open them. It's against school security policy. You gave your combination to your advisor for a locker on third floor. This locker was on first floor."

"I'm allowed to have two lockers, though," I explain. "It's part of my IEP—never mind. Anyway, it's part of my accommodations. It's so I don't have to lug all my stuff around for the whole day."

Her brow creases and she sounds stern. "Well, I'm sorry, if it was part of your official accommodations, it should have been logged by the student accommodations coordinator, and as of this afternoon, it wasn't."

She walks around her desk and knocks on the door that belongs to one of our hall monitors. The door opens partway. "Sorry to interrupt, but the girl in the wheelchair is here to claim her things."

They both go inside to gather all the items removed from my locker, and I'm left sitting alone in front of the main desk.

"Effie," I correct her, barely above a whisper. "My name is Effie."

CHAPTER TWO

The woman in the office hands me a grocery bag filled with my notebooks and folders, my water bottle, and my pencil case. At first glance, everything's there. Stuffed in the bottom, making the bag bulge from the sides, is the locker shelf Katie Hollins helped install.

"Would you like some help with your things?" The secretary's voice is so fake sweet. After inconveniencing *me*, they wanted to help? Where was that energy before they broke into my locker without a second thought? Nudging the bag down the hallway with my footplate isn't the most effective method, but I'm not going to give her the satisfaction.

Out in the hallway, alone, I push forcefully and the bag crumples before tipping over, loose syllabi sliding out of a folder and onto the floor.

I'm so done. I want to go home.

"Wow, they kicked you out of school on the first day? Harsh." The voice comes from behind me. I don't need to turn around to know whom it belongs to. I crack a tiny smile, in spite of myself.

I play along. "Yeah, the standards just keep getting higher and higher around here and it turns out I do not make the cut."

"Jeez," Wilder says, walking forward and then in front to face me. "If Ef-phalm-maya Galanos is out, there's really no hope for the rest of us."

I glare at him. But then a second later, I feel another smile forming. I have to hand it to him, he knows what he's doing.

Effie is short for Euphemia, which as you can imagine, presents a challenge for teachers calling roll on the first day of school. What Wilder uttered was the attempt of our new Student Council advisor in our shared fourth-period class.

On the very first day of high school, our Algebra I teacher butchered my full name in such a heinous way that I will not repeat it. Seriously.

"It's Effie," I'd managed to croak, but not loudly enough for the teacher to hear.

Just when I could feel my face turning beet red, a loud voice I now know as Wilder's perked up from behind me. "She said her name is EFFIE!"

The apology was made immediately, the taking of attendance continued, and the embarrassment mitigated. He is the only person who I let make jokes about my full name. Harper and Cam don't even dare try, but I suspect it's because they're not even sure how it's actually pronounced.

(It's You-phee-mia, if that helps. Why my parents cursed me

with that when they intended to call me Effie from the start, I'll never understand. Maybe they wanted something more than my thick, dark, curly hair and olive skin tone to scream, *She's Greek!* loud and clear. "You were named after a saint from the Orthodox Church! She was known as being 'well spoken of.' What more could you want?" my dad always asks me. A lot, Dad. A lot.)

Wilder kneels down to pick up my papers. Up close, I see his medium-brown hair lightened over the summer, no doubt thanks to lifeguarding at the outdoor pool in St. Louis Park. I only know about his summer job from social media. Lots of photos of Wilder posing with the other lifeguards in a white lifeguard shirt, red shorts, and black Ray-Ban–style sunglasses, the dimple in his left cheek popping as he grins.

Wilder and I are in-school friends. Although we have a fair number of mutual friends, we've never quite figured out how to make the jump to truly hanging out outside school, with the exception of maybe one or two group parties. At the end of every school year, I add my phone number underneath my name when I sign his yearbook, but he's never taken me up on it. I know I could get his number from someone else, but that's not what I want. I want *him* to call *me.*

Wait. If we only hang out in school, and this is our last school year together, what does that mean? I swallow, pushing that thought to the back of my mind.

He points at the folder and asks, "These go in here, right?"

He tucks the papers inside, turns the bag upright, and drops the folder back in. I know I said I didn't need help, but this is okay.

"So what actually happened?" He stands, dusting off his hands on his knees. "We both know they'd never kick you outta this place."

"They cut the lock off my locker, no warning or anything." The words come out flat, and I'm feeling both exhausted and sad that I had to say them at all.

"What? Why?" He pauses for a second. "They finally found your secret stash, huh?"

"No, that's still hidden, thank god." I wink at him. "I'm allowed to have two lockers to make it easier for me and to be able to carry around less stuff. Ms. Wilson was supposed to make note of the second locker so it didn't end up as unassigned, but she must have gotten too busy and forgot or something. And now here I am."

Wilder grabs the handles of the bag. "That sucks. I'm sorry, Effie."

A bit of the anger leaves my chest. "Don't be," I say. "It's not your fault."

"Yeah, but you're the one who has to pay for their mistake." He looks me in the eyes. "Anyway, where to?"

"I think I'll just stash this in my registered locker until I can hopefully get the one I want back. I was trying to get this stuff up to the third floor."

"Lead the way."

I roll the fifty or so feet to the elevator, and he falls into step next to me.

"You know," he says as he examines the padding that hangs from the elevator walls to protect them from getting dented or scratched up, "I think I've only ridden the elevator maybe three times since I've been a student here."

I don't really have anything to say to that. I don't know what staircases in our school lead where, which ones get crowded during certain times, which ones students hide in or sit on to do last-minute homework assignments before class. I've never climbed them, never looked up them. There is a whole other layer to our school's architecture that I don't understand at all, a subsection of this world that doesn't belong to me. The elevator, however, I recognize every inch of.

"So," he says as we walk down the hallway. "I noticed no STOMP shirt for you either, huh?"

He nudges my shoulder jokingly and my body jerks up half a millimeter as my muscles stiffen under his touch. Not in *that* way. Having cerebral palsy basically means that because of a brain injury I got from being born too early, my brain is extra about everything: *extra*-tight muscles, *extra* sensitivity to startles like loud noises or, like now, Wilder touching my shoulder. It's like having those bang snap fireworks that you throw on the ground explode inside you when you most want to keep your cool.

"I'm a bad senior Student Council rep," I reply. "And you're a terrible co-chair!"

Wilder laughs, "I played basketball over the summer with Seth and all those guys who guard the 'endowment fund.' Trust me, they have more than enough resources to throw big parties without my twenty-dollar 'donation.'" He pauses again before asking, "Do you have Andersen for AP Lit, too?"

"Yeah."

He exhales. "What do you think about that college workshop we have to go to on the fifteenth?"

I pause, unsure of what to say. For a second, I consider telling him the truth. Instead, I shrug. "I don't know. I guess I haven't given it much thought."

"Yeah, but before the meeting, we have to have an initial list of schools we might apply to." Wilder sounds worried. Yet another reminder that most kids haven't been working on theirs for years.

"I know," I tell him.

"And you're not wigged out about that?" He pauses for a second. "I mean, I think I know at least one school I for sure really like, but still . . ."

I don't want to tell him that Mom and I started that list sophomore year. About the plastic file folders she recently moved from her office into the living room. My list isn't just a list of places I might apply, but also includes info on climate, campus size in square miles, whether or not they have an accessibility coordinator, and if they are able to connect me to a current student who also uses a wheelchair to answer my questions.

"Not really," I respond.

Once we reach my locker, I undo the lock and open the door. I hold out my hand expecting Wilder to give me the bag and get back to whatever he was doing before he stumbled upon me.

Instead, he reaches for the retractable locker shelf, pulling it out to examine it. He squats down to my height to make sure he puts it in where I can easily reach it, and snaps it into place.

"Is this good for now? Once you get your second locker back, if you want to move the shelf there, just let me know."

I don't feel as sad or as tired as I did a few minutes ago. "Thanks, Wilder. This was really nice of you."

"Least I could do."

He touches my shoulder again lightly, and a bang snap pops inside me again.

When I finally make my way out to the parking lot, I'm twenty minutes late.

"Sorry," I mumble as I get in the front seat, but Mom doesn't answer, getting out of the car and popping the trunk open to put my chair inside.

"You left me sitting here, Effie. You should have texted." Since I depend on rides from my mom, she expects I stay on her schedule. She slams the car door shut and puts the car into reverse.

"They cut the lock off my second locker," I explain. "All my stuff was taken to the office and I had to go claim it and move it to the other locker that I still have."

Mom immediately puts the car back in park.

"You have got to be—" She exhales loudly, pinching the bridge of her nose. "I'm officially counting down the days until we don't have to deal with Ms. Wilson ever again. If she can't do her job correctly, *somebody* in the school has to speak up for you. They should've known it was yours, or at the very least held off a day until this could get sorted out."

I wait for her to get out of the car. I expect to blush bright red as she marches right up to the door of the school, flings it open, and goes inside. Instead, she shakes her head as though clearing it and reverses the car again, backing out of the spot.

"Besides that," she asks, "how was your first day?"

I glance at the brown bricks of the school one last time. I still only have one locker. I want to ask Mom if she plans to call and go off the moment we get home. But then she squeezes my knee and launches into a whole other type of dramatic.

"My big senior; I can't believe it!" She lets out a fake sob.

It's unavoidable, so I just roll my eyes. "You already went through the routine this morning!"

"Indulge me, Effie. You're my youngest and I can do whatever I want. I just got used to the idea of your sister not living at home and now I have to get used to the idea of losing you, too."

My sister, Cora, is a sophomore at Cannon River College in a town called Northfield, about an hour away from where we live in Minneapolis. If you ask Mom, though, it was as if she had moved to Siberia.

Now seems as good a time as any to tell her about my workshop. "For AP Lit I'm required to go to a college-application workshop on the fifteenth. I need to have a list of places I might apply to by then."

"Well," Mom says, "you're ahead of the curve there. Just print off a copy of our spreadsheet."

She completes a turn onto Theodore Wirth Parkway. I look out the window at the green grass and lush trees, barely starting to turn color. A biker zooms past in a blur.

Mom blinks suddenly. "You were able to move all the stuff in the locker by yourself?"

I shake my head no.

"Who helped you, honey?" Mom asks.

"My friend Wilder." My voice goes quiet, his hand on my shoulder suddenly feeling scandalous.

Mom's voice goes up slightly. "Wilder? Do I know him?"

"He's on Student Council with me."

"Where's he applying to college?" There she goes again. Only the first day of senior year, and I can't even ease into it.

We drive past Lake of the Isles, where the floating dock bobbing in the middle of the lake reminds me that summer was just a few days ago, and arrive in our neighborhood. Our house isn't *on* the lake, so it's not one of those mini-mansions, as Cora and I always call them. It's a small one-story with enough room for the four of us: Mom, Dad, Cora, and me.

Mom pulls into the driveway, then gets my chair out, and I do my transfer from the car seat to the chair. I release the brakes and roll to the door. By the time Mom comes in from getting the rest of her things out of the car, I'm in the kitchen scouring the pantry for an after-school snack.

"Effie?" Mom's voice sounds distant.

"Did you get more of those trail mix packs?" I ask, my head still inside the cabinet. "Not the ones with the dried fruit, the ones with the M&M'S."

I hear Mom put her keys back in the drawer, then say my name again. I look at her.

"You can get a snack in a minute. I want to talk to you about the locker situation."

"I know, Mom," I say, because I do know exactly how this will go. Mom's mad, and she'll call Ms. Wilson and leave a choice voicemail, and follow up on it tomorrow morning. Ms. Wilson will find me in the hallway tomorrow and apologize profusely, promising me that this will *never* happen again, which, of course it won't. I'm graduating.

But Mom's eyes look stern.

"Tomorrow, I think you should talk to Ms. Wilson. It's just that, well, you've heard me complain to her before. And I know you won't have a locker issue in college, but you will have other issues. But you also won't have me there to help every single time."

A small lump rises in my throat. I swallow it.

I know this is reality, but . . . this is senior year. I want to have an easy start.

I don't even know half the things I'm going to face next year. And I certainly don't know how to face them alone.

Mom and I look at each other for a moment. I can't tell if she wants to fold and I can't tell if I want her to. But she doesn't. So I relent.

"That sounds . . . good." The "good" comes out flat. It's not how I feel, it's just the word that came to me the fastest. I close the door to the cabinet and mumble something about getting started on my homework. Suddenly, my appetite is gone.

I guess I don't know how things are going to go anymore.

CHAPTER THREE

When I hear the buzz, I lift up my Human Biology textbook and notebook, looking for my phone.

It's a FaceTime call from Cora. I answer, happy for the distraction.

My sister looks a lot like me, but I think she's prettier. Her hair is less frizzy-curly than mine, and she's able to tame it into waves rather than boing-y curls. And her name isn't, like, Cornelia or something, in case you were wondering. She has it easier than me in every conceivable way.

I watch her on the screen as she stands up from her desk chair, climbs onto her lofted bed, and flops down with exuberance. She makes it look so simple. Because for her, it is.

"So," she asks. "What's new in the hallowed halls of Mill City High?"

Cora looks at me expectantly. I bite my lip. I could tell her about the locker, but I don't want to bring it up again. Not after that conversation with Mom. So instead I say, "The senior word this year is STOMP."

"What's the best guess for what it stands for? My word was SURGE. I think it meant *Seniors Urge Rough*—"

"I don't wanna know!" I yell, covering my face with my free hand.

"Fair enough." Cora giggles. "I still can't believe you're a senior! I'm so excited to have you here for a weekend next month. I'm going to take you to the caf and we'll chill in the dorms. But we're definitely going to do some stuff Mom will never need to find out about." She wiggles her eyebrows up and down.

My stomach sinks a bit. In the background of Cora's FaceTime screen, I see the corner of a poster for her favorite indie band, The Left Behinds, with the black scrawl of the bandmates' signatures in Sharpie just barely in frame.

Cora discovered the band online, made up of three women in their twenties. She took the initiative and asked her college's music committee to bring them to play in Northfield. And of course, she met the band afterward. Cora does things like that. While I wheel through the world trying to keep things safe and easy, my sister always ups the ante, all in, all the time, double or nothing.

In college, could I do something, become someone who does something like that?

"Hey," Cora speaks softly. "Look at me."

My eyesight has gone elsewhere, as it often does when I am

25

doing too much thinking. For the last several minutes, I've been staring at a distant spot on the wall unknowingly, instead of at the screen. My brain being extra again. If I look away, it's because I'm focusing extra hard on what someone is saying. It just doesn't always look like I am. *Eye contact*, I remind myself. *Eye contact. Eye contact.*

I look back at Cora, smiling sweetly at me.

"You're gonna figure all of this out, you know that, right? And we're all gonna help you, Mom, Dad, and me. Whether you end up at Cannon or not. You shouldn't feel like you have to come here just because I did, no matter what Mom's lists say."

I laugh. I bet Mom would love it if I stayed close to home, just like my sister.

"You're going to forge your own path, just like you have a zillion times before, 'kay?"

"'Kay," I reply.

When we hang up, I click the screen on and off a few times, to make sure the call is really over. I know my sister can't hear my thoughts from miles away.

But they're so damn loud.

I'm scared. Because next year I won't have my parents or my sister. And I have to somehow find the right place for me. And I'm pretty certain the right place is not on my college spreadsheet.

My chair is across the room from me, so I stand and take a few steps over to my bookshelf. I pull out the brochure that I've kept hidden between old magazine issues.

The thing is, I think I've found the right place. If right means scary, exhilarating, freeing. I just haven't told anyone yet. If I'm a little scared, I can't imagine getting everyone else on board.

I run my fingers over the raised embossing on the cover: *Prospect University, New York City.*

"Effie, was that your—"

I stuff the brochure back into place as fast as I can, kicking the edge of it to try and jam it in farther back between the magazines.

"—sister?"

I try to play it cool and smile at my dad, pretending I'm not hiding my biggest secret. I inhale sharply and take a few wobbly steps before plunking down ungracefully in my chair.

I hear the *click, click, click* of my ankles thudding fast against my footplate. Immediately, the clonus starts. My leg muscles shake like when you release a stretched-out rubber band, as if I am shivering just from the waist down. I place my hands on my knees hoping to quiet them, and I feel the slight bounces into the palms of my hands.

Dad looks at me a little suspiciously. "I was wondering if Cora's financial aid stuff all went through?"

"Didn't ask," I tell him. "You'll have to text her."

He leaves and I wait a full minute before I pull the brochure out again, placing it on my lap and covering it up with a stack of magazines.

I look down at the magazine on the top of the stack, the glossiness of its cover reflecting the overhead light of my bedroom. An old September issue of *Cosmopolitan.* I read all the articles online now, but I can't bear to part with a few favorite print copies. The address label in the bottom left-hand corner still reads CORA GALANOS. *This* is how it started.

When she went away to college, I started reading her magazines. I thought I'd eventually lose interest, but the more I looked the more I became interested in what I wasn't seeing in the pages—people like me.

I don't need stats to back up what I already know: Disabled people almost never see themselves in the media, in magazines, in ads, in any space.

And one night at the beginning of the summer, I was reading a profile of one of my favorite digital editors, just a few years out of college and changing the game. She was an alumna of the Prospect University Mass Media and Society major.

Ten minutes browsing their website, and I was infatuated.

I pull out the brochure again and unfold the letter that came with it:

Dear Euphemia,

We are delighted by your interest in Prospect University, and especially by your interest in our Mass Media and Society major. In this program, we are dedicated to asking questions of the media

**that populate our daily lives and are committed
to taking on the key issues in the field to shape
the media landscape of tomorrow. Rigorous
and thoughtful curriculum meets real-life hands-
on internship experience that you can only get in
the heart of New York City at the nation's top mass
media corporations. Our alumni win top industry
awards, start the next viral social media campaigns,
become respected editors, or launch their own
imprints.**

Maybe it seems silly, reading a couple of my sister's magazines and then charting my major, but the more I look into this
field I find something else to like. I can learn about journalism,
social media, and the way they all intersect. And then there's
the prized Prospect attraction—a semester-long internship at
Hearst Communications, the global media company. I don't
know exactly what I want to do yet, but I know this will help
me answer that question.

That's what led me to email Mr. Andersen a few weeks
ago to ask if I could have a piece of college-related mail sent
to his faculty mailbox instead of my home address. It feels
like a dream still, and I'm not ready to deal with the reality
of it all yet.

"You know, Effie," he said kindly as he handed it to me
when I went to select my second locker two weeks ago. "I
couldn't help but notice where this is from." I looked away

shyly, feeling my cheeks get a little pink. It was only fair and all since he had to sort through the mail, but I wanted to keep this dream mine for a little longer. "Prospect is a really excellent school, and they'd be very lucky to have you."

For the rest of the day, I didn't wheel anywhere. I simply floated along.

I page through the brochure. I know these things are created to impress you, but this is something else. The campus in Park Slope, Brooklyn, is stunning. There are Georgian-style buildings in red brick with white trim. There are leafy trees pictured in the different seasons and big green lawn spaces. The campus looks like classic New England mixed with a countryside castle, but condensed to fit in the middle of a big city. It's where you'd go to think important scholarly thoughts or learn web design in their state-of-the-art lab.

I haven't visited in person—haven't even been to New York—but I can see myself getting up and wheeling across the quad, wearing cute sweaters in the picturesque autumn. Strolling down streets lined with brownstones. Learning from the incredible guest lecturers who pass through the Mass Media and Society department. Wheeling along and feeling the rumble of the subways beneath me or falling asleep to the sound of a car honking on the street. Hearing different languages spoken around me. Buying coffee at a bodega. Learning all the five boroughs and finding a favorite spot in all of them . . . not a tourist spot, but a little piece of it that only I love. Springing for a cab to Little Italy for dinner with my future new friends after a workday at my internship in Manhattan.

On my phone, I pull up the Galanos System Spreadsheet that Mom and I have been working on since the end of sophomore year.

I try to imagine adding in Prospect University, but all I could think to type would be "Mom, would you even let me consider going here?" She's made comments about not wanting to send me out of the Midwest because it's too far away. New York seems so big, too far, too much.

I put the Prospect brochure back inside the *Cosmo*—one dream tucked inside another—and place it back on my bookshelf.

CHAPTER FOUR

The next morning, I knock on Ms. Wilson's office door and wait a few seconds.

Maybe she's in the staff lounge or in a meeting. I can come back tomorrow. Tell Mom I tried, and it'll be the truth.

Instead, I knock again, and this time I hear footsteps. *Crap.*

The door opens. "Effie!" Ms. Wilson says, so friendly, like yesterday didn't even happen. "Sorry, I was just finishing up a phone call. Come on in." She holds open the door and I wheel inside. "What can I do for you?"

She sits down at her desk.

My breathing starts to quicken and I feel a prickle on the back of my neck. "My locker," I croak out. I've gone over every moment of this conversation in my head. Each time, I'm forceful and persuasive, and I always come away impressing Ms. Wilson. Croaking was never involved.

Digging through a pile of papers on her desk, she pulls out a spreadsheet and flips through until she finds my last name in the G's. "Let me see . . . you have a locker on first and a locker on third?"

"They cut the lock off the one on first yesterday."

"I thought . . ." She flips through the sheet. "Oh, Effie. I'm almost certain I let the front office know . . ." She ruffles through the papers a few more times before looking me in the eye. "The start of the school year is so busy . . . there's always one thing that slips . . ."

I want to tell her that I'm mad. That their system of claiming lockers doesn't make any sense. That she made a mistake at my expense.

Instead, I can't make words come out of my mouth.

Ms. Wilson clicks her pen up and down a few times, and when she speaks, her voice is stern. "Effie, I really am sorry. But you have to know that it's dangerous to have items in lockers if we are even a little bit unsure of what contents might be inside them."

I gear up for another shot at what I know I need to say. But instead I hear myself say, "Okay."

Okay?! My head slumps. This is a disaster. I wanted to handle it all on my own for once.

Ms. Wilson opens her mouth to say something, but then the warning bell rings. She knows I'll be late to class and so do I.

"Effie, again, I am *so* very sorry." She stands and opens the door for me. "I'll let you get to your fourth-period class, but I'll give your mom a call and we'll get everything sorted out by the end of the day."

33

My whole body goes soft.

I go out into the hallway and I want to yell at myself.

I'm a senior in high school and I can't even get a simple locker mix-up fixed without my mom stepping in to save me.

I blew it.

❧

My fourth period is Student Council, which counts as a credit as long as seniors do something to give back to the school by May.

The first order of business on the Student Council agenda is the endowment fund.

Seth Collins, a fellow senior and Wilder's Student Council co-chair, calls the meeting to order.

"We've seen great profits from the senior shirts, no thanks to the support of my co-chair." He glares at Wilder, and I wonder if I'll be implicated, too.

"I never said I didn't support Student Council," says Wilder, grinning slyly. "I'm mostly against the fast fashion industry. Did you know that thrown-away clothing accounts for nine percent of the world's non-recyclable waste per year?"

"I did not," Seth deadpans. "*Anyway*, the endowment fund is in good shape, which is exciting, because it's never too early to talk about the School Beautification Project." Seth passes around a sheet of paper. "Here's some administration-approved projects we can choose from."

The document is printed on official Mill City High School letterhead, with our mascot, the hummingbird—fierce, right?—pointing its beak toward me with intense eyes. Since when do birds have eyebrows?

> *The School Beautification Project is meant to keep our school clean, up to date, and welcoming to all who enter. Approved projects include repainting of surfaces (doors, benches, parking lot lines), donations of books to the school library . . .*

Welcoming to all who enter? The door openers don't even work. I skim the rest of the list. Of course, there's nothing about accessibility on it.

Wilder speaks up. "As Student Council co-chair—"

"Who didn't even wear a shirt!" Seth shouts.

"—I'll be heading up the project and will need at least one other member to take on shopping and organizational duties with me. Reach out to me if you're interested."

The conversation switches to various project ideas, but I don't contribute. I'm still stung over my utter locker failure.

They settle on painting the benches outside school, then Seth moves the topic of discussion to the homecoming dance.

❧

I'm not even all that excited about going to senior homecoming. But when Harper comes up to me and Cam the next day at school, she's vibrating with excitement over how she asked out Calvin, her very new love interest from her club hockey team. She cut letters out of poster board and taped them to different items—his skates, his gym bag, his hockey stick, the puck—all spelling out HOMECOMING, with Harper left holding the question mark at the end.

"And . . ." Harper drags out the word. "He even posted a photo of us!" She holds her phone up: a shot of Harper and Calvin together on the ice. Immediately, I see what she sees in him; he has big brown eyes, with a bright, friendly smile. His hair is styled in a short Afro, faded on the sides.

They're both wearing their green jerseys, and his arm is slung over her shoulders.

"Nice!" Cam smiles. "Social media official!"

It was such small interaction, but for the rest of the day, something eats at me that I can't quite put my finger on.

Harper looks so happy. She *is* so happy. And I'm happy for her.

But once—just once—I wish that specific kind of happiness for me.

❧

That evening, I go across the hall to Cora's room and open her closet.

Her dusty pink dress is right where I thought it would be. I hold the hanger in one hand, drape the dress over my body, and look at myself in the mirror.

It hits just below the knee, so I don't have to worry about it getting caught in my wheels. The color will bring out my olive skin tone like it did for Cora. The top is really simple, with thin straps and nothing fancy for the neckline. But it would hit my waist in just the right way.

And maybe it would shimmer as I dance with my friends, and for one moment, Wilder and I would dance together, laughing, having a good time.

I'm well aware: If I want that specific happiness, it comes with putting myself out there. But it's hard when I can't see anyone *like me out there doing it.*

I picture myself in this dress, at homecoming, once more. Only this time, at the end of the night, I tell Wilder, "I like you."

It's a nice thought. And I hang the dress up and shut the door behind me to go back to reality.

❧

It's Thursday, and I'm just trying to get to Bio. I've already had to dodge Abe and Sarah, having to move so close to get around them that I could see Sarah's tonsils. So it's been a day, and it's only third period.

And then as I get on the elevator and punch the button, I see a boy approaching and I notice what he's carrying. I debate getting off, but he's the one invading *my* space, *my* passing time. I don't want to be hospitable today.

When he realizes I have no plans to leave, he frowns. He carefully considers his options and I know that he knows he has none.

The doors close behind him and he doesn't hit a different button than me. Perfect. We're both going to the same place. He's a junior, I think. I don't know his name and I'm sure he doesn't know mine. As we ascend, he unrolls his poster board.

He clears his throat. "Hey, um, do you think you can move behind me? Like, you know, over there?"

He wants me to sit in the corner. I ignore him.

I eye the quickest way to beeline out of here. A foot and a half from the corner to make it out the door into the hallway, including a sharp left turn so I don't have to bump into whoever awaits me on the other side. The junior is bouncing up and down on his heels. This is the longest thirty seconds of both our lives.

The elevator is approaching the sixth floor.

Right on cue, I can hear a female student's shrill, confused voice saying, "I swear to you, I did not skip class! You can ask my teacher. And since when do you even single people out for skipping class anyway? This is ridiculous!"

The doors open, and one of our hall monitors is standing next to this poor girl. She looks close to tears. They always do.

But then she sees the boy. He grins, holding his sign. He can barely get out "Will you go to homecoming with me?" before she lets out a loud squeak.

"*Omigosh!* Really? Omigod! Ryan, you got me *so* good."

He drops the sign to the floor so they can hug and I run over the edge of it as I try to book it out of there as fast as I can.

I'm not sure when the elevator-ask became popular, but it's a fad I can't wait to see die out. The asker finds a hall monitor and asks them to pull their potential dance date out of their class just seconds before passing time, feigning some concern about a call in the office or like today, skipping class. The whole goal was to lead them to the elevator. And well, you know the rest.

I can't even count how many asks I've inadvertently crashed over the years. The people in this school co-opt elevators and kiss on ramps and don't let their Beautification Projects actually change anything.

But maybe—*maybe*—I am also a little bit bitter because it would actually make sense to ask the girl who uses a wheelchair out in the elevator (super cute, even!) but it has never happened to me.

It's just, this is my last homecoming. I thought maybe, maybe by now, by this dance, I'd have someone ask me to go, too.

But then my phone trills. A text from Harper: Hey, Wilder is now in our group. Hope that's cool with everyone.

I could think about how surprising it is—that in the

random ways homecoming groups come together and all the various friends he has, he ended up with us.

Or I could think about how I don't think he is seeing anyone, and how it seems likely he'll be alone at the dance.

But all I can think about suddenly is that dusty pink dress. How I will look in that dress. And Wilder getting to see me in that dress, for real.

From the homecoming ticket line, I respond: All in. ☺

CHAPTER FIVE

"Lift from the front, girls!"

Mom has parked her car in the driveway of Cam's house, dropping me off to get ready for homecoming tonight. The Cordes house has two small steps to get inside. Mom is lifting me a foot or two off the ground using the handlebars on the back of my chair, and Harper and Cam are lifting from the frame of the chair in the front, one girl supporting either side. Once I am safely in the entryway, Mom hands over my garment and makeup bags.

"Okay!" she says excitedly. "Have a ton of fun! Take lots of pictures."

I turn around to wave goodbye, greeted by the sound of the car door slamming shut. She's already backing out, not looking at me. Mom's been a little extra hover-y since I failed to handle my locker situation by myself, and she was clearly upset she had to step in. But tonight, I'm glad she's letting it go.

Pop music blares from upstairs, and I wonder if we're going to be walking up the stairs after all.

"Oh," Harper says. "The other girls are in the upstairs bathroom since there's more mirror real estate. I told them we'd use the smaller bathroom on this floor, if that's okay."

"It will be more fun, too," Cam jumps in right away. "This way, we'll get ready together, just the three of us."

It sucks to feel like the person who forces everyone to recalibrate their plans. On the other hand, I am happy that I get to be with my two best friends, and I'm happy that they know to make that call instead of placing that burden on me.

The downstairs bathroom is pretty small. I park my chair in the hallway and, using the doorframe, take the two small steps to be able to sit on the toilet. With all of us inside, we're packed in like sardines.

When Harper lifts her arms to put her hair up, she winces.

"Your shoulder?" Cam asks.

Harper nods. "I'm worried it will hurt my chances of playing in the tourney against Wayzata. I really want to."

"Oh man," Cam says. "You've been looking forward to that for weeks."

She has? And she has a shoulder injury?

I wonder why I'm so out of the loop, but then Cam pins two big sections of my hair back so that two curls fall down nicely in front to frame my face, and we start to talk about other stuff.

"Ef, what do you have planned for your makeup?" Harper asks.

"I was hoping you would just do it for me?" My voice is intentionally high-pitched and sweet. I've never been any good at this stuff. I normally don't care about looking super different for a dance than I would otherwise, but tonight feels different.

For my makeup, Harper uses some shimmery gold eye shadow and some rose blush that will bring out the color of the dress.

When it comes time for the dress, I stand, both hands holding on to either side of the sink. Cam kneels down, laying the dress on the floor so I can step into it. As Harper lifts the dress up my body, I wobble a bit and feel my muscles stiffen.

"You're not going to fall," Harper says. "I'm standing right behind you."

I know that, but sometimes, my body doesn't. She zips the dress just as the burn starts in my ankles.

"And, you're in." Harper's hand lightly grazes my back as she guides me so I'm sitting down on the toilet again. She's known me for since forever, so she knows when I've been standing for too long.

Harper's dress is a longer aqua dress, Cam's is a medium-length black one. They walk out into the foyer, but I pause for a second in front of the hallway mirror.

43

Maybe it's the fact that this *is* the last homecoming, or maybe it's how pretty Cora's dress truly is, but I bask in it. The thing is, when you're in a wheelchair, you sometimes feel like you can't be beautiful—that's for *other* girls. Non-disabled girls. I look in the mirror at how the pale pink dress accentuates my chest in the right way—without being too much—and my foundation that doesn't even have one crease (thanks, Harper) and the mauve of my lipstick, and I realize maybe that's false. That beautiful feeling is for *all* girls. That beautiful feeling is for me.

In the living room, before the dates come, we take lots of combinations of photos. Ones of the whole group, a smattering of people we know from classes and a few friends from the art club Cam is in at school. And of course ones of just me, Cam, and Harper.

They kneel down to my height so they can wrap their arms around me. For a moment, I let myself buy into it: our *last* homecoming. Some were fun, and some were just okay, but all of them were ours. And I'll miss them. Next year, I don't know who I'll be hanging out with. But it probably won't be my two best friends.

I hug them extra tight.

Around seven thirty, the doorbell rings. Before I even have a chance to turn around, I know by Harper's face, a mixture of elation and a bit of apprehension, that it's Calvin.

He's taller than he looked in pictures. Good thing Harper is wearing heels tonight. He shakes Mrs. Cordes's hand and that same big, bright smile is out in full force. He's wearing a blue dress shirt to match Harper's dress, and a white tie. He's carrying a tiny box, which I know contains a corsage.

He gives her a quick kiss on her cheek, and she lights up another few watts.

"These are my friends!" Harper sweeps her hand out to encompass all of us.

Cam leans over and whispers in my ear, "I creeped on all his photos last night and went so deep I think I ended up on his cousin's best friend's profile."

"Nice work," I say back.

He makes his way over to us and we straighten up.

"And this is Cam and Effie."

"Hey," Calvin says. "Oh man, I've heard so much about you guys!"

"Only good things, I hope." Cam puts on a fake-serious look for half a second before smiling. "Just kidding, like Harper has anything bad to say about us." It's a rare glimpse of Cam's feistiness coming out, especially in front of a new friend, and I love it.

"I might if you keep this up," Harper deadpans.

45

When Calvin shakes my hand, I wonder if he's surprised to discover his girlfriend's friend uses a wheelchair. I search his face for any hint of surprise, but it's normal.

"I'm so excited to meet you guys and hang out tonight," Calvin says. "We're going to have a great time."

The doorbell rings, and Cam immediately dashes off to greet her girlfriend, Ali. Cam and Ali met teaching at a kids' summer arts class two summers ago—Ali does sculpture and Cam is an amazing sketch artist.

I watch them for a second, before my eyes catch who walked in behind them.

Wilder is standing in the doorway. A bang snap goes off inside me, even though I'm not startled.

He's wearing a crisp white dress shirt with a black bow tie. An actual bow tie.

My lips twitch upward into a smile. I am not sure I can make it through this night.

Especially after I see who walks in the door after him. Sameerah Watson, a junior. She has perfectly sleek black hair without any frizz and is wearing a sparkly gold minidress. As a flushed feeling builds from my stomach throughout my whole body, I repeat to myself, *She just drove with him. This isn't what it looks like.*

But then he touches her elbow and she grins. I notice the corsage on her wrist and all my hopes fall like a house of cards.

I'm not getting his number tonight. I'm not getting time

alone with him. And he's certainly not going to notice me in my dress with Sameerah looking like that.

I nudge Harper in the ribs and whisper, "Are Sameerah and Wilder dating?"

Harper looks toward the door, and if she can pick up on my sadness, she thankfully doesn't say anything.

"No clue," she says. "He didn't say he was bringing anyone. But wow, she looks great."

The next few moments are a blur. I catch Wilder meeting Calvin and them casually chatting about hockey and this year's Frozen Four.

And suddenly, he's in front of me. "Effie, do you know Sameerah?"

I don't, not really, but suddenly I want to know every little thing about her. I want every bit of information I can find until I discover what it was about her that made him want her.

My eyes catch the corsage again. And I think about how, if he gave me that, I'd accidentally tear it up while wheeling.

I fake a smile and respond, "Nice to meet you."

❧

The Homecoming Gods have officially cursed me—the only vehicle my chair fits in is Wilder's van. And to make matters worse, we have to put most of the seats down to get the chair in, leaving little room for another passenger. This leaves

Sameerah squished between two girls in the middle seat of Calvin's red Toyota.

"You should be with her. This is . . . awkward." I blush.

But Wilder seems unfazed. "Don't worry about it."

I try to protest, but I see all the other cars pulling out of the drive, oblivious to my pain. It's me and him.

Surrendering, I secure my foot on the bottom frame of the van. I grip tightly on the door handle, and quite honestly, from here, I just hope for the best.

Two strong hands grip my shoulders, and I momentarily forget what legs are even supposed to do. I gather myself, and sort of half sit, half flop into the front seat. It's not pretty, but it does the job.

But Wilder's still standing there, looking at me.

That's the thing with never hanging out with me outside school. He's never had to see me try to navigate things without my chair. He's never seen me stand up.

"Hey, Effie. I'm really sorry my car is so high," he says, as if he built it himself.

I shrug. "I'm used to it."

At first during the ride, there's silence. I don't know what to say. So he turns on the pop music station.

And suddenly, he's singing along, tapping his fingers to the beat. I can't stop looking at him. This is exactly what I wanted in exactly the wrong scenario.

"So, Sameerah," I say during a commercial break. I don't want to talk about it, but it feels weird not to.

"Oh, yeah, we had a class together last semester. She's great."

Last semester?

A whole summer since then?

Did I miss all the signs?

But Wilder changes the subject, complaining about a boring novel we're reading in Mr. Andersen's class. And we're off, talking about teachers we like and complaining about useless worksheets.

Wilder looks at me. "So not to be *that* person since I know literally everyone is asking this, but I'm super interested in where you're looking at colleges."

Super interested? I don't know how to read that. I start to answer him, but realize we've arrived at the hotel, and the next moments are tied up with finding parking.

And after that, Harper and Cam are helping take my chair out of the van, and Sameerah is back by Wilder's side, and he's not super interested in me anymore.

❧

When we're finally on the dance floor, it's the five of us: Harper and Cam plus their dates, and me. Most of the group splits off, including Sameerah and Wilder, so I make myself try to forget about them. I don't want it to ruin my fun.

I rock back and forth on my wheels. I vogue and do goofy things with my hands and arms while I lip-synch to the lyrics. I look wild, but I don't care.

And I am doing okay, until the first slow love song comes on.

"I'm gonna get some air," I say. Cam smiles and mouths, "See you later," but Harper doesn't notice.

Back in the hallway, I sit against the wall and click through social media, seeing clips from the same dance I'm currently attending.

What am I doing?

I put my phone down and pull myself together. I have the dress. And the makeup. Everything about tonight is exactly how I hoped.

Except I don't have the boy.

I shake my head to clear it. I can still have a good time.

Back inside, my friends have moved deeper into the dance floor. I spot the edge of Harper's dress peeking out as bodies jump and thrash around them. If you think school dances are not a contact sport, you clearly haven't attended one in a wheelchair.

I see my first break: Two boys have turned to holler at each other during a part of a song that everybody yells out. It creates a tiny space between them, and I push through. I am still three clumps of people away from my group.

I bump into someone and hear the customary "What the . . . ?! Oh. *Oh!* Oh shit, I'm sorry."

This is my version of crawling under the alarm lasers in the spy movies.

One guy almost ends up sitting in my lap as he backs into

me by accident, and we are both embarrassed. That's one way to get a lap dance.

When I finally make it back to the group, the song that just retired as the song of the summer comes on, and I look across the dance floor to see Wilder dancing with Sameerah. It's like swallowing an ice cube, cold and hard, as it sinks slowly down to my gut.

But suddenly, my chair jolts back. Calvin has grabbed the handles and is moving me around in a circle so fast, the room is blurring. "Let's *gooooo!*" he shouts in a deep, rumbling voice.

This has happened to me before, and unless you're my close friend, I don't really allow it. But when you've felt on the outside for a whole night, there are just some things you will grin and bear to get your mind off other stuff.

"Whoo!" I shout, and resume fist pumping, and it earns a big laugh. I let it wash over me.

Toward the end of the night, one of the songs that Wilder was singing along to in the car comes on. I have to admit, it's a great song. Full of a thumping pop bass beat and catchy lyrics you can't help but want to belt at the top of your lungs.

There's a yank and my chair is being whipped around again. I look up, expecting to see Calvin at the reins, but bang snap when I see it's Wilder.

"Mind if I cut in?" he asks cheekily.

I don't have a chance to answer before the room

becomes a blur again. He tips me back like I'm popping a wheelie.

I don't know what to think, and I don't know where Sameerah is, and I know it's just a dance. But I also know I will never again hear this song without thinking of him.

CHAPTER SIX

In the morning, I open my phone. I look at all the photos I was tagged in from the dance. Cora's liked every single one. Calvin has requested to follow me, and I follow him back.

There's a direct message to me on the app, which was sent around 12:45, when the group started going home.

It's from Wilder: Hey! Great night. Forgot to ask: Mr. Andersen told me you're interested in going to Prospect? I think it's my first choice.

Wait. What?

It feels so unbelievable, and yet, now I know why he was so eager to ask me about colleges last night. And that's all my brain needs . . .

Imagine if I go to Prospect. And I'm far away from Minneapolis in the hugeness that is New York. And despite meeting new people and everything, Wilder is the only person who I would know really well there. He'd know what I mean when I say I miss home: being able to walk around a lake

53

while still being in a city, being able to go to the same Dairy Queen I took a field trip to in kindergarten, how some people talk about Prince like he's a personal friend of theirs, the way the seasons change, and the way the first time it hits forty degrees in the spring, you laugh at all the people running around the lake in shorts. It takes a long time to build to that level of familiarity with new friends.

Maybe we'd hang out more. At college, there are probably no more "in-school friends" because you're living on campus. I might see him at a Saturday-night party. Or maybe I would see him at a restaurant somewhere near campus in Brooklyn. Him waving me over to his table, clearing a space and removing the chair for me so I could roll right up. Us talking till midnight about philosophy or Western religion or whatever you talk about when you're at Prospect University.

I imagine seeing him on a Sunday morning, studious in the library, hunched over his laptop. Does he wear glasses when he does schoolwork? I picture him wearing sweatpants and a Prospect hoodie. He would look so cute in a hoodie.

I shake my head, trying to center myself. I remember how happy he looked with Sameerah, and how I shouldn't even be thinking like this.

Just as I start to settle into my worksheet on Punnett Squares for the unit on genetics, my phone buzzes.

A text from Cora: Who's the cute boy in your homecoming group?

Right underneath it, she adds a winky face.

Real-life perspective is overrated, and can wait until another day. For the ninth time today, I hit Play on that song that Wilder spun me around to, turning the volume all the way up.

❧

In the library, Mr. Andersen writes out the agenda for our ninety-minute college-admissions session on the whiteboard, his black marker squeaking.

Harper is coming late from hockey practice (I'm fully expecting she'll be beaming about getting asked to go to Calvin's homecoming) and Cam has an eye doctor appointment after school and will go to next week's makeup session, so I'm sitting alone.

"All right." Mr. Andersen claps his hands to get our attention while I'm still copying the agenda into my notebook. "Thank you for coming out this afternoon! Hopefully we'll provide you with some good information to get started on this whole scary, exciting process of applying to college."

Start? I think. Maybe Mom should have come to this workshop. Hell, she could lead it.

A backpack makes a loud noise as it hits the floor next to me, and I startle two bang snaps' worth. My heart rate starts to settle and a blush fills my cheeks as I hear the scrape of the chair next to me being pulled out.

"E-prew-nefria . . . is it okay that I sit here? I had another meeting with a teacher that ran late. Have I missed the secret of how to get into all the colleges yet?"

"No . . ." I catch myself feeling shyer than usual. "No, he just started a minute ago, so you're right on time."

Wilder leans down to unzip his backpack, retrieving a notebook and pen. While we wait for Mr. Andersen to say something, Wilder taps the pen against the page.

"You excited for the start of off-campus lunch?" Wilder asks me.

At about six weeks into the school year, all seniors are granted off-campus lunch privileges. The conversations are already bubbling up, my peers asking, "Where are you going to lunch?" Panera, Chipotle, burgers and fries—the possibilities are endless, but what I'm looking forward to is that first taste of real freedom. To be able to go anywhere I want with my best friends.

I grin at him. "Can't wait."

Mr. Andersen claps his hands to get our attention. "I thought to kick things off, we'd start by sharing our understanding of what the college-application and admissions process is like," Mr. Andersen says. "Feel free to call out any words or ideas that you think of when you think about applying to college."

He points to one girl who shouts, "Stressful!" We all laugh.

"Indeed," Mr. Andersen agrees as he adds her word to the board.

Another guy adds, "Competitive."

Other words shared are: "time-consuming," "confusing," and "deadlines."

"Different for each school!" Wilder calls out, and I bang snap again.

"Sure is. Hopefully, now you can see that the emotions you feel about applying to college are normal and shared by your peers. Now I want you to take a moment and share with the people sitting next to you what you're each looking for in a college."

Everyone immediately turns to their full tables and the dull roar of group chatter fills the room. There is no one else at my table except for Wilder. The universe is taking no prisoners today.

"Well," he starts. "You already know which college I want to talk to you about. So, Prospect for you, too?"

"Yeah . . . I mean . . . I . . ." I take a quick breath. "It's a really great school and I'm only just starting to look into it but . . . I like what I see so far."

"I visited over the summer. Effie, it's . . ." He leans back in his chair, like he's blown away just thinking about it. "My dad went there, and for that reason, I was dead set on hating it. I wanted to do my own thing. But he insisted we go, and I loved it right away. It's *so* cool. And New York is . . . well, to me, there's no place quite like it." He's talking with his hands animatedly, and takes a hurried breath, like it's exercise just to say everything that he wants to. "So, why do you want to go to Prospect?"

I swallow, and say quietly, "Um, the classes."

I hoped he'd jump in here and take over, but he wants me to say more. Which, of course he does. Everyone goes to college for the classes; it's, like, the main draw.

I try again. "Prospect's Mass Media and Society department, actually."

He leans forward to hear more, so I keep going.

"It might sound kind of silly, but I started reading a lot of my sister's magazines when she went off to college, and it made me realize how, in media targeted toward women—and really, any media—disabled people don't see themselves represented. And thankfully, that's changing, but I've been thinking maybe I can be part of that change."

Did I really say that out loud? I haven't told anyone this— well, unless you count the drafts of my admissions essay on my laptop as telling. My body flashes hot, then cold, and my arms itch to push away from the table and roll away as fast as I can.

Finally, he speaks. "Effie, that's . . . that's really *cool.*"

"Really?" I hate that it comes out like I'm surprised. But truth is, I am. When you dream up something on your own, it's so scary to share it. But as a new feeling settles over me, I realize it feels like a relief, too.

"*Yeah,* hell yeah. And I think if that's what you want to do, you should do it. Just promise to remember me when you're the next high-powered digital-content manager."

For the first time, I'm not thinking of any of this as silly anymore. I'm thinking about how awesome that would be.

Just then, I notice Harper has arrived, sitting in the back. Her face lacks its normal energy. She motions to me like she wants me to come sit at her table, but this conversation with Wilder is going so well. I look away. I can't bear to burst our perfect Prospect bubble.

Wilder tells me how he wants to go into International Relations. He talks about classes that bring in dignitaries from the UN as guest speakers. I hear myself mention how much I want the internship at Hearst. He pulls out his phone and types something in.

"There's an internship in the same area that I'm interested in. How wild would that be, two Minneapolis kids interning in Manhattan?"

Imagining the two of us at Prospect no longer feels like a daydream. I see us commiserating over our shared work-loads and stress. Him catching sight of me as we go off to our internships, two people rushing with everyone else in rush hour. Would he text me to see if I want to grab lunch from a street cart? I can see us eating together in Bryant Park.

"Where else are you applying?" I ask, to ground myself.

Wilder lists off his other choices, then says, "I really want it to be Prospect, though." He's all in. Then he asks, "So what about you?"

My knees bounce up and down under the table. I tell him about Cannon River and the University of Minnesota. I mention I'll apply to Northwestern University in Illinois, though it feels like a stretch. I'm a strong student, but I'm not sure I'm "one of the top in the country" strong. Last, I mention Cal Berkeley, but it comes out like a question because, to me, it feels like one still.

"California?" Wilder's voice is surprised.

"Remember that national college fair for juniors at the Convention Center last spring?"

Wilder says he didn't go.

"Well, my parents made me," I say. "And the representative from the California system called me over to her booth to make sure I knew Cal's history of supporting disabled students."

"How'd that feel?" he asks.

"Kinda weird," I admit. "But it's not common to hear that about a college, so I added it to my list."

One of my hands balls up in my lap. I'm luckier than many, I know. I'll have to take out some loans for school, and I'll look for scholarships. But by and large, my family's financial situation isn't putting any of my choices out of reach.

Accessibility might, though. Privileged in some ways and not in others.

I take a deep breath. "I want it to be Prospect, too."

I realize that if I'm really going to do this, I have to get to work.

❧

The bright red Prospect logo loads on their website with a picture of the city skyline at night. The same excitement surges through me. I hover over "Student Life," then under "Resources," click "Disability Services."

A banner loads of a woman sitting behind a desk, a smiling student on the other side wearing a backpack. Underneath the header, text reads *Prospect University is committed to helping every student achieve their academic goals.*

There are links for current students to register for support services, links to assistive technology and on-campus resources. There's a list of medical professionals and medical device rental and repair companies in New York City.

I open Excel—my own spreadsheet, separate from Mom's and mine—and as I read through the links, I copy the details in. Across the top in the categories *Classroom Support, Dedicated Disability Coordinator, Outside Resources* . . . Prospect is checking the boxes. But the categories like *Current Student in a Wheelchair—Can we connect?* or *Dorm Room Accessibility* I know can only be answered in one way.

I open my email and start on one to the contact listed for DisabilityServices@prospect.edu:

Hello Cynthia,

My name is Effie Galanos and I am a high school senior in Minneapolis. I am very interested in Prospect University.

I take a deep breath before I type the next sentence: *I consider it to be my top-choice college.*

I click Save as Draft.

With big cities come big distances to travel, and the places I would be going to could no longer be measured in feet or whether Mom could pick me up or not. I know I'm lucky: Being able to walk even a little bit means I can get into a cab, and I have a wheelchair that folds. Not everyone has those options or the flexibility they afford me.

I type "New York City + wheelchair accessible" into the search bar and scroll through the results. What I see stops me right in my tracks.

New York City has to be one of the least accessible cities in America. I read that there are fourteen hundred famous yellow taxicabs that are accessible—out of a fleet of nearly fourteen thousand. Only 10 percent.

I click a link to a video that the *New York Times* made about a guy in a wheelchair who asks his non-disabled friend to make the identical trek from the same starting point in Brooklyn to a Manhattan coffee shop. The friend gets there using the subway, only three stops. It takes him thirteen minutes.

Meanwhile, the guy in the wheelchair can't get a direct bus into the city, nor can he access his neighborhood subway station. And even if he could, he can't be sure all the transfer stations or his final stop in Union Square has an elevator. The map is unclear. So he's forced to take the East River Ferry. And worse yet, once he exits the ferry, he still has to take two buses to get to Union Square. It takes him an hour and forty-three minutes.

One of Prospect's selling points is that they claim I could be just a twenty-minute subway ride from Manhattan. It doesn't look that way for me, at least on the surface.

But I've made things that aren't accessible work for me.

Who's to say that this couldn't be one of them?

I open the Common Application like Mr. Andersen taught us in the workshop. I change the password to something Mom doesn't know. I add Prospect to the list of schools I'm applying to.

I will tell my parents, eventually. Just not tonight.

CHAPTER SEVEN

Dear E_Galanos10,

We've noticed multiple log-in attempts on your Common Application account. If this wasn't you, we recommend you change your password immediately . . .

Dad notices my eye roll and asks, "What's wrong?"

I put my phone down, closing the email along with it. I shrug. "Mom is trying to log in to something and it's . . . it's nothing."

I can tell he doesn't completely believe me, but he lets it slide.

We pull into the parking lot in front of the Cannon River admissions office. It's the first weekend in October—my weekend with Cora. Yeah, I'm staying with my sister, but seeing the word ADMISSIONS big and bold on a building sign reminds me that it's much more than that. The last time I was here, we were moving my sister into her dorm two years ago. I wasn't thinking yet of how, eventually, it'd be my turn.

As if he can read my mind, Dad says, "Your job, Effie, is to be an observer this weekend. Notice the things that you like about the campus. This can be both in terms of accessibility or anything else. You're allowed to like a college just because, you know."

As we wait by the information desk, I squeeze my pillow to my chest a little too tightly.

I hear my sister before I see her approach. It's the quick *click-click-click* of a perfect heel-toe walk of boots hitting the floor. It makes me so jealous that Cora can create that sound. It's a power walk. The strength she must feel from that added height, the rhythm created by an even walk, is an experience I'll never have.

When she rounds the corner, she's wearing her boots with jeans—the perfect cool-college-girl look. I hope the clothes I packed are cool enough.

She hugs Dad sincerely but quickly.

Dad hands her my duffel bag and she leans over to give me a light one-armed hug. "Hey," she says, "ready to experience the wild college life?"

Dad chuckles. "I guess that's my cue to leave you to it." As he leans down to say goodbye, he whispers in my ear, "Remember what I told you, okay? Have fun, but not *too* much fun." Dad's voice drops low in warning. He shoots Cora a glance that reminds me that I am definitely the baby of the family, even if college is on the horizon.

Alone together in the elevator, Cora asks, "What did Dad tell you?" Her eyes are glued to her phone, texting.

"Just to keep an open mind about everything and not try to have all the college search factors in my head the whole weekend."

"Ugh, oh my god, right? Mom and Dad rode my ass the whole time I was applying. Do this, go here, meet this deadline." She doesn't have to look at me; I can hear her eye roll in her voice.

Luckily, the elevator dings and I don't have to say anything back. Cora chose to go to Cannon the night before the May deadline. She claims she was deliberating whether she wanted to be that close to home after all, but I think she waited partly to drive our parents up a wall. Mom threatened that if Cora didn't decide, she would spin her around with her eyes closed, pin-the-tail-on-the-donkey style, and Cora would have to go to whichever one she pointed at. Because technically she could've, if she'd wanted to. They were all accessible to her and could accommodate her perfectly.

Cora steps off the elevator and I follow, feeling like a lost puppy already. The walls of the café are a pale yellow and the tables and chairs are typical cafeteria style. Some people are chatting, laptops and textbooks spread out next to them.

Cora walks up to an empty table and pulls out a chair for me. "I'm ordering for us. Trust me." She walks off, campus card in hand.

I look around. Can everyone tell that a mere five hours ago, I was sitting at B-period lunch, hearing Cam talk about her latest art project, and fretting about what I got on my paper about *The Bluest Eye*?

Cora comes back with two sandwiches oozing with cheese on thick bread and served with chips. When I bite in, the warmth fills my mouth. I manage an "Oh my god."

"I told you," Cora says, grinning.

This part of college, I think I can handle.

All of a sudden, Cora sits up straight, her eyes fixed on something behind me, and before I have the chance to turn around, a guy wearing athletic-style joggers and a Cannon River Cross Country shirt approaches our table. He grins at both of us, and Cora springs to her feet.

"Hey!" Her voice is a little too pitchy. "Here." She pulls another chair over, making a loud scraping noise against the floor. "Join us."

He sits down, putting his red-and-black backpack on the floor. He has shaggy, short, curly brown hair and his face has a dusting of freckles.

I notice then that despite Cora's relatively simple outfit, she took the time to put on eyeliner. And now I know why.

"Hey!" he says. "I'm Drew."

"Drew is my friend from my American Cinema class. It's a good one. We analyzed *Fight Club* last week." She's trying to play it cool but her lips are fighting a smile.

I shoot Cora a look that says, *Friend, sure,* and she shoots me one back that says that the first rule about Drew is that we don't tell Mom and Dad about Drew.

He turns to me. "You must be Effie! Welcome to Cannon. What do you think so far?"

"I just got here," I explain. "So far, my official report is that the grilled cheese sandwiches are top-notch."

He laughs. "That they are. I heard it's a big prospective student weekend?"

"It is," Cora confirms. "A lot of students from the Cities have tomorrow off and are fitting college visits in."

"Ah," Drew says. "I'm from Duluth, so I don't always know about those big weekends for local students."

I guess, in most people's minds, I am not at all far from home.

Drew asks if I have any ideas of what class to sit in on. "One recommendation," he says as he picks his backpack up by one strap. "Don't go to any class with the word 'cinema' in the title. You'd think a class where you get to watch movies all the time would be easy, but *nooo*."

Cora looks at him wryly. "I think they mostly only let prospectives go to intro classes anyway."

He pretends to wipe his brow. "Phew! You're safe, then." He stands, fully slinging his backpack over one shoulder. "Unfortunately, I've got to go to the science library. But will I see you guys over the weekend?" He directs the question more toward Cora than at me.

"For sure," she says. "We'll be around. Isn't there a party tomorrow night in your dorm?"

His face lights up. "Yeah, I was going to ask if you were going to be there."

"We will be." She looks at me to warn me not to react in any way.

"Cool." He turns to me. "Enjoy your class tomorrow, Effie. Here's my official endorsement: Cannon is great and you should come here."

"I'll take that into consideration," I say, and he walks off.

As soon as he's out of earshot, I turn to Cora.

She knows exactly what—or who—I'm going to ask about, so she changes the subject. "Are you nervous to go to a class tomorrow?"

"A little," I admit.

Cora smiles. "High school used to be scary too, but you figured that out. Ef, *everyone* is scared to start college. You'll see it in everyone's faces when we go to check you in tomorrow. Trust me."

A beat of silence settles between us, the faint sounds of the radio playing over the speakers from the kitchen.

She picks up my duffel bag and holds my pillow under her arm.

"Okay, but we have to talk about Drew," I tease, and she takes off running toward the elevators, and I race to catch up.

"Home sweet home," Cora says as she unlocks the door. She kicks it open with her foot. As I look around, my first thought is whether my wheelchair would even fit through the pathway created by the two beds. Both my sister's and her roommate Rhea's beds are lofted, allowing space for storage shelves underneath. There are two desks situated against the walls on both sides near the window in the back. Besides the closet that's near the door, this is the entire space.

Cora climbs up and plunks her backpack down on her bed, which is covered with a purple-tie-dye-patterned comforter. I eye the other bed, covered in a blue quilt and some light pink pillows.

"Rhea works as a card swiper at the gym. She usually gets back around nine," Cora explains, looking down at me. "I guess even though you're my sister, I'm probably obligated to give you the official prospective student experience."

I back out into the hallway because the space is too tight for me to turn around in. The hallways are also narrow, each gray wall lined with lots and lots of doors, each one decorated with a different cartoon character from movies that were popular when we were kids.

"There's a bathroom on either end of the hallway." Cora walks toward one and I follow her. No door opener. She pushes open the bathroom door.

While Cora fluffs her hair in the mirror, I open the door to the accessible toilet stall. Surprisingly, it's one my chair can fit all the way into, and not just a slightly wider stall with grab bars. I wheel over to the banks of showers. All the showers have doors on them that lock, like the doors of a bathroom stall. I open the door to the accessible shower and am pleased to see that it's big, big enough that I could fit my chair inside and park it far enough away from the stream of water so that it won't get wet. There's a fold-down bench with a removable showerhead and grab bars. I am about to add this to my list of things that could definitely work well for me when a thought jolts through me.

"Are these bathrooms co-ed?" I close the shower door and go out to face Cora, who is looking at me, leaning with her back against the sink.

"No, the men's bathroom is at the other end of the hall," she answers. "Some halls have co-ed ones, I think, but it's determined by the residents who live there each year. The dorm itself is co-ed, of course."

It takes me much longer than most people to get dressed. What if, after finishing my shower and taking the time I need to put on my clothes, someone knocks on the door for me to change faster? Like anybody, I have days when I like my body and days when I don't, but I am also hyperaware of how skinny my legs are because I have no calf definition, and of the scars that run the sides of my hips from orthopedic surgeries when I was a kid.

Cora senses what's on my mind. "Oh, come on. I know it's awkward at first, but you're going to have to figure out how to share your space with other people at some point. And besides, there are worse things than letting a guy get a peek at your body."

I know she's being cheeky, that this is what sisters do, and that I am supposed to drop my voice a bit lower and say something like "I know, right?" But how do I explain to her that the only thing worse than wanting something is wanting something I know I might not be ready for?

But then I think about Drew and all the other boys who wanted to date her. She'll never understand.

So I just feign exhaustion and ask to return to her room.

Back in the room, Rhea is here. Her thick hair is pulled back under a baseball cap, her work uniform. She beams when she sees me.

"Our distinguished guest is *here!*" Her voice goes all singsongy and I can't help but smile.

"Hey! Thanks for having me." I feel a bit more comfortable talking to her, as we're probably the only two people who know what it's like to live with Cora.

"Are you kidding? I was so excited when Cora told me you were coming. I've never hosted a prospective before, so I'm living vicariously here." Rhea darts back and forth around her corner of the room. She's digging through her laundry hamper and slamming the drawers to her dresser.

She holds some gym shorts and a T-shirt over her arm and mumbles, "Where is my—"

"Towel? Over the desk chair." Cora points, and Rhea smiles, grabbing it.

"Thanks." I am amazed by the ease of their rapport.

While Rhea showers, Cora helps me spread out my sleeping bag in the space between their beds. I use this time where it is just me and my sister to change into my pj's. When Rhea returns, there's so little space that she has to awkwardly step over me.

"How has your visit been so far? Have you met Drew yet?"

Even in the dark, I can see the look Cora shoots her.

"Jeez, okay. Message received. I just thought with him *coming over here all the time.*"

Cora groans, and Rhea peeks over the bed at me and says, "See, college is fun!"

❧

In the morning, the campus feels like a completely different place. Students mill about, and every once in a while, someone on a bike whizzes by.

One look around the dining hall and I wonder why anyone would skip breakfast. There are stations where you can get eggs, and a place to make waffles. There is a cereal dispenser that has both Cinnamon Toast Crunch and Cocoa Puffs, which is basically everything I could ever want in life.

After breakfast, a clump of people clutching folders are standing in front of a table outside the dining hall, looking as lost as I feel. This must be the check-in area.

"Hi! Welcome to Cannon River prospective student

weekend!" This girl is way too peppy for 7:45 a.m. "I can help check you in."

"Yeah, hi, my name is Effie Galanos."

"Effie . . . Effie . . ." She hems and haws as she looks over the name tags. "I have a . . . Erifem—"

"Yeah," I interject. "That's me." I let out a breath of air and grab my packet. Of course this will still happen to me in college.

Once I get back to Cora and Rhea, I take a look at the class list. I select an Introduction to Sociology class on Rhea's suggestion.

Cora examines the schedule and remarks, "Perfect, on the way to my nine a.m. class."

I follow my sister outside and through the campus. Some of the paths are smooth sidewalk, but parts are uneven and hilly, and it makes it hard to wheel on. I already feel my arms getting a little tired. When we reach the building, I look down. My hands are streaked with dirt.

Cora wishes me a good class, smiles, and then she is off. I watch her go, blending into the crowd perfectly, like the normal college student that she is. And now I am left on my own. I wheel up to the door, press the door opener, and go inside.

CHAPTER EIGHT

7:56. I stare at my phone screen. *I'll go in when it's 7:57,* I tell myself. The time comes, and I don't budge.

"Are you a prospective?" My head shoots up. A girl smiles at me. "Are you coming to Intro to Sociology?"

"Y-yeah," I answer.

"That's my class! It's a good one; you'll like it, I promise. Come on in."

There is no good spot for me, so I sit awkwardly off to the side of the classroom. The professor enters. He places his papers down on the desk and smiles at the class as he shrugs out of his jacket.

"Good morning, everyone." A few people mumble good morning back. "And a special welcome to any guests that are joining us for prospective student day." He smiles and looks my way. I remember the things that Cora told me and don't look away. "Let's dive right in."

After Cora gets out of her class, she meets me and walks me to the Student Life Office.

"Man," she says. "A meeting with the dean of students! You're so fancy. I'm not even sure I know who the dean is, and I already go here."

Mom set up this meeting, and it was clear to me that any other college visit I go on will have this meeting on the itinerary. As I wait near the couches inside the office, my phone buzzes. It's a text from Mom: Take good notes. In a way, this feels like my follow-up test after the locker.

"Effie?" I put my phone on silent and tuck it away, and follow Dean Smith into his office, which has white walls and a white desk in the center. Next to the bookshelf packed with particularly impressive academic texts, old black-and-white photos of campus hang on the walls. Sunlight comes through a window that looks over a green space and one of the more picturesque buildings on campus.

"We've had a number of students with disabilities on campus in the years I've served as dean, and we have a number of students currently who identify as students with disabilities," he tells me. "I can tell you're independent, taking this transition on by yourself."

Was that meant as a compliment? I ignore it, and start asking my questions. "What's the accessibility on campus like?"

He laces his fingers together. "Well, as you know, Cannon

River College has been around for almost a half century. And that means we're an old campus. So while we've made some updates, we do have a ways to go."

I'm confused. Aren't all campuses old? Are all of them using that as a cop-out?

I try again. "Are the dorms accessible?"

The dean's eyes are calm, his voice even. "We do have accessible dorm rooms here on campus. They have en suite bathrooms with showers." I am instantly put at ease. I wouldn't have to worry about sharing the space with boys or with anyone else. "Those rooms are singles," he continues.

Even though the dean seems fine with all of this, I'm not. I take a breath. "Singles?" I ask. "Does that mean I wouldn't have a roommate?"

"That's correct," he says. "If you chose to live in an accessible room, it is for one occupant only. If you wanted to live with a roommate, you would live in one of our more traditional dorm rooms and would use a standard dorm bathroom and shower."

I am silent for a second. Yeah, I was wigged out about the shared bathrooms, but why should I have to choose between accessibility or a roommate? Isn't having a roommate a quintessential part of the college experience? I think about Cora and Rhea. How easily they get along and how they're able to banter together. It's clear to me that they have a lot of fun. How am I supposed to accept not getting to have something like that just because I use a wheelchair?

As I leave the meeting with the dean, I text Mom: I learned a lot of things at the meeting. I will fill you in at home.

Maybe there was a reason for the Galanos System Spreadsheet all along. Maybe Mom was trying to protect me from feeling like this.

◆

"Here." Cora throws me a shirt from her closet. It's a black short sleeve that has crisscrosses of fabric where the V-neck is. It shows just enough to be fun but not enough to feel like I am showing too much off.

"Thanks."

"No prob," she says back. "Not everyone gets to go to their first college party when they're still in high school. You should look good for it."

"Okay, but what are you going to wear when you see Drew tonight?" We're headed to a party in his dorm, and Cora is smiling shyly. "So you *are* together, then?" I press.

"We are . . ." She trails off as though trying to find the right words. "Something. At least, I hope so."

"He's definitely into you. Anyone can see that." I take off the shirt I'm wearing and slip Cora's shirt on over my head. "Why don't you want to talk about him?"

Cora sighs. She steps away from her closet, where she is flipping through clothes on hangers. She comes over to sit on her bed. "Maybe I think that by keeping Drew just to myself, I can minimize the hurt if something goes wrong. But I've been thinking about it," she says, springing to her feet, pulling a black jumpsuit and jean jacket from the closet. "And I think I should just go for it. I mean, the worst thing he could say is no, right?"

But after all the work of getting to the point where she can admit that she likes Drew, put herself on the line like that . . . just the thought of being rejected would be so hard.

Instead, I mumble, "Yeah, shoot your shot."

❧

At first glance, college parties aren't that different from high school dances, except that nobody's dressed up and with less focus on trying to impress people. But the music is the same, all pop and rap songs blaring so loud that the beat rumbles off the walls. The room, which is a dorm room's communal lounge space, is basically completely dark except for a few colorful lights. The couches are pushed to the side and someone has thrown what looks like a bedsheet over the television. Also, college parties start really late. It's ten thirty and things are just starting to pick up. I am not used to staying up this late, and after the long day I've had, I'm tired.

While Cora dances with her friends, I roll around the room to stay awake, and end up beside a guy who turns to face me. He waves a flask at me—something I suspect he snuck in, and I freeze at his offer.

"Effie!" The voice is shouting a bit over the sound of the music. Drew pushes through the people on the dance floor, wearing jeans, sneakers, and a gray shirt. "You good?" he asks, eyeing the flask, and I nod. "She's good," he tells the guy, and leads me away to a quieter corner.

"Thanks," I say, and I mean it. I'm not ready to deal with that yet.

"No worries." He slumps down so that he's sitting with his back against the wall. He's tall enough so that we are almost eye-to-eye from this position. "How has your weekend been? How has this fine educational institution treated you?"

I don't know why exactly, but I tell him about my meeting. When he hears about the dorm rooms, he's surprised.

"Really?" He's quiet for a second. "I know I said Cannon is great and you should come here, but truly, the best advice I can give you is, if you can picture yourself on a campus, that's where you should be."

I do not know if Drew and Cora are together, or if they ever will be. But right now, in this moment, he earns the sister stamp of approval. He stands and starts to head toward the dance floor. I watch as he goes over to my sister and they start to dance. Their hands are up, just another couple in this sea of people. His hands find her hips and she smiles.

I smile, too, happy right now to just be a wallflower and watch something new blossom in front of me.

CHAPTER NINE

As we ride home through our neighborhood, Dad rolls down the windows, the autumn sun soft on my face. The blur of the oranges and reds of the trees matches the intensity of my nerves.

My visit to Cannon made me realize that maybe it isn't the place for me. But I know what place might be, and I shouldn't be wasting any more time keeping it a secret. It's time to try to make it happen. If Cannon doesn't feel right for me, I have to work on what is.

I'm telling my parents about Prospect. Tonight.

When we get inside, the house is empty. Mom must be at the store. Setting my bag on my bed, I look around my room. How weird that in less than a year, I won't be living here.

There's the sound of Mom's car pulling in the drive and the rumble of the garage door opening. I hear her greet Dad and the sound of the grocery bags as they get placed on the kitchen counter. The *clink* of her putting a pan on the stove. I'm sure she's making spaghetti and meatballs, my favorite comfort food. I didn't think I could deal with dinner tonight, but when I smell the garlic bread, I give in.

When she calls me to the table, I roll out meekly, trying to play it cool.

"Hey there," she says, all happy. "There's our college student!"

Not yet, I want to cry out. *Please not yet.*

"I made your favorite. I can't wait to hear all about your weekend."

Once we sit around the table, I busy myself with spinning my fork around the pasta.

"Do you want to tell Mom about your sociology class?" Dad starts.

"I—uhhh . . ." I try to say something but it comes out guttural, the words crumbling once they hit the air. "I really liked the class, but I'm not sure Cannon is for me."

Mom puts her fork down. "Why?"

Dad, clearly surprised, frowns.

"They don't have fully accessible dorms, at least not ones where I could also have a roommate. Having a roommate is a huge part of college."

"Effie." Dad looks at me, brow creased. "Is this why you were so quiet on the drive home? Why didn't you say anything?"

Mom cuts in. "Did you set up a time for a follow-up call with their office—"

"No," I say, a bit too forcefully. But I don't want to advocate for anything tonight. I want what I want. "Because I think there's a college I would like a lot better." *Say it.* "I'm interested in Prospect University."

She opens her mouth to speak. Then closes it. Then she says, "In New York?"

"Yes," I squeak out.

She looks at Dad to see if he knew, but his face is as blank as hers.

But he jumps in first. "Effie, that's . . . how . . . when?"

My secret feels like something physical that I put out on our kitchen table. And so I unwrap it, bit by bit. I tell them everything about the Mass Media and Society major. And now I tell them something new: how I found a whole page on their website devoted to disability scholarship. There are so many classes related to disability that they break them down by subject. There's even a class on disability and the entertainment industry.

Dad looks like he wants to say something, but Mom speaks first. "It all sounds wonderful, Effie. It really does. I'm glad you told me." She takes a moment to inhale, and I can tell she is choosing her words carefully. "I . . . I guess I'm just having a hard time seeing you in New York."

A rock sinks in my stomach. "But it's big and it's amazing and it's the epicenter of the digital-media scene—"

She waves her hands in front of her as if to erase and try again. "It's not like I don't *see* you there, I can. I can see what you like about this school and their program. That all makes sense to me. But, Effie . . . New York City?"

Mom gets up to clear her plate even though I notice she hasn't eaten much. After rinsing it, she puts the sprayer back and leaves the plate in the sink. "You are almost an adult, so I am going to be honest with you like I would with an adult." And that's when she looks me right in the eyes and says, "I'm not sure you're ready."

Dad stands, too. "Now, let's hold on—"

"I'm not saying no!" Mom's voice gets a bit more forceful. "But I do have to say that I'm simply not thrilled to send my daughter to the biggest city in the country when she can't even get a locker back by herself."

And there it is. The locker isn't everything, but it was my first big test, and I fell on my ass.

Mom and Dad go into the living room, and even though they speak in hushed tones, I pick up Mom saying: "She has a way to go in order to prove . . ."

I pick up my fork and swirl the spaghetti around it. My favorite meal has never looked so unappealing.

I want to prove I'm ready for Prospect so bad.

I may have been spoken to like an adult, but I've never felt more like a little girl.

But I'll change that. For Prospect, and for me.

❧

"Hey," Harper says, a hint of a laugh in her voice. "Off-campus lunch, baby!"

"Heck. Yes." Cam tucks a piece of her hair behind her ear, deep in thought. "Where to today? Panera? Nah, it's our first jailbreak. We should go big . . . Chipotle!"

"Today does seem like a 'yes, I'll have guac even though it's extra' kind of day," Harper agrees.

It's the second week of October—the start of off-campus lunch for seniors.

Today is guac-even-though-it's-extra day.

We arrive to homeroom, and Harper sits down next to me.

"I'm glad we're early—I really wanted a chance to talk to you. It's about what's going on with my shoulder."

"Sure," I say, turning to her. Behind her, I notice Wilder walk through the door into the classroom. He looks so cute in a black sweatshirt and ripped jeans, but my stomach flips when, right as the door is about to close behind him, I catch a glimpse of Sameerah standing outside.

Wilder waves at us as he walks by. "How's it going, Effie?" he calls.

I can feel myself blush, but right away the teacher clears his throat.

"I'm supposed to read this announcement . . ." He holds up an official bulletin from the front office. "Senior students in good academic standing will be allowed off-campus for lunch beginning today." A few students let out a whoop.

He continues. "Provided they return to class at the end of

the thirty-minute period." The same kids boo. The teacher's voice goes an octave higher, talking over them. "*All* students must present their school IDs to the official at the front desk before leaving the building through the main entrance on the second floor."

I sit up straighter. Cam turns to me and mouths, "What?" I shake my head. It can't be true. At the main entrance, one of our front office staff members sits at the desk to provide late passes to people who enter after the final bell in the morning and have access to the security camera feeds. Having her check us out for lunch makes sense. Expecting me to exit through the front entrance that has three flights of stairs does not.

"We'll figure it out . . . I'm sure it's a technicality. They have to send someone down to let us out of the West Parking Lot door. They have to. Like, *have to*." Harper is reassuring Cam that Chipotle is still in our future today, but I can't say anything in response.

From being friends with me, Harper and Cam know that accessibility isn't perfect, but I doubt they'd believe our school views the ADA as optional. Institutions translate *have to*'s to *should do*'s, which become things that are never done unless someone screams and bangs their fist. In the minds of Mill City High School, the door is not the technicality. *I* am the technicality.

By the time homeroom concludes and we're on our way to first period, I'm calculating how much cash I have on me and whether I should spring for a gross slice of cafeteria pizza. By second period, I'm thinking of work-arounds. I think I could do the stairs if someone carries my chair behind me and we wait for the stampede of people to exit before us, but then I quickly change my mind. Stairs are tough and slow for me anytime, but especially those outdoor concrete steps that lead to the sidewalk.

Plus, I factor in the probable ten minutes it would take in total for me to walk down to the sidewalk while Cam carried my chair. Our original timeline already accounted for Harper having to make a mad dash to her car anyway, and with this added obstacle, it will be too tight. Twenty minutes there and back is not enough time.

By third period, I am sad. All around me, my peers are asking, "Where are you going to lunch?" There are plans to try multiple places in one week, which now seems like luxury.

It's not my classmates' fault, but their excitement feels like bragging. *Look how easy it is for me to get around! Look at all the things I never have to think about!* I'm already down about Mom telling me I can't handle Prospect, and now this. It feels like maybe she's right.

At the start of lunch, Harper and Cam look a bit too excited when they see me coming.

"So!" Harper claps her hands together. "Since this school is a bureaucratic mess, we thought we'd celebrate only having to be here six more months."

"And," Cam says, "everyone knows the best way to celebrate

is with guac even though it's extra." She pulls a brown paper bag out from behind her.

"You skipped class to go to Chipotle?" My lip quivers for an entirely different reason.

"It turns out they deliver." Harper hands me a foil-wrapped burrito. "It cost a fortune, but not as much as I would have to pay if my parents got one of those automated emails saying I was marked absent last hour."

I'm pretty sure this will be the best burrito I'll ever eat.

"You don't know how much I needed this," I say.

There's a weird feeling in my gut, because I know what Mom would want me to do in this situation. I have to confront Ms. Wilson. And unlike with my locker, I have to say what I want to, on the first try.

It's what will get me closer to Prospect in her eyes. And I want to try, for me.

Here we go.

CHAPTER TEN

Sitting in the stuffy beige room of the administrative offices, I fidget with my hands in my lap. I try to calm myself, to tell myself it's all for Prospect, and for the enjoyment of the rest of senior year.

"Effie?" I bang snap. Lovely. Off to a great start.

Ms. Wilson opens the door to her office. She pulls aside the chair that usually sits in front of her desk, then goes around to sit behind it. "Thanks so much for making an appointment. What would you like to talk to me about?"

"Well, I'm a senior," I start out.

She shakes her head, cutting me off. "Time just *flies*, doesn't it? My goodness, I remember when you were a freshman."

If you had started working on this issue then, we wouldn't need to be having this conversation right now. "Yes, so anyway. I get off-campus lunch privileges, starting today, but I wanted to discuss the protocol for entering and exiting the building with you, and to see if we couldn't find a work-around."

"A work-around?" she asks like it never occurred to her that anyone might need one.

"The bulletin that was read said that all seniors with good academic standing will be granted the privilege of off-campus lunch," I try. I state my case: It doesn't work for everyone, and if I tried to make it work for me, I could get hurt. It's not worth the risk, and something like this shouldn't involve risks anyway.

"I understand that." She's speaking to me in a customer service voice. "Unfortunately, what this comes down to is a security issue."

A shiver goes through me, and my hands tremble in my lap. "I'm not saying you can't check my ID," I say calmly. "I'm just wondering why it isn't possible for a hall monitor or some other staff person to come to the accessible door downstairs and check mine and my friends' so that we can go out to lunch like everyone else."

She puts her hands up, stopping me again. "During regular school hours, every door on campus locks via a magnetized system, with the exception of the front door. The doors are only to be unlocked in the event of an emergency evacuation or drill. The reason the main door is the required door to enter and exit from during the school day is so we know we always have a staff member present at that front desk to be able to keep track of who traffics through our building during school hours."

I ball my hands to keep them still. She doesn't care about

me, so I shouldn't feel nervous to stand up to her. I'm mad. "Again, I don't understand why that means—"

"Effie, if we were to unlock the accessible door for thirty minutes to an hour for you to go out to lunch, we can't guarantee that we'd be able to keep a staff person there for the entire time. If the door is left open for you, that also frees other students to leave—some of whom are not seniors and do not have off-campus privileges—as well as anyone from our community to enter our school as they please. As I've stated, that's a security risk." She looks and speaks at me calmly, like she could take out a book on the school code, and it would explain this all clear as day.

But watching your disabled student get jostled on the stairs? Watching her fall? That's not a safety risk at all, apparently. "I . . ." Everything about this is an excuse. Can't she see that?

She taps her finger on the desk, marking the end of our time, her voice crisp. "Thank you again for coming in, Effie. This is of the utmost importance. We've got to figure this out."

A coldness settles over me. I understand now why sometimes Mom gets so worked up. I'm ready to go off.

"We've recently learned that it's likely we'll have a ninth grader next year in a chair. Someone to take the reins from you."

My heart sinks. It's going to be so hard for them, but hopefully not as hard in the same ways that it was for me. Maybe the administration will listen to me. Hopefully, they will learn.

"Trooper" or "fighter" are words people love to throw out at disabled kids. "A little fighter." It's so patronizing. But for once, I'm glad I'm a fighter.

I hope that incoming student is, too.

CHAPTER ELEVEN

Normally, I would have ignored Seth's Story with the text in all caps: *STUDENT COUNCIL PARTY—MY HOUSE—TONIGHT—BE THERE!!* without a second thought. I don't even like Seth. I barely like Student Council.

But Harper is out with Calvin, and Cam texted me to say she had plans to visit a one-night-only art exhibition in Northeast. Maybe it's silly, but I feel like my friends are already moving on a bit, and I don't want to be the only one without something to do tonight.

So I look up at the house, one of those beautiful, old, ornate ones in the Kenwood neighborhood. Something that looks like the backdrop to a Christmas movie, with the windows that light up just enough from the street so you can guess at all the sweet family scenes that happen inside.

But that means stairs. Two small flights. The breeze blows and a porch swing creaks. I'll have to somehow find somebody to get me up the stairs, across the porch, and into the house. This wouldn't be a problem if I were here with Harper or Cam. And the only person I really know well at this party is Wilder. And I don't have his number.

What am I doing?

I should've sucked it up and had Dad help me in when he dropped me off. Instead, I made up some lie about how it was a yard party and we'd be playing night games. I don't think he believed me, but who wants to have their dad walk them into a house party?

I hear footsteps behind me.

"Hey." It's a voice I don't recognize. It's a boy, who I think is a junior, wearing black skinny jeans and a Mill City Basketball shirt. "Are you going to Seth's party?"

I consider saying no but that would mean that I'm weirdly sitting here staring at this house. So I say yes.

"Okay." He looks down at my chair. Everywhere but my face. "Uhh . . . how are you going to get inside?"

It comes out before I even know I thought of it. "Can you go get Wilder?"

He swallows and mumbles a yes, still looking at my legs and not my face.

When he bounds up the steps and opens the front door, I hear the low thumps of trap music before the door swings shut behind him. Faintly, I hear a couple of people call out hellos to him. Will anyone greet me?

I press my lips together, trying to quell the anxiety about

what's going to happen next. It's Wilder; I know I'll be okay. I don't have a choice.

I hear the door swing open again and I bang snap quickly. Wilder comes out wearing blue jeans and a long-sleeved burgundy shirt that's a little tight in all the areas I want it to be. Now I'm the one looking anywhere but somebody's face.

"Effie! Hey!" Wilder grins and bounds down the steps, skipping every other one, his feet so nimble it looks like a complicated dance move. What is that like—for your brain to tell your feet to do something complicated, and they *do* it? Now he's standing in front of me. "I'm glad you came." It's not in the brush-off way that most people say it. He means it.

"How do you want to do this?"

"Umm . . ." I roll up as close to the steps as I can get. The door slams again, and I look up to see Seth has joined us. I think through my options, then look at Wilder. "Can you help me and Seth can grab the chair?"

He extends his arm and I grab it. It is strong and firm. He isn't going to let me fall.

I grab the railing with my other hand and beg my legs to cooperate. Thankfully, this time, they do. Also thankfully, Seth is not as clueless as I peg him to be and manages to get my chair up the steps.

"This thing is so light," he remarks. *It better be,* I think. *It costs as much as a car.*

When I sit down, I smile at Wilder.

"I like your jacket," he says. I'm wearing my army green jacket with embroidered pink flowers. It's probably too cold to be wearing it in mid-November, but I'm trying to look cute without looking like I'm trying. I'm glad he noticed.

"You look nice, too."

He smiles. His dimple appears on his left cheek. It's the best thing I have ever seen.

Wilder holds the door open for me and I bump my chair over the threshold. He kicks people's shoes out of the way to make a path for me and a thought comes to me like a bang snap: Why can't I tell him I like him? I might not know my future or get off-campus lunch, and I might not even have my friends for much longer, but I can have this. I haven't seen him with Sameerah since that day I saw her outside homeroom. I can still try to tell him how I feel. Plus, *I* made him smile like that.

But once I get through the path, I realize I've lost Wilder. Even worse, I realize what I already knew: This is a party filled mostly with people I don't care about.

The last time I felt this out of my element was at the college party at Cannon.

The latest pop song to hit the Billboard Top 10 radiates off the walls, then quickly fades into an indie hit but layered over each other. Someone is playing hipster remixes from the internet. I look at the kitchen and see a bowl of chips sitting out. At least I know what to do with those.

I roll up next to them, put a few on a napkin, and go over

what I'll say to Wilder. I face the living room and see him out of the corner of my eye.

I like you. It's only three words. I've said it to my friends, about a song on the radio, about an ice cream cone. This is just . . . elevating it a little.

I like you. I imagine the words passing through my lips. *I mean, I always have. Well, not always in this way. But now it is definitely, absolutely in the I'd-like-to-kiss-your-face way. But you know, consensually, if you were game for it.*

I crumple the napkin and put it in my lap, and take stock of Seth's house. There's a staircase with a dark oak banister, and a long hallway leading to a small bathroom. I go down the hallway, where photos of Seth and his siblings line the walls. There's one of him wearing denim on denim as a little kid and cheesing hard. I snap a photo of it. I start to pull up my texts to send it to my friends—and then I remember they're busy.

A gaggle of junior girls pop up behind me. I could use a friend tonight, so I give them my friendliest smile. One smiles slightly, so I approach.

"H-hi," I say tentatively. Another girl eyes me—first my face, then my chair—and turns her back to me, closing me off from their circle.

My face heats up, and then a coldness rushes through me. I move away quickly, wishing the bathroom were large enough for me to wheel into and shut the door.

Look, there's a reason I've clung so tightly to Harper since fifth grade and kept every single hand-drawn card or sketch Cam has ever given me—even the ones on the back of math worksheets. My wheelchair is a filter. If people don't want to be in my life because they're scared of the chair, because they judge it, they bounce.

And yeah, it filters the crappy friends out. But it doesn't mean the bounces don't hurt.

I miss Harper and Cam. *We're all leaving soon either way*, I think to myself. I just have to build more, stretch more, push myself outside my comfort zone . . .

Wilder catches my eye and smiles at me warmly. "Effie," he calls out. "Come join us!"

Tell him, I remind myself. Just the thought of it makes the back of my neck prickle with sweat.

I wheel back down the hallway and look in at the living room. A couple of people lounge around on couches while others stand in clumps chatting. Seth is sitting in an armchair while a girl lies across it, her legs dangling off the arms. I bet she found the photo of him in the hallway charming.

The music picks up to a faster song, the pounding beat matching the rush of my adrenaline as I move closer. *Tell him tonight. And then you'll have your answer. And if he doesn't feel the same way, then you'll have all the rest of this school year to get over the awkwardness before Prospect.*

And then I see it. Wilder is talking to three girls. And one of them is Sameerah. Oh no.

"Anyway," one of the other girls says, "you're totally going to be like one of those hip, celebrity boys who goes to school at NYU."

"Actually, it's not NYU . . ." Wilder smirks and glances at me. She doesn't understand like I do.

Sameerah, however, does. "It's Prospect, actually."

I thin my lips and feel a pinch near my ribs when I realize he's told her about Prospect. Of course he has. That thing that's supposed to be ours.

Wilder smiles slightly, then looks at me again. "Effie's actually interested in going to Prospect—"

But then Sameerah interrupts him by saying, "Wilder, this would look so good on you!" She takes the pink baseball cap she's wearing off her head and gets up on her tiptoes to place it playfully on Wilder's head. I expect him to pull back, but he doesn't. He laughs, and readjusts it. "Thanks, it's definitely my color."

I notice the muscles in her calves through her jeans and how her knees don't bulge through the distressed holes. Wilder bends down to give her hat back. Their height difference is cute—him having to bend and her having to stretch just a bit, like the couples in the magazines.

I nod vaguely toward the bathroom and retreat.

In the hallway, I'm alone and the pictures of baby Seth mock me. *Tell him. Tell him. You can't tell him. You're a wimp. A wimp with no friends. And wow, how are there so many pretty girls at this party, and why are they all by him?*

Through the rods in the banister, I watch. He's moved on to

talking to one of the girls from my class. Her contour is amazing. I thought I was going all out by putting on mascara.

She says something and he laughs, big, with his head thrown back. He high-fives her, and when his hand lowers, it hovers just next to her hip for a second. And then his hand moves away. But a second is all you need.

Three seconds were all I needed and I didn't take them. And now what's the point? He's probably with Sameerah, and besides, he has his pick of girls; there's no way he could like me.

There's a nudge on my shoulder and one of the unnamed girls from the living room pushes past me to get to the bathroom.

"Hey," she says. "Wilder told me you're thinking about going to NYU, too. That's so cool!"

I say three words with no problem. "It's not NYU."

❧

I'm back with the chips. The hipster remixes have stopped, and now the Party Jams playlist is playing K-pop. Some people are playing Scattergories around the coffee table. The category is modes of transportation that start with *T*. I think of *taxi*, but don't shout it out. In fact, maybe I'll have to take one home.

It's past ten o'clock, the cutoff time that Dad was willing to swing back and pick me up. He's gone to bed.

"Ask Harper or Cam at that point," he'd said. I didn't have the energy to explain that (a) they aren't on Student Council and wouldn't be at this party, and (b) they had other plans tonight.

This whole night was a bad choice, and now I'm stuck without a way to get home.

A loud roar of laughter comes from the living room. I haven't seen Seth in ages. He's probably off with that girl. The only place I want to be right now is on my bed recounting every meticulous detail of this night to my best friends. But I can't. Now I'm alone and so, so lonely.

"Hey."

I bang snap, then look up to see Wilder.

"Didn't mean to scare you."

"It's fine."

"You, uh, look like you're ready to get out of here." He smiles.

"Is it that obvious?" I ask, and he laughs.

"Do you need a ride?"

I start to say yes, then pull back. "Are you sure?"

"I'm offering."

"Then I accept."

"Okay. Let me go pull into the driveway, then I'll come back." He fishes into his jeans pocket and pulls out a set of keys. There's a silver key chain engraved with WILDER in cursive and then the words NEVER DRIVE FASTER THAN YOUR GUARDIAN ANGEL CAN FLY underneath it. He sees me staring at it. "Yeah . . . my grandma got me that when I got my license and I keep it on there to make her happy."

He's never one to let anyone down.

Back outside, he's driving the big van again. "God, I'm sorry you have to get inside this giant thing, Effie. This is the worst."

"It's not the end of the world." But I'm thankful I'm wearing sneakers and not flats that fall off.

I'll ride in the front seat again this time. He opens the door and I use the railing on the inside under the window to stand up. From there, I grab the handle on the roof of the car and hoist myself up.

"That was . . . easier," he remarks.

"Always helps to have done it once before."

Out the window, I watch him lift my chair, smoothly, and with respect. The trunk slams and he comes around to the driver's side.

He starts the car. "It's a little chilly. There's a heated seat button right there if you want yours on."

"Okay," I say stiffly. For some reason, I don't want him to know I'm cold. But this cute jacket isn't cutting it.

We pull out of the driveway and start driving through Kenwood Parkway. "Did you have fun?" he asks.

"Yes," I lie.

Wilder launches into the latest Student Council drama, complaining about how no one has stepped up to be his partner on the School Beautification Project, and how Seth doesn't even care about finding someone. I feel like I could care about the project, if we did something meaningful with it, but my thoughts are interrupted when my foot crunches an old Noodles & Company cup on the car floor.

"Oh, sorry," Wilder says, glancing over. "Carnage from going out to lunch. Where have you gone?"

The question makes me squirm. It's been two weeks and still not a word from the administration about lunch. I sent an email to Ms. Wilson for follow-up and got no answer.

I feel so stuck. So I tell the truth: "I actually haven't gone out for lunch."

"What do you mean?" he asks incredulously. "Not even for a bagel?"

"I can't."

"What do you mean you can't?"

"Like, I physically *can't*. The school says that everyone has to use the stairs on second floor and they won't make an exception for me."

Out of the corner of my eye, I see Wilder's knuckles whiten as he grips the steering wheel. "Are you . . . *kidding me?*" His voice is a tone I've never heard before, deeper, more raw, angry. He extends his arms farther and presses his back against the seat. "Effie, that's *fucked up*."

I would be surprised about his language if he wasn't right. "It really, really is."

It comes to me all at once. Who says the Beautification Project can't be meaningful? "What if we did the School Beautification Project together?" He glances back at me. "I've been trying to get through to Ms. Wilson about the lunch stuff, but she isn't responding. We could do something about accessibility? I don't know . . . fixing the automatic door openers so that all of them actually work?" It's the first idea off the top of my head, but I actually love the concept.

Wilder grins. "Sure beats benches and some plants outside school. It'll probably have to wait until I finish my college apps, but I can start looking into some prices and companies. I'd love to work on this with you!"

Tell him you like him. But what if he decides he doesn't want to do the project anymore? I finally have someone on my side, I don't want to screw it up.

Instead, I tell him thanks, then change the subject. "How goes everything with college apps?"

He relaxes his grip slightly. "I've actually decided to apply to Prospect early decision, so it's really crunch time."

Early decision apps are due next week, and you find out if you got in in mid-December. "That's awesome," I say. "Congrats."

"Thanks. Of course, for now I obviously have the fear that it might not work out, but I figure that Prospect is what I really want, and if I do get in, the sense of relief will be great."

I have no doubt he'll get accepted to Prospect—he's got great grades, good extracurriculars, and obviously comes across as extremely likable in interviews. But I can't help feeling jealous he was able to select his perfect school so easily. As everything stands right now, I'm not even sure if I can convince Mom to let me apply, let alone attend.

As if he can read my mind, he glances at me. "Do you think you'll visit the city soon?"

He is already calling New York "the city" like a real local. When he does go to Prospect, he'll fit right in. He launches into the things to check out: Times Square even though it's mega-touristy; the High Line; get the "cronut," the cross between a doughnut and a croissant that people line up around the block for.

I'm trying to commit all of these things to memory, but it's too much to even think I might get Mom on board to visit. Wilder gets to know fun things about the city while I have to research accessibility facts and prove I'm ready.

As we round Lake of the Isles all too soon, I realize my body has warmed up. I look at the console, and see Wilder turned on my seat for me.

A beat of silence, then he says, "Do you think you would go there?" I look at him. The orange of the passing streetlights lights up his face in flashes. He's looking back at me earnestly; he wants to know my answer.

"I don't . . . I don't . . ."

"I know," he clarifies. "It's a long way away, and I don't know if I'll get in there yet and neither do you. But if you got in . . . do you think you would go?"

I look down, fighting the urge to play with my hands. Just by telling him about the lunch stuff, I feel like he might understand a tiny bit more when I say, "There's a lot I would have to figure out. But if I could make it work, I would really like to go there."

The beat of the turn signal. "I would really like that, too," he says.

Say it.

Say it.

What is wrong with you?

Just say . . .

"Turn in here," I say instead. How are we home already? Why does Seth have to live so close to me? He ruins everything.

Wilder looks at me, smiling, his keys still in the ignition. And I swear that almost for a second, despite Sameerah, despite everything I saw this evening, it feels like . . . something. His hand lingers on the door handle before he pulls it open. "I'll go get your chair."

I exhale.

In the driveway, I try again.

I like you. The words get to my throat and then—

The rumble of a neighbor pulling their recycling out to the curb. Then Wilder's van starts chiming that the door's been open with the keys in the ignition too long.

"Well, have a good night, Effie."

The moment is gone.

"Thanks for the ride."

"Of course. Anytime."

"Are you headed home?"

He reaches behind his neck, looking down. "Nah, I think I'll head back to the party."

Back to Sameerah. Message received.

I hear the driver's side door slam shut. As I put my key in the side door to the house, the headlights still illuminate me. He's waiting to see that I get in safely.

Inside the door, I switch off the hallway light that my parents left on for me so he knows I'm in.

The headlights move across the wall before flashing up toward the ceiling as he backs out. Right before they flicker out altogether, I whisper it quickly.

"I like you."

SECTION 28

SECTION II: WINTER

CHAPTER TWELVE

Over the next few days, I start to get a few unexpected DMs on social. *So unfair about the lunch issue!* accompanied by an angry-face emoji from one of the girls from my freshman Civics class. A guy from my French class sophomore year messages, *This sucks! I'm so angry on your behalf. My dad is a lawyer. Let me know if you need help with anything.*

I assume they're reaching out in response to Cam's latest social post: a video of her talking about how the one off-campus lunch exit isn't accessible to everyone. And while she didn't single me out by name, being the only person in a wheelchair in my school singles me out anyway. I'm not mad about it exactly, but it sucks that a social post gets more action and anger than meeting with or emailing Ms. Wilson.

And now it's lunchtime, and I'm sitting in our usual spot. But my friends are nowhere to be found. Suddenly I'm not hungry as the cold, sad hollowness of the realization that my friends really did it—they went out to lunch without me—sits like a rock in my stomach.

Cam texts: Come up to the front desk!

When I get to the second floor, she's waiting outside the elevators. "Effie!" She sounds a little excited and a bit nervous. "This is wild!"

"What's going on?" I'm very confused. "Where's Harper?"

"She said she has an appointment." I fish out my phone and see that Harper texted that to the group text . . . I must've missed it while I was busy making up other scenarios.

My stomach and my heart lighten as I start to see it was all in my head. "So you guys didn't go out to lunch?"

"Without you?" Cam says. "Never."

My shoulders sag slightly against the back of my chair and I take a deep breath. "Okay, so what's happening up here?"

Cam has a slightly unsure look on her face. "Well . . . come see . . ."

She leads me down the hallway, then stops when we have a view of the desk in front of the main entrance. Around six students—including Wilder—are sitting on the floor directly in front of the desk, eating their lunches, while the staff member looks on.

"They're having a sit-in," she explains. "They say they won't go off-campus for lunch until all students who choose to are able."

Cam watches me closely. It dawns on me that she didn't bring me up here at first because she wasn't sure how I would react. Cam has a funny look on her face, and I put two and two together and realize this was her doing. I'm touched that she would organize this for me, and I don't know what to say, so I squeeze her hand, and she squeezes back.

"Can we . . . ?" My eyes go to my feet. "Can we go back to our regular spot?"

"Of course." Cam smiles.

The rest of the day, my brain is in a fog. I don't want this to morph into the Protest for Effie Galanos. I want to acknowledge it, but I don't want to become the face of it.

After much back and forth, that night, I decide to send Wilder a DM: I'm a little overwhelmed by it all. Thanks for the support.

The three dots appear under the message, indicating more . . .

Effie, you know I've always got you. ☺

⌒

"Effie!" I look over the door of my locker to see Wilder barreling toward me, weaving through all the students.

I close my locker door and look at him expectantly. It's mid-December. Celebratory announcements from my classmates that they got into their first-choice college started popping up on social media late last night. I'll admit it: I refreshed Wilder's social twice today, finding nothing.

I don't even need to ask, I can tell just from his face. He has a smile like a broken egg yolk, unable to stay in its contained space, spilling all over.

"I got in. I got into Prospect!"

My stomach seizes for a second in jealousy before I smile a genuine smile. "Of course you did! Who wouldn't want you?"

It happens in an instant. He leans down and his arms are wrapping around me. I smell the floral scent that must be his laundry detergent and feel the straps of his backpack press against my shoulders. I move my hands up from my sides and reach around him. I gauge the force of his hug: light, friendly, the tips of his fingers just barely landing on my shoulder blades. I hold back, and reciprocate accordingly. "Congratulations, Wilder," I say.

He pulls away as the warning bell rings, his eyes level with mine. "Thank you, Effie. You're so great." He walks away, still looking at me. Then he extends his forearm all the way out, pointing at me. "You! You're next!"

A tickle in my stomach happens that I recognize first as dread, as uncertainty. Upon further examination, I only feel a great sense of hope.

❧

On Friday before winter break, Cam texts me: Pit stop by parking lot door before lunch? Have to transport some art class stuff from my car to my locker first.

When I meet her there, she's holding the art room door open

with one foot as she attempts to balance a cardboard box full of paint and sketchbooks in her arms. She explains the art teacher unlocked the door for her to be able to get her materials. I hit the door opener for her—which thankfully, this time, works—and she shifts her balance in relief. I'm reminded of the proposal for fixing door openers Wilder sent over this week. The cost of fixing even one is way outside our tiny budget. So we might have to stick to the benches, unless we can come up with something better. I'm so bummed, and so far have nothing else to contribute.

Just as Cam almost makes it inside, a rogue sketchbook slides off the stack and lands outside the door, taking a couple paintbrushes with it. Loose papers blow in the December cold, and water starts to soak the pages from the ice on the sidewalk.

"Oh shit!" Cam sets the box inside the door and we both scramble outside. Cam starts frantically picking up the pages, fanning one in the air to try to dry it out. I go after a paintbrush that is dangerously close to rolling into a grate. I bend down and grab it, and when I sit up, that's when I see it.

Across the street, parked against the curb is a red Toyota that I recognize from homecoming—Calvin's car. And strolling out of the school, like she doesn't have a care in the world, is Harper. Calvin gets out of the driver's side and they kiss. Just as I watch her throw her backpack in the backseat, I realize Cam has walked up behind me.

"Did you get it?" she asks, referring to the paintbrush that

I've tightened my grip around. "What are you looking . . . ?" She follows my line of sight before simply saying, "Oh."

That *oh* settles like a pit in my stomach, and confirms what this is: My best friend is going out to lunch without me, behind my back.

I look at Cam, who is biting her bottom lip. "Did you know?" I ask.

"She said she had another appointment. I know she's been keeping up with a lot of intense physical therapy," Cam says. At the blank look on my face, she adds, "She has that thing with her shoulder because of hockey."

It dawns on me that I've been so caught up in my own stuff that I forgot about her shoulder injury.

Together, we watch them drive away.

Suddenly I remember just how many appointments Harper has gone to throughout November and December. At least three a month. I feel a tightness in my chest when I realize she had an appointment the day the sit-in started. Has it all been a lie?

Cam puts her hand on my shoulder. "Come on. It's cold. Let's go inside."

CHAPTER THIRTEEN

After school, I expected to feel nervous, but I feel weirdly calm. It's almost winter break and I can't let this sit and fester for two weeks. When I see Harper heading toward the side door, I go after her.

"Hey," she says, all casual. She pulls out a wad of receipts from the front pocket of her backpack. I want to take them and track the dates and restaurant locations of every one, evidence of her deceit.

"How's your shoulder?" I say. She looks up toward me, no doubt reacting to my not-so-caring tone.

Her eyes get a bit cloudy, and her tone a bit sharp. "Still sore, but getting better."

"And how was lunch today?" I spit it out forcefully.

She jerks her head back slightly as she puts two and two together. "Listen . . ."

"How many times have you gone out?"

She looks down at her feet. And I know that I caught her.

"All my actual appointments for my shoulder have been before or after school." I was right. "Effie, I . . ."

"Save it." Harper and I have been friends for almost eight years, and we've never had a real fight. But I know from the deep, raw hurt in my gut that we are fighting now. "You are so *selfish*." I can't take it back. I don't want to. "You *lied* to me about going out to lunch. You'd rather be with your boyfriend than support me. Even when our school is discriminating against me, you still put yourself first."

Harper's face looks blank. For a second I think that's it, but then she says quietly, "Of course I want to go out with my boyfriend and of course I want to go out to lunch, Effie." Then her voice goes sharper. "But apparently I can't focus on me at all." She pauses, considering what to say next. "I was told I might have to get surgery on my shoulder, the day of the college-application workshop. I got the call from my doctors when I got out of hockey practice, after they'd reviewed my X-rays."

A rock sinks to my stomach, remembering how I waved her off so I could keep talking to Wilder. And how I was too distracted the day we learned about the lunch issue to listen to her.

"I was scared, Effie. And even though it turned out that I *just* have to do physical therapy, it still sucks. I missed playing in the Wayzata tourney, my big moment." Harper blinks twice. "And so, yeah, I wanted to go out to lunch with Calvin instead, because he's been there for me. Cam's checked in, too. But who

I really wanted and needed was you, because I know you've been through that sort of thing."

I look at my feet. She's right. I had no idea. Surgeries and PT are second nature to me, but it's a big deal for my friend.

"But all the support goes to Effie. Even when you got your own sit-in, it's still gotta be all about you, huh?" Harper looks straight at me. "Noted."

It's then that I see her eyes are wet.

I made my best friend cry.

In eight years of friendship, our first fight.

I back away slightly. She doesn't step forward.

She turns her back to me, and walks away, and I am alone.

⌐

Describe a problem you'd like to solve. It can be research-based or ethics-based, anything that's important to you, regardless of its size. Explain why you think it should be solved and the steps you would take in order to solve it.

I know they call them personal essays for a reason, but when the problem *I'd* like to solve is how to patch things up with my best friend, it hits a little too close to home.

It's the awkward few days between Christmas and New Year's, and I'm sitting at the kitchen table, watching the red blinking cursor of my Word document. Dad has gone into the office to take advantage of the quiet time and get some work done, Cora is in her room upstairs ordering her textbooks for next semester, and I can hear the scraping outside as Mom shovels the dusting of snow we received overnight from the front walk. Everyone is accomplishing things but me, and with the deadline looming for the Common Application, my time to obsess over every line of this essay is dwindling.

At least they're not asking me why I'm not hanging out with my friends. Cam sent a generic "Happy holidays!" group text, but Harper hasn't answered. It didn't feel like a merry Christmas this year—my last Christmas before college, and I couldn't bring myself to feel any cheer.

Cora walks in, snatching an apple from the counter, shining it on the hem of her T-shirt. She pulls out her chair and sits across from me. "Still tinkering with the essay?" I nod as she swallows a bite of her apple. "I can proof it for you if you get it done in the next two days."

"You'll be in Duluth," I point out.

She shrugs, smiling. "I hear they still have email up there."

One of my biggest questions was if she ever told Mom and Dad about Drew, but her trip to spend New Year's Eve with him answered my question. They weren't thrilled having to breach the territory of an overnight stay with the boyfriend they'd never met, but they didn't say no either. Last night as I finished brushing my teeth, my elbow bumped her toiletries bag and I caught a glimpse of her birth control packet.

Nothing like a reality check to make me feel meek when I've been living off the high of Wilder's hug. Sometimes, I wish I knew what it feels like to let someone see all of you, to open up all the way. How open do you have to get? How brave do you have to be?

Without warning, Cora angles the laptop screen toward her to see what I've written. I stretch across the table, trying to pull the computer back, but she picks it up and reads aloud, "'Like any girl who survived middle school, I have memories of lying on the floor of my friends' rooms, looking at teen media sites on our tablets, music blasting. This led to conversations about which celebrity was dating whom or what tactics would actually work when asking out our crushes, or what outfits would fit our bodies. But the question those websites never answered was how to talk about my disability when it came to any of those topics. In fact, disabled people are rarely, if ever, seen front and center represented as independent people who thrive in every-day life.'" She skims farther down. "'I never got to see disabled voices represented—so I want to be able to make my voice count.'"

Cora stops reading, stands up from the table, and smiles. She pushes the laptop back to me. "You should definitely go with this topic." She smiles. "College in New York City . . . changing the culture of a whole industry . . . you're braver than me."

Before I can even process what Cora said, as if she summoned it, my email pings with a notice from Prospect. I open it. "They're inviting me to do an admissions interview," I tell her.

"Who is?"

I bang snap at Mom's voice, having just now realized that she came in from shoveling.

When I tell Mom which school, she sits down at the kitchen table, then looks up. "Cora, would you mind giving your sister and me a moment?"

She nods, and as she walks away, I don't feel brave anymore.

Mom runs a hand over her face and takes a breath. "I know the deadline for your college applications is fast approaching, and so it's time to talk about Prospect."

My mind races from the failed meeting with Ms. Wilson to the lunch issue that my parents don't even know about. My only decent plan for the School Beautification Project is a no-go and so far, I've got no other ideas. In the fall, Mom said I had a ways to go to prove myself—and so far, all I've got is a bunch of failed starts.

I unravel like a string in desperation. "I'm so interested in Prospect, Mom. I know there's a ton to figure out still but I'm trying to get better at advocating for myself. I really am. I really *want* to." I take a breath. It's not a strong card, but it's something, so I play it. "I'm even partnering on the School Beautification Project for Student Council with my friend Wilder. We're working on ideas to enhance accessibility at school. It was my idea."

Mom smiles brightly. "That's wonderful, Effie. What are your plans for the project?"

I bite my lip, pulling back, and mumble that we're still deciding.

She pauses, eyes soft. "I've been doing a lot of reflecting and this interview opportunity comes at an interesting time." She takes a deep breath. "It's just that, with Prospect . . . I'm still not sold. Even if the school does a great job at supporting you, how would you get around the city? The subway is so inaccessible. You couldn't possibly cab everywhere."

I'm afraid of all the same things. But I don't want to put off my dreams because of what might be. So I try again. "I want to apply to Prospect, Mom. It's still a possibility and I deserve to at least explore it."

Mom looks at me, her lips parted down. I can't quite read her expression. "You're right, Effie." A rush of pure surprise and elation rushes through me as I realize I may have just bought myself more time.

"You can apply to Prospect." But she holds up her hand and I know not to get ahead of myself. "I think it's a good idea that you do this admissions interview. That way you can use the opportunity to find out more information about the accessibility on campus. From there, we can reassess."

I hold eye contact. It's not a yes by any means, but it's more hope than I've had in a while, and she is being fair.

"Deal."

Please type your name to signify an electronic signature.

I'm sitting in front of our Christmas tree in my red flannel pajama pants and Mill City High T-shirt I've had since I was a freshman.

The branches of the tree are starting to droop a little, more and more pine needles lining the floor. We haven't bothered to clean up. It's December 30, and we'll take the tree down in two days . . . on January 1, when my college apps are due.

I did think maybe I should change into real clothes, considering what I'm about to do. In the end, I settled on washing my face and brushing my teeth.

I close my eyes to gather myself. I've double—triple—no, quadruple-checked everything. Cora and Mom both approved my essay. I said I wanted my voice out there. And this is the logical next step.

My fingers hover over the trackpad. I feel like I can't breathe, but I take a deep breath anyway.

I click.

Your Common Application has been submitted.

In the end, it's the most anticlimactic thing. At the very least, I expected those little fireworks to light up my computer screen like when I win a game of Spider Solitaire.

On pure muscle memory, I reach for my phone to text my friends the obligatory *Submitted ✓* text. Cam did it when she sent off her app to Georgetown, and Harper when she applied to her first choice, a school in Iowa called Grinnell. I type the text out, and then delete it. My phone screen lights up but all I see is the confirmation email from the Common App.

It's hitting me how this is it. Next fall, the three of us will be spread across the country—none of our college lists overlap. I thought we would be fine with FaceTime and texting and school and summer breaks, but we're already pulling apart. Normally, we would be hanging out together, but right now, Cam is seeing the new Marvel movie with Ali. And even though I'm not talking to Harper, I'm sure she's hanging out with Calvin.

Who am I kidding? We've already separated.

CHAPTER FOURTEEN

During lunch on the first day back from break, Cam meets me at my locker with a sullen look on her face. "You won't believe it—they shut us down."

"Who shut what down?" I ask, zipping my backpack and slamming the door shut.

"The sit-in!" That gets my full attention. "Ms. Wilson gave some BS line about how we were no longer permitted to gather in front of the desk upstairs."

A lot of people think rage is hot, but it comes over me coolly.

"And people tried to push back. We tried to say that what really shouldn't be allowed is their inaccessible policies," Cam explains. Her voice is quiet, and I instantly can see that she's trying not to get visibly upset in front of me. "Wilder was livid—he tried to explain to her if they just made a change, this would all be over. And then she tacked on that, if we tried to keep this going, we would get detention."

My mouth falls open. "What?"

Cam tucks a piece of hair behind her ear and her eyes fall to the floor. "I'm sorry we couldn't do more for you."

I reach up and wrap my arms around her. It goes unsaid—that a mark on their records, when most of the participants haven't yet been accepted to colleges—is too high of a risk right now.

"You did what you could," I reassure her. And it's true. And even though I have my Prospect interview coming up, and I'm nervous for everything that rides on that, I know I'm not done here.

It's time for me to take over from here.

❧

After school, I knock on Ms. Wilson's door, and this time, it feels different. This isn't about me proving myself to Mom.

This is about me, going after what I know is right, for me.

I knock, and the door opens. "Effie!" Ms. Wilson sounds confused. "You didn't have an appointment. I was just about to head out to a staff—"

I cut her off. "Please, I only need a minute of your time."

She presses her lips together, then nods, and holds the door open for me.

My legs shake in a way I know isn't clonus. Unlike the locker conversation and our first conversation about lunch, I haven't rehearsed this. I simply take a deep breath and tell her what I feel: "I think it is wrong that the school still has not been proactive on the accessibility of off-campus lunch when you've had months, even after I followed up . . . but to tell my classmates—my *friends*—that they'll get detention if they speak out . . . to me, that's even more hurtful than your nonresponse."

Ms. Wilson looks down at her desk, blinks, then looks back up at me, and I can't tell from her blank expression what she's thinking. "Effie, I appreciate your passion with this, but this is a complicated issue that—"

"It's not." I'm not sorry for interrupting. People love to say that accessibility is "too complicated" or "too much to ask for" but I tell her the truth: "It's easy if you make the choice to do it."

But I can see there's no fixing this on my own. So even though I'm not grateful, I thank her for her time, and show myself out.

CHAPTER FIFTEEN

My phone buzzes, and out of habit, I expect to see Harper's name pop up. My sadness is softened that it's a text from Cam: Go out there and CRUSH your Prospect interview, baby!

I text back thanks with a heart emoji. Harper hasn't eaten lunch with Cam and me since we got back from break. I'd hoped that the news that the sit-in was a bust would make both of us put the fight behind us. I'm crushed. Crushed that she would treat me this way, that I said the things I did, and crushed that now it's awkward for Cam, too.

I've drafted a million "I'm sorry" texts and picked up the phone so many times to call. But none of it seems quite enough, and I don't know how to fix this—to fix us.

But I can't focus on Harper or whatever will happen with lunch right now, because we've arrived for my interview.

In the driveway of my interviewer's house, there's a fancy car. I guess maybe that's a nice indication that a Prospect degree might set me up for success. There's also—I wait until

Mom's headlights pull farther into the driveway and illuminate them before I count—six cement steps up to the front door.

Mom looks at me. It hasn't snowed in a few days, but it's bitter cold. The steps will be slick, and there's only one cast iron railing.

Underneath my North Face parka, I'm wearing a floral blouse and navy blue sweater. I've jammed my feet with their thick Smartwool socks inside short silver booties. For a Prospect interview, even Mom agreed I shouldn't take the risk of wearing snow boots. Although she may not yet be completely open to the idea of Prospect, she still wants my first impression to be professional.

Mom sighs when she puts the car in park, leaving the keys in the ignition to keep the heat running. She suggested I call and ask him to meet me at a Caribou Coffee nearby, but I said no. What if I startled when the coffee grinder went off, and don't even get me started on agonizing over whether I should pay for his Americano (yes, right?), or . . . oh well. It doesn't matter, I'm already here. *Focus, Effie.* (Is it tacky if I tell him he has a beautiful home?) I'd wring my hands, but my gloves are too thick.

Mom knocks on the door and talks for a minute; now the headlights show the exhaust from the car frosting in the cold. Mom says something and starts back to the car. Then the front door opens again, and a man who can only be my interviewer comes out, slipping a peacoat on hurriedly.

Mom opens the car door. "He's going to help you enter through the garage. I'll go get your chair."

I unbuckle my seat belt and contemplate whether to shake his hand while I'm sitting right here in the passenger seat. Mom brings my chair around before I even have time to think about it, and I do my chair transfer trying desperately not to contemplate what my body looks like when I do it. In Mr. Andersen's college workshop, he reminded us to sit up straight, no slouching, to look the interviewer straight in the eyes, and smile, with a nice firm handshake. He didn't prepare me for what to do in this situation.

I block all those thoughts from my head and get into my chair like normal. Because for me, this is normal.

"Effie." Even though it's dark, and things are chaotic, my interviewer has a nice, warm smile. "Andrew Goldberg. We'll officially get acquainted inside, but I'm really glad you're here."

Despite the cold and the awkwardness, I manage a smile complete with eye contact. With the handshake question answered, I let Mom take control of my chair, leaning me backward on my wheels as it's easier to get through the snow that way. Mr. Goldberg opens the garage door. Out of the corner of my eye, I see him rummage around and pull out a shovel, and Mom quickly replies, "Oh, I've got it! No need."

His garage smells like dust, dead leaves, and faintly of motor oil. He's got another nice car, and I tuck my hands tightly against my lap, praying there's enough distance between the car and my wheels so I don't scratch the sides.

There are two small steps to get from the garage inside the house. Mom climbs up to the threshold first.

"On three?" Mom asks, and I say I'm ready. "One . . . two . . . three," she counts, before lifting me so that the back of my wheels touch the edge of the first step, and my chair and my body, by extension, are aiming downward at a sharp angle. I tighten my core and lean back as far as I can to avoid sliding out. The incline gets sharper as she bumps me up onto the second step. When we hit the threshold, I'm leaned backward instead, so that my tiny front wheels go up in the air, and my back leans sharply against the back of my chair. A few seconds later, and I am once again on flat ground.

Before I can process Mr. Goldberg's reaction, which I'm sure is that mix of horror and new understanding that I have seen many times, Mom is whispering that she'll be waiting in the drive in about an hour. She's probably off to that Caribou Coffee I am now wishing I would have agreed to.

A wave of shaky heat washes over me as I realize that sometimes I don't want to ask for accommodations because I want to feel "normal." But it is in those moments where I am not accommodated that I feel the least normal. Most students don't have to worry about walking two steps.

Closing the door behind him after Mom leaves, Mr. Goldberg hangs his coat and mine in the mudroom where I came in.

"Welcome!" he says, flashing a friendly smile. Now we shake hands.

"Thank you so much for having me."

As he leads me through his kitchen and offers me a cup of tea (which I decline . . . what if holding the hot cup makes my muscles tense and I shake too much?), my stomach clenches as my adrenaline rises. This is really happening. This person is going to record my responses and formulate an opinion of me and send that opinion on to the folks at Prospect.

When he eyes the white carpeting in the living room, he suggests that we sit at the dining room table. It's one of those long, rectangular wooden ones. He pulls out a chair and I wheel in, snapping the brakes into place when he isn't looking so if I fidget nervously during the interview, it isn't obvious. He sits down directly across from me, and I am pretty sure a single bead of sweat just rolled down my spine.

"Thank you again for coming out tonight, Effie. As an alumnus of Prospect, it always delights me to meet the next generation of students interested in attending. I like these one-on-one experiences in a private home, as opposed to an admissions office, because they offer a more casual environment to just have a simple conversation."

That's ironic. As casual as this setting is, my entrance was anything but.

He clears his throat. "I do hope you know that you could have let me know about your obstacles, and that I would've been happy to meet you anywhere else."

An obstacle is a traffic cone. A hurdle. A mild inconvenience that you sail over and continue on your way. A human being shouldn't be called an obstacle.

It's a disability; just *say the word.* It isn't a curse word.

My lips fight against my brain like a fish swimming upstream. My lips curl into a polite smile. "Oh, don't even worry about it. Everything is fine, and I'm here now. You have a beautiful home."

Mr. Goldberg smiles kindly, then rests his hands together in front of him, and it feels like it's time to begin the interview. "Like you, I grew up in Minnesota," he explains. "When it came time for college, I just had this hankering to really get out into the world. I knew I wanted to go into something related to the law field I eventually found myself in, and I discovered that Prospect and New York itself provided me the opportunity to do that." He looks directly at me. "Tell me, Effie, what is it that makes you interested in Prospect?"

Eye contact, eye contact, eye contact beats in the back of my brain, almost as loudly as my heart. I hear Mom's advice echo in my head: "Don't be shy, show him what you're made of." I remember Wilder telling me that my dreams are cool, that I could be a high-powered digital-content editor if I really worked at it. Cora's voice whispers, "You're braver than me."

"Prospect's Mass Media and Society department really appeals to me. I want to help minorities, but more specifically disabled people, be more visible in mass media, like magazines and the digital space."

Now it's his time to sit up in his seat, and a bit of electricity jolts through me, the type of high you can only get when you know you've struck a chord in exactly the way you want to. "That's an extremely ambitious and worthy goal, Effie. When I say I like meeting young students, it's for moments like this. The drive that your generation has to make change and alter the status quo is immensely inspiring, and I count your ambitions among them."

I smile a smile that is not for pleasing anybody but myself.

As the interview gets ready to wrap, I know I've nailed it, and I've done it by being nothing but my authentic self. But when he asks me if *I* have any questions for *him*, I know there's one thing I have to ask. I promised Mom, and after taking on Ms. Wilson, it's easier.

"I've never been to New York City. Do you . . . do you think a student in a wheelchair could be successful on campus?"

He sits back in his chair a bit, like we're in it for the long haul. My shoulders slump a little. "Well, clearly, I need to start with the caveat that I am not a current student, nor was I a student who navigated campus with any challenges. It has also been several decades since I lived on campus and in the city. I certainly hope that my alma mater has kept up with the times and made the changes that the current laws require." He drums his fingers on the table for a moment. "And I suppose that as an alumni interviewer, my official line should be to tell you to consult the school's Disability Services department to find the best ways they can make accommodations for you."

Accommodations. There's that word again. That word that again reminds me that I have to ask so many more questions than anyone else in this situation.

"But, as I mentioned, we are in my house, and I think that affords us the opportunity to have a more honest and straightforward conversation. So I'm going to take off my official admissions-office hat and speak to you, Prospect alumnus to Prospect hopeful."

He tells me about a path that cuts through the campus; he calls it a main artery of campus. It's tree-lined and unpaved, marked with gravel. From being an active alumnus, he says he knows there's been talk to pave at least part of the path to make it easier to manage for students with disabilities, but to no avail.

"Alumni are very attached to that path." His voice gets quieter like he's letting me in on a secret he knows he's not supposed to be telling me. "I myself have very fond memories of walking down that path in the fall with the leaves changing. It's extremely nostalgic for me and many others in the Prospect family. I happen to know that many alumni are reluctant to make any changes to this path because of their strong connections to it."

He goes on to say that he doesn't want to speak for the city itself, for its subway systems, its possible lack of curb cuts, or even things like the state of the dorms on campus.

But in telling me this one thing, I fear he has told me all I need to know.

"I know I'm not the official voice on this, but I want to tell you, Effie. I think you would do very well at Prospect. Your ambitions for a major are focused and admirable. The campus and the student body would strengthen by having you become a member. Based on our conversation this evening, I personally see no reason why you wouldn't excel academically there."

I want to smile. I want to bounce up and down in my seat. I should want to celebrate with ice cream on the way home, but I hold myself back.

I thank him for his kind words and also for his honesty. One is sweet and the other one sour. I have reassurance that I'm capable of getting into my top-choice college, no simple feat. And yet . . . I might not be able to get from one building to another.

Alumni who love their university should want to help anyone who wants to go there have the same life-changing, fabulous experience that they had. And yet if there's a path, you literally wouldn't pave it to make it easier for someone to get through? What is your nostalgia worth then?

Before I know it, Mom is bumping me down from the garage the same way she did on the way in, in reverse. Mr. Goldberg offers to help, lifting from the front.

"I've learned a great deal from you this evening, Effie." He means it as a compliment, but I feel the burden over and over again when it's like I personally have to show up to open someone's eyes to something they never would have thought of otherwise.

When he walks us out to the car, he turns to Mom. "You have a wonderful daughter."

Mom waits until we're both in the car and the door to his

house has shut before letting out a shrill squeal. "Effie!" She squeezes my knee three times in quick succession. "Baby, I'm so proud of you."

As we make the drive back, she presses me for details. I tell her the stuff about how he thinks I am a good fit and how I would excel academically there. She asks about the campus, and I tell her I got solid info. I leave out the stuff about the path. I'll have to tell her eventually, I know. Both about the way Ms. Wilson treated me and about the things Mr. Goldberg told me tonight.

But I can't bear to right now. Not when she has a smile brighter than the full moon that's following us all the way home.

"Should we stop for ice cream?" She answers yes before I can say anything. And I decide that tonight, I deserve it either way.

CHAPTER SIXTEEN

The next evening, when we sit down to dinner, Mom has a funny look on her face. As soon as she starts the conversation, I know why: "I got a call from Ms. Wilson today. About needing to make some changes to the exit for lunch at school."

I put my fork down and blurt something out. "Mom, I—"

She puts her hand up to stop me. "You aren't in trouble, Effie. I only wish you had told me sooner." She shakes her head. "You haven't been able to go out to lunch since *October*?"

"Yes." My face falls. "It started the first day that seniors were allowed out for lunch." I take a deep breath. "I didn't want to tell you because I wanted to be able to handle it on my own. That was when I met with Ms. Wilson for the first time, who said this was all of 'utmost importance' and then didn't do a single thing."

"She told me you were quite up front with her. It sounds like you really gave her a piece of your mind." I look at Mom, expecting her to tell me I was in the wrong. Instead, she smiles softly. "Effie, sometimes you have to. It's the only way they might actually pay attention."

She looks at my dad, and he nods, and I realize there's been a conversation between them about this earlier that I didn't know about. "I still have to follow up with the school tomorrow." Mom looks heavyhearted. "I wasn't happy with any of the so-called changes they wanted to make, and I think it's going to mean taking a stronger stance."

Mom takes a deep breath. "It's made me think about what you said, how you deserve to explore the possibility of Prospect." Mom takes a sip of her water. "I have to say you've really impressed me these past few weeks. I can see the changes in you. You stood up for yourself in front of Ms. Wilson. Plus, you asked important questions during your Prospect interview."

For maybe the first time ever, my heart sinks at the thought of Prospect.

"I can tell how much you want to go to Prospect and how hard you've worked for it, both academically and in other ways. I know it hasn't been easy, and you haven't always received the best news, but you keep trying and clearly, from your interview, the school is interested in you. And . . . based on the feedback from your interviewer about how well you would do in the program, your dad and I think it's time we went to visit the Prospect campus."

I should smile. I should be thrilled. This is my victory. I earned this.

Instead, I break silently like a twig in winter, brittle and weak. You can hear each individual splinter of my pain in my voice, the anger and the resentment, and, biggest of all, sadness.

"I don't think I can go to Prospect," I whisper.

"Why?" Dad asks, clearly surprised.

I take a shaky breath and settle enough to get it out. "There's this path—one of the main ways to get around campus. It's gravel and inaccessible."

Mom opens her mouth like she wants to contradict, but I stop her. "It's true, Mom. Mr. Goldberg basically confirmed it during my interview. He didn't want to say it, but I pushed, and that's when he told me."

It's quiet for a moment.

"His whole answer about accessibility wasn't great. He skirted around the truth. Everything he had to say about the school was positive but that." Under my breath, I whisper, "It isn't fair."

It isn't fair that I started researching colleges a full two years before everyone else. It isn't fair that Mom and I know way more about all of this than the Mr. Andersen at every school in the district combined. It isn't fair that I've worked so hard in all my classes and still might not be able to attend my dream school. It isn't fair that however much I want to go off into the big city and live my own, fun, wonderful life,

I'm still so scared about leaving my safe support system. It isn't fair that I'm nearly eighteen years old and still need my mom and dad to literally lift me up and carry me sometimes.

"You're right," Dad agrees. "It *so* isn't fair. But, Effie, the perfect college isn't out there."

I jolt a little and look at him.

"It's not," he presses. "The perfect college isn't out there because it doesn't exist. Even if you find a college that you absolutely love—and even if that college is Prospect—it won't have absolutely everything you're looking for. Even if it has great accessibility, there will still be ups and downs. But the college where you are happy, where you can be successful, and there are people there who want to support you, that's the *right* college. And that one does exist, and we're going to find it."

Needle in a haystack. Finding a polar bear in a blizzard. It may be out there somewhere, but the odds certainly don't feel as good as one out of six. And it's too late to increase my odds by applying to any other schools.

I look at Mom, who is looking at me kindly. "I don't think it's reasonable to write off a school because of a path, at least until we see it and decide for ourselves."

I sit up taller in my seat, finally starting to feel excited. She may be right.

"Effie." Dad looks at me. "I think it's possible that, if Prospect is interested in you attending, they might push themselves to make more improvements to the campus that can help you, and in turn could help other students. It doesn't hurt to visit and see what we find."

They're off to look at flights for mid-February, and while I'm still buzzing with the idea of visiting Prospect in person in three weeks (!!) . . . I'm also stuck on what Dad said about improvements that help other students, not just me. Isn't that the point of the School Beautification Project? To pass something better on to the new class of students?

I pick up my phone and DM Wilder: Meet me in the auditorium after school on Tuesday. I have an idea.

❧

I wait for Wilder in the auditorium. I don't know if my new idea will work, but I decide it's worth a shot. I face the stage, looking at the two benches that are normally outside our school. They've been brought inside for the winter, and were once a dark green, but are now so weathered you can't tell.

Behind me, I hear the door open, and turn around to see him walk in. With a jolt, I notice the hoodie he's wearing: bright red background with gray stitched-on letters reading PROSPECT UNIVERSITY.

"Effie, hey!" To my surprise, Wilder walks up to me and squeezes my shoulder, but I only bang snap a little. "I'm so, so sorry about the end of the sit-in." He takes off his backpack and then turns back to me. "But I heard they finally came up with a solution. Took them long enough."

I roll my eyes. By "them," he means Mom, who made good on her promise for change and called the school district attorney. Together, they demanded that the school install a new set of cameras above the accessible door on the first floor. At the sight of the attorney, Ms. Wilson folded immediately, and they'll be installed within two weeks' time. It's a solution so obvious and simple that I wish I could say I can't believe it took all it did to get here. But I do believe it. They don't care about me unless someone forces them to.

In addition to the cameras, a buzzer will be placed on both the inside and the outside the door. At lunch, I can buzz out, and they can clearly see it's me coming and going. I am the only one who knows about the buzzer, to keep other students from abusing it.

"I swear, when Ms. Wilson told us we had to put a stop to the sit-in, I don't think I've ever been that mad about anything ever."

Coming from Wilder, that's a big deal.

"What if we could still make them listen about changing the exit?" I ask. Getting to this point certainly wasn't easy for me, but I want to keep trying. I know it's "fixed" now, but I've lost my trust in this school making any sort of change that lasts. Wilder raises his eyebrows, so I propose my new idea. "What if we put together a detailed proposal to change the exit for off-campus lunch to the first floor? We could even use our budget to cover new signage for it."

He grins. "That's a great idea. I think it makes a lot of sense, too. Most classes on the second floor are freshman and sophomore ones, anyway. So why not put something for the seniors where the seniors actually are?"

"But . . . hear me out on this . . ." I say. "We keep the benches."

Wilder looks over at me, his brow furrowed. "For the outdoor sitting area, like we'd originally planned?" he asks.

"No," I clarify. "They're not going to listen to us when we hand over the school lunch plan and call it a day. The sit-in got no response. So I say we paint the benches, and make them think we're going through all the motions of the plan we promised them. But when we present them, we do it in a way they aren't expecting so that maybe, this time, they have to take notice."

And maybe, if we do it right, we can help some future students in more ways than the obvious.

When I fill him in on the full plan, his grin matches mine.

"Totally in, Ipfrenia."

We high-five to close the deal, and to my surprise, he grabs my hand at the end, holding on to it for only a few seconds. But even after he lets go, I swear I can still feel his fingers wrapped around mine. I tell him I'm officially visiting Prospect. His smile lights up ten watts, and he asks if I remember his lists of suggestions in New York.

It's funny how he believes I am capable of forgetting, as if our every conversation and interaction haven't been a constant private screening in my brain for months.

"How about this?" he asks. "You go crush the shit out of the Prospect visit, blow them away, and totally fall in love with the campus, and then we'll regroup on this project when you get back?"

"Thanks," I say, grateful for the opportunity to focus and let the visit take up my full attention. "And thanks for being a part of the sit-in, no matter how it turned out." I smile and look him straight in the eye.

"No need to thank me. It was honestly the very least I could do." He looks at me in return. "I mean, when I had the idea, I figured only a couple of people would join me, and it wouldn't run as long as it did, you know?"

No, I don't know. "What do you mean? It was you? You organized it?"

"Yeah!" He blushes slightly and lifts up an arm to scratch the back of his neck. He's nervous. "Like I said, it was the least I could do. I didn't want to go through Harper and Cam, because I figured you wouldn't want it to seem like you got all of us together, and I knew if I'd asked you for permission, you probably wouldn't let me do it."

I can't even try to play it cool. I smile.

He smiles back. "See! I knew you wouldn't."

He knew it. He knows me so perfectly well.

I'm stunned. All this time, I was sure it was Cam.

I don't want to ruin our friendship, but I also can't make sense of these signals. He started a whole sit-in for me. That has to mean . . . something.

It's scary to have this much hope, to feel my crush this strongly. My cheeks flush and my heart races.

With Wilder on my team, I feel unstoppable.

CHAPTER SEVENTEEN

The moment the chime sounds that, upon landing, it's safe to unbuckle our seat belts, the entire plane jumps up like popcorn kernels in a microwave. All except for me.

Mom stands to pull our stuff down from the overhead compartment. She stays standing, facing the aisle, her back to us. Dad springs up by habit, then sits back down with me.

I turn to look out the window again, even though I know all I can see is the metal sides of the jetway and the glow of those light sticks the guys on the runway wave around. It's just after eight o'clock at night on the East Coast, and thanks to some clouds and the gray February sky, my first glimpse of New York City was nothing more than a mass of blurry lights. And yet, in some ways, it's living up to my expectations already: Each of those bright lights represents a person, all of them moving together in this massive, dynamic place.

"I saw them put it on, Effie." Dad's voice pulls me back to my seat, in this stuffy plane that smells like stale air and spearmint gum. "I know it made it."

I glance up and Mom is watching the front of the plane like a hawk. She's holding her carry-on in one hand and the cushion to my wheelchair seat in the other. As the people from the far back of the plane start to make their way out, a flight attendant comes through, picking up the last few crumpled napkins and wrappers to those biscuit cookies that never taste as good as you want them to.

"Is the wheelchair up yet?" Mom asks her.

"A wheelchair?" Her eyes come up from the seats so fast that the topknot on her head bounces back like when you press down on the top of a perfectly baked cake. "We have a wheelchair on this flight?"

"*My daughter* is on this flight—" Mom starts in, but Dad nips this in the bud.

"I saw the wheelchair get loaded on in Minneapolis. We'll start making our way up to the front of the plane now, so if you can keep an eye out for it, that would be great." He turns to me. "Ready?"

I stand as quickly as I can. I am so ready to get off this flight, for more reasons than one.

I turn so that I'm facing the aisle, steadying myself by holding on to the back of the seat that was in front of me.

"Stretch first," Mom reminds me. I grimace, but she's right. My hamstrings feel like iron rods after spending three hours straight in the confined space. I flex my calves and heel chords as much as I can.

Stepping into the aisle, I place one hand on the seat to either side of me. Like climbing a rock wall, I grab on to the next set of seats each time before taking my next steps forward. At one point, my heel chord spasms in protest, and I inhale sharply, stopping to try and regain my balance. Dad's hand lands lightly between my shoulder blades.

"I'm here," he reminds me.

I keep going until I make my way to the first row in the plane and sit down. I look longingly at the complimentary water bottles they handed out in first class. Until I see my chair safely in front of me, my mouth is the Sahara Desert.

"We have two strollers," the flight attendant says, peeking out into the jetway. "But no wheelchair yet."

We do this complicated song and dance every time we fly. Every time it's the same: Did my chair even make it onto the plane? Did they pick it up and throw it on, like they do the plastic foldable strollers? Will it arrive with a broken brake, a dented spoke, or the worst: a bent axle, making it nearly impossible to wheel?

Well, no, that's actually not the worst. The worst is when they mistake your chair for a courtesy airport chair and take someone else away in it—to baggage claim, or in the horror of horrors, to their connecting flight.

I used to think Mom was just overreacting, until a few years ago when she sprinted off the plane and to the check-in desk to stop my chair from going on to South Dakota when we landed back home.

"We caught it just in time!" the airline representative had said, as if that made it any better.

Now my mind races, and I'm wondering if I should Google places to rent a wheelchair in the city just in case.

"Wheelchair's up!"

Mom, Dad, and I all exhale. Mom goes out and puts the cushion on, inspecting for any obvious cracks or damages. Dad helps me stand, we thank the attendant, and I am reunited with my chair. Everything appears to be fine, but I know we'll do second and third checks at baggage claim. I'm lucky—many people who use power wheelchairs don't even dare fly because they feel like the risk of damage is too high and too permanent. I'm lucky I can even consider colleges within flying distance. But that doesn't mean that I don't want it to be better.

Once we move past the gates and get farther out into the terminal of LaGuardia, the first thing I see under the fluorescent lighting is one of those touristy gift shops selling I ♥ NY stuff: the classic white T-shirts, plus the design reprinted on tie-dye sweatshirts, or repurposed on mugs that look like yellow taxicabs. It's a small thing, but even this makes me happy. It's the first sign that I'm really here. *I did this.* Me. The girl from five months ago who asked for a Prospect information packet to be sent to her teacher because she was terrified to tell her parents would be shocked and amazed.

I text Cora that we landed, and she responds with the Statue of Liberty emoji. Three dots appear, indicating more. Then a heart.

Retrieving our luggage and making sure the chair is okay one last time, we get in line for a taxi into the city. Catching my first real-life glimpse of those iconic yellow cabs has me giddy. In line with all the tired travelers and catching the eye of people who I assume are locals because they're walking toward the trains, I try to keep my cool. But I can't stop smiling.

We have to pass on a few normal-sized cars before a taxi van pulls up to take us. Dad loads the suitcases in back while Mom opens the door for me. Right as I start to stand, my phone buzzes in my pocket.

I ignore it and focus on wrapping my fingers tightly around the grab bar that flips down from the ceiling of the cab. I lift one foot up toward the running board; the tightness of my hip makes it so my foot can't get high enough. Mom boosts me slightly so I can make the step, and her hand lands lightly on my back. *She's there.*

"Where to?" the driver asks once we're all in.

"Manhattan," Dad answers, along with the cross streets for our hotel. Manhattan is a forceful, solid word, one that feels so full, holds so much. As we pull away from the curb, in the privacy of the cab, I am no longer afraid to grin like a fool.

I watch the other cars on the freeway, outlined in black and only made visible by the headlights, glowing like flashlights in the night when we drive under the highway overpasses. At one point, a train—a real one, rough and metal and clanking its way along—rolls over one of the overpasses. I've been so focused on the subways that it didn't really occur to me that New York had aboveground trains, too. As we get farther from the airport but not yet into the city, I see outlines of brick buildings and what look like small houses. A hollow pit forms in my stomach. I've spent so long living in my daydreams, fueled by that Jay-Z and Alicia Keys song and the overhead shots they show on the morning news shows before cutting to commercial break. Now I'm starting to wake up to clanky trains and cloudy skies and lonely highways. New York City is a place for dreamers, right? I hope the reality still has some of the magic.

We drive under a sign for the Queens-Midtown Tunnel, Manhattan. It's slower going now, as more cars have joined us on the road. Almost like opening a pop-up book, the city sky-line unfolds before me, all of it, all at once. Among billboards and brick, a building that is tall and ends in a high, pointy spiral captures my attention. There's so much more to explore here than at home. The dreamer in me is wide awake.

The combination of brake lights and the lights that line the tunnel makes it glow an orangish red. I'm glowing too, excited and bright and full of anticipation. The tunnel hangs on like an ellipsis. When I was a kid, I used to make a wish and hold my breath as we drove through tunnels. I may not be holding my breath now, but my wish is as strong as ever.

When we emerge, the streets remind me of those pictures my elementary school art teacher always tried to get us to master, drawing a landscape until the horizon line disappears into the vanishing point. Here, there is no open space between the buildings like there is in the Midwest. All I can see until I can't see any farther is concrete and glass, and I can only assume the buildings go on beyond that.

All too soon, the cab pulls up to our Manhattan hotel. Dad thanks the driver and Mom goes around to get my wheelchair out of the trunk. The thought of having to stand up again makes me exhausted, the weight of the day starting to catch up with me. I've seen so little of this place, and yet I'm already so stimulated. My heart has been beating so fast in anticipation that it feels weird for it to slow for even a moment.

Sitting in my chair on the sidewalk of our hotel, I watch the cars and buses drive by and listen to the sounds of the city: the honks, the snippets of overheard conversations, the noise of people walking in every direction.

In a year, or two, or three, will this be the moment I look back on, as the moment that started it all? A long, complicated, exhilarating relationship with this city and these streets? Maybe at the end of this week, I might have an answer.

My phone buzzes and I fish it out of my jacket pocket.

A new text from Cora:

Soak it all up and tell me everything!

I plan to do just that.

CHAPTER EIGHTEEN

"Come on, Effie! Smile . . . and *not* the fake smile."

Behind Mom, Dad stifles a laugh as she presses the screen on her iPhone, taking a bunch of pictures in a quick burst. Any excitement I had about first seeing the Prospect University sign has been replaced by embarrassment thanks to Mom making me pose with my arm casually leaning against one end of it. A group of college boys walk by and I blush.

I wheel away from the sign, claiming we won't have time to make it through touring some of the buildings where the Mass Media and Society classes are if we keep taking pictures. Mom and Dad dutifully follow, even though they both know it isn't true. This morning, I was up and ready quicker than my previous record of that one Christmas when I was expecting an American Girl doll. Even with stalling in a coffee shop to kill time, we are still twenty minutes ahead of schedule. I'm signed up to sit in on a 10:00 a.m. class called "Digital Media: The Modern Age."

We took a cab from the hotel to the Park Slope campus in Brooklyn. The brochure didn't lie; I love the redbrick buildings, and the energy of all these students bustling about. Even though it's winter, I can tell the campus green space would be lovely.

I remember when Wilder tried to explain Prospect to me and it was like he didn't have the words. I understand now.

I have to admit, I was a little sad to take the over-forty-minute ride outside Manhattan. The city is so huge. I know I can't see all of it on this already too-short trip, but oh, do I want to.

As I start to make my way through campus, I notice every little detail: Are the sidewalks cracked? What is their grade? I glance at the buildings to see if they have door openers on them.

I look up and see a couple walking a few paces ahead of me, big backpacks thumping against their backs with each step. He says something that makes her laugh with her head thrown back. It feels invasive to get even this tiny glimpse into two strangers' lives.

I look behind me for my parents. When I don't immediately see them, my stomach flips, and on second glance, I see that they've fallen at least twenty yards behind me. I'm not wheeling particularly fast, but with the way Mom is scrolling through her phone and Dad is consulting the campus map, I realize it's intentional. They're letting me feel things out for myself, to learn how it would really be if I were actually a student here. I feel a pang when I remember they won't always be right behind me every time something new makes me feel uneasy.

"Are you looking for something?" I bang snap at the sound of the guy's voice in front of me. He and his partner have stopped walking, their hands still clasped, and they're looking back at me. "Are you a prospective student?"

I swallow. "Um . . . yes, I am."

"Awesome! My girlfriend and I love it here." She smiles at me, too. "Are you trying to find a specific building?"

A wave of shyness overtakes me, and I can't get out that I'm looking for the Media and Society building. It feels too personal to say. Then a rush of embarrassment arrives. Who am I to think about interning at Hearst or anything like it if I can't even say the name of a building?

My voice a little shaky, I tell him what I'm looking for.

"We can take you there," he answers. "It's close to our dorm. We're on our way back there now."

I respond gratefully, so happy now that my parents are far behind. As we walk, they ask me where I'm from, and if I've already committed to Prospect. They're juniors, and they can't say enough good things about the school.

They're so kind, taking time out of their morning to chat with me. It makes me feel included, important, mature.

We move toward the academic building, stepping off the concrete path and onto a gravel one. Almost immediately, the chair stalls in the frozen ground. Softly, I ask, "Where are we on campus right now?"

"This is one of, like, the main paths on campus. The main artery, they call it." His brow crinkles a bit and his lips thin as he kicks a particularly big chunk of icy gravel out of my way.

I've spent weeks thinking about this path, and now we finally meet. My speed significantly slows, and my new acquaintances notice.

"Do you need help?" the girl asks. She sounds a bit nervous.

I shake my head no, but I already feel my biceps burning from the extra effort. They keep up the friendly chitchat with me, but my answers become shorter as I exert more effort. If they pick up on it, they're polite and don't say anything. My parents thankfully don't come running to my rescue, but truth be told, I'm not sure I could manage this path on my own.

After what feels like ages, we make it. There is no door opener, and they hold the door open for me. My arms are burning, and I notice that my gloves are streaked black with dirt. I try to hide them as best as I can.

"Sitting in on a class?" the guy asks me.

When I tell him, surprising myself with how forthcoming I am, he lights up. "That sounds so awesome! Man, I'm a math major. Your class sounds way cooler than any of mine."

I thank them both, and as I wheel away, I have to agree that I *do* feel cool. But that familiar question eats at me, asking if I could really make this work.

Inside Prospect's Disability Services office, black-and-white photos of New York City landmarks hang on the walls: the Brooklyn Bridge, Times Square, Central Park, Broadway. I wonder how I would even get to all of those places.

On the Maps app, I check "subway" and "accessible trip" on the subway route from Park Slope to Manhattan for the internship and a pop-up on my phone says, "Please be advised there may be elevator outages along your route."

I knew it wasn't going to be easy. I've done my research. But I also know I owe it to myself to try. And so, dammit, I am going to try.

"Effie?" A woman who looks to be in her midforties has come out an office door and into the waiting area. "I'm Cynthia, the coordinator of Disability Services here at Prospect. So great to finally meet you."

She leads us through the door to a side office full of cubicles, and to her own private one. She's already pulled out one of the chairs, so I wheel in, and Mom and Dad sit in chairs on either side of me. Cynthia sits down at her desk across from me, a file folder in front of her, which, with a jolt, I realize is about me.

"I have to say," she says, clapping her hands together a bit for emphasis, "we all have been *so* excited for your visit, Effie. Prospect has needed a student like you for a long time."

A student *like me*? I'm not sure how to respond to that, so I just nod.

We chitchat, but it's stalling. So I take a deep breath and jump in.

"I met some students today and they were wonderful. It makes me so excited about the prospect of joining your student body." Cynthia smiles at me, and I gather myself. "Do you have other students on campus who use wheelchairs?"

Her smile quickly turns into a tight line. "At this moment, we do not. We had a student who used a wheelchair with us for a while, but he chose not to continue his studies here."

Mom pipes up, her voice stiff and straightforward. "Chose not to, as in . . . ?"

"He transferred to another institution," she clarifies. Mom nods, and I sit still. This school is well over 150 years old. She can't possibly be saying . . . "But before that . . . at some point . . ." I press.

Cynthia removes the reading glasses she was using to look over my file. "Effie, your application is so strong. Your drive makes you exactly the type of student we want to see go out into the world and make a difference."

I need her to stop dancing around it and tell me a number that is too low but is still something.

"At this point, no, I can't say we have had a student in a wheelchair successfully graduate from Prospect." Oh. I feel a thud that must be my heart hitting my stomach. I grimace slightly, then look down.

Imagine saying that out loud about any other minority. Imagine the size of the recruitment efforts to change it if it was for anyone else.

I zone out for a second before realizing my parents have asked her about the path.

Cynthia squares her shoulders and leans in toward us. "I want you to know that we've brought forth a petition to the board of trustees in regard to a partial paving of the path in light of Effie's high interest in attending Prospect. At this early stage, I can't definitively say if it will happen."

I look down at my hands, and underneath them sits the Mass Media and Society booklets, or as I've heard the students call it, MMS. On the bottom, I see the Prospect logo printed with the slogan *Prospect University: Your Key to the City.* But for me, it's a big lie. *Prospect University: My Key Can Barely Open One Door.*

When the three of us head back outside, we stay together as a unit, no one falling behind or going on ahead. I watch the students mill about my dream school, a mirror of what I saw before the meeting. Only now it's like the mirror has a big crack across the middle.

Dad's voice is low and sweet. His hand lands lightly on my shoulder. "Let's go have some fun."

CHAPTER NINETEEN

"There's no elevator at this station." This poor guy, just a random passerby my parents approached on the street for directions. "There may be an accessible stop about five blocks that way." He points forward. "But I'm not sure. I know the buses go that direction." Mom thanks him for his help, letting him off the hook. He gives me a shy, apologetic smile as he walks away, putting his earbud back in.

"Five blocks to an accessible stop," Mom grumbles. My parents thought it would be fun to try the subway, and this is how it's going.

Dad walks up to the entrance of the subway station. "Two full flights of stairs." He looks at Mom and then at me. "Should we try it?"

Both of them now look at me. I eye the stairs and the rush of people coming and going. This is life in New York. And if I want to be a part of it, I have to try.

"Let's go," I say. I wheel to the edge of the stairs and Mom and Dad spring into position. My brakes snap into place. I place one hand on the metal railing and Mom comes around to support me on the other side. I stand, pausing when I'm upright to make sure I'm steady. When I don't waver for a few seconds, Dad takes the chair from behind me, and he starts carrying it down the steps.

One foot down, wait for the other foot to land on the same step. Repeat. I notice a few people walking up the stairs look at me and then look away really quick. At one point, I glance behind me. There's three or so people waiting to walk down the stairs, but thankfully, they're giving me space, waiting.

A gaggle of college-aged girls race down the opposite side of the stairs, avoiding me altogether. The way that they are able to bound down the stairs looks almost unreal to me, like on TV when the Flash runs so fast there's a cloud of dust behind him. They're all decked out in jeans and jackets and shimmery makeup. They got there in twenty seconds. It's taken me two minutes and I'm still not there.

I get to the bottom of the stairs and sit in my chair, which Dad has prepped, ready at the exact angle I need it to be. I press my hands to my thighs to try to beat the clonus, but it comes anyway, and I welcome it. It's a sign that I can push myself and that I've learned to use my body to the best of its abilities.

Once on the platform, people wait for the train, commuting toward their homes, toward their friends, toward their futures. And I am moving with them.

As we wait, the same thought tumbles around in my head, like a rock that gets smoothed over by moving through the same silt so many times: *I've been able to do so many things in my life that I didn't think were possible. Who's to say that this couldn't be one of them?*

I scroll through my phone, and I wince when I see that Wilder has responded with a heart-eyes emoji to the photo of campus I posted to my Story.

What did you think? he asks. He told me to crush the shit out of the visit, blow them away, and totally fall in love with the campus. That all happened, but the campus didn't love me back. And I don't know how to handle that, much less how to tell him.

To get into the subway car, there's a gap the size of a stairstep.

Mom steps inside the car, grabbing on to my handlebars. I lean back into my chair, bracing myself, then stiffen as my wheels make contact with the inside of the subway car when she lifts me. The front of the chair rises as Dad grabs the frame.

Some of the fellow riders offer to help me, and some keep their distance. There are no MTA workers on-site. On the train, there are spots designated for passengers with disabilities. Ironic. Doesn't the song go, *If I can make it there, I'll make it anywhere?* I couldn't even make it onto the train by myself.

The electronic announcements overhead tell me this is the

Jamaica-179 train. I have no idea what that means or where that is. Maybe, four years from now, I'll look back and laugh at how little I knew about the layout of the city and how to get around. Millions of people live here. Some of them have to have the tips and tricks that I don't yet know.

The stops blur by as we pick up speed. The colors of the tile and the figures of the people blend together like an Impressionist painting as we pull away from the station.

When the next stop is announced as Herald Square, I get an inkling where we're headed.

Dad comes up behind me. "Ready?" I flash a thumbs-up.

Thankfully, here, there is an elevator. Inside, I hold my breath, partly due to excitement and partly due to how bad it smells.

When we get out onto the sidewalk, we walk a few blocks, until, suddenly, it truly feels like an opening out into a whole new plane. As I take in all of the lights, the flashing screens, the taxicabs, and the pulse of the moving people that seem to match the beat of the street performer's bucket drums, I realize all those songs about New York, they all got it right. It's like the city is singing to me right now, a first verse that is building to a chorus that will be stuck in my head for a long time.

As we walk, I see screens advertising plays I would love to see. Even simple things I've seen my whole life—banks, Gap stores, and Hard Rock Cafes—feel more than what they are. I smell the street meat and the spiced nuts, feel the thrum of too many voices in my ears, and bang snap at the chime of the little bells on those bike taxis. It's so much to take in, and I am only one tiny dot in this moving mass. But maybe, right now, a plane is flying over, and they see that big mass of lights. Today, I'm a part of that, too.

Once we see Times Square, we walk for about ten minutes before my parents stop in front of a building, all gray and glass and modern. Mom consults her phone. "Yep, that should be it. Columbus Circle."

"Why did you bring me here?" I ask.

She shows me the map on her phone screen. *You have arrived at your destination. The Hearst Communications Building.*

"Don't you want to see where you'll be interning in a few years' time?"

I'm not sure you're ready, she'd told me a few months ago.

And she's probably still scared, but she's willing to let me go.

No, she's telling me to *go for it.* She can't be there to fix everything, every time. And I'm not sure I need her to be—not anymore. She sees that this is my dream, and she's going to let me try.

I wheel right up to the front door. Regardless of the circumstances around it, what coast I end up on and the opportunities I take, I still see myself here, at the end of it. Prospect or no Prospect, I'll find my way back here.

"Effie," Mom says. "Turn around."

I wheel around, and I smile for her picture. This one's anything but fake.

This time, my question isn't *What if I can't?*

I know I can, and someday, I will.

~

Back home, right away I wheel down the hall to my bedroom, where Dad has already put my suitcase on the bed. As I open it to unpack, I move my hand over the cotton of my pajamas, the roughness of my blue jeans. As much as I hate to admit it, a part of me wondered—and even hoped—that a brand-new Prospect sweatshirt would be folded right on top, the suitcase springing open due to stuffing in the extra item.

I can picture the sweatshirt, like the one Wilder has: the kind with the letters big and stitched on, with the strings you can chew on. But if I'm honest, I can't picture the name of the school that will be on it.

I move to my window. Our house looks out at the whole block, so I can see not only our driveway but straight down to the next cross street. The world is so much bigger than my tiny street. But my tiny street is big enough to count as its own world, too. It's big enough to be the only home I've ever known.

I change into my pajamas. It's only 8:45, but I consider crawling into bed. I could read, but I can tell I wouldn't be able to concentrate.

Out in the living room, I hear TV. It's one of those HGTV shows. I can't tell if it's the one where they choose between three houses or the one where they have to decide if they want to stay in their old house after renovations or buy a new one. It doesn't matter; the shows are all the same, and I bet Mom and Dad have seen every episode of all of them at least twice. I always know my parents can't sleep at night when I startle awake to hear the words "open concept floor plan" at 2:00 a.m.

I wheel down the hallway and into the kitchen. I stay there a moment, partly to get a glass of water and partly to hear if my parents are talking about our trip, debating which one of them knows best what's currently going through my mind.

At the sound of the tap turning on, Mom calls out, "You headed to bed, Effie?"

I join them in the living room.

"They're going to pick house number two." I blurt it out.

"Hey!" Dad sounds fake hurt. "Spoiler warning, please."

"It's always house number two. Or whatever house lets her get a bigger closet or him get a man cave."

I get out of my chair and crawl onto the couch, in the space between my parents, where I feel at peace for the first time today.

A comfortable silence settles between us. Mom spreads the blanket over me, and I cup the edges of it to my face.

She takes a sip of her wine. "Those countertops are stunning," she remarks. "Can we do that in our kitchen?"

"Maybe someday." Dad chuckles.

No matter what changes are coming, tonight, this is home.

CHAPTER TWENTY

"How was it?" Cam's enthusiasm makes me bang snap as I shut my locker door. She's bouncing on her heels, practically vibrating in her skin. "I need to hear everything. Is Prospect perfection?"

At that, I swallow a lump in my throat. I haven't seen her all morning, and I've been dreading this conversation. Because the answer to her question is yes. It's so absolutely perfect, in every way but the ways I need it to be.

"Um, it's . . . good." I'm panicking a bit. The lump in my throat is quickly becoming a rock. I've avoided Wilder today, but next period is Student Council. So I blurt the first thing that buys me more time. "I actually have to use the restroom."

I'm off before I can look Cam in the eye; all I can hear is her confused "Okay" in response.

In the bathroom, traitor tears start to fall. I grab one of the brown paper towels to wipe my eyes, but that only makes it worse.

And then, to add insult to injury, I hear, "Effie?"

Harper is standing just inside the door, one strap of her backpack over her shoulder. "You're crying," she says softly. "What's wrong?"

And even though things have been rocky between us for weeks, and even though she hurt me and I hurt her, this is still my best friend, and I am the girl crying in the bathroom.

"Prospect," I choke out before a fresh wave of tears falls.

Harper sets her backpack down and ushers me into a corner past the bay of sinks, away from the door. "Okay, what happened at Prospect?" I realize two things: She's standing in front of me so that other people don't see me crying, and that even though we haven't been talking, she still knows I went to New York. She looks sad. "Hey," she says. "I've really missed you."

It's then that my shoulders start to shake, and in between shuddering breaths, I tell her everything. The path, the problems with public transit, how they have my perfect major, and how they've never had a student in a wheelchair.

"It's so messed up, but I still want to go there so bad, Harper."

"Oh, Effie." She steps forward and leans down and wraps me in her arms, and I melt into her. "That sucks so much."

The bathroom door opens. Cam looks concerned, but when she sees us hugging, the worry leaves her face. "What's going on?"

"Group hug," Harper answers, and makes space for Cam to join us.

It dawns on me that lunch is half over. "I don't want to go to Student Council. I don't want to have to talk to Wilder about Prospect."

"Then don't." Harper's voice gets a bit mischievous.

I could blame the busy few days preparing for my trip as the reason I haven't gone out to lunch until now. But truth is, I didn't want to go out without Harper. As hard-fought as my ability to be able to do this was, on my first time going off-campus for lunch, I buzz the three of us out without a second thought. This isn't how I pictured it at all, but I'm so glad to be able to do it.

❧

Thirty minutes later, we're parked outside McDonald's. I'm dipping fries into a chocolate shake. Cam's run inside to grab more napkins after an unfortunate ketchup spill.

"Hey, Effie?" I turn toward Harper. She's put her food down, and is looking at me. "I'm sorry I went out to lunch with Calvin, but most of all, I'm sorry I said those awful things to you. You have a right to be mad about what the school is doing to you."

My lips feel quivery again, but I settle myself not to cry again, even if it's in relief. "I'm sorry I said you were selfish," I tell her. "You're not. You're my best friend, and I've missed you so much."

She reaches over and squeezes my shoulder. "The lunch drama was awful, but I know you'll find a way to get the administration to listen to you." I open my mouth to tell her about the steps I've taken, but she holds up her hand to stop me. "Look, I get that I'm never going to completely understand everything you go through and shit people say to you. I can witness it, but I'll never live through it. But I know that how our school has treated you is wrong."

It doesn't fix everything, but it's nice to hear nonetheless.

"I'm so sorry I haven't been there for you during your shoulder injury. I don't have an excuse for that, no matter what was going on in my life." I look her in the eye. "I know surgery—even the possibility of it—is scary, and I hate that I was so in my head that I couldn't see when you needed me."

Harper nods. "Thank you for saying that, Effie." Then she grins. "I'm back playing at full force now."

I grin. "How does it feel?"

"Incredible." I can hear her happiness in her voice. "I get to play in the Winter Classic on Thursday."

"I'll be there," I tell her, and I mean it. "Me and Cam. With signs. Maybe pom-poms."

When Cam gets back into the driver's seat, she looks around. "Everything okay in here?"

"We're great," I answer, and reach behind me to squeeze Harper's knee. Cam lights up. "We're going to watch Harper's hockey tournament on Thursday, by the way. With signs."

Cam looks confused, but agrees.

I clear my throat. "I want you to go out to lunch with Calvin, Harper," I say. I'd been thinking about it for a while. "And you too, Cam. I want you to go out with Ali, if you want."

They both look at me, eyes big with confusion.

"Not like *every day*," I clarify. "But if you want to, you should feel free. Now that I can go out too, I'll eat in the green space out in front of school. I don't want to hold you back." And it's true. I've been scared my friends will leave me behind because of their relationships, and I'm afraid of all the changes next year will bring. But I'm realizing things are *already* changing, and the way to honor my friends is to celebrate the changes in their life. It's not always easy, but it doesn't have to be so hard.

⌒

"What if we, like, get arrested?" It's Friday night, the day after Harper scored a goal at the tournament, and we're celebrating. Cam is sitting behind the steering wheel, biting her bottom lip. We've parked, but haven't gotten out of the car, so without the lights on, it's as dark inside as it is out.

I'm sitting in the passenger side, and Harper lets out a sharp yelp. "Ah, Effie, your frog wheel just jammed into my head."

"Sorry!" I say, but it comes out more like a laugh. This is a last-minute excursion, and the only car available to us is Cam's mom's Kia, a compact that wasn't meant to fit three people plus a wheelchair. While they got the wheels into the trunk successfully, the frame of the chair is in the backseat next to Harper. I can see the little front wheels sticking up in the air in the rearview mirror.

"Guys, I'm serious. What if we get arrested?"

"Cam," Harper says. "There's no way I'm letting any of us get arrested for the first time at some hotel in downtown Minneapolis. There's just no way."

I snort while Cam whines, "Harper!"

I may be a bit worried too, but I'm so happy to have Harper back with me, with us, that I would do just about anything with her right now.

"I'm texting Calvin and he's Googling it right now." She holds up her phone, I assume to prove it to us, but all we see is the screen creating a blinding orb of light.

"Oh shit!" Harper's mouth falls into an O, her face glued to the screen. "Calvin sent me a link to a legal forum that says we definitely *could* get arrested."

Even in the dark, I swear I see Cam's face blanch.

"Oh, wait, wait!" Harper squints closer at her phone screen. "He just sent me another link from *GQ* about how you definitely can sneak into a hotel pool if you play it right."

"Oh, good!" Cam's voice is anything but enthusiastic. "Because when you're trying to decide whether or not to do something that could go on your record, *GQ* is absolutely the source you should consult."

"That's exactly what I think!" Harper sticks out her

tongue and quickly opens the backseat door. Cam and I both blink as our eyes adjust to the burst of the overhead lights turning on.

A rush of excitement pulses through me as Harper pulls the frame of my chair out. She asks Cam to pop the trunk so she can get the wheels. Cam groans but gets out, partly to assist and partly to convince her that we shouldn't be doing this.

We came prepared, wearing swimsuits under our jeans and T-shirts and thick down parkas. It's the very end of February, and at eight o'clock at night, it's a whopping fifteen degrees.

Twenty minutes ago, we were all lying on Cam's bed, complaining about how cold it is.

"I just want to be *warm*," Harper whined. "Like, sitting-beside-a-pool warm."

When she got that glint in her eye, Cam and I knew we were in for trouble. But this is our girl, and we missed her.

Harper looks around the hotel lobby like she is casing the joint. Cam and I hang back, watching the man behind the desk. He is talking to someone on the phone about their reservation, placing the phone between his shoulder and his ear and pressing some keys in quick succession on his computer.

Harper waves us over to a quieter part of the lobby. "Take your coats off."

Cam eyes the automatic doors, which at any moment could fly open and expose us to the giant deep freezer that is happening outside.

"Who tries to get into a pool fully clothed? Look the part!" Harper speaks under her breath, but it almost sounds like hissing. We have no choice but to oblige. Cam takes her coat and mine and balls them up behind a large potted plant. Harper flings hers against the little green velvet armchair like this is her home. Cam rolls her eyes and stuffs Harper's behind the plant, too.

I watch Harper walk up to the desk like she's walking into Target. She looks back at me. And I don't quite know what I'm thinking, except that tonight, my best friend and I are going to have the kind of fun together that will carry us through any future hard times.

I roll up next to Harper.

"Hi!" Harper's voice is breezy, effortless.

"Hello. Welcome! Do you have a reservation?"

The words come out before I even realize it. "We're actually already staying here. My cousins and I are in town for our aunt's wedding."

Cam coughs loudly. Between my olive skin tone and curly hair, Harper's brunette hair in a bob, and Cam's red hair and green eyes, we are some set of cousins.

"There's not a wedding booked here this weekend." He's about to punch some more keys on the computer to check, but Harper doesn't miss a beat.

"The wedding's in the suburbs. Our moms booked the hotel too late, and by then, the block of rooms they set aside at the other hotel were full up. You know how it goes."

The guy actually cracks a half smile. We are magic.

"So how can I help you ladies?"

He looks at me and instead of getting shy, I say it. "We came down here to use the pool and forgot our keys, so we can't be buzzed in."

He cocks an eyebrow. "All *three* of you forgot your key?"

"Well, you only gave us two to begin with. And our aunt has the other one."

He looks at Harper, and then at the three of us, considering each of us carefully. Based on his facial expression, he probably doesn't believe us. But maybe he is feeling soft tonight, because when another group comes down actually dressed to enter the pool, he calls out, "Hey, would you mind letting these girls in with you?"

❧

Inside the pool area, it's a good seventy-degree difference. "I can't believe it!" Cam is giddy. Harper lets out a little yell, and tonight, I let myself cheer a little, too. My heart is loud, both a celebratory beat and a warning siren. I don't have to tell Mom about this. I can lie and she'll never find out. Cora would be proud.

We shed our jeans and sweatshirts. Upon first look, the prize does not necessarily equal the valiant effort to win it. Besides the view of downtown Minneapolis out the windows, it is the same as any other hotel pool: small, weirdly oblong shaped so that it prohibits any real swimming, with a tiny hot tub. But none of that matters.

Harper goes whole hog with a cannonball. Cam giggles, but takes a more conservative approach and sits and slips in the pool from the side. I wheel over to the stairs and park my chair there.

For a second, I consider myself sitting here in my swimsuit. It's a one-piece, not anything super revealing. But even in this, the scars along the sides of my hips from my long-ago surgeries are on full display. I remember the conversation Cora and I had in the bathroom at Cannon. I was so frightened by the idea that a boy could potentially see me, all of me, on display in that situation. Somehow, though, I don't have any issues with my friends seeing my body like this. I already know they won't care. Why do I hold boys to some sort of lower standard, then, even though I know I shouldn't?

With the support of the railing, I walk in slowly. While my friends shriek and splash and swim breaststroke with their heads out of the water, I stay mostly in the same area, shivering a bit.

I look out at the Minneapolis skyline. I can make out the Foshay Tower, because it has the name lit up on its side. I see something that I think is the IDS Center, and the building with the top that lights up in fun colors. I've seen this skyline my whole life and I still can't identify all the buildings. Maybe it's a sign that I'm not ready to trade it in for the shinier, bigger, brighter model. To be honest, sometimes it still doesn't make sense to me how I could be the one who came up with the Prospect idea in the first place. Perhaps maybe there is a part of me deep, deep down that really believes I can do what I want to. I only wish that she would assert herself loudly and more often.

"Effie?" I realize both Cam and Harper are staring at me. I look back at them. "You're shivering. Hot tub?"

I laugh, and Cam smiles. "Your lips are purple!" With muscles that are already incredibly stiff, it doesn't take much of a change in temperature to make me shake like a leaf.

Once the air hits my wet body, the clonus kicks in almost before I can fully sit down. I place my hands on my knees in an attempt to get it to stop, but my ankles just won't stop jumping. I can't look at my friends. I'm not ashamed of my body, but I don't like those rare moments where I feel disabled in front of them.

Harper grabs a towel and wraps it around my shoulders, giving me a little hug from behind in the process. "Come on," she says. "Let's get you warm."

From the hot tub, the three of us look out the window together. You can tell it's cold because our view is obstructed by the condensation coating the windows.

"California's looking better and better, right, Effie?" Harper smirks at me.

"What do you mean?" I ask.

"Well, you're the only one of us smart enough to put a warm-weather college on your list. I want to go to school in *Iowa* for god's sake, and Cam in Washington, D.C. Both of us know where we'll be taking our spring breaks!"

The words get caught in my throat. It feels strange to me to think of anything other than Prospect. "I mean, if I go there."

"Right, sure," Harper clarifies. "All I'm saying is that right now, it sounds pretty damn good."

Cam smiles at me through the steam of the water. "If you went to Prospect, though, we could take the bus to see each other." In this very moment, that's maybe a stronger sell than the idea of being near Wilder ever was. Maybe it's the time I lost out on during the fight with Harper, but even though I haven't left my friends yet, it's already feeling like there's not enough time.

"Isn't that where Wilder's going?" Harper says, as though reading my mind.

"Yeah, he got in early decision," I blurt.

They both look my way, smirking at me. They know.

"You were fast with that fact."

There's no point in trying to wear armor. I surrender. "Yeah," I say. "I've thought about the fact that he's going there a lot. Like, a lot a lot."

Now Cam smirks, too. "I called it. I win."

Harper giggles. "Well, it's not like it was too hard to figure out."

My cheeks are burning hotter than the hundred-degree water temp.

"Not that I blame you, Effie," Harper continues. "Wilder's so cute."

"Have you talked to him about it?" Cam asks, a kind smile on her face.

"We talk about a lot of things. Just not about that."

"Why not?" Harper shoots back. "What's there to lose?"

Nothing. And everything.

Right then, the bubbles cut off. The water swooshes as Harper stands and walks out of the tub to restart the timer. I am grateful for the silence.

She walks back down the steps, then pushes to glide on her stomach back to where she was sitting.

"I think you should go for it, Ef." The water droplets on Harper's face make her shimmer.

"I'm partnering on a Student Council project with him," I say, unsure of how else to answer.

"I can't be sure but I think guys only do that type of thing if they want to kiss you," Harper says as she pokes me in the ribs, and I bang snap. "And you want to mack his face, that's pre-established." Harper looks at me pointedly. I try to protest that I haven't said that about Wilder, but my squirm gives me way.

"And the only way to know if it's *mutual* is to *go for it.*" Harper says the last three words like they each have their own exclamation point.

My friends make it seem so easy.

"I don't know if I can." It comes out like a whisper.

They look at me, and I'm tired of hiding, tired of pretending it doesn't matter to me. "I've just never . . . I've never really been able to be honest with boys that I . . . want to spend more time with them."

I expect them to laugh, to tell me it's nothing, to be shocked I haven't done it yet.

"Effie." I turn. Harper is looking at me right in the eyes. "I haven't just been hanging around you all these years for no reason. It's because you're super nice, and thoughtful, and funny, and I love being around you. No one's in your life because they have to be. And any guy who is now or might someday be in your life will be there because he wants to, too."

Harper's support makes me feel emboldened. I wish we'd never had our fight, but I'm glad it's brought us here—supporting each other. I had fun watching her play hockey, and now here she is, cheering for me.

Maybe I was so worried that me being in a wheelchair would scare other people off that I was scaring myself off instead. A tightness arises in my chest. I always think, no matter how many friends I have or whatever I accomplish in life, the first thing anyone will think about me is "she's in a wheelchair."

Feeling newly braver, I say, "I almost did. He drove me home from that Student Council party and I almost did. I swear."

"We believe you." Cam's voice is steady.

I surprise myself by what comes out of my mouth next: "I want to tell him. And I will."

"You can do it," Harper assures me. "Keep trying. You can have that and you deserve that. And I want that for you, too."

﹏

When Mom picks me up the next morning from Harper's house, she asks, "How was your evening?"

"It was fine," I respond. "We really didn't do much of anything."

SECTION III: SPRING

CHAPTER TWENTY-ONE

Wilder and I agreed to go Wednesday after school to get supplies for the bench painting. He's parked in the same space where my mom usually picks me up, but not in the big van he had at homecoming and Seth's party. This time, he has a brown hatchback.

"I thought this would be easier for you to get into than my monster truck," he explains, and I smile.

I open the passenger-side door and do a transfer into the car seat.

"Um." He chews his bottom lip. "I'm not sure how to get this to fit in the trunk."

"I can show you." I sit with my feet still hanging out the car door, my back facing the driver's side. After flipping up both of the brakes, I tell him the wheels have to come off. "Press the big button in the middle by the axle. Then push in and pull out at the same time." My voice is matter-of-fact, as though I am explaining how to put toothpaste on a toothbrush. I have given this explanation so many times.

Wilder follows my instructions, and when the first wheel comes off, the frame of the chair thuds against the asphalt, and he gasps.

"It's okay!" I assure him. Everyone has that reaction. "They're built to withstand stuff."

Tentatively, he removes the second wheel.

"Sometimes that's enough to get it in some people's trunks."

"Okay, let me try."

I hear the rumble of him rearranging everything in the trunk. Just by the sound, I can tell he put one wheel in, and is trying to fit the rest of the chair frame before putting in the other one. There is silence for a second, and then he's opening up the back door.

"There is one more thing we can do if you can't fit it as is!" The back of the seat can fold down if you remove the cushion.

"Nah, I've almost got it. I knew all those hours playing Tetris would pay off in real life somehow." He pushes some boxes and a bottle of antifreeze from the trunk into the backseat.

"Sorry to make you have to rearrange your whole trunk."

"It's all good," he says. "That bottle has been sitting back there since last winter anyway."

When he goes back out and I hear the trunk slam shut, I exhale. There's always the worry that the chair won't fit. We've always managed it somehow—truly like Tetris sometimes—but it is just one more thing I always have to worry about.

"And we're *in!*" he says triumphantly as he slides into the driver's seat.

I can taste another apology on my lips, but Wilder will tell me it's not my fault. And really, there isn't anything to be sorry for. And so I answer, "Let's roll. Figuratively or literally, in my case."

He laughs, a real, genuine one. I make him laugh. He thinks I'm funny.

As soon as he starts the ignition, the radio turns on, and the notes of the opening to NPR's *All Things Considered* chime out.

"Gah! Sorry, this is my mom's car. It's her preset station." He flips to the Top 40 station, where it's currently running a commercial for buying a Honda with zero-percent APR financing, but we don't change it.

"What would your name be if you were a public radio host?" he asks me.

I pretend I'm thinking for a second for the effect. "Euphemia Galanos. It's perfect. No one would ever mispronounce it."

He laughs again, and this time his head rocks back with it. "I walked right into that one, didn't I?"

"What would yours be?" I ask.

His face is pensive, and I can't tell if he's concentrating harder on his driving or my question. "It would be something that looks easy to pronounce based on spelling, like Michael Tutti, but in reality I'd have to be snotty about it and be like it's *Myy-keel Tell-thai.*"

Now it's my turn to laugh. "I would have pegged you for an Adrian Norwell or something."

"Nope," he says, "I truly feel like *Myy-keel Tell-thai* is an extension of my truest self now."

"Well, I can tell you having an easily mispronounced name is not all it's cracked up to be."

"I can imagine." He's quiet for a minute. We pull onto the highway. The radio station announces the start of a commercial-free hour featuring all our favorite hits, and Wilder decelerates a bit as we join up with all the other cars in rush-hour traffic coming from downtown.

Being a professional passenger, I notice a lot more about how people drive. How cautious they are, how soon they signal (or if they signal at all), if they take charge, or if they do that Minnesota four-way-stop thing where we're all too nice to assert ourselves as the car that gets to go.

Wilder is a safe driver, but he doesn't drive ten-and-two, or whatever they teach you in behind the wheel. He's just got one hand gripping the top of the wheel. His other hand is at the bottom of the wheel just resting, his fingers drumming softly to the beat of the latest country-pop crossover hit. I imagine that he's not this easygoing of a driver all the time. I don't know why, but I do.

"How do you actually say it?" he asks, and I look over to face him. "Your name."

"You-phee-mia."

"Euphemia. I like it. It's pretty."

"Thanks." I am blushing hard-core. I don't want him to notice, but there's no way I can hide it. I no longer have to wonder what it'd be like, just me and him. This is what it's like. And I like it so much.

"But I love the name Effie, too. It's just you. It suits you somehow."

This is the only time I've ever felt extremely grateful for my name. "Thanks," I say again. "I can't take credit for it, but it has served me well."

That's it. I have to ask him if he's still dating Sameerah. "Wilder, I was wondering . . ."

"Why don't you ever speak up about it, though?"

"Huh?"

"In class, teachers always mispronounce your name, which, okay, it's an unusual name, whatever. But you never correct them. You just sit there and take it. It's your call, but it's not like people aren't capable of learning how to say your name."

I should be taken aback, but I'm not. If he knew that some people in our school call me "the girl in the wheelchair," what would he say then? I *know* I shouldn't take *that*, but sometimes I don't know how not to.

"Anyway, I wanted to ask if you—"

A car cuts us off on the highway. Wilder brakes quickly, and my chest becomes tense against the pressure of the seat belt.

"Son of a . . . Aw, okay, real nice, buddy! Superb driving, simply A-plus."

I slump back into my seat, snickering. I *knew* it!

"Are you okay? Sorry for the fast brake . . . and I should mention that I have really bad road rage. It's one of my faults, and if my mom mentions it, I'm totally working on it."

"I'm okay," I say. "No complaints here."

And then, once we're out of traffic and coasting, he asks me what I knew was coming: "So, are you totally in love with Prospect?"

I could tell him. But I also know, given how mad he was when the sit-in broke up, that'd he'd be even more angry about this. And he has that glimmer in his eyes, the same excited one I had for months until I went to campus. I can't ruin this for him.

"The classes, and the MMS program, are absolutely incredible." It's not a lie.

"And isn't the campus just amazing?"

I want to agree wholeheartedly. It *is* beautiful. But it's hard to see something as beautiful when it isn't accessible to you.

"So, do you think you'll go?" he asks, and the question looms larger than when he asked me in the fall.

"I haven't gotten in yet." Acceptances come out in just a few weeks' time.

He doesn't fall for my bluff. "Effie, c'mon. You're going to get in and we both know it."

I'm not so sure, but I do smile at his confidence in me. "There's a lot I would still have to figure out, and a lot of things that might be . . . challenging for me."

I have an appointment coming up to look at mobility scooters and power assists. My parents and I decided to explore the options after my campus visit. I'm not thrilled at the thought of having to get one, but it might make the path at Prospect more doable for me, and so, I'll look into it.

I thought Wilder might press me for more details, but he only nods. "Okay, well, my fingers are crossed."

When we pull into the parking lot of Menards, Wilder is thrilled when I mention I have my parking pass with me.

"Yesss! I've never been able to park this close anywhere." When he cuts the engine, he turns to me, grinning. "I'm going to take you everywhere from now on."

He makes me triple-check that he put the wheels on correctly. Each time I tug at them. "See? Secure. Not sliding or anything." I can tell if they are loose just by looking at them, but he doesn't know that.

As I wheel the first few feet toward the storefront, he asks again, "Are you sure I did it right?"

"All good."

"Okay. Don't want you losing a wheel in the middle of the paint aisle."

He grabs a cart, even though we probably won't need one. We're here for a few small cans of paint.

I hold on to the edge of the cart without thinking about it. It's something I always do when I'm out shopping with my family; enjoy the easy, free momentum of their push.

"Hey!" Wilder laughs. "No freeloaders."

"You try pushing up the ramp on the main floor three times a day and then tell me that."

"That's fair," he says. "Do you ever notice how Abe Crawford and Sarah Smith make out all the time on that ramp?"

"Do I notice?" I ask. "How could I not?"

"It's dis-gus-ting! It's like, calm down, no one else cares about your love."

"Harper, Cam, and I call that ramp Swapping Spit Slope."

"Oh my god. So good! Hey," he says. "Let me try to push you and you see if you can push the cart."

I grab on to the cart handle and he pushes me. It works, but steering is a challenge. We veer too far left at one point.

"Oh shit!" Wilder lets go of me and pulls the cart back before it crashes into one of those displays of batteries at the end of the aisle.

"You're going to get us kicked out of here, and where else can we go to save big money, *Wilder?*" I chide him jokingly.

"Suddenly, Seth looks at our receipt and is like, 'How did you go one hundred dollars over budget?' and we're just like, we got kicked out of Menards for clowning around and suddenly everything was priced ten times higher at every other store."

We get to the paint aisle by me holding on to the edge of the cart and Wilder taking a run and jumping up to stand on the rack underneath.

"Now we both get a free ride." He grins.

Our school colors are black and yellow, and I suggest that we could paint one each color.

Wilder shakes his head, scrunching up his face. "Too bumblebee. What about a blue-green?" he suggests. "Like a seafoam?"

"Seafoam? Someone watches their HGTV."

"Shut up. I think it could look good. Plus they'll be bright. People will stop and notice *where* we've put the benches and *why*, which is what we want, for them to notice the whole thing."

I smile. He gets it.

I watch him thumb through the wall of paint chips, so focused. And it dawns on me that this may be my only chance to get my answer. And maybe I was scared of it before, but it's been on my mind for months. So I ask.

"Wilder?" He turns to look at me, and the softness of his eyes makes me bang snap. "Are you still with Sameerah?"

He frowns slightly. "Why would you think that?"

I stare back at him, like it isn't obvious. "Well, you went to homecoming with her, and I see you together . . ."

Moments flash before me. Him touching her elbow at homecoming. Her flirting with her baseball cap at Seth's. The glimpse of her outside our homeroom. It seems impossible that those type of moments can add up to nothing of significance.

But he confirms it. "The homecoming thing was . . . well, she asked me last minute and I said yes. We're friends, that's all." He looks me straight in the eyes when he says, "Effie, I was never with Sameerah."

A baby wails in the background. The employee walkie-talkies beep. A country song from five years ago plays faintly in the background. It is the same place as it was a moment ago, but the ground has shifted underneath me.

We somehow go through the motions of deciding on the seafoam-green color and adding paintbrushes and sandpaper to the cart.

Wilder grins. "This is going to be so awesome. I just wish there was a way to make it huge."

We walk toward the register as I try to make sense of this new elephant in the room. *He was never with Sameerah.* Now when I play back those moments, everything looks slightly different.

And maybe everything can *be* different.

"Wilder?" He turns to look at me and I smile. "Next weekend is my eighteenth birthday, and I'm having a party at my house. Would you like to come?"

He grins. "I wouldn't miss it."

We use the self-checkout. When the prerecorded robot voice says, "Thank you for shopping at Menards!" Wilder says, "It was my absolute pleasure."

Back home, I close the door to my room and think about our bench plan. It's exciting, but I only wish there was a way I could make it even bigger.

While working on an assignment on my laptop, I find myself opening a new document, writing down new sentences:

School Beautification Project doesn't solve real issues.

It doesn't benefit all students.

Disabled students should have a voice.

These aren't just ideas; they're a thesis.

I look up the guidelines to submit an op-ed to our school newspaper.

I'm going big.

CHAPTER TWENTY-TWO

Do you feel any older? That's the question everyone asks you when you have a birthday. But the truth is, I don't. Not really. Eighteen is weird. Now I can vote. I can go out and get a tattoo (not that I'm planning on it). But for the time being, things are still pretty much the same as they were yesterday.

My morning started out by being served a big cinnamon roll on a red plate that says YOU ARE SPECIAL TODAY. It's the same plate Cora and I have had our birthday breakfasts on since we were little kids, so it's got a few chips around the edges, but it's never not made an appearance. At least for me, I realize. Cora has spent her last two birthdays on campus. Maybe this is my last birthday where I will feel exactly like this, my birthday the same as I have always known it. A year from now, I'll have my first birthday without the birthday plate. I try to ignore the combination of weird and sad that I'm feeling.

Dad makes a comment how it seems nearly impossible that

it's been eighteen years since the day I was born. A lot of parents tell their kids about the day they were born, but I don't think any of them do as frequently as mine do. I bet Cora knows more about my birth than her own. It's the story I'm the star of even though I have no memory of it. But each time I am told it, I feel fortunate. It reminds me that going off to college is indeed a very big deal, and there are so many people who cared for me from day one.

Dad gives me one of those cards that sings that Stevie Wonder song. It's such a Dad move. He also wrote on the inside, *I'm excited for all that you've accomplished so far and all that's yet to come.* It's also a very Dad thing to say.

Cora arrives around noon and we go out to lunch at my favorite restaurant. Drew drove her down, and gets out of the car to meet my parents. I watch as Dad shakes his hand, gripping a little too tightly.

"Join us, Drew," Dad suggests.

"Oh, I don't want to intrude," he says.

"It's my birthday and I insist, so you have to do it." Drew grins at me.

Over lunch, Drew shares that he's planning to study abroad in Spain in the fall, and Cora is hoping to go visit him. I catch him put his hand on her knee under the table and she smiles. I may be officially an adult, but my sister is out here being one, for real.

❧

When we get home from lunch, Mom, Dad, and I head to the kitchen while Cora and Drew are unloading the car.

"So, about tonight, Dad and I will be here during the party—" Mom starts, but feeling brave, feeling older, I cut her off.

"Can you go to a movie during the party? Everything will go all right here, and Cora and Drew will be here if it doesn't anyway."

Mom and Dad look at each other, evaluating what I've said, and just how much they're willing to let me grow up tonight.

Dad delivers the verdict. "Yeah, sure, honey, that sounds good."

I sit a bit taller as I go into my room and start to put my gifts away and my new clothes in the hamper. Ten minutes later, I hear a knock.

"Hey, birthday girl." Cora opens the door a crack, smiling. "Can I come in?"

I tell her yes, and she slips in, closing the door behind her.

She lies down on the bed and I join her, both of us leaning against the big pillows. Our brown curls fan out and intermingle with one another.

"Extremely bold of you to announce you're planning a trip abroad," I tell her. "Mom and Dad will want to talk that over later."

"Oh, I know," she laughs. "But I've been saving up all semester. I can't go four months without seeing him." I've never heard her talk about a boy that way. "But I'm sorry I planted the seed on your birthday and stole your spotlight a bit," she says, laughing softly. "Classic Cora."

"It's okay." And I mean that. I have a lot of experience running interference between my parents and my sister. "Everything okay out there?" I can hear Mom and Dad and Drew carrying on a conversation. "You're really leaving him out there to fend for himself?"

"Oh yeah. I figure if he survives this, we can keep dating. *Anyway*," she chirps, her voice all singsongy. "I wanted to give you this." From behind her, she pulls out a small gray box, with a navy blue bow on it. "I picked this out a few weeks ago. I sent Drew to pick it up and get it wrapped. He took it so seriously. He was all"—her voice drops lower, mimicking—"*I can't mess up your sister's eighteenth-birthday present.* He wants you to know he picked out the color of the bow."

"It's a very nice bow." I catch a glance at my sister, who has a silly grin on her face. It is the look of a girl who is completely smitten with her boyfriend, and, from the laughter coming from the kitchen, whose boyfriend is completely winning over her parents.

I pull off the ribbon and lift the lid off the box. Inside white tissue paper sits a bracelet on a thin, dainty gold chain. Connecting the chain in the middle is a charm in the shape of a key. I squint, and see that in the middle of the key the word BRAVE is engraved.

ONCE
upon a
BOOKCLUB
Open your gift

that she's sitting
e key."

"Do I?" I ask, part joking, part serious.

But my sister doesn't seem to think it's funny. "Effie, yes. You *are* brave."

Everyone around me believes it. And maybe, now that I'm an adult, I guess, I should start believing in me, too.

"Do you like it?" Cora asks.

"It's beautiful."

"Good." She takes it out of the box and undoes the clasp, placing it on my wrist.

"Thank you, Cora."

"Anything for my not-so-little little sister."

❧

Cora lets me borrow a blue dress with bright flowers on it, which I wear over black leggings and black booties. She does my makeup and applies a gold shimmery eye shadow. It glints in the light just like the bracelet on my wrist.

Harper and Cam are the first to arrive, and nervous excitement fills my chest. They're surprised to see Cora, and she gives them both a quick hug before introducing them to Drew. It's the first time I've heard her introduce him as "my boyfriend."

While the two of them slip away to take Harper's and Cam's coats to the bedroom, Harper says, "Okay, Cora, I see you. He's *hot*."

Their gift to me is they're letting me borrow Cam's Polaroid camera, and they brought some funny props, like those way-too-big sunglasses in neon colors.

Drew goes back into full photographer mode. "Okay, ladies. Let me see you strike a pose."

While we're busy posing, the doorbell rings. Ali and Calvin show up, followed by a few of the people who were in our homecoming group. My sister has everything set up in the living room, including the pizza, the snacks, and the party hats. Drew seems content to manage the playlist as an impromptu DJ, although he has to take requests from Calvin every five minutes. A ways in, Cora has the great idea to break out our Bluetooth karaoke mic.

I try not to worry too much about whether Wilder shows, even though I am very aware of every minute that ticks by without him here. I distract myself with the karaoke, which is a hit. We've already worked our way through most of Taylor Swift's hits. Right as I belt the last line of "I Knew You Were Trouble," I realize Wilder has walked in.

He grins, dimple and all. He nods toward the mic in my hands. "Put me down for a rendition of Ariana Grande's 'Into You.' It's my go-to for karaoke."

He said he wouldn't miss it, and he wasn't lying. Wilder is in my house, at my birthday party.

I don't hesitate. I wheel right over and hug him. He returns the hug, and it's tighter than the one he gave me when he was accepted to Prospect. I don't think about anyone or anything else in that moment, I just do what I want.

"Happy eighteenth, Effie." His voice rumbles in his chest and I feel his breath in my ear, whispering something that's only for me to hear.

I watch him say hi to my friends and clap Calvin on the back like they've been friends for a million years.

Cora saunters up behind me. "I saw that hug." Her voice drops low. The heat rises in my cheeks. "That's the guy you went to homecoming with, right?"

"I didn't go to homecoming *with* him, he was in my group. And we're just friends."

"Are you sure about that?" Cora asks.

I was, I think. But now the line is blurry.

I watch her slink away, a smirk on her lips.

She walks right up to him and extends her hand for him to shake. Over the pop beat, I hear, "Hi, I'm Effie's sister, Cora."

He's here because I asked him. And it feels right.

Eventually, Drew has to leave to drive back to school. Cora will stay one more night, and Dad plans to drive her back in the morning.

When I go back to my room for a second to take my phone off the charger, I can hear them saying goodbye at the side door.

"Do you think I did okay?" he asks.

"You did great, baby," she reassures him. There's a slight

pause, and I know they've snuck a kiss. "You won my parents over, my sister . . ." Another pause. "And me."

I smile to myself. I wouldn't mind having something like that for myself someday. Who knows what the future will hold, but I wouldn't mind if Drew stayed a part of our family's.

I'm absentmindedly checking my phone and closing the door to my room to go back to the living room when I hear "Effie?"

Wilder has come out of the bathroom, switching off the light.

"Is that your room? Can I see it?"

My brain races, trying to remember if there are any dirty socks on the floor, or if any bra straps are poking out from the top drawer. "Y-yeah." I fumble, then recover. "For sure."

I reopen the door and turn on the light. My bed is in the middle of the room, the baby blue comforter a little rumpled from Cora sitting on it, but otherwise, everything looks fine. I move to the side and let Wilder step inside. I try to imagine it as he sees it. The light yellow walls that I chose when I was ten. My little bookshelf that's been there since I was a baby, some of my picture books mixed in with some YA novels and a romance novel I stole off Mom's shelf. Can he see the leftover remnants of sticky tack that I once used to put glow-in-the-dark stars up above my bed?

My bedside table is white, and in middle school, Mom had a piece of glass fitted for the top of it so that I could slide photos underneath. Wilder walks over and looks at them, and with a jolt, I now remember I haven't swapped out the pictures since then: me and Cora, Harper and me in our Girl Scout vests, a photo of me and Dad when I was in the awkward acne-and-braces phase.

"This is nice," he says. "Girl Scout uniforms are super attractive."

I blush, even though I know he's only teasing.

I have a boy in my room. Like, *in my room*. My parents and I have never had to set rules for this type of thing, because it's never happened.

I watch him standing, his hands politely clasped behind his back. I wish he was more relaxed. I wish I was next to him. I wish his arms were wrapping me up. I wish, I wish, I wish.

He takes a step backward and trips a little, knocking into something on the floor.

He speaks fast. "Oh! Oh no. I'm sorry." He kneels down, and I hear paper being shuffled. It takes a minute for it to connect. *My college file folders.* Since the applications are in, Mom moved them in here. I wheel over right away.

"You don't have to . . . I can pick that up . . . Don't . . ." I stumble. I see papers from Prospect, Berkeley, and more. Printouts that clearly read OFFICE OF DISABILITY SERVICES with Mom's highlights and notes in the margins.

It's like he's seen me naked.

Wilder is smart, and I know he knows now what all of this entails. He gives me a look that suggests maybe he should have guessed this, but is embarrassed it took this long. Like possibly he knows why I was so vague about whether I might actually go to Prospect.

He stuffs everything back into their respective file folders as best he can, then places the crate upright, and the files back in place.

I clear my throat. He stands up.

"I think . . . I think we're going to do cake pretty soon."

He grins. "I'm always down for cake. Lead the way."

❧

Once everyone's left and we're cleaning up, I'm sad to see that it's past midnight, my birthday officially over. On Harper's Story is a clip of her singing Beyoncé's "Single Ladies" while Calvin attempts to do the dance in the background. In the corner, I eye Wilder laughing.

I pick up the thick stack of Polaroids and head back to my room to call it a night.

I plug my phone in on my nightstand. My eye catches my wrist, and I decide not to take the bracelet off. I want it to be the first thing I see when I wake up. I set the photos down on the nightstand, a new collection to update my collage with, finally.

I notice inside the stack sits a small envelope. I'm certain it's from Mom, a last-second attempt to get all sappy and emotional.

I open it, and a scrap of paper flutters to the floor. I bend down to grab it. It's one of those HELLO, MY NAME IS name tags. EFFIE is written big and bold, the smell of Sharpie ink still fresh.

The Post-it is stuck to the inside of the envelope. I pull it out carefully.

> So you never forget to speak up about
> your name, or about anything else.
>
> Happy birthday!
>
> —Wilder

With a sharp intake of breath, I tuck the note back in the envelope. I slide the name tag underneath the glass, for safekeeping.

CHAPTER TWENTY-THREE

3:37 p.m.

I am about to burst. Every nerve in my body is electrified. When Mom sees me check the time on my phone again, she snatches it from my hands.

I give her a look.

"For the last time, Effie. This place books out appointments weeks in advance. If I'd known, I wouldn't have scheduled it for right now, obviously. I'm sorry." She tucks my phone deep into her purse, which lets me know that I'm not going to be getting it back for a very long time.

When I slump in my chair, she's the one to give me a look. "This is important. Getting something with power could make your college experience very different. And you're the only one who can communicate what would and wouldn't work best for you. And so, *for the next hour,* I'm going to need you to be present, *fully* present."

I want to say that learning which college campuses I might

actually get *a chance* to be on would positively affect this appointment, but I know to keep my mouth shut. Of all the days, of all the times, Mom *had* to schedule this appointment at my medical supply center on March 28 during the hours of the late afternoon when my phone might ping, *There has been an update to your admissions status posted on the Common Application portal.*

Looking around, this is not the place I want to find out my fate anyway. The waiting room of this company is also their showroom. The room is sterile, the carpets tan, with matching uncomfortable seats like you'd see in a doctor's office. Next to us are tiny end tables covered with six-month-old issues of *National Geographic* and *Marie Claire.* Circling us around the outside of this expansive room are things that make me feel, well, to be honest, like I'm way too *young* to be here.

Little corners of the room are meant to look like model bathrooms with fake toilets behind fake tile, showcasing the large grab bars and the emergency alarm pull chain you can install in your own home. There are various sizes of shower benches with and without backs, and with varying degrees of sturdiness. There's even that electric chair that slides you up and down a full flight of stairs in your home.

In my direct line of vision are the power wheelchairs. And next to them sit the mobility scooters, the purpose of this appointment.

I wheel over to get a closer look. One is bright red, one is blue. The sign next to it reads *Our FastMove 3.0 model has been magnificently redesigned to make a splash in the industry!*

I snort so loudly that Mom gives me a look.

I go back to studying the scooters. It's not that their sign is so strange. Well, mostly. I've always used a manual chair. Having a power option to go long distances across a campus *could* make a real difference. I look at the specs advertised: 360-degree-pivot turning radius, reaching top speeds of four miles per hour. *About the speed of a bike ride,* the representative on the phone had said. I could get places in half the time, basically without expending any physical effort. That sounds amazing.

But Mom doesn't get it. The only time I've ever seen people in scooters are inside Target and Home Depot. Last night when Mom was researching special bags and attachments you can put on them, the copy for one read *Perfect for attending craft swaps!* My favorite activity.

I likely need, or at some point will need, a lot of things in this showroom. But none of it is marketed toward me. None of it shows a girl like me just trying to get to the dining hall before it closes, or zooming across campus to catch the latest episode of my favorite TV show with my friends, increasing the speed, as there's only ten minutes before it starts.

I'm already "the girl in the wheelchair" everywhere I go. And now, right as I start college, making a first impression in front of all new people, I have to be "the girl in the grandma scooter," too?

"Effie?"

The sales representative calls my name and Mom stands. He takes us to a private space where he's set out several types of wheelchairs and a FastMove 3.0.

He smiles at me warmly. "You still liking your titanium manual?"

"It's great."

"It's definitely one of the most popular wheelchairs we sell. Very high-end. Lots of satisfied customers." He talks about my wheelchair like it's a Mercedes-Benz. He sits, scribbling a few things in his clinic notes. When he checks the date on his phone, I catch that it's now 3:48 p.m. It's one hour later in New York. My Prospect decision could be coming out any minute.

"But what we're here for today is to look at getting you something with some power as you prepare to go to college?"

"That's the plan," I say.

"Where are you headed?" he asks.

Give me my phone and I might be able to tell you right now.

Mom decides not to give me an opening, filling in, "She wants to go to Prospect in New York City."

"How wonderful!" he exclaims. I can tell by the tone in his voice that he's genuinely impressed. He's quiet for a second, brow furrowed. "What's the city like for a chair user?"

"Well, truthfully, tough," Mom answers. "Maybe with power, even just to get around the campus, things could be easier."

Provided I get in. Maybe they saw the challenges during my visit and put me in the no pile. Maybe it all stops here, in this sad office, right now.

"Let's get you in something fit to cruise those city streets!"

❧

My first option is power assist wheels. They would attach to my regular manual chair, and I would switch between them and my regular wheels when needed. I transfer from my own chair to the show version. Sitting in someone else's chair feels a bit like I imagine driving a rental car would: close, but not quite right.

Instinctively, I put my hands on the rims and give a big push forward. The wheels make a sound like a revving engine and I pop into a wheelie that I wasn't expecting. Forget a bang snap, I startle a firecracker worth. The chair zips across the room and I almost run into a wall on the other side.

Mom and I look alarmed, but the guy just smiles. "So, what you're noticing here is that you don't have to push the power wheels anywhere near as hard as you do on a manual chair. A slight tap will do."

I'm still waiting for my adrenaline to settle, shaking slightly. I tap the wheels, and the chair zips quickly across the room again, almost too quickly for my liking. I'm lacking the control I usually feel.

Once happily back in my own chair, he has me practice taking off the power wheels. They weigh significantly more than what I'm used to, due to the motor. What about having to take them off to charge every night? I imagine my friends having to put them in the trunks of their cars, or having to carry the extra weight down the subway stairs because the elevator is out.

Provided that NYC is still on the table.

The nail in the coffin is that they can't get wet, which makes them not too useful for plowing through a snowbank. We move on to a power wheelchair with a joystick.

I am not any good with the joystick. I blame Mom for not letting Cora and me have video games as kids. I only move the chair in inch-by-inch increments, stopping and starting in little jolts like I just got my learner's permit.

"Honey, hold the joystick down and keep it down. Only release it when you want to stop." Even with Mom coaching from the sidelines, I suck at this. They suggest I try turning onto and going up the small ramp in the showroom, but I can't even get myself properly turned in that direction.

The moment I sit on the scooter, something feels different.

"I can tell just by the way you're able to sit in it and the look on your face that we may be onto something here," the guy remarks. Dang it. I don't want to like this. The two speeds are marked on the dial by a rabbit and a turtle, for god's sake. But on turtle mode, I'm able to turn and make my way up the ramp, cautiously weaving around everything else that was in the main showroom where we came in. He lets me put my coat and gloves back on and drive out into the parking lot. Even with the added thickness of my gloves, I can operate the throttle and steer just fine. The fact that simply releasing the throttle makes the brake click on immediately makes me feel in control.

"Come on," Mom says, smiling. "Crank it all the way up!"

I turn it to the rabbit icon and go all the way around the edge of the parking lot. The scooter immediately breaks through the gross, wet gray slush, remnants of winter that would normally be a fight in my chair. I've done three laps, and I'm not even tired. This wouldn't solve all my problems, I know. But I can actually picture myself on the path at Prospect right now. Instead of struggling, I'm keeping up with everybody else. It's in a slightly different way than most people, but similar to Mr. Goldberg, maybe I can have nostalgic moments of scootering through campus with the leaves changing.

I mean, you know, if I got into Prospect after all.

When I pull back up next to Mom, I hear her say, "I'll have to go over everything with my husband first," but let him know it would be a good idea to draft an order. He slips her a couple of flyers on the scooter, and she tucks them into her purse.

When I get back into my chair, it feels a little anticlimactic. If I had both, I could have the best of both worlds. True flexibility.

As Mom snaps a photo of both the scooters on the floor, the red and the blue, I think the blue is kind of cool, actually. Maybe I could put some bumper stickers on it to make it more me.

As we go out the door, the bell above us dings. "Hey, Effie!" the rep calls out. "Good luck with the college decision! I can't wait to hear where you'll go."

Me neither, I want to say. But I call back, "Thank you!"

❧

In the car, Mom doesn't give me my phone, and I don't ask for it either. We don't talk, and everything is quiet save for the clicking of the turn signal and the public radio playing in the background. I don't make a sound even when I hear Wilder's voice in the back of my head saying, *"Myy-keel Tell-thai."*

Today doesn't feel like a day when my whole life could change. The sky is gray and cloudless, like it might sleet. Even though it's spring by calendar time, it never is by Minnesota time, and we have the heated seats on still. I shiver, even though my body feels warm. Maybe my whole life won't change, exactly, but maybe all the pieces of this puzzle I've been putting together for months and months will fall into place. Maybe.

❧

We pull into the driveway and it hits me: This is the last moment my future will be a big, blank abyss. In a few minutes, I am going to open the door just a crack.

Mom gets my chair out of the trunk like always and sets it

next to the passenger-side door. I thought I would be bounding through the door, but instead I unbuckle slowly, thankful for the silence. When I get into the chair, Mom is standing there, looking at me. Suddenly, I feel a strong and unexpected desire for her to wrap her arms around me and tell me it will all be okay.

I don't give in to the urge, but maybe she can tell what I need, because she smiles. "This is big, kid. It's so exciting." I smile, too. "So proud of you, no matter what."

When we go inside, Dad is sitting in the living room chair, waiting for us. "Well?" His voice is high, the question loaded. He means my admissions decisions, not the scooter.

"She hasn't checked yet," Mom says, her voice a bit hushed. Mom rummages in her purse and pulls out the flyers on the FastMove 3.0. Dad examines them, brow furrowed.

Quietly, I hear her whisper, "I think she really liked it." Louder, she says, "Tell Dad what you thought, Effie."

I want to explain about how I never thought I'd be the type of person who needed a scooter. About how I'm already thinking about how it could possibly fit in my dorm room. About whether it will impact how people at whatever college I go to view me and what I am capable of.

Instead, I say, "I think it will make some of . . ." I move my arms around, gesticulating broadly. "All of *this*, more possible for me."

Dad grins. It is gentle and loving, like the smile he gave me when I first told him I wanted to go to Prospect.

Mom rummages in her bag again and pulls out my phone. She holds it out, screen down. I take it, but don't look at it. Instead, I climb up on the tall chair by the kitchen island. I pull out the laptop. My future deserves the big screen. Mom and Dad walk over and stand behind me.

"Can't wait to see what all your options are," Mom tells me. And there's something about the way she emphasizes "all" that I know that she still sees Prospect as an option, if I wanted that. If I chose it, she'd be happy for me.

They are all in my email, all lined up together: the six notices of updates to my admission decisions at six schools.

I start low stakes, with Wright University, the college in Wisconsin. My cursor hovers for just a second—the final seconds of this phase of everything. I click "View Decision" and log in.

The screen loads, going blank for a second before showing a scan of a letter on official university letterhead. One word stands out: **Congratulations!**

"All right!" Dad exclaims.

"You're going to college, officially," Mom adds.

Officially. Getting to this moment has taken two years, but in reality, my whole life.

Off to a good start and the nerves slightly at bay, I move on to Cannon River.

Dear Euphemia,

We are pleased to inform you . . .

"Excellent!" Mom exclaims. She looks at Dad. "Both our girls could go there. Wouldn't that be something?"

I don't want to check Northwestern, because if I do, then I am only left with three schools: University of Minnesota, Berkeley, and, of course, Prospect.

But then again, I want to check Northwestern right away so I don't have to wait any longer to find out about the three schools I care most about: my close-to-home safety, my California adventure, and my dream school. I bite my bottom lip nervously. Dad's hand lands lightly on my shoulder. *The decisions are already out*, I remind myself. *I've done all I can do. I deserve to know, so I can move forward.*

I click "view decision."

We regret to inform you . . .

"I didn't get into Northwestern," I say, even though they can read the screen behind me. It was always a reach. But still. To know that my essay, something I put so much time and energy into, about what is right now my biggest goal, didn't strike a chord makes me feel a bit sad.

I shake off the disappointment just as soon as the cool surge of adrenaline washes over me again.

Here we go. "View the update to your University of Minnesota admissions decision."

The screen loads with a maroon background with gold font, nice and big: **Congratulations! You're in.**

"Effie, that's so wonderful!" Mom sounds genuinely excited. And much to my surprise, I am, too. Weirdly, it makes me feel like the time when I was a little kid and Mom said it was still okay to bring my teddy bear to my first sleepover. I don't want to go to the U; I've said it before and I still mean it. But as excited as I am about my future, I am not quite ready to give up my security blanket. I am glad to still have my fail-safe, even if I hope not to have to use it.

There are now only two unread emails in my inbox. I start to tremble a little bit. Damn tight muscles always giving me away when I most want to keep my cool. I wish that they still sent out the letters first. At least then, I would know by looking at them—little letter is a no, big packet is a yes, right? That seems less stressful.

It's time to rip the Band-Aid off. Resisting the urge to go to my bedroom and pull the covers over my head, I click open the email from Berkeley and click the link to the update. Dad tightens his grip on my shoulder.

The screen loads. There's a video that starts playing automatically. A group of enthusiastic students in Berkeley sweatshirts exclaim, "We're thrilled to welcome you to the Cal Bear family!"

My hands fly to my face before I even realize it. "Omigod!" I yell out in one breath, surprising myself.

Top-twenty material. Look, I know rankings aren't everything.

But when I submitted my final list of colleges to my guidance counselor, they told me that, of the few students from my school who have applied to Cal in recent years, they've only taken one.

And this year, they took me.

I'm the girl with the difficult-to-pronounce name. I'm the girl who wants to work in digital media. I'm the girl in the wheelchair, too. But today, I get to be the girl who got into Berkeley.

Now Mom is wrapping me up, in the same way I wished she would only a short while ago. Only now, I don't need the hug to tell me everything is going to be all right. She's telling me that everything has turned out just the way it was meant to be.

"I am so, so proud of you, Effie. You're amazing." This is a sentence that moms say to their kids a lot. And it can be something disabled people hear a lot. Go somewhere on my own? So amazing. Push through the blatant discrimination toward me at my high school? So proud. And so I usually brush it off. But right now, I have to admit that I'm proud of myself, too.

Now this is truly it. Mom, Dad, Cora, even Mr. Andersen, they've all told me the same thing. My life will go on if I don't get into every school I wanted to. Plenty of people don't get into their first-choice colleges every year, and they go on to be thriving college students and successful adults.

I don't want to ruin this moment. But I also want to see if the moment can get any better. So with glossy eyes and shaky breath, I open the email from Prospect.

Dear Euphemia,

Congratulations! We are pleased to welcome you to the Prospect University class of . . .

My hands completely cover my face and both my parents wrap themselves around me.

"I got into Prospect," I squeak. I don't want to say it too loudly, as though it's like a house of cards that the wind could topple over at any second.

Prospect isn't perfect. But I can do hard things and be successful. My acceptances prove that. And that with my possible new transportation options and creativity and hard work, it might just work.

"You got in, indeed!" Dad says, a chuckle in his voice.

"Effie, honey, read the rest!" says Mom. It is only then that I notice Dad's hand is no longer resting on my shoulder. He's wrapped his arm around Mom, in a sideways embrace. They've told me that I was going to go to college for as long as I can remember . . . they didn't exactly know how, but the expectation was set. Maybe a dream of their own is coming true right now, too.

I scroll down, the words blurring through my tears. Toward the bottom of the letter, I make out:

Based on your exemplary application and the strong feedback from your interview session, we would like to award you the Women in Media Scholarship for $4,000, renewed annually, to support your education at Prospect. This scholarship is handed out to a select number of incoming students in Prospect's Mass Media and Society major, indicative of their promise in the field. We hope you view this honor as an

indication of how much we would love to have you join the Prospect family.

My mind goes to all the students, all over the world, logging on to their laptops or refreshing their phones at this moment, waiting to find out their fate, same as me. Maybe there are a lot of students who deserve something like this. But today, I remind myself that I deserve it, too.

I got into my dream school. They aren't ready for me, and even they've admitted that. But they want me.

Prospect University wants me. They want me just as much as I've wanted them.

CHAPTER TWENTY-FOUR

I stare at the words inside the notification on my iPhone screen.

It's the first week of April. The bell rang ten minutes ago. Even though the hallways are mostly emptied out, I'm still looking over my shoulder for Wilder. *Did you get in??* He'd DM'd earlier that day, explaining that he had a dentist appointment and would be missing Student Council. I hate to admit it, but I was relieved. I didn't lie, but it was easier to type this half-truth than to try to bumble through it in front of him.

I look at the message one more time. *I got IN!*

. . . But . . . my DM makes it seem like I'm so excited, and in reality I'm so conflicted.

. . . But . . . Wilder deserves to know, and I *am* so excited.

. . . But maybe . . . I don't know.

I stare at the blinking cursor for a few seconds longer before impulsively pressing Send and promptly tucking my phone away. I only have three weeks before I have to sign my name away to a college, and I'm leaving tomorrow for Berkeley, during our spring break. Now that I've gotten in, it's time to see the campus. I can't rely on the experience portrayed by glossy booklets and flashy websites. Those lie and let you get your hopes up.

My phone buzzes, and I wonder if it's Wilder responding. But it's Mom letting me know she's here to pick me up. I text back, saying I'm on the second floor and I'll be down soon. I don't usually roam the halls after school, but today, I need space to clear my head. Or at least try to.

~

Mom, Dad, and I fly into SFO late that night and spend the next day doing touristy stuff around SF (I read online that you're never supposed to call it "San Fran," as it's a dead give-away that you're definitely not a local. I keep reminding Dad, but he keeps reminding me that we're *not* locals, so why does it matter anyway?)

We go to Fisherman's Wharf, a place with a ton of restaurants and tourist attractions like a Madame Tussauds and one of those walk-through exhibits that claims to be historical but it's basically a glorified haunted house playing up the Alcatraz stuff. We eat at the sourdough-bread place where you can watch them in the window as they make bread loafs shaped like turtles. We watch the sea lions (they have actual sea lions here. Like, in public) barking low and guttural, their flabby skin wet from the water and glistening in the sun. Honestly, just from the tiny bit of the extremely hilly city I've seen, I'm not sure how a person in a wheelchair could live independently in San Francisco, and I'm nervous about what Berkeley might be like.

Looking up from the dock, I can see the Golden Gate Bridge, tiny in the background in the expanse of blue water, but there nonetheless. The real thing, red and regal.

Dad catches my eye and says, "Can't get that in New York."

While we wait for the BART to Berkeley, I can't get his words out of my head. Because he's right. I can't get any of that in New York. Because this isn't New York. All day I've tried to suck it up, to be a good sport and keep an open mind. But it's hard, trying not to think of Fisherman's Wharf as the Times Square of the Bay, the Golden Gate their Statue of Liberty.

I wonder if this is what it feels like to go on the first date after you've had your heart broken. Nothing about this new place is the same, and of course, why would it be? But I can't help but look for all the things that remind me of that other love, wasting my first impressions finding second-rate comparisons instead of trying to find new things to like just as much.

The BART train toward Richmond pulls up. It feels similar but different to the subway. The doors open and the next thing I know, I'm on board and securing my brakes in place in the accessible seating area. I realize I've missed the point. It's not the New York City subway. Because I just boarded completely independently.

Mom and Dad sit behind me, my back facing them. I'm glad they can't see my face, grinning like a little kid. I'm embarrassed for letting anything get the best of me.

The train picks up speed and it's *loud*. I'm not even comparing anymore, but it's louder than any train I've ever experienced, buzzing so much, almost like a high-pitched howl. As we cruise along, the scenery is still urban, but without feeling crowded. I can see individual houses with brown roofs. Green plants. And the water. I can see the water.

Once the train passes Embarcadero Station, we're leaving San Francisco and crossing into the East Bay.

West Oakland Station.

12th Street/Oakland City Center.

19th Street.

MacArthur.

And then we move underground and it's dark.

When we surface, and Ashby Station is announced overhead, there's a rush of excited nervousness. I'm in Berkeley. Not only that, but I traveled several miles on public transit, through three cities and across a body of water without anyone helping me. That's an experience I've never had before. It's something I haven't even imagined, because I wasn't sure it was possible.

We advance to the next stop, darker tile and underground with 1970s-style architecture. When the doors open at Downtown Berkeley Station, I don't wait for Mom and Dad, I just roll right on out to see what's next.

◆

I swallow thickly, trying to quell my nerves. I'm here on Cal's campus. The part of the campus where I entered, with big evergreen trees and shallow creeks, reminded me of Minnehaha Parkway in Minneapolis.

But near me now there are all these twisty, knobby, leaf-less trees that look like nothing I've seen in the Midwest. I move a few feet and notice another shallow creek right below me. It calms me a bit, makes me feel less far from home.

I triple-check the details in my email:

Subject: Overnight Stay at Cal

Hi, Effie!

This is just a reminder that your prospective-student host, Talia Givens, will be picking you up out in front of Sather Gate at 5:30 p.m.

I look up. The green gate welcomes me, large and almost auspicious. It doesn't surprise me that they arrange for prospective students to be greeted here; it's impressive, a grand entrance into a new chapter.

I don't open social—I don't want to post anything from this trip . . . not yet. I learned that with Prospect. Also, I can't bear to see Wilder's response to the news that I got in. Just seeing the bright red *1* icon indicating a new message is enough for now.

I look down at my duffel bag. I think back to my overnight back in Cora's dorm. I was nervous then, and sure, I'm nervous now. I'm staying with a stranger, after all, not my sister. But I don't feel like a little kid going off to her first sleepover anymore. I'm here to figure out how this all would work for me. I'm an adult taking control.

"Effie?"

I jolt at the unfamiliar voice, the bang snap being the one thing I'll never get control of.

"Oh, do you have a startle? Some of my friends do, too."

"Yeah," I get out, though it sounds higher than I expected. Rarely does anyone just get it. Except for this girl with her black hair pulled into a slick ponytail, wearing a green camouflage jacket and sitting in the wheelchair in front of me. Instinctively, I look at her hands, and notice she has the same callouses on the base of her thumb that I do, rough spots from wheeling.

"Are you Talia?" I ask.

Before I have time to wonder if she'll shake my hand, she goes in for the hug, the front parts of the frames of our wheelchairs tapping together when we do. It feels strange to hug someone at my level height.

"Welcome to Cal!" she says.

Prospect never had a student like me. Cal welcomes me with one.

Before I can finish saying, "These are my parents . . . ," she's over there shaking their hands.

"Nice to meet you," Dad says, but it comes out more as a question, his voice rising slightly at the end, like he can't quite believe what he's seeing. Neither can I.

Mom beams, then whips around again to face me. "You ready?"

It comes out before I think about it. "Ready." I don't know quite what I'm getting into. But I am ready.

So I don't overthink it.

With a quick wave to Mom and Dad, I balance my duffel bag on my lap and I follow Talia through the gate.

I'm ready to try again.

CHAPTER TWENTY-FIVE

"So the grade of the sidewalks here is . . . well, it's *fine*."

I'm trailing behind Talia, trying to take in the campus but mostly trying not to lose sight of her as she weaves around students walking through on a Sunday evening.

"Mm-hmm," I reply. It's not that I'm not interested in what she has to say. Quite the opposite actually. It's not often that I find someone who will talk openly about sidewalk grades. I'm having trouble keeping up and balancing my duffel bag at the same time. If I was with a non-disabled person, they probably would have asked if I needed help at least twice in the last ten minutes, or, god forbid, just started pushing my chair without asking. Maybe this is how it is to be with people who automatically understand—they always let you figure out how to manage your own stuff.

"I mean," Talia continues, "the campus is pretty hilly. Are

you thinking of getting a power option for school? You're going to want one."

I think of the application for the FastMove 3.0 that I have open with the insurance company. I'm hoping to be approved soon, and to have the blue model before the end of the summer. "Yeah, I'm working on it," I huff, hoping she doesn't notice I'm falling too far behind.

"Good," she says, putting her hands on the rims of her wheels and slowing to an almost stop. Thank god. "I used to be so anti-power chair or anything like it. And then I thought about how there's, like, no shoulder replacements or anything, and it's ten times harder for us to get to class, so screw my own assumptions or anything other people might think, and got a power assist. It's been a lifesaver." She launches into a story about how one time a cloud broke open right as she and her friends were walking back to the dorms, and she took off at top speed with her power assist. But I'm still back on the last thing she said. About screwing her assumptions or what anybody else has to say about a scooter. "—And my friends thought it was totally unfair, but of course it wasn't. If they really wanted out of the rain, they could've just run." Her eye catches mine. "You good?"

"I'm fine."

"Look, no one at college gives a shit about whether you get around in a chair or a scooter or whatever else. And if they do, then that's ableist."

"I know," I say. And I do. I've been telling myself that every day since I first decided on the scooter. But it takes a lot of work to unlearn all the bullshit you've unknowingly been fed your entire life.

"You hungry? We could go to the dining hall. You'll get a guest pass."

I accept, grateful for something other than a big helping of the truth, served hot.

❧

During dinner, I learn three things: (1) Talia's from Portland, is a sophomore, and is majoring in Political Science, or as everyone at college seems to call it, "poli-sci." (2) There are people at the Berkeley dining hall who will help you carry your tray and dish your food for you. I didn't know that going in, but I followed Talia's lead. It was a little awkward at first, telling someone else what you feel like eating and then communicating your preferred portion size, but it was better than the fear of dropping my tray in front of everybody. (Cora says at Cannon if someone drops their tray, the whole hall applauds loudly. Super embarrassing.) And (3) Talia has a boyfriend, who is really cute. His name is Brennon and he's non-disabled.

That was the first thought to enter my head, about two seconds after he walked up to our table and I realized who he was. And I hate myself for it. I swat it away as fast as I can. I should be focusing on the adorable squareness of his jaw or how he lets Talia steal fries off his plate. But the thing is, in my high school, you don't see a non-disabled person and a disabled person just *being together*. Enjoying each other's company. In fact, the more I think about it, I don't think I've ever seen a non-disabled and a disabled person dating. Ever. In my whole life.

As I watch the couple seated across from me, I wonder why it took so long. As I'm looking at Talia, I'm not thinking she's pretty . . . for a girl in a wheelchair. She's pretty, period. And despite only knowing her about ninety minutes, I can tell she's special, and Brennon is lucky to be with her.

Maybe this is another thing people won't give a shit about once I'm in college. Maybe I can learn not to get so hung up on it either.

They say you can't be what you don't see. Well, I just saw it. So I can have that, too.

❧

It's like magic. Talia presses a little remote no bigger than a Bluetooth car key and her dorm room door opens.

I must look shocked, because she smiles, then shrugs, showing me a blue-and-gold lanyard with CAL BEARS stitched down the sides. "It's a remote that attaches to your keychain. They can get you one for your dorm if you want one. I had the same reaction. In my high school they couldn't be bothered to replace a door opener if it stopped working, and then I got here and it was easier. I felt like there had to be some sort of catch."

We both wheel inside, and instantly, I know Cora would be jealous of Talia's room. She has a roommate, so there's two beds, but it's much larger than the double room my sister has. In fact, I know I haven't seen a ton of dorm rooms, but this one might fall in the category of "huge," as much as a dorm room can be called that. There's room for both my wheelchair and a scooter.

"Yeah, I know." Talia is smiling, taking in my reaction. "We also have our own bathroom."

I look at her for a permission of sorts, and she nods. I go to check out this luxury. It's also quite large, with grab bars by the toilet and in the shower—a private shower!—with a fold-down seat, a removable showerhead, and grab bars. I think about showering at home, where I sit on the floor of the tub. If I came here, I would actually miss my dorm bathroom when I went home for breaks. How many people can say that?

I hear the squeak of wheels on linoleum and realize that Talia is behind me.

"Just know that with a bathroom like this, your room will be Getting Ready Central for every party, regardless if you decide to go or not."

At other schools, I might not be able to have a roommate. Here, my room could be a place for everyone to be. "I can see that, for sure."

"My roommate and I decided to live together for two years and I honestly don't know if it's because she loves me or this room, but she's great, so I'm willing to take my chances." She tells me a story about when Jaqui, her roommate from New Orleans, came home from a party at 3:00 a.m. and had lost her keys somewhere on campus. Talia let her in using the door remote without even getting out of bed.

Talia gets out of her chair and flops down on her tiny twin bed with the wooden frame. "There's a saying out there: 'Disability is an art. It's an ingenious way to live.'"

I look at Talia, and there are so many things I want to ask her, I don't know where to begin. How did she become this comfortable with her disability? I love that quote; who said it? How long did it take her to feel this at home at college? Is she really this happy here? Does she think I could be happy here, too?

I watch her, reclining in her bed, but with her knees up at an angle. She's scrolling through social media, holding her phone high above her, and it's primed to hit her in the face at any second. Something else I'd love to ask her is how she knew Brennon liked her back. When we left the dining hall, he'd been off to a meeting with the baseball team, and they'd shared a quick kiss. He'd leaned down to kiss her. How long did it take to figure that out? The first time, was it awkward? Did he try to bend down and did she try to prop herself up a bit and did they laugh or did she blush and pull away? How long did it take for them to get into a rhythm?

Does she ever stand up to kiss him? If she doesn't, does he care?

And as I look at that tiny bed, I can't help but wonder about how they go about ... well, everything you presumably go about when you're in an adult relationship. Not in a crude or creepy way. It's just ... you barely learn any of this stuff when you're non-disabled, and there's absolutely nothing when you're disabled. Information on the web for disabled kids just stops after pediatric care.

Googling *How does alcohol affect spasticity?* brought up a bunch of weird Reddit threads that I didn't want to click on, and Googling anything more than that gave me the same feeling I got when Cam admitted that she once watched porn. The feeling that there was just less to figure out for other people.

Don't get me wrong, I can't imagine sex is all *that* hard. But when I was a kid working on the best way for me to sit and walk, my physical therapists always reminded me that it's like my knees have magnets in them; always touching, they never want to move apart.

There's some things even your big sister can't help you figure out.

Talia's phone dings and she swipes out of social media and into her texts. She snorts a quick laugh at the newest message. "Wanna come meet my friends?"

That's a question I know the answer to. "Yes, absolutely."

It's clear to me that this isn't some informal hang from the minute we enter the basement of a different dorm complex. A guy jumps up to open the door for Talia and me, smiling.

"You came!" he says to me, and now I see that our attendance is not random. He puts out a hand for me to shake. "I'm Will."

"Effie," I respond.

"We have a prospective on the premises!" Will announces to the room.

Talia snorts. "Leave her alone, jerk." Then in a voice turned slightly mad scientist, she says, "She's mine, all mine."

He juts out his lower lip. "Dude, I'm just jealous. Admissions has never asked me to host an admitted student."

"That's because you'd scare everyone away," Talia retorts, and everyone laughs.

I look around at the room. The white walls and white linoleum and the assortment of mismatched furniture, some with holes where the foam insides spill out.

A girl pulls away a chair to make room for me in the group. I suddenly feel super shy, but the loud scrape the chair made when she pulled it away almost mandates that I take the space.

"Hey, I'm Kelsie." She smiles warmly.

When I tell her my name, she reveals that she's a senior. When I congratulate her on her impending graduation, she looks a little down. "I'm definitely feeling all of the emotions." She smiles wistfully for a second before adding, "I'm a bit jealous of you, having it all before you."

I'm not sure I would say the same thing about my high school. "How did all of you guys meet?" I ask, looking around the room. Besides Talia and me, one other person is in a wheelchair, a larger power Permobil that reclines. There's about eight other people in here, all different class years, just hanging out.

Kelsie laughs. "I guess I'm the last OG member, but when I took Gender Studies my first year, I served as a notetaker for another student with a disability. When I mentioned I have a chronic illness, she and I started this on-campus group called the Divinely Disabled. It started off as a group to talk about gender and sexuality and has morphed over the years into a general pride group. It's wonderful. I'm so happy to see what it's become."

It's almost as though I can feel the gears in her head moving, as she processes yet another thing she'll miss. "Anyway, we call these Sunday-night gatherings meetings, but they're more often than not just an excuse to get together and procrastinate on writing papers and stuff."

Another girl in a wheelchair rolls in and the guy in the Permobil lights up. I eye them as they break off from the group. She gets out of her wheelchair and climbs up into his lap. I hear him ask her something, pushing her bangs out of her face. She buries her face in his chest. It's sweet, but I look away, feeling like I've seen enough.

"Oh yeah." Kelsie chuckles. "Austin and Ivy. They're cute, and they definitely don't care who knows it."

I've always thought dating was some big, secret society–type thing that I was never going to be able to get into. But I think now that maybe it's like I've been watching a game of jump rope, wondering when it'd be the best time for me to jump in. Maybe all that waiting only meant I'd been passing on my turns for years.

I'm not sure if I'll date a non-disabled person or a person who's also disabled, and it honestly doesn't matter to me. But I'm excited to finally take a turn.

"Are you staying with Talia?" Kelsie asks.

"Yes."

"She's a firecracker."

I laugh. "I've noticed."

"She hosted a panel for Divinely Disabled on disability and politics last semester and got great feedback on it. I'm sure she's going to become the next group president when she becomes an upperclassman next year. You should totally join, too."

The response *If I come here* sits on my lips, and I can almost feel the vibrations of the words buzzing to be said.

At home, I have friends who love and support me and, I now know, will stand up for me when I need them to. But they're never exactly fighting on my same team. I've never known what it's like to be a part of a group that is unequivocally fighting for the same thing. And who knows what I could learn from that? I'm only one person, with one unique set of needs. What else should I be advocating for? What else do members of our community need?

Our community.

I've never had one of those.

Turns out, maybe it was waiting for me all along.

All I had to do was look for it.

CHAPTER TWENTY-SIX

"How'd you sleep?" Talia's raspy voice asks. In the gray glow of the still-dark room with just a little bit of morning through the curtain, I see a single, bright light and realize she's probably on her phone texting Brennon good morning.

"Good," I lie.

She sighs, putting her phone down. She sits up in her bed, pulling the covers off of her, and swinging her legs around so that her feet touch the floor. She transfers to her wheelchair by pushing up with her forearms and twisting around fast enough so that her bottom lands swiftly in the seat. It's a move I've done a million times, but only watched from the outside once.

With the familiar snap, she releases her brakes and heads toward the bathroom. She doesn't get more than two wheel turns away before her phone buzzes, and she races back to her bed to retrieve it. When she reads the notification, her eyes light up like she just found a box of Girl Scout cookies in the back of the freezer that she forgot she had. I'm pretty sure my suspicions about who she was texting were correct. I wonder what that feels like, to have someone who can make you feel that good with a simple hello, over and over again.

I hear the same snap of brakes, and crane my neck from my sleeping bag on the floor to see Talia moving my chair closer to me, pushing it like a bumper car.

"You didn't have to do that," I say.

She shrugs. "I know. But scooting on your butt really sucks."

I peek to make sure Jaqui is still sleeping before pulling a pair of jeans and underwear out of my duffel. Keeping my pajama shirt on, I change only my lower half before getting into my chair, waiting for Talia to be done in the bathroom.

Once I'm in the bathroom and have changed into my flowy navy blue blouse and long gold necklace, an outfit that's trying to be serious yet casual, I look at my reflection, running my hands through my larger ringlets.

It's a little past ten o'clock in Minnesota. I'm missing second period, which for me is World History. We've reached the modern period, which isn't vital for end-of-the-year tests, and the teacher is relying on the assumption that we've probably heard about the recession and President Obama's election anyway. Right now, Cam is in Advanced Art and Harper in Spanish. I start to text them to say hi, but purposely resist the urge. I have to learn what it's like to not talk to them every day, to not have the comfort of knowing where they are at every hour, who they're hanging out with, or the outfit they wore yesterday. It won't be like that when Harper's at Grinnell and Cam's at Georgetown, and I'm . . . somewhere.

After breakfast, Talia says she's off to her class and I freeze. I don't know why, but I guess I assumed she would escort me to my class.

I check the time on my phone. Twenty minutes till class. According to the map, I don't have far to go. But I feel my heart rate picking up and a prickly feeling in the back of my throat. I'm on my own, in college.

I start off heading in the general direction I think is right.

I type the name of the hall into Maps on my phone. It tells me to "head south," which is not helpful. My brain injury makes me terrible with directions; I only know how to find things by landmarks.

I look at the photo of the building. Colleges always brag about the unique architectural structures of all their buildings, but right now, they all look the same. A big, scary mass of concrete academia.

I'm beginning to feel like I want to call it quits and go home, but instead I remind myself I can do this. There is no one who can do this for me but me.

I keep going, following the map as best I can. At one point, the blue dot strays from the line, and I panic, but make a guess of which way to go, and it corrects.

And then I look up and see that I found it. I am buzzing. I want to text Cora or Harper and Cam and tell them that

I did it, but I decide this accomplishment is just for me.

I arrive three minutes late to the lecture hall. My hands are streaked black with dirt.

I'm smiling.

❧

In the half hour before I'm set to meet Mom and Dad for our meeting with the Disability Resources office, I head to the Campanile Esplanade.

The bells in the Campanile, the eight-story clock tower that ends in a triangular point, begin to chime just as I get there. Everyone says it's this campus's most recognizable symbol, and here, it's like it's watching over everything. I watch as a guy learns to skateboard on the sidewalk. I see a mom in yoga pants and oversized sunglasses pushing a stroller, and a guy walking his dog.

And no one here is pausing to say that I shouldn't be here. No one thinks I don't belong. I'm beginning to believe them.

Looking out past the tower, I can see the blue of the Bay. Minnesota is known for its lakes (in fact, we always brag that we have more shoreline than the whole of California's coast) but it still feels remarkable to see open water here. On this clear day, I see the Golden Gate, which doesn't look red from so far away.

My phone buzzes in my lap, and I bang snap. It's a text from a 612 number I don't recognize.

Okay, so you're killing me here. You're really not going to respond to my message about you GETTING INTO PROSPECT?!?

Three dots, indicating more . . .

Then: This is Wilder, btw. I got your number from Harper. Can't believe I didn't have it until now!

All those years of writing my number in his yearbook, wishing and hoping that he thought I was cool enough to hang out with, and it happens *now* and *here*? I always thought going to the same college was what would bring us together. I had so many moments imagining two of us sharing the same cab ride into the city because we'd be on the same flights coming back from school breaks, the way he'd support me in the MMS major, and the way we'd have four more years together.

But now I'm on the opposite coast, on the campus of a school that couldn't be more different, seeing a place that might actually support me, being around people who might actually understand what I go through.

I select Add a New Contact, and type his name.

Maybe I wasn't ready for all of this back in ninth grade. Maybe I wasn't ready at the beginning of the school year, when he brought my things to my locker. Maybe it's okay that it happened right now, even if it's not anyway how I imagined it would be. It's okay because it's real.

And in realizing that, I know I don't need to text back.

I call.

He picks up on the third ring. "Effie?"

"Hey." I can't help myself. At the mere sound of his voice, I grin wide. "How are you?"

I can hear his smile through the phone. "I knew it! Congratulations, Effie. They'd be majorly missing out if they didn't want you."

I light up at his compliment but dial it back quickly. They want me, yes, but a want is just a want. They haven't done the work.

He pauses for a second. "Harper said you were out of town. Where are you?"

"On the West Coast, with my parents." I wince at my half-truth. He would understand, if I told him, but I'm not ready. I want to stay here one more moment, where it's just me and him and the dream of Prospect—the thing that was always ours.

"Oh, nice." There's a pause, and then he says: "Well, hurry home."

And at one point, I would have convinced myself he was talking about how we need to paint those benches, that's all.

But my heart does a funny little flip, because I'm fairly certain he's talking about me. And then he adds, "I owe you a hug."

❧

My duffel bag swings back and forth in Dad's hand as we walk away from the campus. I picked up my things from the cubby

247

in Talia's hall before heading out, since unfortunately, she was in class. When I texted her to say thanks and that I wish we'd gotten a chance to say goodbye, she texted back, Why would it be goodbye? ☺

Our meeting with the Disability Services team confirmed what I already sensed was true. UC Berkeley had their first student in a wheelchair attend in 1962, decades before the ADA, when it was commonplace to tell disabled students they had no business attending college. Within a few years, many disabled students were attending Cal and living in a wing of a hospital. By 1970, they were living in on-campus apartments. Those accessible on-campus apartments are now co-ops where many disabled students prefer to live. Talia mentioned wanting to live in one next year.

By coming here, I wouldn't be the only student in a wheelchair. In fact, I could join a distinguished line of people who came before me.

I'm sure Berkeley isn't some disabled utopia. It's not perfect. There would be challenges attending here. There will be challenges anywhere that I go. But the difference here? They're trying.

❧

On our way back toward Sather Gate, we pass the Student Store. When Dad asks me if I want to stop in, I say yes.

Under the fluorescent lights of the store, I know they're

watching me. I roll past the display of navy blue coffee mugs and water bottles toward the rows of women's sweatshirts.

I find one in that navy color with the yellow stitched-on letters, with a hood and the strings you can chew on. Getting this sweatshirt will be the type of commitment I've been dreaming of for months, but even as I touch the soft lettering of BERKELEY and the stitching of CALIFORNIA GOLDEN BEARS, ESTABLISHED 1868 and even though I can practically feel Mom and Dad holding their breath, I can't make myself pick it up and take it.

I take my hand away.

"Can we go get ice cream?" I ask. They exhale, then nod.

❧

Telegraph Avenue is no Broadway. It's quieter, but still a main hub of a city. I smell the exhaust from the buses and hear the chitchat of students milling about on a Monday evening. With its used bookshops and record stores, restaurants and the promise of street vendors on the weekends, Berkeley seems unassuming, like it doesn't take itself too seriously. It reminds me of Minneapolis in that way.

I continue to coast down the incline. Mom trails a few feet behind me, and out of the corner of my eye, I see Dad catching up, a block behind. They're doing it again, letting me do this on my own.

I can do this, I remind myself. I really, really can.

Mom and Dad come through on the promise of ice cream and we reach CREAM (Cookies Rule Everything Around Me . . . apparently acronyms aren't only for senior shirts in high school). My parents are eating their ice cream sandwiches with birthday cake sprinkles auspiciously, but the tension hangs in the air like a thick layer of humidity.

This school year, I've been challenged and I rose to it. I stood up to Ms. Wilson, and soon Wilder and I will reveal my idea for the School Beautification Project. I now know how to stand up to systems and to the people who put them in place.

But I think that next year, I don't want to have to do that anymore.

I thought I wanted to move to New York City and ride the gritty subways and be among the skyscrapers. Wilder would be there, and we would have so much time to get to know each other so much better. I saw it all, except I never saw its faults.

And now here's a new option. It's still a big, bright city for me to explore. I actually can take the train. And I know I'll have at least one friend in Talia. And my future? I have four full years to figure that out. I can't see it all, and for once, that's the exciting part. I'll have to dive in and see what happens.

Dad told me several months ago that the perfect college doesn't exist. But the one where I can be happy, successful, and where the people will support me? That's the right college. That's my college.

My palms are sweaty, my lips are sticky from the ice cream, but my heart is full.

I thought when the time finally came, it would feel so hard. But it's simple.

I clear my throat.

Mom and Dad look at me expectantly.

"I think . . ." I take a deep breath. "I think I really want to go back and buy that sweatshirt."

Mom's lips start to pull up at the corners. "What do you mean?"

Dad's eyes are still fixed on me. "Are you announcing something?"

I start to nod, but stop myself. I want to say it out loud. "I'm accepting UC Berkeley's offer of admission."

Mom squeaks in excitement. She pulls me into a hug and Dad leans across the table to kiss my cheek.

I don't feel any grief for the possibilities I let go. I'm welcoming new ones.

Dad reaches under the table and pulls a plastic shopping bag from the Student Store out from my duffel bag. He was a block behind Mom and me for a reason. "I had a feeling, honey. But I kept the receipt just in case you surprised me." He hands me the bag. My sweatshirt is inside. "Effie," he says. "You never cease to surprise and amaze me. I hope you never stop."

"This is only the start," Mom adds, watching me as I unfold the sweatshirt on my lap. "You'll need a water bottle and a pennant for your dorm room next."

Dad looks at her. "You and I need those Cal Mom and Cal Dad T-shirts for sure."

Mom claps her hands jokingly. "Cling stickers! For our Toyota van."

"What empty nesters celebrate by buying a minivan?" I laugh.

Dad laughs. "Your strange and embarrassing parents."

Mom picks my phone up off the table. "Hold it up," she instructs, making a motion toward my lap.

I hold the sweatshirt up and smile while Mom snaps a photo. I see Dad smile, his almost as big as mine. But not quite.

I text the photo to Cora, with no explanation or context. After a beat, I do the same on my group text with Cam and Harper.

My phone practically explodes.

> Harper Jeffries: EFFIE.
> Cam Cordes: EFFIE!!
> Harper Jeffries has sent a link: YouTube—The Beach Boys—"California Girls"
> Cam Cordes: YES (sent with confetti)

The screen changes rapidly: *Cora is requesting to FaceTime.* I hit the talk button.

"Are you kidding?!" She's so loud, it's as if my sister is right here in this ice cream shop. Mom and Dad laugh.

"Yeah, I'm totally kidding." Mom and Dad look confused for a second as I let it play out. "No, but seriously, I'm going to go to Cal."

"What a casual announcement. Congratulations, you massive troll. I'm so, so happy for you."

"Thank you," I say. "I'm happy for myself."

CHAPTER TWENTY-SEVEN

A new text from Wilder: I missed homeroom. Are you back?

Staring at it as I wait in line is making my stomach both flutter and hurt. Flutter as I remember the sweetness in his voice when he told me to hurry home. And hurt when I remember that I have to tell Wilder that I won't be joining him in New York.

I know he won't react rudely, but I'm scared that in not being fully honest with him, I was rude. And now that May is approaching, everything is wrapping up so quickly. Thinking back to that party in November, Wilder and I had no idea where we would be headed in the fall, and we hoped that our futures might hold a space for each other. Or at least, I did.

Instead of the typical third period, we're ordering our caps and gowns. I peer down the line of my classmates ordering golden yellow gowns with bold black tassels. Cam follows my gaze to the poster on the wall of the Commons: *Upperclassmen!*

Buy a ticket for prom today! "I still cannot believe they picked 'Old Hollywood' as the prom theme. In *this* climate?"

"Because nothing says 'glamorous' and 'party time' like harkening back to an extremely sexist and racist era," Harper adds.

We didn't go last year. Harper didn't want to go single, and none of the three of us had much money for a ticket anyway, so Ali and we stayed out past midnight at a diner and went to the latest cheesy rom-com movie at the Southdale AMC.

"Blame it on the juniors. They're the ones who pick the theme," I say. While all prom themes don't add anything to the event besides a few hanging decorations, something like "Under the Sea" clearly would have worked better. At least my branch of the Student Council can't be blamed.

"Well, clearly, this school will be lost without us." Harper sighs wistfully, and then adds, "I gotta talk to Calvin about tickets, though."

This year, it will be different. Of course it will be. We're seniors, and it feels worth shelling out the extra money for a ticket. We've been talking about all the "lasts" for months now, but now this truly is our last high school dance. Nostalgia is hanging heavy over all of us seniors. Even if we pretend we don't feel it or don't care, it's as if every interaction we have is soundtracked by the first few bars of "Time of Your Life" by Green Day.

Even I can't deny it. These are the lasts of the lasts.

This year, we're going to prom.

We order our gowns, and the bell rings for lunch. Harper looks at Cam. Cam looks at me. It's one of the first truly beautiful days of spring, seventies and sunny. After lunch is fourth period, and I don't want to go to Student Council and face Wilder. I want to be with my best friends.

Harper pulls up in the parking space my mom usually picks me up in. I hop into the front seat and Cam hops out the back to put my chair in the trunk.

As we pull out of the school parking lot, Harper sticks her tongue out at me and gives two quick honks on the steering wheel. I can see the big smile on my face reflected in the lens of her sunglasses.

The windows are all down and the air fills our ears with a loud thrumming sound as we cruise. Cam leans forward from the backseat and grabs the aux cord, plugging in her phone. The beats of what is sure to be the song of the summer vibrate through my seat and fill my chest. I catch lyrics about just being here for a good time, and hoping it will last. There are times when you feel like a song finds you at the exact right time, like the only explanation is someone got into your brain and put your thoughts to a melody, matched your constant looping rumination into a catchy chorus.

We drive through Linden Hills, past the library where I checked out my first books and participated in the summer reading challenge. We pass the little shops where I used to beg Mom for toys, and the boutiques that Cora likes.

We pass the park where Harper and I came on the first

night of summer after eighth grade. If I look at the swings hard enough, I swear I can see us dirtying our shoes as we see who can make the biggest streak by digging our heels into the sand on the down slope. I can picture my younger self, with frizzy hair and no conception of makeup, who thought that the teenage characters on kids' shows were still a little bit cool and aspirational, even though she knew she wasn't supposed to admit it.

I remember feeling excited to start high school because that's what I was supposed to feel. But I was scared out of my mind, too.

Some feelings never really go away, I guess.

～

Harper makes the turn toward Lake Harriet, and I look out at the sparkling blue of the lake. When the thought of trading it so soon for the Bay comes into my mind, I push it away. I need this moment exactly as it is. I focus in on the downtown skyline on the other side of the water. For now, I am home.

～

We buy an extra-large popcorn and lemonades from the Bandshell. It's a place for outdoor concerts overlooking the lake with a concession stand.

"My mom used to take me here as a little kid, and we would

throw popcorn into the water for the ducks," Cam says. "I only recently learned that it's super bad for their stomachs. Definitely a glass-shattering moment."

We head to the open green space and I get out of my chair. None of us thought ahead to bring blankets or towels, so we put Cam's and Harper's backpacks side by side and lie down, resting our heads on them as lumpy pillows.

As it's lunchtime on a weekday, the lake is pretty quiet except for a few parents with young kids or a senior speed walking. I hear a cry and crane my neck to see a toddler getting scooped up by her mother, leaving her tiny shovel and pail behind in the sand area. Down on the bike path, a slightly older kid scoots by on his Razor. We make eye contact and I half smile. He looks away fast. That's the thing about always living in your hometown. In this space, I've been the baby with her mother and the kid who's slightly scared to acknowledge the high school kid skipping class. Who will I get to be in a new place?

For a while, we sit in comfortable silence, scrolling through our phones and not updating our social so we don't get caught sooner than we have to be. Grease from the popcorn slicks our fingers and the lemonade makes our lips sticky.

Harper clicks the screen off on her phone and places it face-down on the grass next to her, sighing heavily. "Do you ever think of where we'll be four years from now?" she asks.

I almost laugh. Four *years*? I'm worried enough about what the next four months will look like. Senior year moves in such distinct phases: you apply, you wait, you get accepted, you deliberate, you decide. Next, we'll graduate. I haven't come up for air since September. And then a new cycle will start: graduation parties, roommate requests, and a million trips to the Container Store. It should make me excited, and it does, but I know that at the end of this phase is goodbye.

A minute passes as we each try to imagine one of the million ways our futures might play out. The breeze ruffles the leaves but we don't say a word. No one answers Harper's question out loud; perhaps the weight of it is the answer itself. She takes hold of her phone and extends her arm, clicking the camera open on the screen.

"Come here," she says, and Cam and I squish our heads closer to hers so that we are cheek to cheek. We smile, and she takes the photo. We look silly, our hair all matted together on top of this backpack, our chins at unflattering angles.

"It's cute," she remarks, and Cam and I agree. When my phone vibrates a second later, I'm happy she's sent it to me in the group chat. It's not anything we would ever post, but it's a photo I know I'll cherish four months from now. The photo is a lot like today has been: unplanned, unpredictable, but happy.

We'll keep moving forward just like this. In four years, things will be different, no doubt.

But the three of us will be absolutely fine.

❧

There is still the ellipsis hanging. The end to the sentence is different than I thought it would be, but . . . I need to finish the sentence nonetheless.

I'm sitting on my bed, the glow of my laptop screen lighting up my face. When I pull the computer out of my backpack, a piece of paper slides out with it. The Cal bumper sticker I picked up for my new scooter.

But with every yes, you have to say no to something else.

I type *prospect.edu* into the browser. I think of all the nights exactly like this, sitting here with my door shut tight, browsing this website and feeling so scared to tell my parents. In the end, my parents were never the biggest obstacle.

I've heard that you never regret chasing a dream, because then at least you'll always know how things turned out. You can look back knowing you did that.

I did that. I did that and so much more.

I log in to the portal, and click the option to update my admission status.

I check the box that says I will decline Prospect University's offer of admission. When I do, a text box opens underneath, asking for the college I will be attending instead. I type my answer.

I stare at the screen for a few seconds more. Nothing can change anything, and I don't need anything to change. But in the last few moments before this chapter closes, I reflect on everything it brought me. Closer to Wilder, yes. But even more so, closer to myself.

I click Submit.

A new page loads. Underneath the Prospect logo, text reads *Thank you for your interest in Prospect University. We wish you the best on all your future educational endeavors.*

From there, I open a new email, and address it to DisabilityServices@prospect.edu. I remember first drafting an email to them in the fall, and feeling so much hope for my future at this school. I know so much more now. I gave it my best effort, but it wasn't enough. Prospect has to want to do the work, too.

Dear Cynthia,

I've submitted notice officially that I've decided to attend the University of California, Berkeley next year. This was a very tough decision for me, as there is so much to love about Prospect and so many reasons I was interested in attending there. I wanted to let you know that ultimately, UCB has the accessibility and services that I need to be successful in college on every level, and that was the deciding factor for me.

As you're aware, accessibility improvements to a campus can take many years and a significant amount of funding to complete. I simply could not take the risk of attending Prospect knowing these

**projects were not in place and may not be com-
pleted by the time I graduate. It is my hope that
Prospect invests the time and energy in these
projects now so that future students can benefit in
ways I will not be able to.**

Even though I still feel excitement for my future, there's a
lump rising in my throat. I blink twice, but no tears come. I
exhale. I've lost something, sure, I remind myself. But they've
lost something bigger. They don't get to have me.

Next year, I'm going to be a college freshman. I'm going to
have to adjust to living far away from my parents, my friends,
and my sister. I'm going to be taking harder classes, figuring out
how to live on my own, eat my own meals, and figure out life
in a brand-new city. And the thing is, I would've had to do all
of that anywhere. But at Prospect, I would have had to be an
unpaid accessibility consultant, too. It's completely unfair to
ask anyone to take on anyone's full-time salaried job for them.
I already have a job and that's to focus on being a student.

I close my laptop and reach for my phone. It's solidified now,
and Wilder deserves to know.

I open my texts and type out: *Hey! I wanted to let you know
that I decided to attend UC Berkeley. Sorry.*

I remember that I have nothing to be sorry for, and delete
that part before typing: *It was just a better fit for me.*

I delete it and try again: *There were just so many things that
worked better for me there.*

I delete that, too.

A notification pops up so fast that I bang snap, wondering if maybe I hit send by accident.

Talia Givens is requesting to follow you.

I open the social app and click Accept.

As I swipe to close the apps on my phone, I go back to my texts. There's a reason no combination of words feels quite right. He told me in person. I should do the same for him.

I delete the whole message, and in response to his message about when to paint, I type instead: Can you meet me at the benches tomorrow? I have something I want to tell you.

I set my phone facedown on my bed. I get back in my wheelchair to finish getting ready for tomorrow.

When my phone buzzes, I lunge for it.

One new text from Wilder: Sure. See you then.

CHAPTER TWENTY-EIGHT

Words tumble around in my head as I go through all the ways I could blow this: *Hey, you should know we're not going to college together!* Or maybe: *Hey, I know we had all these hopes and dreams together but I threw a wrench in all of them! (I mean at least I hope it was you, too. No? Just me? Well, this is awkward . . .)*

My phone buzzes.

We still on for meeting at 3:15?

The clock on my phone changes to 3:07. I decide to keep it casual and respond with a single thumbs-up emoji.

I turn and head off toward the auditorium. Here goes nothing.

❧

"So I primed them last weekend . . . when you were on the West Coast. Anyway, that's set. So do you want to work on one and I'll work on the other?"

The two benches are sitting on the stage, ready to be painted.

I try to say, "Wilder, about that thing I have to tell you . . ."

What comes out instead is "Sure, I'll paint the bench on the left."

The seafoam-green paint has the look we intended: bright, cheerful, fun, in contrast to how I feel right now.

We settle in across from each other, and I dip a brush in, careful to wipe the sides of the brush extra times on the can so the paint doesn't drip onto my footplate. When I see that Wilder has painted almost a whole arm of the bench in the time it's taken me to paint a tiny patch, I wonder if it's because I'm being so careful or because I'm stalling.

I hear a noise and look up. Wilder is whistling. He's incredibly pitchy and off-key, but still.

When he notices me listening and looking at him, he laughs. His laugh is so amazing. Deep, but with this funny high-pitched wheeze at the end. How did I not properly appreciate it all these years? I'm going to miss hearing it on a regular basis. "Sorry," he says. "Annoying habit."

"We all have them. No worries."

We go back to work, sans whistling.

"Are you going to go to prom?" Wilder asks. My mind races for a second, then realize of course, he's only asking me if I'm going, not *going* as in with a date.

"Oh yeah," I say. "Harper, Cam, and I will all be there." I look at him. "You?"

He looks at me and answers, "I plan on it." We go back to painting.

For a second, I hope and hope and hope. I've been hoping for so long. And I know I haven't fully put myself out there yet, but I've come so far, and . . . he brought it up.

But there's still that thing I need to tell him. I wonder about listing all the reasons. All the challenges. Every little factor that factored into my decision. I know he would get as mad as I once felt. But the thing is, I'm not mad anymore. I'm good. I repeat it again to myself for good measure.

I am good.

I have to disrupt this comfortable silence that is only comfortable for one of us. I take the deepest breath I've taken all day. "Wilder." At the sound of my voice, his blue eyes come up to meet my gaze. I put down the brush. "I wanted to let you know that I've decided to attend UC Berkeley next year."

Silence. One beat, two beats, three, and then, right as I'm about to sink into the hole that I swear is opening up beneath me . . .

"So when you said you were out of town . . . what you meant was . . . you were—" His response comes so fast that all I hear is anger.

I sputter into overdrive, cutting him off. "I didn't mean to keep you out of the loop. I wanted to tell you, I promise. I was just so in my head that—"

He holds up his palm, splattered with green paint. "Mr. Andersen told me that one person from our class got into

Berkeley this year. I didn't know it was *you*. Effie, that's . . . that's absolutely incredible."

I allow myself a beat to calm down. He's not angry. He's telling me that I'm good. He's telling me that *we* are good.

Now, months later, it's my turn to have the broken-egg-yolk smile—spilling out all over my face.

"I'm so, *so* happy for you!" He takes a step forward, then reconsiders. "I would give you that hug I owe you but my hands are covered in paint."

I hold up my hands with matching stains, laughing. We air-five from several feet apart instead.

"I—" Wilder's speech stops in its tracks, like he said something he wasn't sure he was capable of saying. He tries again. "I guess, selfishly, I'm sad."

I meet his gaze again. It's important that he knows. "I know. Me too."

"I mean, I always knew that there was a chance you could choose . . . or that I might not . . . but then I did and I thought . . ."

"I know. Me too."

These were secrets I held in for so long. Whether they were front of mind or something I pushed back, I always held on to them, thinking they were mine alone. Now I knew they were Wilder's, too.

I would hug him. But the paint.

The comfortable silence settles back in. So much has changed in the past five minutes; at the same time, nothing at all.

"So," Wilder says. "What are you going to do when one of your professors butchers your name on your first day of college, Erithrema?"

I look directly at him. "It's pronounced Euphemia, but I go by Effie."

"Attagirl." He laces his fingers together, palms facing outward, and flexes them. "My work here is done."

❧

The next day at 7:00 a.m., the janitor remarks he doesn't usually let students in the building this early. And while he looks a little confused at the request, he agrees to help Wilder move the now-dry benches into the West Corridor.

Wilder and I affix a sign above them that says **Seating for those who are low mobility—a School Beautification gift from the senior class.**

Wilder turns to me. "Hey. You're quiet. Are you sure you still want to do this? Just say the word and these can go outside—"

I hold up my hand to stop him. This isn't only for me. After I started thinking about how I could make a change for future students, I researched simple but effective accommodations online. And this one—to allow those who need one a chance to rest while walking this endless corridor—seemed perfect. "I'm doing this, Wilder. This is my chance, and I'm ready."

Then, next to the sign, we hang another: **Mill City High School is not accessible for all students. Please review our**

proposed School Lunch Plan to fix one issue on our campus.

Last weekend, I laminated two copies of my school lunch proposal, highlighting where the new exit on the first floor should be. Now I punch a hole in both and affix a copy to the arm of each bench using yarn.

On the other arm of each sits a clipboard with a pen attached to it. **Students, sign a petition encouraging Mill City High School to enact the following proposal.**

We admire our work, months in the making. I think back to how I felt, looking at this assignment in Student Council in September. I felt so defeated after not getting my locker back, I could never have imagined I'd pull off an act so public and so forceful. But I did. And I'm proud of myself. I'm not the same girl I was eight months ago.

❧

By the time the bell rings for passing time to first period, the final piece is in place. Editions of this week's school paper are distributed around school, with this above the fold:

ACCESSIBILITY CONCERNS HINDER EXPERIENCE AT MILL CITY HIGH SCHOOL

By: Effie Galanos

Mill City High School's School Beautification Project promises an opportunity, along with financial support from the school, to make the building welcoming to all who enter. Yet the project suggests only superficial changes, when physical and attitudinal barriers prevent the building from being a place where disabled students can thrive.

At the end of my op-ed, I invite students to visit the West Corridor to view the benches.

I'm scared. Scared my classmates won't understand, or worse, won't care.

But what's done is done.

And now we wait.

I notice a few students noticing me a bit more than usual in the hallways, but that's about it. *Even if this doesn't amount to much,* I tell myself, *it was still important.*

But when the lunch hour arrives, Cam shows up at my locker just as giddy as the day she took me to discover the sit-in. We meet Harper in the West Corridor to learn that they were both the first and second signers of the petition. Both of my friends, together, supporting me. I hug them tight.

Harper looks at her phone and grins. "Calvin says this is badass. And if he went here, he and all his friends would be signing it." She swipes through to a different app. "Also, you're blowing up on social."

I open my phone to find I've been tagged in several people's posts. They've taken photos of the op-ed and of the benches.

Something I didn't realize was happening, a sophomore who will be joining Student Council next year writes. *We must do better. Sign the petition!*

Even Seth shares it: *This is really important. I'm sorry I didn't do more to help. Glad I can now. Thank you, Effie.*

By the end of the second lunch period, we have forty signatures. By the end of the day, we have sixty.

After last period, I head back to the benches. Abe and Sarah are making out on Swapping Spit Slope, but today, I've had enough. "Would you please get out of my way?"

Their eyes go big, and they only move about two feet, but it's progress.

Wilder comes barreling toward me, and I get that hug he's been promising. It's so forceful, he pushes me back a bit.

"We did it," I say into his ear.

"Oh, no. I was happy to help, but this is you, Effie." He finally lets go, and is grinning. "This is all you."

I'm half expecting all of this to be removed by the time I come to school tomorrow, but today, I have this.

Today, I *did this.*

CHAPTER TWENTY-NINE

"I mean, what even *are* the wall decorations for an Old Hollywood–themed prom supposed to be?" I ask. "Instead of streamers, will old rolls of film be hanging from the ceiling?"

Neither Harper nor Cam look up from their phones.

"I'm ready to head out to lunch," I tell them. It still feels great to be able to say that, and even greater to get to do it. But my friends still don't seem to hear me, let alone register that I'm willing to talk about prom.

I don't get it. I spent years dreading the constant dance talk that started weeks in advance: if we would go, or who we might go with. Or at least, who *they* would go with. For me, it was mostly deliberating if I was up for going without a date.

But this is senior prom, and I'm going to go, and I am going to have a great time. And I even want dance talk, because even though it isn't a "last" I'm going to miss, it's a last nonetheless.

I try again. "We're buying tickets today, right?" I looked up the prices online last night, sixty dollars for a single ticket and one hundred and ten dollars if you buy as a couple. I don't like how couples get a discount, and it's something I would've normally griped about for at least a week, but this year, I'm calm and casual.

I just wish my friends would take notice and appreciate it.

Still nothing.

When I ask again, Cam finishes typing out a message. "The tickets will still be there tomorrow and the day after. I'm not rushed."

The thing is, as soon as the tickets go on sale, school becomes a lawless land. Guys come in mid-class strumming guitars to ask girls to go with them. Signs start popping up in the hallways. Girlfriends co-opt the morning announcements to broadcast proclamations of adoration to the entire school. The infamous elevator asks haven't started yet, but, oh, they will, and I'll have the scoop on who's going with who because of it.

Harper is working out a way to ask Calvin to our prom (he'll have to ask her to his school's, of course) and I know Cam asked Ali in a more simple way already. I get wanting to be private, but no fretting over what dress to get? Not even one bit of swooning?

I'd want to swoon if it were me.

Suddenly Cam says, "By the way, Effie, I need your and Harper's opinion on which pieces to submit for my senior art exhibition. It should take thirty minutes after school."

"And I'll drive you home," Harper volunteers quickly.

"Okay, sure." I grab my phone to text Mom.

"It's all good." Harper bats at my phone, making me lower it. "Your mom knows and is fine with it. You're going to have to trust me."

❧

It's 3:15 and I'm sitting outside at the usual spot, waiting. Most students left right at bell, and I see no sign of Harper's car pulling up, despite her jogging off telling me she's parked around the corner. Right as I'm about to text her, my phone buzzes.

I look down, expecting a *Be there soon!* text, but instead, I see this:

Wilder: Hey, would you mind coming back inside?

It's three days after we planned the stunt with the benches. The administration ended up taking our proposal and signatures, saying they would "look into it on the strong recommendation of the Student Council." It's not everything, but I try to hold on to hope that things can change, for me and for students to come.

I comb through recent interactions with Wilder to see if I forgot about something we needed to discuss, but nothing sticks out. I head back toward the door anyway, thinking it's still wild that we text now, that we talk so much I can forget to follow up on something.

When I press the door opener, something crunches under my palm. I pull my hand away to see a folded piece of notebook paper taped smack-dab in the middle of the wheelchair symbol. I would take it off anyway, but especially because EFFIE is written on it in all caps.

I unfold it: The bottom is crooked, the top section of a lined notebook page quickly ripped out, the fringes from the spiral still left on. Partly in the heading and in the remaining lines is the same messy scrawl:

Eou—Pre—Maia Galanos...all the mispronunciations of your name are such a pain.

But what do you say...are you up for a few clues leading you down memory lane?

Remember that fateful moment during roll call?

Let's kick off this hunt by going to the place that started it all.

This isn't Harper's or Cam's handwriting. This handwriting matches the one on the name tag that's underneath the glass on my bedside table. This note was written by Wilder. My heartbeat starts to increase. Sweat prickles my neck. He isn't . . . This isn't . . . Isn't it?

The place that started it all for us? My first thought is his car that we drove in to go to Menards.

But there are no cars in the lot now, so that can't be it. I work backward, back before I had his phone number, back before I was a senior. All the way back to when I was a freshman.

I press the door button and go inside. I'm the only one in the halls, so I move quickly. Past the lockers, down the hall, to the door of the classroom I haven't been in since ninth grade. I don't see a note on the door, so I open it cautiously, unsure of what to expect. Thankfully, my teacher from my days in Algebra I is nowhere to be found, and the room is empty. The door slams to a close behind me.

The room looks practically unchanged, like a time warp, the same stack of Texas Instrument calculators on the bookshelf in the back. If I close my eyes, I can almost hear it: "Efumia? Efumia Galanos?"

Yeah, I said I would never repeat the worst-ever mispronunciation of my name ever again. But my teacher did, several times, and slowly, naming each syllable: *Ef-u-mia*.

The mispronunciation of all mispronunciations.

My cheeks on fire as I mumbled, "It's Effie."

And if it wasn't for Wilder being the only one to hear and calling out, "She said her name is EFFIE!," dulling the roar of laughter, I probably would've changed my schedule. Or transferred schools. I didn't even know him then but I smiled at him, and mouthed, "Thank you." He smiled back.

I was sitting . . . *there*. On my former desk, there's another folded piece of paper sitting on top. I race to grab it.

Go to the place where you keep all your scholarly possessions.

(The fact that you have more than one keeps this school stressin'!)

Your next clue will be nested in the spot where your textbooks are most neatly kept in.

My locker. Specifically, the one that Wilder helped me move into on the first day. I want to get to the elevator as quickly as possible, but I look around for a second longer, thankful that he took an embarrassing memory and replaced it with a good one.

❧

Riding in the elevator, I consider how I am obviously not naive. Wilder is doing *a thing*, and if I'm right—and I'm pretty sure I'm right—he is doing The Thing. My stomach flutters, but not in the romantic butterflies type of way, but in the I-have-spent-so-long-imagining-this-but-never-actually-thought-it-would-happen-like-seriously-ever-and-now-it-is-happening-and-holy-shit-I-do-not-know-how-to-process-this-except-to-throw-up-or-cry-and-I-do-not-want-either-of-those-things-to-happen type of way.

I look down at my jeans and boring old T-shirt. I am going to *kill* Harper and Cam. They could have told me to dress cuter today.

My hands shake as I undo the lock. The door squeaks as it opens, and sticking out between two books is my next clue:

In Manhattan they're famous for making this hand—tossed and super thin,

In Chicago, it's deep enough to dig your face in,

In California, I don't know how it will taste...

But it certainly will taste better than when it comes from THIS place.

Deep . . . Chicago . . . dish? *Pizza.* There's only one place to get pizza in school, and it's disgusting. I hop back into the elevator.

Underneath the fluorescent lights of the cafeteria, the heat lamps are turned off and the trays all put away. But in the area where slices would usually sit in bubbling grease is one single pizza box. I open it, and a piece of paper is taped to the top lid:

You and the lunch hour have a history that's deeply fraught.

For your ability to go out, I'm so proud that you fought.

You beat the bad policies this school sought,

And your next clue rests where justice was wrought.

The desk that Wilder and crew sat in front of on the second floor? I start to head off toward the elevators again, and then stop. I'd passed that desk, no note. The sit-in helped, but it didn't fix everything. The true fix (if you can call it that) was the cameras.

Sure enough, when I go back to the same door I came through with the first note fifteen minutes ago, a ribbon hangs from the camera, and on the end of the ribbon dangles a note. I laugh. It's hanging right at my height, which is absurdly low for anyone else.

My adrenaline rushes, realizing that maybe Wilder was here just minutes ago, putting this into place. I almost bang snap at the notion that the next clue could lead me to him.

I grab the note, and unfold it:

The good news is that Sarah is moving on to undergrad

Where her obnoxious make—outs with Abe will surely make other people mad.

Your last clue lies in the place where they kiss.

Running them down every day will surely be something you will not miss.

Swapping Spit Slope! I make toward the ramp in the Commons. Weirdly, my mind has gone blank, like my brain is pushing out all of the trivial things to devote all of its energy to this. I want to remember how I feel in this exact moment. I thought I would feel a weightiness, an importance. But truly, the overwhelming feeling is happiness.

Taped to the wall at the very bottom of the ramp is my last note. I position my chair so that I'm heading straight for it. I bomb the ramp, a rare pleasure, and tear it off.

Unlike the STOMP shirt—to Seth's despair

I've now found a shirt that I'll actually wear.

I like this one better, it has another short phrase

I'd like to run by you today.

You'll find it behind the doors of the place where you move from floor to floor.

The elevator? I was in there ten minutes ago . . . he couldn't be . . . but I go up to the elevator anyway. I look down at my lap, at the six little scraps of paper. I take a deep breath and exhale. When I push my finger against the button to call the elevator, my hand trembles.

And then . . . I wait? A nervous laugh titters out of me as I watch the floor indicator above the door light up from six . . .

Five . . .

Four . . .

Three . . .

Two . . .

One.

Ding.

The doors open. My mind goes blank for me again, recording every second.

There's crepe paper hanging from the ceiling of the elevator, along with a mini–disco ball.

Below it, Wilder is standing there, smiling brightly. This is the sweetest thing anyone has ever done for me and it was done by the sweetest boy I know. I don't throw up. I don't cry. I beam.

And then I see it . . . his shirt. It's the same black-and-yellow tie-dye of the senior shirts we both hate. But instead of STOMP in white block letters, his shirt reads PROM?

I spent all this time thinking getting asked out was complicated. But it's actually simple: He smiles, I die. That's all there is to it.

Wilder spreads his arms out. "Effie . . . will you go to prom with me?"

It's really happening. It's here. It's now. No deep breath needed.

"Yes, of course I will!"

I go into his open arms for a hug. The elevator doors try to close and buzz loudly at us when we're in the way.

The door magically opens and I look behind to see Harper

pressing the up button to keep it open. Cam is behind her snapping pictures with her phone.

Harper gives me the look that only your best friend can give you when it turns out they were right all along. It's not a stern look, but a sweet one. I think back to sitting in that hot tub with Harper when she told me I could have moments like this and I deserve moments like this. It's an "I told you so" in the best way. And now it is so.

And it's perfect.

CHAPTER THIRTY

It's 10:37 p.m. I don't expect Cora to answer, but I try her on FaceTime anyway. It's the evening after I've just been asked out for the first time ever, and it was in the best way ever.

I need to tell my sister.

"Hello?" I jolt, surprised she answered. Cora's voice sounds hushed, and the lighting around her face is dark, so I can't see where she is.

"Hi . . . Did I . . . I didn't wake you, did I?"

She sighs. "It's Hell Week, Effie. There is no sleeping. I'm in the library."

That's right. It's the last week of classes before heading into finals week.

"Why aren't *you* sleeping?" I swallow her unintended dig that I would be in bed before eleven on a Friday night. (She's usually right.)

"I got asked to prom." I try to play it cool, but the buzzy high pitch of my voice tips my hand right away.

"WHAT?!" My sister's voice goes up at least twelve octaves. There's a muffle at the other end, like she's putting her hand over the phone. "Oh shit—I forgot I'm in the library for a second and am getting so many rude looks. Omigod, Effie. Hold on, don't hang up."

"Okay."

A moment later, through the sounds of walking and shuffling, I hear the echo of a door slam, and then her face reappears and she lets out another shriek, now in the brightly lit hallway. "Okay, tell me *everything.*" She pronounces it like *ev-err-eey-thing*, so I know she means it. "How? When?" Her eyes get big and she sputters, "Wait . . . start with *WHO!*"

"Wilder." I singsong his name without even trying to. I hate being like this. I also love being like this. Having someone who makes me feel like this. "He's the—"

"The guy from your birthday party. Obviously. Insert the 'I knew its' and the 'I told you sos' et cetera here. So when? How?"

"Today, after school." I launch into the whole story.

I hear squeaks on the other end, the screen blurs as she moves it quickly. "I'm jumping up and down," Cora laughs. "Oh my GOD, Effie. That is amazing. Truly. You don't know how lucky you are. First off, I got asked, like, a week before the dance. And when he finally did, it was a text message because his original idea was to make it seem like my car was being towed and then he was going to, like, emerge from the bushes and ask me to go to prom." Cora's laugh is loud and happy.

I snort. "You can't make me laugh like that. I'll wake up Mom and Dad."

There's a beat of silence. Then Cora speaks. "So we're going to the mall this weekend, right?"

I shake my head. "You're in Northfield."

"That car from the aforementioned story? I still own it."

"But it's Hell Week, Cora."

"One day off isn't going to kill me. Not being there when you pick out your prom dress, now, *that* will kill me."

After the day that I've had, I'm not even sure I have a heart anymore. A ball of warm goo beats in its place.

"So . . . see you tomorrow?"

"See you tomorrow."

"This," Cora says, "is *definitely* it."

I look across the floor of the Macy's salesroom to see Cora holding up a hot pink dress with a sequin-filled top and a puffy tulle bottom. It looks like something Barbie would pick on *Say Yes to the Dress*.

I snicker. "It's perfect."

"So, what are you actually looking for?"

To tell the truth, I don't have any idea. This is the first time I've bought a dress for a dance. I've either borrowed one of Cora's or, one time, from Cam. "All I know is that I don't want a long dress." I glance around. All the mannequins are wearing long gowns, none of which would look good on a person in a wheelchair.

Cora starts pulling any short dresses she sees. While we roam, she asks what the prom theme is. When I tell her, she recoils. "Does no one read the room? Watch the news? Jeez."

I don't have a color in mind, so we pull all sorts of things. Every once in a while, Cora holds up a dress to my arm or my hair and shakes her head. "It doesn't match your skin tone," she says.

I pull one longer dress that's not floor-length but does go past the knees, just to see, and head to the accessible dressing room. Inside, Cora locks the door, then piles the dresses on the bench. "Where do you want to start?"

I point at the longer dress. "I want to make sure I can rule that one out."

"Okay," she says, removing it from the hanger while I remove my jeans and T-shirt.

Cora is about to hand me the dress, but hesitates. "Okay . . . just making sure . . . you do have a nicer bra and underwear for the actual dance, right?"

I blanch, then blush bright red. "Cora! Yes. And anyway, we're not . . . God!"

"I mean, we are at the mall, so I could help you if . . ."

"We're not!"

Cora balls the dress up and tosses it at me playfully. Then she throws up her hands in surrender. "Sisterly duty. And hey, when I was in your shoes, it was *Mom* asking that question. I'm sparing you here. Plus, you are headed to college, and girls have these things. It's not a bad idea for you to at least think about, when you're ready."

I glance at myself in the mirror, my strong shoulders that seem too big for my frame, my pale skin, my surgical scars. I'm not ready yet. But someday, I will be.

It's pale pink, strapless, plain. It's pretty, but I don't love the length. "No," I say flatly.

"Oof, out so quickly? It's not bad."

"It's too similar to the dress—your dress—that I wore to homecoming. Wilder has already seen me in this color."

"Aha. Noted. Yeah, that's fair. We're on the hunt for a knock-out here."

We try a burgundy dress next. It's short, above the knee like I want, but it's one of those hip two-piece dresses. The top isn't quite a crop top, but it's meant to show a playful bit of stomach. If you were standing. When I'm sitting, the edge of the top folds over the top of the skirt like it's too big, even though it's the right size. I shake my head, and Cora agrees.

Cora digs through the shrinking pile and finds one I barely remember pulling. It's an emerald-green satin halter dress that hits right at the knee. The straps are thin, and they crisscross to make a sexy open back. There's a sparkly belt in the middle.

I slip it on, my back to the mirror. When I finish adjusting the straps, I turn around to look. My breath actually catches, something I thought only happened in the movies. The straps of my bra still show, but I mentally remove them. The dress is the perfect length for me, and as Cora would say, this dress compliments my skin tone. The belt hits right at my waist to cinch perfectly. It's so flattering, and I don't need a mannequin to show me that *this* is how you look good in a wheelchair.

"Ladies and gentlemen, we have our knockout. Hot damn." Cora smiles. "Wilder is going to lose his shit. It fits you like a glove, Effie." She gets a sly look on her face, then asks, "Do you own a strapless bra?"

When I shake my head, she snorts. "See! We'll get one, don't worry."

❧

We're browsing the jewelry rack, looking for something pretty but simple so as not to detract from the bling the belt already brings. I hold up a pair of teardrop earrings to get Cora's take, but she's looking at her phone.

I see her type out a quick response to a text. From my angle, I catch a glimpse of it: *Love you too.*

She switches her phone off. "Those look nice, but I don't think they're it. Drew says to tell you hello and to have fun at prom."

I look at my sister as she goes back to browsing. She and

Drew are saying that they love each other now. I suspected it, but having it confirmed feels different.

I swallow, and the words are out before I realize I'm saying them. "What did you tell Drew about me, when you first met?" I've been wondering for months. If she went technical, if he Googled stuff afterward.

"What do you mean?"

"Did you tell him about the wheelchair and . . ." I wave my hand in front of my body. "You know, all of that?"

"Well, I mean, yeah. I mentioned it."

"Did he have a bunch of questions?"

She looks up, like she's racking her brain. "Honestly, no. And it didn't even come up for a while."

"Really?" I say.

I must sound surprised, because she stares at me, wide-eyed. "Effie, yes, seriously. I don't go around telling everyone how my sister is in a wheelchair. I told him that we were close. I told him you were looking at colleges. I told him you were super tight with your friends, something I envied. And then I told him the rest of the stuff at some point, probably before you visited me. And by then, I had told him so many other things about you that he was just kind of, like, oh . . . okay. It was just another fact." There's a beat of silence. "You should know that with anyone, that's never going to be the thing I lead with, like, ever." She's not mad, but she is being stern with me. "And for the record, I barely even filled him in with anything about how unstoppable you are. You did that all on your own."

Relief floods into me, like the last missing puzzle piece.

Cora reaches for a pair of sparkly studs. Not too big, and pretty without being over the top. "You should go with these."

I agree. We've settled on shoes: a pair of silver strappy flats that I already own from a wedding a few years ago.

"Now, come on. I want to hit up Sephora before we go."

"I don't need any new makeup for prom," I point out.

"Yeah, but Mom and Dad are paying and they don't know that. And besides, this is for me."

We leave the mall with the dress, the earrings, a dark pink matte lipstick, a tiny metallic clutch, and wrapped in tissue paper, a new strapless bra and matching pair of lacy underwear.

"I know you're not," Cora said as she pushed me to spring for it. "But you can pick out something nice that makes you feel sexy just for yourself. That's the secret of this whole industry, honestly. It's all girls doing it for themselves."

❧

We drive back around 2:00 p.m., the pop station blaring, and the worn-out AC in Cora's car doing the best it can, blowing lukewarm air in our faces. The stench of Cora's food court burger and fries that she bought to eat on the way back fills the car.

As she pulls in the drive, a tightness arises in my throat. "I'm so happy you came today."

"Me too," she says. She gets my chair out of the car. Leaving the car still running, she gives me a tight hug. "I'm always one call away. But you already know that."

"I do."

She's gone as quick as she came, laying on her horn until she turns the corner on the end of our street.

CHAPTER THIRTY-ONE

Today feels like a normal Saturday, except every once in a while, I remember and my stomach seizes, half nerves, half excitement. I spend twenty minutes shaving my legs, making sure I get every single stray hair. Mom makes me scrambled eggs, which I pick at. I browse aimlessly on my computer until four o'clock rolls around and the doorbell rings.

Harper and Cam pile into our house to get ready. Mom's in full "cool Mom" mode, with fizzy lemonade and chips, veggies, and hummus set out.

Harper, Cam, and I head to my room and I close the door. We made a deal for the last time we all get ready for a dance: not even a hint about our dresses to one another until we're wearing them. Luckily, I can put this one on without assistance.

Cam takes the guest bedroom and Harper heads off to change in the hallway bathroom. Alone in my room, I take off my normal clothes and begin my transformation. I slip the dress over my head, pulling my arms up and through the straps and checking in the mirror to make sure the dress crosses the way it's supposed to in the back. I put extra deodorant on, in case I sweat buckets from nerves, or dancing, or both. On second thought, I put it in the pouch underneath my chair to be on the safe side.

Smoothing out the skirt with my hands, I still think it's every bit a knockout.

There's a knock on my bedroom door. "Ready!" I call out.

My friends walk in. A burst of joy moves through me. Cam is wearing a bright blue dress, short in the front and long in the back, which makes her red hair and freckles pop. Harper is wearing a simple but lovely long peach-colored dress that ties in the back.

"Honestly." Harper's voice drips with the smile that's on her face. "We almost look *too* good."

"*Yup.*" Cam agrees matter-of-factly.

It is fact. We look so incredible. It is in these moments, when it's me and my friends, hanging out, having fun, encouraging one another, that I feel the happiest. We are incredible.

"That *dress,* Effie!" Harper beams at me.

"It's a great dress," I agree.

"No, it's *your body* in that dress." She smirks. "Wilder's heart is going to drop into his butt."

Cam shrieks. "What does that even mean?"

"Not sure. But it's happening."

Cam helped me twist my hair into a bun with a couple of loose curls hanging down from it. I'm in my bedroom again while the two of them are in the bathroom both trying to perfect the "Beachy Waves with a Flatiron" tutorial they found on YouTube. About every five minutes I hear "Don't forget to like and subscribe and give this video a thumbs-up!" before one of them says, "Wait, I swear you almost had it. Play it again."

I slide the new earrings in, and then look over at my dresser. I put my bracelet from Cora on, the word *Brave* where I can see it. It's a label that this time, after everything I've been through, I know that I've earned.

There's a knock on the door. Mom calls out, "Can I come in?"

I open the door and Mom has that melty smile on her face. "Oh, Effie. You look so gorgeous and grown."

She helps me set my makeup with powder, and putzes over various spots in my foundation that I've already gone over three times.

"Close your eyes." I feel her hand in front of my face while she douses me with hairspray.

"Well, that's not moving for three days." I laugh.

"Good," Mom says. "That's exactly what you want."

She stands behind me, admiring at me in my finished look in the mirror. My eyes meet her reflection. She takes a breath.

"Effie, when you were born, I knew it wasn't going to be easy. They told me it would be hard. And it has been. For me, your dad, and especially for you. And if I've pushed you to advocate for yourself, it was only because I wanted you to be happy and I wanted people to treat you right."

"I know," I say.

"I can't believe how far you've come this year. Every single thing you've faced, you've handled with such grace, and poise, and spunk that I know you're going to be fine." She swallows thickly. I do, too. "I hope you enjoy tonight because you deserve it. It's been hard, but it's also easy. You make it easy for me because you're you."

She squeezes my shoulder. I feel the weight of it, and the release.

❧

Don't think of it as your first date ever. I am going out with Wilder. Who I know. Who will be sweet, and kind, and fun.

The pit in my stomach is still there, but I don't listen to it.

We pull up to Minnehaha Falls, the fifty-some-foot waterfall in the middle of Minneapolis. Over the roar of the water, I hear the voices of other prom-goers, their families yelling, "Look here! This camera now, one . . . two . . ."

Ali spots Cam and calls to her. Cam runs, her gold thong sandals thwapping against the grass.

In five minutes, I see that Calvin has already found Harper, their parents getting the shot of her pinning on the boutonniere.

I'm sitting all alone, by the stone wall overlooking the water. The last moments before . . .

"Effie?"

Six . . .

Five . . .

Four . . .

Three . . .

Two . . .

One.

I turn around to see Wilder. The pit in my stomach disappears.

He's wearing a black suit with a white dress shirt underneath. He has a skinny emerald-green tie. He's holding a box that has a corsage. For me.

He breathes out some combination of "whoa" and "omigod" that comes out as "Whoamygod." He hugs me, pulling back slightly only to say, "In case that wasn't clear, you look absolutely amazing."

My heart is most definitely in my butt.

Ending the hug and looking up at him, it feels like I'm actually riding in a hovercraft, floating five feet above the ground. "Thank you. You look amazing, too."

Looking around, I see a small, sweet woman with her hand on her chest.

"This is my mom, Nicole." Wilder introduces us sheepishly.

"Hi, sweetheart." She wraps me in a warm hug right away. "You guys are going to have so much fun tonight."

I introduce Wilder to my mom, who gives him a hug, too. I am still hovering, powered by happiness. Dad grips Wilder's hand a bit too tightly.

"So, um." Wilder fumbles, taking a calculated step away from our parents. "I hope you don't mind, but I took some creative liberties." He pulls out a floral arrangement that's . . . bigger than a corsage? I stare at it for a second. No, it's not bigger, it's *longer*. He unfolds it, an emerald ribbon with three white roses pinned in the beginning, middle, and end. "I know it's not traditional, but I thought it would look good on the back of your . . ."

"Oh!" I turn around so that the back of my chair faces him. He kneels down, and I feel his weight as he pushes three pins through the back of my chair. I hear a camera click, and he stands, showing me his phone.

It fits perfectly underneath the handles of my wheelchair, a little extra ribbon hanging off both ends. "I love it."

"Really?"

"Oh my god, yes." No other girl at prom will have a corsage like this. This is from Wilder, just for me.

I take out the white-rose boutonniere from underneath my chair, and make a little guttural noise as I try to reach up to pin it to his sport coat.

He kneels down, his blue eyes level with mine.

We hold that gaze a second too long. I pull myself away, like defying a magnetic force.

I pull the pin out. My hands shake as I position it on the lapel. I would blame spasticity, but this isn't its fault. After a few tries and some encouragement from our parents, I stick the pin through the right way. My hands stay there. Finally, I pull away, slowly. He stands up, slowly.

The various photo arrangements begin. Wilder and Calvin. Then just the girls: first, the three of us with Ali. Then of course, just the three of us. Our moms go wild. Harper and Cam bend down to my height, and we get some where they stand behind me. For the last shot, Cam wraps her arms around me and Harper wraps her arms around Cam, a continuous embrace. We hold the pose for longer than necessary.

While Cam and Ali take their couple's shots, I overhear Wilder's mom ask my dad, "So, you're sending your baby to an opposite coast in the fall, too?"

Dad sighs. Out of the corner of my eye, I see him run his hand through his hair. "Sure am. I'm not sure I'm ready, though." I look away, then hear him say, "But she is."

When it's time for Wilder and me to do our couple's pictures. I open my mouth to talk logistics. Does he stand? Do I sit on the cement wall behind us?

But in a second, he's kneeling, one knee up, and we're the same height. It's so natural, I don't know why I worried. All these things I thought would be so hard are easy with Wilder.

He wraps his arm around me, and I lean into him, and we both smile, unable to hold it in.

"Come on, *let's go!*" Calvin calls from Wilder's big van that we are all taking.

"And they're off," Cam's mom laughs. My parents are going out with Harper's and Cam's parents for dinner, which is about the sweetest thing I can think of.

Mom gives Wilder a quick hug, and then turns to me, squeezing tight. "Remember, you deserve it," she whispers.

Dad claps Wilder on the back and then pulls me aside. He hugs me, and kisses my cheek lightly, so as not to mess up my makeup.

"You're just the best kid, you know that?"

"Better than Cora?" I try.

His laugh rumbles. "Trying to catch me in a weak moment. You know I don't play favorites." A beat of silence. "You're *so* ready. For this, for everything."

I don't hesitate. "I know."

As I head toward the van, I turn at the last second to see my parents walking across the grass to their car, their backs to me. I know if I called out to them, they would come running to help me. I know they'll be helping me, in the future.

But I don't need them tonight.

So I turn, give my chair a push, and let them go.

CHAPTER THIRTY-TWO

They've decorated the hallway leading into the Radisson with yellow construction paper stars. We were handed a Sharpie at check-in, which makes sense now that we see a sign reading ADD YOUR NAME TO THE MILL CITY HIGH WALK OF FAME!

It's tacky, but Cam and Harper both take one off the wall, so I reach for one, too.

Wilder positions it on the floor, uncapping the marker, he pens big and bold:

Effie and Wilder

"Hold up," he says, taking his phone out of his jacket pocket. He positions his feet on one point of the star, and I arrange my footplate to be over the point on the other side, the silver of my shoes sparkling. He snaps a photo.

I'd expected to be a nervous wreck tonight, but after all the imagining and all the worrying, it all feels so normal. Besides making sure I didn't order anything too messy or with too much garlic for dinner, I've been focusing on having fun.

At one point, I passed Wilder the water pitcher, my hands wrapped around one side and his around the other, the tips of our fingers touching. I've never been impressed by magic tricks, but I've never wished I could make an object disappear more.

Inside, there's a red carpet with gold ropes on the side, leading to the official photo area, a marquee that reads MILL CITY HIGH SCHOOL PROM with the date underneath.

All of us decide to take our photos now, while we're still wearing our shoes and before the boys untie their ties, undo their collars.

I don't think about it until it's our turn to go up. I look around me, and gulp. It was one thing when it was just our small group. But here are all my peers, about to see me *with* Wilder. I can almost hear the whispers:

"*Wow! Look at that!*"

"*He took the girl in the wheelchair? How big of him.*"

"*Man, good for her.*"

I wheel up. There's a literal spotlight over us. I feel its heat in more ways than one. It's like being onstage, when you can't fully see the faces of the people in front of you. I await the verdict of the peanut gallery.

Someone makes an alarm sound with their mouth. "Hot couple alert!"

Wilder blushes, then waves him off with his hand. "Sorry. That's Chase from my Psychology class."

"Chase? From the football team?"

"Yeah."

An endorsement from a member of the football team is, like, top honors in the court of high school.

Someone else calls out, "Stunning, Effie!" It's Jenna from the track team. I smile softly at her.

Someone I don't recognize whispers, "Oh, *cool*! Look at the back of her chair."

I don't like being on display, but I relish this moment. After all, I deserve it.

❧

Different color lights flash down on us on the dance floor. I start out dancing stiff, my arms close to my body.

The sound fades while the DJ builds into something new. It's a fast beat, a pop-y first verse. It can't be. But of course it is.

It's the song Wilder and I danced to at homecoming.

We both burst out laughing. Sometimes, the universe pulls no punches, but sometimes, it does you a major solid.

Wilder grabs my hands and extends me at full arm's length, and then pulls me back in. He has a way of doing that. We don't look like anyone else dancing out on the floor, but that's okay. No one else cares. And tonight is for us.

Harper and Calvin, Cam and Ali come over and we start the night off right. They jump and I raise my hands up in the air. We scream the lyrics. We do funny dance moves, the fisherman, the bunny hop, the robot, and we don't care who watches us.

When the DJ salutes us from his stand, laughing, we cheer like we scored a touchdown. Wilder fist pumps.

I've always ended up having a good time at dances, but I've never understood people who say they wish the night wouldn't end. I always feel sweaty, tired, and sore at the end. But tonight, I get it. I want to freeze time. I want to stay in this moment as long as I can.

I know that's not possible, but there are some moments where your mind doesn't need to go blank to remember everything. You just know you will, because it was that perfect.

I didn't mean to look at my phone; with a jolt, I realize it's 10:30, about an hour to the end of the dance. This whole school year has been about time, how much of it is left, how fast it's passing, and now, strangely, how I wish I had a little bit more. I'm happy to see high school end, but possibly could be persuaded to take one more pop quiz if it meant I could have a bit more time with my friends, in this comfortable space, a space I will never be able to re-create again.

The first bars of a new song come on. A slow dance song. I thought this through ahead of time, and though I know Wilder wouldn't mind, I don't want him to kneel down to dance, and I don't want to stand up. I don't need that validation to feel normal anyway.

"Do you want to get some air?" he asks.

"Let's go," I say.

I turn, looking for Harper and Cam. I catch their eyes, dancing with their dates. They both stop dancing for a second to turn to look at me. I give them a thumbs-up.

"We'll be here when you get back!" Harper calls.

I mouth "I know." And smile.

They smile back.

They're not going anywhere.

❧

We go down the Walk of Fame, my wheels crunching the construction paper. We're allowed just outside the automatic doors of the hotel, but not any farther. We walk through the lobby, and through the doors. There's a tiny bubbling fountain there, and a little bench, a meager attempt at making you forget you're not facing a parking lot.

Wilder sits down on the bench, resting his chin in his hands. I sit across from him. Our knees are so close they could touch. I move a centimeter closer. They're touching. He doesn't pull away.

"It feels good out here," he sighs. "At least twenty degrees cooler than the dance floor."

"I didn't notice," I say. It's the truth.

"What are you most looking forward to about college?" he asks. It's a question we've been getting asked everywhere. Teachers, parents, random students. But we haven't asked it of each other. Usually I say something about the California weather or the Media Studies program.

But now I keep it simple. "I'm excited for my future . . . just . . . everything it will hold." Our eyes meet. The same magnetic pull engages. The decor must be effective, because we're not in a parking lot. We're in a bubble, our own world.

"What are you least looking forward to?" he asks.

"Cafeteria food," I admit. Then, without a second thought, I add, "And not being around you."

Like so many things this year, I thought it would be hard. Finally speaking up. But it feels right, like what I should have done all along. I just did it on my own time.

I take a deep breath, and shoot my shot: "Wilder, I like you." I look at him for his reaction, but his eyes are hard to read, so I force myself to continue. "And I was going to tell you. I tried so many times. And maybe it's silly now, or maybe it's too late. But tonight has been—*you* have been—everything I've—"

It's quick like lightning. No, like a bang snap. Wilder's lips touch mine; then he quickly pulls away.

His brow softens. "Can I kiss you?"

I don't say yes. I lean forward, and give him my answer.

In my imagination, kissing seemed hard. There were so many steps. So many ways to wonder if you were doing it right. But I see now that there is no right or wrong way. I feel the way

305

Wilder's lips move and follow his. I don't wish to freeze time. It's already stopped.

Finally, we pull apart. His hands are still cupping my face. He exhales, putting his forehead against mine. "In case that wasn't clear, that was my answer. I've been wanting to do that for a long time, too."

My heart is firmly in my chest, beating wildly. Pun not intended, but it absolutely works.

We work.

"I'm glad you told me," he says.

I smile. "It was hard, but it was worth it."

We were supposed to have years and now we only have weeks. But we still have tonight. Why am I worrying about having more time when tonight isn't even over yet?

Wilder takes my hand. "You ready?"

"I'm ready."

My future is before me, everything, all of it.

But first, I go back inside to enjoy everything I already have, right now.

ACKNOWLEDGMENTS

A week before I left for college, I wrote this in my diary: *As you are currently on the cusp of your college career, I guess you must qualify as "college-aged," no matter how bizarre it sounds to you at this very moment, sitting on your bed. Exactly one week from this time, you will be all moved into your dorm room . . . waiting to officially start it all.*

I could not have known at age nineteen that the memory of those weighty feelings would stay with me for over a decade— or that they would become the basis for this book. Publishing my debut novel evokes those same feelings of nervous excitement and anticipation. But—same as back then—I am calmed by knowing that I have the best people in my corner to support me.

To my wonderful editor, Emily Seife: I am grateful for the love and care you have shown this story. You helped me realize its full potential and supported me as I executed my full vision for it. I am fortunate to have you as this book's champion.

To Patricia Nelson, agent extraordinaire: Thank you for taking a chance on me, and for loving this book so fiercely from the start. You are a wonderful advocate who has held my hand at every stage of this wild ride to publication.

I'm deeply indebted to Mary Rockcastle and the entire faculty, staff, and community of the Hamline MFAC program. It was a tremendous honor to learn from and alongside all of you. In particular, thank you to my faculty advisers: Phyllis Root, Marsha Chall, and Nina LaCour.

Phyllis, during my first attempts at drafting this manuscript, I asked you, "Am I doing okay?" And you responded, "You have your hands on a good story, and you're telling it well. Keep going." Thank you for your kind and gentle demeanor, which provided a safe space for me to create.

Marsha, thank you for guiding me through my critical thesis, which helped me define what writing about disability in YA can and should be. That foundation guided every revision of this book that came after it.

Nina, I don't know how I got so lucky to have you as an adviser once, let alone twice. In your first letter to me, you told me you wanted to help me get this book in the hands of as many readers as possible. You have more than held true to your word. Your influence is all over these pages, and though I feel like I'll never be able to thank you enough for everything you've taught me, I'll keep trying.

Thank you to Anne Ursu, for all the mentorship and advice you've provided me, and for all our conversations about disability in the publishing industry.

To my cohort, Megan Ciskowski, Landra Jennings, and Tracey Sherman: I'm so glad we dared to climb!

To the members of my writing group, the Uncommon Writers: Monica Gomez-Hira, Jonathan Hillman, Meg Gaertner, Katrina Soli, Amanda Moon, and Kristin Walker:

Whether it's over a drink at a café, beside a lakeside bonfire, or during a champagne toast, I'm always ready to celebrate our wins and discuss our works in progress. There's no one else I'd rather be in the trenches with.

I'm grateful to the entire team at Scholastic who brought their talents to this book: Cassy Price, designer; Janell Harris, production editor; Kassy Lopez, editorial assistant; Shannon Pender, marketing manager; Rachel Feld, senior director of marketing; Lia Ferrone, senior publicist; Lizette Serrano, vice president of educational marketing; and Emily Heddleson, director of educational and library marketing.

Adams Carvalho illustrated a beautiful cover that I still can't believe is for *my* book!

I'm grateful to Dahlia Adler, Elana K. Arnold, Brandy Colbert, Nicole Kronzer, Nina LaCour, Lillie Lainoff, Anna Meriano, and Melissa See for generously taking the time to blurb my book.

I wish to thank Jennifer Krohn, formerly of Grinnell College, for all the work you did to make my college experience accessible to me. Your advocacy allowed me to focus on being "just another college kid," and those experiences helped me become the person who would write this book. I reflected on what I learned from you many times while writing it. You are a true ally.

To list all my many friends who have supported me along the way would require a separate acknowledgments section. So, to all the Harpers and the Cams in my life, who know who they are: Thanks for being in my life. It's an honor to be in yours. I love you all.

I am beyond fortunate to have a family who has supported me in everything I've wanted to do, but especially my writing. Thank you to my entire extended family for the love and support. But especially to Mom, Dad, Stephanie, Matthew, Angela, Emerson, and Bennett for being my biggest cheerleaders. I love you.

And lastly, to any disabled readers of this book—but especially disabled teens—it is my sincerest hope that you found comfort, escape, and maybe even some joy in these pages. May you never forget that you, too, can be the hero of your own story, and that we deserve to be seen—and celebrated—just as we are, in all spaces, always.